A Practical Theology of
Bible Translating

A Practical Theology of
Bible Translating

By Dr. Steve Combs

ISBN 978-1-7339247-9-5

Published in the USA by
The Old Paths Publications
www.theoldpathspublications.com

Copyright © 2019 by Steve Combs

All rights reserved. No part of this publication may be reproduced or transmitted in any form or by any means, electronic or mechanical, including photocopy, recording, or any information storage and retrieval system, without permission from the copyright owner, Steve Combs, in writing, except for fair use.

ISBN 978-1-7339247-9-5

All Bible quotations are from the Word of God the Authorized Version (the King James Bible), Occasionally other versions are used for specific purposes and are named.

Published in the United States of America
By The Old Paths Publications
http://theoldpathspublications.com/

A Practical Theology of Bible Translating
Contents

	Major Definitions	7
	Important Abbreviations	11
	Preface by Dr. H.D. Williams	13
	Forward by Dr. Steve Zeinner	15
	Introduction: The Purpose of This Book	17
1	The Division of Languages: Babel and the Great Need	19
2	Inspiration, Preservation, and Authority	33
3	The First Translator	51
4	The Great Commission and the Plan of God	56
5	The Scriptural Definition of Translating	76
6	The Scriptural Method of Translating	84
7	The Scriptural Method Applied	102
8	Translating, Bible Study, and Teachers	114
9	The Qualifications of a Translator	130
10	The Septuagint and the Hebrew OT	135
11	The Traditional Text of the NT	167
12	The Received Greek Text, the KJB, and the UBS	200
13	A Short History of Bible Translating	219
14	The Future: Bible Translating and Prophecy	238
15	Unto the Uttermost Part of the Earth	247
Appendices	Introduction to the Appendices and Bibliography	259
Appendix 1	A Bible Believer Asks, Why Use Greek and Hebrew?	260
Appendix 2	Problems of the Greek Text 1 Jn. 5:7; Jn. 1:18; 3:16; Mk. 16:9-20; Rom. 8:1; 1 Tim. 3:16; Jn. 7:53-8:11	264
Appendix 3	A Historical Summary of Unbelief	305
Appendix 4	A Few Passages in the KJB that are Disputed from Greek Mt. 1:1 and 1:17; 21:13; 27:35; Acts 19:37; Heb. 10:23; Jude 8; Rev. 21:9	333

Table of Contents

Appendix 5	Translation Challenge-God or Lord? Acts 19:20	343
Appendix 6	Translation Challenge Judgment, Condemnation, and Polysemy John 5:24	354
Appendix 7	Translation Challenge-Diligent Study 2 Tim. 2:15	357
Appendix 8	Translation Challenge-Faith or Faithful? Rom. 3:3	361
	About the Author	365
	Index	366
	End Notes	372

Major Definitions

Allegory or Allegorical Interpretation: Interpreting scripture as being figurative or symbolical in meaning.

Alexandrinus: A 5th century manuscript of the New and Old Testaments.

Alexandrian Text: A set of Greek manuscripts that associated with Alexandria, Egypt. Vaticanus and Sinaiticus are its most famous manuscripts. The Alexandrian text-type is contained in a very few manuscripts, about 5% of the ancient evidence, but it is held as the most important and accurate text-type by modern scholars.

Bible: The Bible is a book that contains the 66 books of Scripture as we have them in the Protestant Cannon from Genesis to Revelation. The term Bible comes from the Greek word Βιβλος (Biblos).

Codex: An ancient manuscript in book form.

Critical Apparatus: The primary source material behind an edition of the Greek New Testament.

Critical Text: See **UBS Text**

Dynamic Equivalence: A translation method that seeks to produce a translation that affects the modern audience in the same way the original affected its audience. It is a phrase-for-phrase or meaning-for meaning translation as opposed to a word-for-word translation.

Exemplar: In textual criticism, a text used to produce another text.

Essentially Literal Translation: A translation method that seeks to translate the exact words of the source text into the target language in such a way that it is correct according to the grammar and syntax of the target language.

Family: a smaller division of a nation that is made up of related peoples, but much larger than our "nuclear family."

Formal Equivalence: A translation method that has the same goals as the Essentially Literal method. It seeks to translate all the words, grammar, and idioms of the source language into the closest equivalent words, grammar, and idioms of the target language in such a way that the resulting translation is consistent with the usage, grammar, and syntax of the target language (Also called **Word-for-Word Translating**).

Functional Equivalent: A translation method that is closely related to Dynamic Equivalence. This method seeks to translate words of the source language into words in the target langue that serve the same "function" as those in the source. For example, "the lamb of God" could became "the seal of God" in a translation to the Eskimos or "the pig of God" in a translation in Papua New Guinea.

Idioms: 1) The peculiar grammatical and syntactical structure of a language, 2) an expression which cannot be understood by the normal meanings of the words of the expression, for example, "keep tabs on," the cat is out of the bag," kick the bucket," hang one's head," etc.

Idiomatic translation: a translation that does not seek to transfers the words of the source language into the target language. Rather, it focuses on transferring meaning only.

Inerrant: Containing no mistakes

Interpretation: 1) to determine or explain the meaning of, 2) in a Biblical sense, to translate, to transfer words and meaning from language to another.

Literal Translation: a translation that reproduces the words and grammar of the source language exactly in the target language.

Manuscript: An ancient hand-written document.

Method of Translating: The philosophy and procedure used by a translator to translate the Bible.

Minuscule Manuscript: A manuscript written with lower case or cursive letters. Also referred to as **cursives.**

Mother Tongue: The first language learned after birth.

Nation (Also called **People Group**): Biblically, a group of people characterized and united based on common ancestry, common language, common laws or customs, and (usually) common area in which they live.

Palimpsest: Parchment that has been written on, erased, and reused.

Major Definitions

Received Text (Also called **Textus Receptus**): A printed Greek text of the New Testament in several editions. The first edition was dated in 1516 and the last one in 1881.

Revision: A text that has been *changed* for good or bad.

Scripture: The written words of God found in the 66 books of the Bible.

Septuagint: An New and Old Testament in Greek that is generally assumed by scholars to have first been translated starting about 250 BC in Alexandria, Egypt. Its authenticity is disputed by many. The current form of the "Septuagint" is the Codex B, Vaticanus, manuscript dated about 350 AD and found in the Vatican Library.

Sinaiticus: A manuscript of the New Testament, supposedly found by Ludwig Von Tischendorf in the monastery of St. Catherine at the traditional site of Mt. Sinai in 1844. It has been dated in the 4th century.

Source Language: The Language that is being translated another language.

Source Text: The actual written text in the source language used for translation purposes.

Target Language: The language into which the translation is being made.

Target Text: The writing in the target language produced by the translation procedure.

Textual Criticism: The attempt and methods used to restore a text to its original condition.

Textus Receptus: See **Received Text**.

Tongues: Languages

Transcribe: Make a written copy

Translating: (Most basic definition) Transferring words from one language into another.

UBS Text: A printed Greek text published in the 20th century by the United bible Societies.

Uncial Manuscript: a manuscript written in all capital letters.

Vaticanus: An ancient manuscript of the Old and New Testaments dated in the 4th century and kept in the Vatican Library.

Verbal Plenary Inspiration: The miracle of God whereby He gave the words of Scripture to the world through men. "Verbal" means every word of Scripture is inspired. "Plenary" mean all Scripture, the whole, is inspired.

Verbal Plenary Preservation: God has preserved each of the words He inspired (verbal), and He preserved all of the words He inspired (plenary).

Word-for-Word Translating: See Formal Equivalence

Word of God: the Bible, the Scriptures.

Words of God: Each individual word inspired by God.

Important Abbreviations

A = Codex Alexandrinus
AD = Anno Dei, Year of Our Lord
B = Codex Vaticanus
BC = Before Christ
BHS = Bilbia Hebraica Stutgartensia
Ca. = circa
CEV = Contemporary English Version
DE = Dynamic Equivalent
e.g. = For example
EL = Essentially Literal
ESV = English Standard Version
FE = Formal Equivalent
FunE = Function Equivalent
i.e. = that is
ibid = in the same place
ISBE = International Standard Bible Encyclopedia
KJB = King James Bible
LXX = Septuagint
MS = Manuscript
MSS = Manuscripts
MT = Masoretic Text
NIV = New International Version
NT = New Testament
OT = Old Testament
p, pp = page, pages
SIL = Summer Institute of Linguistics
TT =Traditional Text
TR or RT= Textus Receptus/ Received Text
WH = Westcott and Hort

Preface

The study of translating is one of the most important hermeneutical topics in modern times, and probably one of the most neglected. Why? Because there are so many issues that have clouded the exegesis of Scripture and the critical concerns in this area of Theology. Dr. Steve Combs has opened the door to these matters so that they may be comprehended in a precise, unambiguous way. A careful reading of this book will assist translators around the world to come to a knowledge of what God expects from those handling His Words "to make them known," just as:

> "[H]e established a testimony in Jacob, and appointed a law in Israel, which he commanded our fathers, that they should <u>make them known</u> to their children:" (Psalm 78:5) [my emphasis, HDW]

Man cannot and should not assume that he can establish the "rules' for how to *"make them known,"* because God has *"hast magnified [His] word above all [His] name"* (Psalm 138:2f), and the following verse indicates how high He has exalted His name.

> *"To the chief Musician upon Gittith, A Psalm of David. O LORD our Lord, how excellent is <u>thy name</u> in all the earth! who hast set **thy glory above the heavens"*** (Psalm 8:1)

Therefore, as you would expect, God has not left us without instruction as to how His Words are to be translated, a topic which Dr. Combs has thoroughly explored.

In my opinion, the call by God to translate the Words of God is one of the highest, most important callings a believer can have. And even though the task is daunting, God gives the Holy Spirit who guides, instructs, encourages, and indwells. The Lord knows the burden of successfully translating His Words is enormous, but he says, *"...I will never leave thee, nor forsake thee."* He will be right there through the entire process.

Yes, there is a process. There are procedures and methods that will keep the Spirit-filled translator on a path that will magnify His Words. The theological principles are not just necessary, they are imperative. The definition of translate is:

> "from Latin *translatus* "carried over," serving as past participle of *transferre* "to bring over, carry over" (see transfer), from *trans*" across, beyond" (see trans-) +*lātus* "borne, carried" (see oblate(n.))" (www.etymonline.com)

This is what Dr. Combs' book is about, "carrying over" God's Words into another language, according to God's principles and not man's thoughts or ideas. No one should begin translating until he has read this book. I have personally been interested in this area of theology for many years and have written articles such as, "The Interpretation of Parables," "Producing an Accurate and Faithful Translation," "Principles of Translating," and two books, *"The Septuagint,"* and *"Word For Word Translating of the Received Text"* concerning some of the issues Dr. Combs has thoroughly laid out in this treatise. May God bless his work, and may it have wide distribution. I believe it will be a classic in the years to come.

H. D. Williams, M.D., Ph.D., President
The Old Paths Publications, Inc.
Cleveland, GA
www.theoldpathspublications.com
TOP@theoldpathspublications.com
February 2019

Forward

By Dr. Steve Zeinner

When opportunity lends itself to seeing someone read or hear God's Words for the first time in their mother tongue it is a moment in time that will never be forgotten. It has been God's will and purpose that all nations and peoples of the earth know of His wonderful love and gift. From the early church to present-day, great effort and sacrifice have been made to translate His Words into the languages of the world. Dr. Combs passion to see all nations know of his savior was evident as we met many years past.

It is with great joy that I share with you the impact Dr. Steve Combs has made over the years and around the world. His qualifications to author this book are evident by his extensive research and teaching of translation. He has spent many years consulting with translators, studying and gleaming from the scriptures. My first encounter with Dr. Combs was on the subject of Bible translation and the need for a ministry to address the complex issues surrounding it. I have traveled the world with Dr. Combs watching him teach and consult with Bible translators. He has modeled the importance of using Biblical principles to produce a faithful, accurate and true translation of God's Word. His tireless efforts and dedication in writing about this vital topic have been years in the making. You will be inspired, challenged and enlightened by this must-read book.

Dr. Stephen Zeinner
Director
Bearing Precious Seed Global/Global Bible Translators

Introduction

The Purpose of This Book

The Lord gave the word: great was the company of those that published it. (Psalms 68:11)

Declare ye among the nations, and publish, and set up a standard; publish, and conceal not: (Jeremiah 50:2)

And the gospel must first be published among all nations. (Mark 3:10)

And ye shall know the truth, and the truth shall make you free. (John 8:32)

This book is written to teach the *Biblical doctrine of Bible translating* and to make some practical applications of it. It is not about translating the Bible into another English version. This book explains what the Bible says about translating it into the more than 7,000 languages of the world. The Bible has a lot to say about this subject

There are plenty of theories about how to translate the Bible. There are books that explain these theories from a linguistics point of view, but not usually from a strictly theological viewpoint. In fact, they can't all approach the theories theologically, because the theories contradict. They cannot all be true. Therefore, they can't all be Biblical, because *"Thy word is truth"* (Jn. 17:17). Since the Bible is truth, there can be only one truth. In this book, I have tried to make the Biblical truth clear.

This is also a **practical** theology. A practical theology is an **applied** theology; applied to *real world* circumstances rather than left to *concepts* only. I have tried to focus on "what the Bible" says, but I have not left it there. I have tried to apply the theology to practice and to history. In the Bible, we find the basic principles of Bible translating. God expects us to take what we learn from His Word and apply it to our lives, circumstances, practice, culture, and methods. As the Scripture says, *"He that handleth a matter wisely shall find good: and whoso trusteth in the LORD, happy is he"* (Prov. 16:20).

Where will we find greater wisdom than the Word of God? We must learn His truth and believe (trust) His truth and follow it.

One application I have made is to the method and practice of Bible translating. Another application is the most extensive. A translator of the Bible must be certain that the text he is translating is the true text of Scripture. To a great many translators active today, the matter of choosing the *right* source text is a non-issue and they are not concerned. They should be. We will answer to God if we have translated a text He did not choose.

There are three major Greek texts that are used for Bible translation. They are all three different. The first and oldest is the Received Text (TR). The second is the United Bible Societies Greek Text and it differs from the TR over 8,000 times. The third is the "Majority Text," which differs from the TR around 1,500 times. There are two different Hebrew Texts of the Old Testament and a Greek text called the Septuagint.

A translator *must* make a decision between the three. How is he to do that? The decision cannot be made without extensive information and insightful spiritual discernment. I have tried to give the potential translator and concerned Christians the information they need. This is an immense issue. Christians want to know all that God has said, so, a translator must translate the true words of God.

I have tried to stay as close to the teaching of the Scriptures as I can. May God bless you and teach you as you read. May God burden your heart about the need of Bible translating around the world. *Every people should have every Word of God in their own language.*

Chapter One

The Division of Languages: Babel and the Great Need

6 And the LORD said, Behold, the people is one, and they have all one language; and this they begin to do: and now nothing will be restrained from them, which they have imagined to do.
7 Go to, let us go down, and there confound their language, that they may not understand one another's speech.
(Gen. 11:1-9)

26 And hath made of one blood all nations of men for to dwell on all the face of the earth, and hath determined the times before appointed, and the bounds of their habitation;
27 That they should seek the Lord, if haply they might feel after him, and find him, though he be not far from every one of us: (Acts 17:24)

In Genesis 11, we find the historical story of the tower of Babel. The significance of this story goes way beyond the rebellion of man and God's way of dealing with that rebellion. Of course, God had commanded them to replenish the earth (Gen. 9:1). To do this they had to scatter, but they chose another way. They remained together and determined to build a name for themselves (Gen. 11:1-4). They became rebels against God. The symbol of their rebellion was the tower (Gen. 11:4). The strength of their unity was the fact that they all had only one language (Gen. 10:1).

In order to force them to separate according to their nations, God confused their language (Gen. 11:7-8). They couldn't understand one another anymore so they had no choice but to gather into smaller groups according to each group's common language. There is no doubt that the languages were divided based on ethnic relationships. Each related family migrated together in the same direction to the same place. For example, the Hebrew word for Egypt is *mitsrayim* or *Mizraim*, as it is in the KJB. According to Scripture and tradition, Mizraim, one of the sons of Ham (Gen. 10:6), led his family group into the land of the Nile and founded Egypt. The same was true of the others. The confusion of languages split the united descendants of Noah into major family groups led by the grandsons and great grandsons of Noah, listed in Genesis 10. Each family had a common language and each family founded a nation.

> *These are the families of the sons of Noah, after their generations, in their nations: and by these were the nations divided in the earth after the flood.* (Gen. 10:32)

Each group went its own way with its own language. From there languages continued to multiply and diversify naturally, so that now the world has over 7000 languages that can be traced to a few great language families.

It is important to understand that the diversity of languages is God's will and part of God's plan. This is clear from Acts 17:26. God Himself "*hath determined the times before appointed, and the bounds of their* (the nations) *habitation.*" The dispersal of the nations and the confusion of languages were supernatural and unchangeable.

The language or Mother tongue of a people is a special language. It is a part of their soul. Each of the nations of Genesis 10 had their own language and it was very special and unique to them. It was part of their ethnic identity. It was in their hearts. The Jews, which nation God formed later in history, are an example of this. The Jews had been dispersed from the holy land for centuries after the Romans destroyed Jerusalem and the temple in 70 AD. They spoke the languages of the countries to which they traveled. Even in Paul and Peter's time, the Jews living outside Israel spoke those languages (Acts 2:5-13). Yet, when the Jews returned to Palestine and re-established the nation of Israel in 1948, they returned to their historic heart language, Hebrew. This desire for the mother tongue, the heart language, is characteristic of every Biblical nation. For example, Ghana, West Africa, has adopted English as its official language. However, in central Ghana, in the Brong-Ahafo Region, the Brong people still speak Twi, their mother tongue and heart language. After the languages in Genesis 10 were divided, the nations were also divided and God led them to their habitation, their land. [1]

The Date of Babel

The events of Genesis 11, took place soon after the great flood of Genesis 6-9. For reasons of simplicity, we will use Archbishop Ussher's chronology, which seems to be approximately accurate. The flood ended, according to Ussher, in 2348 BC. So, when did the division of languages take place? An indication of that is mentioned in Genesis 10: 25, *"And unto Eber were born two sons: the name of one was Peleg; for in his days was the earth divided; and his brother's name was Joktan."* Peleg was the great-great grandson of Shem. He was born 101 years after the flood in 2247 BC (Gen. 11:10-19). He lived 239 years and something of world-wide significance happened during his lifetime.

What does it mean that "in his days was the earth divided"? There are two possibilities. First, some scientists have suggested that in his time the continents split apart in what is called *continental separation.* The other possibility is that the division of languages took place in his lifetime. Larry Pierceon commented on this in an article posted on the *Back to Genesis* web site.

> Some suggest the continents of the earth were divided at this time. However, this seems unlikely, as such a process would have had to occur with in a very confined time period. The resultant geological violence would be overwhelmingly catastrophic—like another Noahic Flood all over again. Any continental separation thus likely occurred *during* the Flood.
>
> The traditional interpretation, which seems more reasonable, relates this verse to the division of people/nations at the Tower of Babel event in Genesis 11. [2]

The dates of Peleg's life fit nicely into other dates indicated by secular historians about the migration of ancient people. Larry Pierceon explains further.

Babylon begins

The year was 331 BC. After Alexander the Great had defeated Darius at Gaugmela near Arbela, he journeyed to Babylon. Here he received 1903 years of astronomical observations from the Chaldeans, which they claimed dated back to the founding of Babylon. If this was so, then that would place the founding of Babylon in 2234 BC, or about thirteen years after the birth of Peleg. This was recorded in the sixth book of DeCaelo ("About the heavens") by Simplicius, a Latin writer in the 6th century AD. Porphyry (an anti-Christian Greek philosopher, c.234–305 AD) also deduced the same number.

Egypt emerges

The Byzantine chronicler Constantinus Manasses (d.1187) wrote that the Egyptian state lasted 1663 years. If correct, then counting backward from the time that Cambyses, king of Persia, conquered Egypt in 526 BC, gives us the year of 2188 BC for the founding of Egypt, about 60 years after the birth of Peleg. About this time Mizraim, the son of Ham, led his colony into Egypt. Hence the Hebrew word for Egypt is Mizraim (or sometimes "the land of Ham" e.g. Psalm 105:23,27).

Greece gets going

According to the 4th Century bishop and historian Eusebius of Caesarea, Egialeus, king of the Greek city of Sicyon, west of Corinthin Peloponnesus, began his reign in 2089 BC, 1313 years before the first Olympiad in 776BC. If Eusebius is correct, then this king started to reign about 160 years after the birth of Peleg.

Note that Babylon, Egypt, and Greece each spoke a different language. These ancient historians have unwittingly confirmed the extreme accuracy of the biblical genealogies as found in the Hebrew scriptures. The Tower of Babel would have had to have occurred before the founding of these other kingdoms. Babel (Babylon), being in the same region as the Tower, would have been one of the earliest kingdoms, of course.[3]

The Development of the Nations

The confusion of languages was a necessary part of God's plan as expressed in Acts 17:26-27.

> He *"hath made of one blood all nations of men for to dwell on all the face of the earth, and hath determined the times before appointed, and the bounds of their habitation; That they should seek the Lord, if haply they might feel after him, and find him, though he be not far from every one of us."*

God's plan included separating the nations. Why? According to Acts 17 there is something about the separation and association with one's own kind that encourages seeking after God. This association includes a group feeling of identity that produces a common way of life and thinking. In today's world, there are many people groups just like this, over 11,000. If God can get a foot-hold in a group like this, the faith of some will encourage faith in others. The specific group will have much of its identity found within its distinct language and through this language they will find a natural wall of protection from the ideas of foreign groups which have a different identity, culture, and language. The gospel itself is, of course, cross-cultural and requires that someone from one culture go to another culture to make it known. However, when this alien, the gospel preacher, arrives in the new group it is necessary that he identify himself with that group and that he become accepted by that group. One of the best ways to do this is, among other things, learning that group's language and communicating with them in that language.

The Jewish first century historian, Flavius Josephus, recorded the results of his research into the early migrations of the nations of Genesis 10. [4] As stated before, the original nations of Genesis 10 separated and dispersed after the confusion of languages. The descendants of Japheth turned north and northwest toward Europe. Early on, they settled from Greece through Asia Minor to the area between and north of the Black and Caspian Seas. Later, they spread all over Europe. Ham's children went to Palestine and Africa. Some of Shem's and Ham's progeny stayed in the Tigris-Euphrates valley, while other Shemites traveled west and east toward Arabia and Asia.

These were ethnic groups in that they descended from a single ancestor. The families of Shem, Ham, and Japheth became nations. For example, Asshur, son of Shem, founded Nineveh and Assyria. Gomer and Magog and Torgarmah settled Asia Minor and later migrated north from there. Javan founded Greece and the Philistines came from Casluhim. Nimrod was king over the Akkadians and sought to build the tower of Babel. Canaan was the father of the Canaanites and settled in Palestine. Put is Libya. Cush is Ethiopia. Aram is Syria (Judges 10:6-Hebrew).

These events actually correlate to the sequence of events proposed by historians, although the dates vary somewhat. Secular history records that the first great civilization arose in Sumer, which is the southern Mesopotamian area, in the valley of the Tigris and Euphrates River. This is the area the Bible calls *Shinar*. After the Ark landed on the mountains of Ararat, the descendants of Noah migrated east and south until they were east of Shinar. *"And it came to pass, as they journeyed from the east, that they found a plain in the land of Shinar; and they dwelt there"* (Gen. 11:2). This was the beginning of the civilization of Sumer.

History also records that the King of the city of Akkad (Biblical spelling *accad*) conquered Sumer and founded the Akkadian Empire. His name, according to archaeologists was Sargon I. The Bible says of Nimrod, son of Cush, grandson of Noah *"the beginning of his kingdom was Babel, and Erech, and Accad, and Calneh, in the land of Shinar."* If secular historians are right, Nimrod lived in Accad and conquered the rest of Shinar (Sumer). It is highly likely that Nimrod is one and the same as Sargon I. "Sargon" is said to mean "the King is established" in Akkadian. [5] So, it may be a title rather than a name.

The Great Need of the Nations

What is a Biblical nation? Charles Turner defines a nation in his book, *Biblical Bible Translating*, by using four criteria: lineage, language, laws, and land. His definition is summarized below:

1. **Lineage:** In Gen. 12:2 God promised to make Abraham a great nation. The nation of Israel was descended

from Abraham, Isaac, and Jacob. Therefore, they had a common ancestry. In Gen. 12:7, God said that He would give the land of Canaan to Abraham's seed. The word "seed" means descendants or lineage. Abraham's son was Isaac and Isaac's son was Jacob and Jacob's sons were the twelve patriarchs who begat the twelve tribes of the nation of Israel. *The nation was primarily a people with a common ancestry.*

2. **Language:** Gen 14:13 calls Abraham a Hebrew. He was called a Hebrew for three reasons. One is that he lived near Hebron at that time; second, he descended from Eber (Gen. 11); third, he spoke a distinct language that became the language of the Hebrew people and was called by that name. A Biblical nation is a people who speak a language that is distinct from others and is generally not understood by people outside the common lineage.

3. **Laws:** A Biblical nation must be bound together in a community governed and organized by laws. God called Israel to receive their law in Ex. 24:12.

4. **Land:** A Biblical nation normally also has a geographic boundary in which they live. In Gen. 12:7, Israel was promised the land of Canaan as an inheritance. Each of the tribes was given distinct geographical portions of that land. [6]

Brother Turner says, "Any group of people who recognize themselves as having a common lineage, who speak a distinct language, who have common laws (written or oral), and who live in a prescribed area of land, are a nation in the sight of God." [7] The Great Commission commands us to take the Word of God to every single one of these nations. That is a much bigger job than simply planting a church within every geopolitical state or country, because most countries have more than one Biblical nation.

The Bible also provides us with other names of people groups. In Gen. 12: 3 the scriptures said to Abraham, *"and in thee shall all families of the earth be blessed."* We are told in Rev. 5:9, *"And they sung a new song, saying, Thou art worthy to take the book, and to open the seals thereof: for thou west slain, and hast redeemed us to God by thy blood out of every kindred, and tongue, and people, and nation."* Here we have references to tongues, families, kindreds, and people. What are these? What is the Biblical definition of these people group terms?

The term, *tongue,* refers to languages (see 1 Cor. 13:1-3). The verse says "every" tongue or language. So, in heaven there will be representatives of every spoken language on earth.

The first use of the term, *families,* is in Gen. 10. The Scriptures tell us, *"By these were the isles of the Gentiles divided in their lands; every one after his tongue, after their families, in their nations."* If we look in verses 2-4, we find that the sons of Japheth produced seven nations, all of whom are named. In verses 3 and 4, the descendants of two of these sons are named. The descendants of the sons of Japheth were the families that made up the seven nations. In other words, a family is a smaller division of a nation that is made up of related peoples, but much larger than our "nuclear family." In Gen 36:40-43, we have a description of the nation of Edom. Esau (or Edom) founded the nation and his sons, who are listed, produced the families. Study Numbers 26.

The nation of Israel (all descendants of Jacob or Israel) were divided by tribes (Reuben, Levy, Judah, etc., descendants of Israel), which were finally divided into families (descendants of the sons of Israel). A family can be traced back to a common ancestor and is a group that feels a distinct identity while also being identified as a part of the whole nation (see 2 Chron. 35:5). While different nations usually speak different languages, families within a nation may also speak a dialect of the nation's language, or they may speak the common language of the nation.

The word *kindred* is similar to the term *family* and refers to related people and can refer to people related across families. *"People"* is a general term for a large group of distinct ethnically related individuals with a distinct identity similar to *nations*.

This is how God looks at the world. Geopolitical countries are secondary. Noah Webster agreed to this definition in his 1828 dictionary.

> Nation, as its etymology imports, originally denoted a family or race of men descended from a common progenitor, like tribe, but by emigration, conquest and intermixture of men of different families, this distinction is in most countries lost. [8]

The Division of Languages

Noah Webster died in 1843. That was about fifty years after the start of the great missionary movement that began with William Carey going to India in the 1790's. Perhaps Webster missed what Carey and others were learning in foreign countries, but he was wrong about the distinction being lost. The great missionary movement has clearly revealed that the "family or race distinctions" have absolutely NOT been lost. They are very much alive in Africa and Asia and South America. The distinctions are very much alive in Europe and North America with the immigration of ethnic groups that identify with one another more than with the political country they occupy.

Jesus said, *"Look on the fields."* (John 4:24) The original nations of Genesis 10 have divided many times and many families have become nations themselves with distinct languages and families. Modern mission leaders have proposed various ways of looking at the nations in order to clarify the targets for evangelism.

Finishing the Task

In June 2000, *Mission Frontiers* magazine included an article entitled "Finishing the Task." After it explained how the Gospel has made amazing progress over the previous 20 centuries, it tells us that two billion people (at that time, now it is more) still live outside the influence of the Gospel.

> The fact is that the Gospel often expands within a community but does not normally "jump" across boundaries between peoples, especially boundaries that are created by hate or prejudice. People can influence their "near neighbors" whose language and culture they understand, but where there is a prejudice boundary, religious faith, which is almost always bound up with many cultural features of the first group, simply does not easily "jump" to the next group, unless that group desires to adopt the other's culture in preference to its own....If all the members of every church in the world were to bring every one of their friends and relatives within the same cultural

> group to obedient faith in Christ, and they in turn were able to bring all their friends and relatives to Christ and so on, no matter how much time you allow, there would still be billions who would never come to faith. They would be held at a distance from the Gospel by boundaries of prejudice and culture. The church does not readily grow within peoples where relevant churches do not exist. One-third of the individuals in the world live within people groups with no church ...
>
> An ethnolinguistic people is an ethnic group distinguished by its self-identity with traditions of common descent, history, customs, and language ...
>
> People blocs and ethnolinguistic lists give us a simple way to identify peoples and make the larger body of Christ aware of their existence and the need to reach them. The ethnolinguistic approach stimulates prayer and initial planning for specific peoples leading to serious strategic efforts to evangelize them ... [9]

The term *unreached* needs some definition. The meaning of this term describes the essential missionary task. That is, it tells us what must be done in order for indigenous Christians to finish the evangelization of their own nation. For this purpose we can define *unreached* by rather defining what a *reached* people is. A *reached people* is a people among whom "a viable indigenous church planting movement that carries the potential to renew whole extended families and transform whole societies" has been established. "It is viable in that it can grow on its own, indigenous meaning that it is not seen as foreign, and a church planting movement that continues to evangelize the rest of the people group." [10]

Many of these people groups do not have a Bible translation in their own language. They cannot read or study the Bible to grow strong spiritually as you can. They cannot quote the Bible to their neighbors in order to win them to Christ, as you can. We take the Word of God for granted, sometimes leaving the Bible lay on a table until it collects dust, but many of these people have no Bible at all. Some have only small portions of the Bible.

The Division of Languages

The Great Need of the World

One of the premier organizations compiling people group statistics is the Global Research section of the International Mission Board (www.peoplegroups.org). They have amassed information on over 11,000 ethnolinguistic groups. These nations are listed by continent and by country. Thus, over seven billion people are catalogued as summarized in Fig. 1 as of November 2018.

Continent	Number Countries	People Groups	Population
Africa	58	3037	1,223,824,511
Asia	50	4630	4,539,462,285
Oceana	29	1321	32,665,620
Europe	52	886	765,542,950
Americas	51	1881	1,017,420,570
Total	240	11755	7,578,915,936

Fig. 1 [11]

The information in Fig. 1 varies slightly year by year as research continues, but it represents a monumental effort on the part of this mission support organization. World surveys are still going on; there may be many more peoples out there than we know. The Toulambi people of Papua New Guinea, for example, were first contacted in 1993. [12] Nevertheless, the table gives a very clear picture of the vast job that is worldwide missions.

The following table (Fig. 2) summarizes those people groups listed in the Global Research information who are considered to be *unreached*. These groups fall into one of four categories, 0) no evangelical Christians or churches-no major resources, 1) less than 2% evangelical-no church planting in the last two years-some resources available, 2) less than 2% evangelical-initial church planting in last two years, or 3) less than 2% evangelical-widespread church planting in last two years.

A Practical Theology of Bible Translating

Continents	Nations/People Grps	Population
Africa	2081	809,504,886
Asia	3347	2,891,924,390
Oceana	137	10,249,000
Europe	762	694,393,225
Americas	758	64,453,260
Totals	7085	4,470,524,761

Fig. 2 [13]

These peoples are the "last frontier" of missions. More than one half of the global population lives in unreached nations and families! This doesn't include the unsaved, who live in reached nations. This sad state of affairs is shown to be even worse by the fact that many of these groups do not have any missionary church planting teams of any denomination. Global Research lists people groups among whom there is no active church planting in the last two years, as far as is known. That is categories 0 and 1. The following table (Fig. 3) summarizes those peoples.

Continent	Nations/People Grps	Population
Africa	1252	216,968,886
Asia	2505	682,769,790
Oceana	128	8,281,200
Europe	461	34,231,525
Americas	596	11,407,160
Totals	4942	953,658,561

Fig. 3 [14]

This is absolutely incredible! No church planting team for almost five thousand unreached nations and families! Almost 1 billion human beings with little or no gospel preaching! I am reminded of the rebuke given by the Apostle Paul to the Corinthian believers: *"Awake to righteousness, and sin not; for some have not the knowledge of God: I speak this to your shame."* (1 Cor. 15:34). We have been at this task for 2000 years. The job the Lord gave us in Mt. 28:19, *"Go ye therefore, and teach all nations"* is far from fulfilled. All of the peoples represented by Fig. 3 are pioneer mission

The Division of Languages

fields. They are named, identified, and located in the Global Research data found at www.peoplegroups.org.

Look on the Fields: The Great Need for Bible Translating

Today's languages developed from Babel. The Ethnologue lists six major language families that exist now: Afro-Asiatic, Austronesian, Indo-European, Niger-Congo, Sino-Tibetan, and Trans-New Guinea. [15] The Ethnologue lists 7,094 living languages. Wycliffe adds sign languages and totals living languages at 7,361. [16]

What about the need for Bible translations among the nations of the world? The statistics in the next table (Fig. 4) were compiled by Wycliffe Bible Translators. The table shows how many languages have the whole Bible, the New Testament only, portions (such as the Gospel of John), and how many languages have no published Scripture.

Continent	Total	Bible	NT Only	Portions	No Published Scripture
Africa	2193	258	417	398	1120
Asia	2411	231	391	309	1480
Oceana	1346	55	332	192	767
Europe	311	71	48	68	124
Americas	1100	68	346	166	520
World	7361	683	1534	1133	4011

Fig. 4 [17]

So, there are at least 4011 languages with no known published Scripture. This amounts to 54.5 % of all languages. Moreover, it involves 250 million individual souls! They have no Bible, nor a New Testament, and not even the Gospel of John to read. How can we turn our backs on these?

Moreover, the problem is greater than that. We have worked with languages spoken in China, Korea, India, Togo, Ghana, Germany, Canada and France, Ecuador, Myanmar, Philippines, and Paraguay. In each case the language in question already had a Bible ... and it was not a good translation. This is a very big, wide-spread problem. The translations are from the wrong Greek text, poorly translated (at least in significant ways), or both.

Regardless, of how one looks at Wycliffe and other evangelical organizations involved in this work, it cannot be denied that they have seen the need and are responding. They have looked on the fields (John 4:35) and the information that they have gathered should burden us and motivate us to action. We should determine to be a part of the great increase in translations they are working so hard toward. As Jesus commanded, we should first respond by prayer (John 4:34-37; Mt 9:37-38). The prayer is to specifically be that the Lord will send forth laborers. Perhaps, God would have you labor as a translator and church planter. Perhaps, God would have you partner with a mission agency that seeks to recruit missionary-translators and remains faithful to the King James Bible and the Received Greek and Hebrew Texts.

Chapter Two

The Inspiration, Preservation, and Authority of the Scriptures

All scripture is given by inspiration of God, and is profitable for doctrine, for reproof, for correction, for instruction in righteousness: (2 Tim. 3:16)

21 For the prophecy came not in old time by the will of man: but holy men of God spake as they were moved by the Holy Ghost. (2 Pet. 1:21)

Man shall not live by bread alone, but by every word that proceedeth out of the mouth of God. (Mat. 4:4)

The very foundation of a good theology of translating is a firm Biblical conviction about the nature of the Bible itself. God has a very high view of Scripture. Every translator must have the exalted view of Scripture that God Himself has. Everything depends on this. The accuracy and clarity of a translation depends on it.

The Bible is a book unlike any other. It gives us the knowledge of God, It is filled with wisdom, it reveals the future, it declares the will of God, and it shows us the plan of God for the salvation of mankind. Its truth makes the philosophies of mankind to appear what they are, foolish. The Bible is the greatest book on psychology ever written. When it speaks of science and history, it is never wrong. The character of the Bible screams to us that it can only come from one source: God Himself. That is what *inspiration* is all about.

So, the Bible, the Scriptures, comes to us from God. He has also declared that He will preserve it word-perfect; therefore, the Bible carries the authority of God. This truth was expressed many years ago in the 1689 Baptist Confession of Faith and in the 1646 Westminster Confession of Faith.

The Old Testament in Hebrew (which was the native language of the people of God of old), and the New Testament in Greek (which at the time of the writing of it was most generally known to the nations), being immediately inspired by God, and by His singular care and providence kept pure in all ages, are therefore authentic; so as in all controversies of religion, the church is finally to appeal to them. [18]

The Scriptures came into the world by inspiration, from that point they were preserved by God's singular care and providence, and they are the final appeal in all matters. When the Scriptures speak, the matter is settled.

Inspiration

The word *inspiration* in 2 Timothy 3:16 in Greek is *theopneustos,* and basically means *God breathed.* However, this means little in English and needs some explanation. It was the Greek's way of saying *inspired by God.* One thing it certainly means is that God is the origin of all Scripture. God is the only author. He used men as His instruments to write the words down, but the words were all from His heart and mind. It has been stated this way: "The perfect author of the perfect Bible is God." [19]

A clear statement of the process and product of inspiration is found in Matthew 4:4: "*Man shall not live by bread alone, but every word that proceedeth out of the mouth of God.*" The words of Scripture proceeded out of God's mouth; they were God-breathed. They may have been spoken by men, they may have been written down by men, but they came out of the mouth of God. Since God is a Spirit (John 4:24), this is a metaphor to help us understand that every word of Scripture comes from God. He is the origin and author of the words, all the words.

We often speak of *verbal plenary* inspiration. That simply means this: *verbal* inspiration is that God inspired every single individual word. Every separate word is a Word of God. *Plenary* inspiration means all of Scripture as a whole is inspired. Nothing in Scripture escapes the label *inspired*. *Every word* of Scripture and the *whole* is inspired.

Inspiration, Preservation, and Authority

The words of God were inspired when they were "*given*" (2 Tim. 3:16). Inspiration points to the time when God first gave them to mankind in Hebrew, Aramaic, and Greek. The term does not belong to any time or period of time afterward. It does not refer to the making of copies and it does not refer to translations. Copies and translations have to do with the *transmission* of Scripture *through* history. Inspiration pertains to the *entrance* of Scripture *into* history. If 2 Timothy 3:16 applies to a copy or translation, then *every time* a translation is made, it is inspired, and *every time* a copy was made it was inspired. If *that* is true, then there would be no mistakes in any copy or translation, because God does not make mistakes. However, some copies have errors and some translations (even those based on the Received Text) have errors.

I do not want anyone to misunderstand me here. When people talk about the inspiration of a translation, they are usually referring to the King James Bible. So, do not misunderstand me. I believe the KJB is the Word of God without error. Some may still misunderstand me, because they prefer to call the King James an *accurate* translation, rather than inerrant. Indeed it is accurate. But what does that mean? The word accurate is defined as "free from error especially as the result of care." [20] If the KJB is an *accurate* translation (and it is), then by definition it is *without error*. However, it is not the inerrant Word of God by *inspiration*. It is the inerrant Word of God by *providentially guided translation* of words that were given by inspiration and then preserved.

Some think that the KJV is inspired, because 2 Timothy 3:16 uses the present tense, "*is given.*" I presume, they reason that if it refers only to the first giving of Scripture, it would say "was given." Since it says "*is given*" that means *inspiration* applied when the KJB translation was "given." It stands to reason, if that is true, then inspiration applies *whenever any* copy or translation is "given" (see comment above).

However, that is not the reason why the KJB and the Greek text use the present tense. The reason is that *at the time* when Paul wrote 2 Timothy 3:16 *the canon of Scripture was not yet complete*. At the time, inspiration was still occurring, hence the use of the present tense. God was still planning to inspire more Scripture. For example, the Book of Revelation had not yet been inspired. Inspiration, then, applies to the miraculous work of God whereby He *first gave* the Scriptures in Hebrew, Aramaic, and Greek.

How did God give Scripture and how did He use men to do it? God used various methods. The Scriptures themselves give us some additional information and examples of what God did. Foremost among them is 2 Peter 1:16-21.

> *16 For we have not followed cunningly devised fables, when we made known unto you the power and coming of our Lord Jesus Christ, but were eyewitnesses of his majesty.*
> *17 For he received from God the Father honour and glory, when there came such a voice to him from the excellent glory, This is my beloved Son, in whom I am well pleased.*
> *18 And this voice which came from heaven we heard, when we were with him in the holy mount.*
> *19 We have also a more sure word of prophecy; whereunto ye do well that ye take heed, as unto a light that shineth in a dark place, until the day dawn, and the day star arise in your hearts:*
> *20 Knowing this first, that no prophecy of the scripture is of any private interpretation.*
> **21 For the prophecy came not in old time by the will of man: but holy men of God spake as they were moved by the Holy Ghost.**

God started with holy men. The Spirit of God "moved" these men to speak words that He chose. These words were written down by an assistant who was listening. An example of this is found in Jeremiah 36.

> *1 And it came to pass in the fourth year of Jehoiakim the son of Josiah king of Judah, that this word came unto Jeremiah from the LORD, saying,*
> *2 Take thee a roll of a book, and write therein all the words that I have spoken unto thee against Israel, and against Judah, and against all the nations, from*

> *the day I spake unto thee, from the days of Josiah, even unto this day.*
> *3 It may be that the house of Judah will hear all the evil which I purpose to do unto them; that they may return every man from his evil way; that I may forgive their iniquity and their sin.*
> *4 Then Jeremiah called Baruch the son of Neriah: and* **Baruch wrote from the mouth of Jeremiah all the words of the LORD, which he had spoken unto him, upon a roll of a book.**

Even Paul used the speaking method. Romans 16:22 says, "*I* **Tertius, who wrote this epistle, salute you in the Lord.**" The letter was sent to Rome from Paul, not Tertius. Paul spoke the words of the letter and Tertius was his assistant writing it down.

However, Paul seems to have written some of his work himself. 1 Corinthians 16:1 tells us, "*The salutation of me Paul with mine own hand.*" Paul wrote the greeting himself, otherwise it appears the same procedure was used. "*Ye see how large a letter I have written unto you with mine own hand*" (Gal. 6:11). It has been suggested that Paul wrote the end of the epistle to the Galatians and used large letters because he had eye trouble (Gal. 4:15). Regardless, at times Paul wrote himself and at times he dictated to an assistant.

A similar method has to do with the law in Deuteronomy. Moses spoke all the law to Israel and Moses Himself wrote the words (Deut. 31:9).

When dealing with this subject, commentators usually reject out of hand the so-called dictation theory; that God dictated the Scriptures. Yet, that is exactly what God did for part of the Scriptures. For example, God dictated the ten commandments and wrote them Himself on tables of stone (Ex. 34:1). God also dictated the law and commanded it to be written down (Ex. 17:14; 24:4; 34:27; Num. 5:23). Much of the Prophecies are written from indirect dictation; dictated by God to the prophets, spoken aloud by the prophets, and written by a secretary.

At other times, especially with narratives of events, God seems to have put into the hearts of the writers the words they should write. "*And Moses wrote their goings out according to their journeys by the commandment of the LORD: and these are their journeys according to their goings out*" (Num. 33:2).

In whatever way God gave the word, it was given by the miracle of inspiration. The Words were given by God. In whatever way the prophets and Apostles were *"moved"* (2 Peter 2:21), it was the Holy Spirit who moved them. They were led by the Spirit. *"The Spirit of the LORD spake by me, and his word was in my tongue"* (2 Sam. 23:2). Because of this, we must conclude that it is not just the meaning of the words that matter, it is the words themselves. When one is translating the Bible, he must be concerned about the meaning of the text and about the words. *God cares about each of His words.*

> *Psalms 12:6 The **words of the Lord** are pure words*
>
> *Psalms 119:103 How sweet are **thy words** unto my taste! yea, sweeter than honey to my mouth!*
>
> *Psalms 119:130 The entrance of **thy words** giveth light; it giveth understanding unto the simple.*
>
> *Psalms 138:4 All the kings of the earth shall praise thee, O LORD, when they hear the **words of thy mouth.***
>
> *Deuteronomy 4:2 Ye shall not add unto **the word** which I command you, neither shall ye diminish ought from it, that ye may keep **the commandments** of the LORD your God which I command you.*
>
> *Proverbs 30:6 Add thou not unto **his words**, lest he reprove thee, and thou be found a liar.*
>
> *John 3:34 For he whom God hath sent speaketh the **words of God:** for God giveth not the Spirit by measure unto him.*
>
> *Revelation 17:17 For God hath put in their hearts to fulfil his will, and to agree, and give their kingdom unto the beast, until the **words of God** shall be fulfilled.*
>
> *Revelation 22:19 And if any man shall take away from the **words of the book** of this prophecy, God*

> *shall take away his part out of the book of life, and out of the holy city, and from the things which are written in this book.*

Inspiration is the miraculous work of God whereby He gave His Hebrew, Aramaic, and Greek words to men, through human instruments. He gave His words in various ways, including 1) holy men spoke the words as they were moved by the Holy Spirit and an assistant wrote the spoken words, 2) God dictated some of the words, particularly much of the Law and prophets. Moses and the prophets, who heard the words from God, spoke them and they were written down, 3) God gave some men the words in their hearts and they wrote them down, and 4) God even wrote some of the words Himself. God did all this in such a way that every word he gave is His, a part of Him, perfect, and carries His divine authority.

The Divine Preservation of the Scriptures

The inspiration of the Scriptures would mean nothing and it would be impossible for mankind to live by the Words of God, if God did not *preserve* His words. This should be self evident, but many miss it. Nevertheless, the Scriptures make it clear that God has preserved His words.

> *But continue thou in the things which thou hast learned and hast been assured of, knowing of whom thou hast learned them; And that from a child thou hast known the holy scriptures, which are able to make thee wise unto salvation through faith which is in Christ Jesus. (2 Tim. 3:15-16)*

Timothy had the Scriptures, but the copies he had were not the original writings. The original pen, paper, and ink had long since perished. Contrary to what many have said, there is no evidence Timothy was using a Greek Septuagint translation (designated LXX-we shall look further at the Septuagint later). Timothy had copies of the Hebrew Old Testament. Paul called these copies "holy scriptures" indicating that they had been copied accurately; God had preserved His word.

The Fact of Providential Preservation

Many have long denied that the Bible teaches the providential preservation of Scripture. Nowadays, some have adapted their teaching to include preservation. I suspect this is because of all the Bible believing voices that have been raised in its favor. However, many have limited preservation to the "message" of Scripture, and have not applied it to the "words." Following are a few of the verses that teach the Biblical doctrine of the providential preservation of the Word of God.

> *__1 Peter 1:23__ Being born again, not of corruptible seed, but of incorruptible, by the **Word of God** which **liveth and abideth forever**.*
> *__Psalm 12:6-7__ The **words** of the Lord are pure words: as silver tried in a furnace of earth, purified seven times. Thou shalt keep them, O Lord, thou shalt preserve them **from this generation forever**.*
> *__Ps. 111:7-8__ The works of his hands are verity and judgment; all **his commandments** are sure. **They stand fast for ever and ever**, and are done in truth and uprightness.*
> *__Is. 40:8__ The grass withereth, the flower fadeth: but the **word** of our God **shall stand for ever**.*
> *__Ps. 117:2__ ... **the truth** of the Lord **endureth for ever**. Praise ye the Lord.*
> *__Ps. 119:152__ Concerning thy **testimonies**, I have known of old that **thou hast founded them for ever**.*
> *__Ps 119:160__ Thy **word** is true from the beginning: and every one of thy righteous judgments **endureth for ever**.*
> *__Matthew 24:35__ Heaven and earth shall pass away, but **my words shall not pass away**.*
> *__Psalm 33:11__ The **counsel** of the Lord **standeth forever**, the **thoughts** of his heart to **all generations**.*
> *__Psalm 100:5__ For the Lord is good; his mercy is everlasting; and his **truth** endureth to **all generations**.*
> *__Ps 119:89-90__ For ever, O LORD, thy **word** is settled in heaven. Thy **faithfulness** is unto **all generations**: thou hast established the earth, and it abideth.*

Inspiration, Preservation, and Authority

Psalms 119:160 *¶Thy word is true from the beginning: and every one of thy righteous **judgments endureth for ever**.*
Matthew 5:18 *For verily I say unto you, Till heaven and earth pass, one **jot or one tittle** shall in no wise pass from the law, **till all be fulfilled**.*
Isaiah 59:21 *As for me this is my covenant with them, saith the Lord; My spirit that is upon thee, and **my words** which I have put in thy mouth, **shall not pass out of the thy mouth, nor out of the mouth of thy seed, nor out of the mouth of thy seed's seed saith the Lord, from henceforth and forever**.*

These are just a few verses that prove providential preservation is a fact. What do we learn from these verses? We learn His Word is kept for all generations (Psalm 33:11; Psalm 100:5; Ps 119:89-90). His Word was kept for *us*, for our good (Is. 59:21). The preservation of the Word of God is a series of supernatural acts by the Lord Himself (Ps. 12:6-7). The Word is alive, with the life of God, which is forever (1 Peter 1:23; Heb. 4:12).

References	What will be preserved?	How long?
1 Peter 1:23; Is. 40:8 Ps. 119:160; Ps. 119:89-90	The Word of God	Forever
Mt. 24:35	Christ's Words	Never pass away
Ps. 12:6-7; Is. 59:21	God's Words	Forever
Ps. 111:7-8	Commandments	Forever and ever
Ps. 119:152	Testimonies	Forever
Ps. 33:11	Counsel	Forever
Ps. 33:11	Thoughts	To all generations
Ps. 100:5	Truth	To all generations
Ps.119:160	Judgments	Forever
Mt. 5:18	Jot and Tittle	Till all be fulfilled
Ps. 119:89-90	His Faithfulness	To all generations

Fig. 5

Finally, some point to Psalms 119:89, *"For ever, O LORD, thy word is settled in heaven,"* and say that preservation is only in

Heaven. However, Isaiah 59:21 counters that idea by explaining *"my words which I have put in thy mouth,* **shall not pass out of the thy mouth, nor out of the mouth of thy seed**, nor **out of the mouth of thy seed's seed** *saith the Lord, from henceforth and forever."* God's Words will not only be in Heaven, but they will be *in the mouth of people* forever. The Words of God are for us to live by. *"And* **these words***, which I command thee this day,* **shall be in thine heart***"* (Deut. 6:6).

The Definition of the Biblical Doctrine of the Providential Preservation of the Word of God

Providential Preservation is a Biblical doctrine and it is proved by the Scriptures I have listed and many others. The Doctrine of Providential Preservation states:

> God has *promised* to *miraculously preserve forever* all of His Word, His Words, and all His teachings with the words in which they are expressed. He has further promised to make them available to mankind for our good and for our lives. He has determined to do this in His own way depending on Himself alone, not mankind.

We may not understand how God has done this. We may be confused by all the unbelieving statements made by modern textual critics. Nevertheless, our responsibility is, *"Trust in the LORD with all thine heart; and lean not unto thine own understanding"* (Prov. 3:3). We may not be able to see how God has preserved each of His Words, but we can rest assured that He has done so, based on His own statements and promises.

Just as the Bible teaches verbal plenary inspiration, these verses teach verbal plenary preservation. Each individual word is preserved and the entire body of the 66 books of Scripture is preserved.

Take special note about *what words* have been preserved. The words that were inspired were Hebrew, Aramaic, and Greek words. They were not English, German, Spanish, or any other language. When God made the promises of preservation, the words He promised to preserve were Hebrew, Aramaic, and Greek words. He did not promise to preserve English, Spanish, German, or any other language words. This is evident by the Scriptures themselves: *"Till heaven and earth pass,* **one jot or one tittle** *shall in no wise pass from the law, till all be fulfilled"* (Mt 5:18). The jot (yod) is the smallest Hebrew letter and the tittle is a small part a Hebrew letter. The promise in Matthew 5:18 is to preserve words of Scripture in the Hebrew language. Clearly the Lord's promise is to preserve the Hebrew, Greek, and Aramaic words he inspired.

> Jesus taught that the same Divine providence which had preserved the Old Testament would preserve the New Testament … The Holy Spirit providentially guided churches to preserve His Words during the manuscript period. **First,** faithful scribes produced many trustworthy copies of the original New Testament manuscripts. **Second,** these trustworthy copies were read and recopied by true believers down through the centuries. **Third,** untrustworthy copies were not so generally read or so frequently recopied. Although they enjoyed some popularity for a time, yet in the long run they were laid aside and consigned to oblivion. Thus, as a result of this special providential guidance, the true text won out in the end, and today the believer may be sure that the text found in the vast majority of the Greek New Testament manuscripts, preserved by the God-guided usage of the Greek churches, is a trustworthy reproduction of the Divinely inspired original. Some have called it the Byzantine text, thereby acknowledging that it was the text in use in the Greek churches during the greater part of the Byzantine period (452-1453). It is much better, however, to call this text the Traditional Text because this text, which is found in the great majority of Greek New Testament manuscripts, has been handed down … to the present day.[21]

A Practical Theology of Bible Translating

The Authority of the Scriptures

The Word of God came from God. It had its origin in Him. Therefore, it was perfect when it was inspired, because God is perfect and makes no mistakes. Finally, God has preserved it, and because He never fails, it has been preserved perfect. Notice how God exalts the Word.

> *I will worship toward thy holy temple, and praise thy name for thy lovingkindness and for thy truth:* **for thou hast magnified thy word above all thy name**. *(Psalms 138:2)*

> *O LORD our Lord, how excellent is thy name in all the earth! who hast set thy glory above the heavens. (Psalms 8:1)*

If God has exalted His Word above His name, then His view of the Word is so high it's immeasurable. The glory of His name is very important to God, but His Word is in a higher place. Consider that. His glory is above the Heavens! His Word is higher! How much must we exalt His Word and hold it precious? How much ought we to support efforts to translate His Word into every language?

Consider this. There was a time in history when people held their reputation to be of highest importance. When they gave their word, they kept their word. If they broke their word, their reputation would be lost. *"A good name is rather to be chosen than great riches"* (Proverbs 22:1).

Consider this. *The glory of God's name depends on Him keeping His Word.*

Consider, the nature of God's Word.

> *And **the scripture, foreseeing** that God would justify the heathen through faith, **preached** before the gospel unto Abraham, saying, In thee shall all nations be blessed. (Gal. 3:8)*

> *For the scripture **saith unto Pharaoh**, Even for this same purpose have I raised thee up, that I might shew*

my power in thee, and that my name might be declared throughout all the earth. (Romans 9:17)

*For the Word of God is **quick**, and powerful (Heb. 4:12)*

There are some important truths I want to note from these verses.

There was no written Scripture when God gave the message in Galatians 3 and Romans 9 to Abraham and Pharaoh. The Scriptures had not been written, except possibly the Book of Job. Yet, Paul said it was the Scriptures which spoke. It was God who spoke. The word *Scriptures* was substituted for the word *God*. This clearly indicates that whenever God speaks to men in words that will eventually be written, His voice and words are Scripture. They proceed out of His mouth. They are God-breathed. The Scriptures are part of God. Therefore, the Scriptures are as true as God is, and the Scriptures are as authoritative as the "King of kings and Lord of lords."

The Scriptures are given the characteristics of God. In Galatians 3:8, the Scriptures exhibit foreknowledge and prophecy. In Romans 9:17, the Scriptures raise a man up, have a purpose, and glorify God's name. In Hebrews 4:12, the Word of God is alive (the word *quick* means *alive*) and powerful. Where does it get its life and power? Obviously, the Scriptures have all these characteristics because they are *part of God.* Sure, we know that it was God who said and did these things. However, by using the word "Scripture," God is showing the greatness and uniqueness of His words. They are not only *from Him*, but they are *a part of Him*, of who and what He is; just as your words are part of you.

Perhaps this should be enough to convince one and all that the Word of God carries God's authority, but there is much more. God's Word must be handled with great care, faith, respect, honor, and submission. This is the only safe way to handle God's Words. We should have this attitude toward every single Word of God. We must not treat God's Words flippantly.

There are many English versions that do treat God's Words flippantly. Let me give you an example from Psalm 138:1-3 in an English translation called *The Message*.

(KJB) *I will praise thee with my whole heart: before the gods will I sing praise unto thee.*
2 I will worship toward thy holy temple, and praise thy name for thy lovingkindness and for thy truth: for thou hast magnified thy word above all thy name.
3 In the day when I cried thou answeredst me, and strengthenedst me with strength in my soul.

(Message) Thank you! Everything in me says "Thank you!"
Angels listen as I sing my thanks.
I kneel in worship facing your holy temple and say it again: "Thank you!"
Thank you for your love, thank you for your faithfulness;
Most holy is your name, most holy is your Word.
The moment I called out, you stepped in; you made my life large with strength.

The Messsage is a complete adulteration of the Words of God. There is no correlation between the exactly translated words of the KJB. The words of the message came from human imagination. The Message (along with other versions) has substituted the uninspired words of men in place of the Words of God. By doing this, they are hiding the Words God chose to use from people. We must always handle the words that God inspired with great reverence. When we translate them we must take care to determine the exact translation of every word.

God's Word is truth. Jesus said, "Thy word is truth." Everything God has said is true from beginning to end. Some have said that the Bible has errors of fact, but it is still the Word of God. Poppycock! If anything is an error of fact, it is not God's Word. When men say that, they value the word of men more than the Word of God. No matter what subject the Bible speaks on, be it any discipline of science, psychology, medicine, dietary advice, history, government, religion, or any other subject, it is true.

Some Christian leaders water down the Bible's authority. I ran across two quotes that show, in some measure, how far we have departed from the authority of the Bible. This preacher seems to be advising us to not reference the chapter and verse when we quote

Scripture. Rather, he thinks it is better to simply say, "Jesus says" or "Paul says."

> I would ask preachers, pastors, and student pastors in their communication to get the spotlight off the Bible and back on the resurrection. Let's get people's attention back on Jesus as soon as possible, that the issue for us is always who is Jesus, [and] did He rise from the dead? And that we would leverage the authority we have in the resurrection as opposed to Scripture, not because I don't believe Scripture's inspired in terms of reaching this culture. [22]
>
> It's time to stop saying, "the Bible says." At least according to Andy Stanley.
> At Exponential, a church-planting conference attended by 5,000 in late spring (with another 20,000 watching via video), the senior pastor of North Point Community Church in Alpharetta, Georgia, said pastors should instead use phrases like "Paul says" and "Jesus says" when citing Scripture. [23]

All the authority of a preacher, the authority of Paul and Peter, was derived solely from the Bible. If you denigrate the Bible, you undermine your own authority. If you weaken the Bible's authority, you lose your own authority to preach, because that's where you got your commission. God's Word is His written authority on earth.

The following verses teach a number of truths about the sufficiency of God's Word:

1) God's Word is to be obeyed

> *9 Wherewithal shall a young man cleanse his way? by taking heed thereto according to thy word.*
> *10 With my whole heart have I sought thee: O let me not wander from thy commandments.*
> *11 Thy word have I hid in mine heart, that I might not sin against thee. (Ps. 119:9-11)*

2) *The Word of God sheds light on our path.*

   Thy word is a lamp unto my feet, and a light unto my path. Ps. 119:105

3) Those who walk according to God's Word are blessed.

   Blessed are the undefiled in the way, who walk in the law of the LORD.
   2 Blessed are they that keep his testimonies, and that seek him with the whole heart.
   3 They also do no iniquity: they walk in his ways. (Ps 119:1-3)

4) It should be the desire of our hearts to learn his word.

   Blessed art thou, O LORD: teach me thy statutes. (Ps. 119:12)

5) His Word should be a joy to our hearts.

   I have rejoiced in the way of thy testimonies, as much as in all riches.
   (Ps. 119:14)

   Thy words were found, and I did eat them; and thy word was unto me the joy and rejoicing of mine heart: for I am called by thy name, O LORD God of hosts. (Jer. 15:16)

Before we conclude this chapter, let's go back to the 2 Timothy 3:16 and quote it again along with verse 17.

16 All scripture is given by inspiration of God, and is profitable for doctrine, for reproof, for correction, for instruction in righteousness:
17 That the man of God may be perfect, throughly furnished unto all good works.

The Word of God is profitable for four things: doctrine, reproof, correction, instruction in righteousness.

Inspiration, Preservation, and Authority

It is profitable for doctrine. That is, it teaches you what is real and right, thereby helping you to make sense of the world around you, even when that world is in a mess. It teaches what is true and false and thereby, enables you to escape deception. It teaches you the will of God, thereby helping you choose the right path to walk, to know what is right, and to avoid the traps of sin. It makes you to understand God, who He is and what He is like. It helps you get to know Him.

It is profitable for reproof. None of us does the right thing all the time. Sometimes we fail and we need to be rebuked for it. *"For the commandment is a lamp; and the law is light; and reproofs of instruction are the way of life"* (Prov. 6:23). Starting as a child, it seems we always have someone telling us we are wrong. This is the way of life and it is good, especially if the rebuke comes from God's Word. *"He is in the way of life that keepeth instruction: but he that refuseth reproof erreth"* (Prov. 10:17). *"Preach the word; be instant in season, out of season; reprove, rebuke, exhort with all longsuffering and doctrine"* (2 Tim. 4:2).

It is profitable for correction. When you are wrong, the Word of God sets you right. *"My son, despise not the chastening of the LORD; neither be weary of his correction"* (Prov. 3:11). *"Correction is grievous unto him that forsaketh the way: and he that hateth reproof shall die"* (Prov. 15:10). The Word of God shows you where you went wrong (reproof) and it shows you how to get right with God again and keep on walking with Him. *"For a just man falleth seven times, and riseth up again: but the wicked shall fall into mischief"* (Prov. 24:16).

It is profitable for instruction in righteousness. *"Teach me good judgment and knowledge: for I have believed thy commandments"* (Ps. 119:66). *"Make thy face to shine upon thy servant; and teach me thy statutes"* (Ps. 119:132). *"Teach me to do thy will; for thou art my God: thy spirit is good; lead me into the land of uprightness"* (Ps. 143:10). *"The fear of the LORD is the beginning of knowledge: but fools despise wisdom and instruction"* (Ps. 1:7).

The Navigators have a good way of explaining these things:

Doctrine – The Bible teaches us what the right path is.

Reproof – The Bible tells us when we have gotten off the right path.

Correction – The Bible tells us how to get back on the right path.

Instruction in righteousness – The Bible tells us how to stay on the right path.

Conclusion

The Bible is God's book. It is full of God's Words. The Words of God entered history through the miraculous process of inspiration. Those words were given in Hebrew, Aramaic, and Greek. Eventually the writings were gathered into scrolls and books. The writings, the Scriptures, were perfect when God inspired them and had them written down. God has preserved them throughout history in the same perfect condition in which they were given. All the words of God have survived and God has made them available to us. We know this because He said that we must "live by every word that proceedeth out of the mouth of God." The Word of God, given by inspiration and kept pure by preservation, is our authority and guide in all issues and matters of life.

The Bible is clear on the power and importance of God's Word. All His words are powerful, precious, and exalted. A translator must bear that in mind when he translates the Bible. Remember, these are the words that God has chosen. He does not take it lightly when you change them or substitute other words for what he has said.

Chapter Three

The First Translator

> *4 And they were all filled with the Holy Ghost, and began to speak with other tongues, as the Spirit gave them utterance.*
> *5 ¶And there were dwelling at Jerusalem Jews, devout men, out of every nation under heaven.*
> *6 Now when this was noised abroad, the multitude came together, and were confounded, because that every man heard them speak in his own language.*
> *7 And they were all amazed and marvelled, saying one to another, Behold, are not all these which speak Galilaeans?*
> *8 And how hear we every man in our own tongue, wherein we were born?*
> *9 Parthians, and Medes, and Elamites, and the dwellers in Mesopotamia, and in Judaea, and Cappadocia, in Pontus, and Asia,*
> *10 Phrygia, and Pamphylia, in Egypt, and in the parts of Libya about Cyrene, and strangers of Rome, Jews and proselytes,*
> *11 Cretes and Arabians, we do hear them speak in our tongues the wonderful works of God. (Acts 2:4-11)*

Bible translating is a subject that we probably do not think much about when we read the Bible. The subject of languages comes up many times, though, and, as we have seen, it starts in the very first book of the Bible. Since God has divided the languages and since we know that he wants the world to be evangelized (all nations-Matthew 28:19-20), he must have made some provision for that in spite of the language barrier.

The Verses above from the Book of Acts describe the situation on the day of Pentecost. The people drawn to the spectacle of 120 people all speaking in different languages (it must have been quite a noise) were from various countries. They were all Jews, but they spoke the various languages of the countries where they lived. They all heard the Word of God in the language of the countries where they resided. Since such a thing was impossible, it was a miracle. *God Himself did it.*

The First Translator

God has moved in history in such a way that makes His desire abundantly clear. History shows a consistent Bible translation movement from the early days of church history. We will look at some of the details of that movement later. Every movement must have a beginning, though. History's line of translators must have a first translator. Who is the first Bible translator?

To find this out, it will be necessary to review a little Bible history. Up until Babel in Genesis 11, the entire earth spoke one language. After Genesis 11, there were numerous languages and people from one language found it hard to talk to people of a different language, just as it is today. Genesis 10 outlines the original nations descended from the sons of Noah. These all had different languages in their nations (Gen, 10:2, 5, 6, 20, 21, 31). Among the sons of Ham was Canaan. He had eleven sons who founded their own nations with their own languages (Gen. 10:15-20). So, when Abraham came into the land of Canaan, he found a land with many inhabitants speaking languages other than his own (Hebrew).

The first description of an encounter Abraham had with someone of another language after he came into Canaan, is in Genesis 12. It was not a Canaanite. It was an Egyptian. During a famine, Abraham and Sarah went to Egypt. They had just recently come into Canaan, so the language of Abraham was no doubt unfamiliar to the other inhabitants of Canaan and to Pharaoh. Yet, Pharaoh spoke to Abraham in Genesis 12:18-19. They must have spoken in Egyptian or a common trade language or through an interpreter. It is highly unlikely they spoke in Hebrew.

There were a number of such instances in Genesis, but let's skip ahead to the history of Joseph in Genesis 37-50. Joseph's ten older brothers were jealous of him. Wanting to get rid of him, they sold him into Egypt as a slave. For a while, he was a slave in the house of the Captain of the Guard. Afterward, he was in prison for a time. While in prison he interpreted the dreams of Pharaoh's chief butler and baker. His entire time as a slave and as a prison inmate was thirteen years. Joseph, then, had years of being forced to learn to speak Egyptian. The conversations between him and the other Egyptians certainly took place in the Egyptian language.

In the Book of Exodus, Moses had several direct conversations with Pharaoh. Moses had grown up in the household of Pharaoh and was fluent in Egyptian. Doubtless, these conversations were in Egyptian.

In the New Testament, there were several languages spoken in Israel: Latin, Hebrew, Aramaic, and some Greek. Doubtless, Jesus' mother tongue was Hebrew. Scholars today try to say Jesus' normal spoken language was Aramaic, but I beg to differ. The conclusion that the Jews in Palestine spoke Aramaic comes from certain inscriptions and writings found that were in that language. However, when the Jews returned from the Babylonian captivity, their everyday language was Hebrew. This is evident by the fact that they wrote their history of the time (Ezra and Nehemiah) in Hebrew. When Jesus was crucified, the inscription on the cross was in Hebrew, Greek and Latin. Aramaic was not there.

The portions of Ezra (4:7-6:18; 7:12-26) that were written in Aramaic, were written for a specific purpose. The Jews were dealing with certain Syrians who were making trouble for them. Two letters were written from the Syrians to the King of Persia. The decree of King Cyrus was referred to, inquiries were made about the authority of the Jews to rebuild, and a request was made for a records search. Aramaic was the language of the Syrians and an empire wide trade language. This section was clearly written in that language to make it easy for the Persians, the Jews, and the Syrians to read and understand. The whole section is a message to the Syrians to leave the Jews alone because the Jews have the authority of the King and the protection of God Almighty. The book is again recorded in Hebrew beginning at 6:19 where the subject changes to the Jews keeping Passover. The language changes to Aramaic once again at verse 7:12. There, a copy of the letter given by Artaxerxes, King of Persia, to Ezra is reproduced. The letter gave authority to the Jews to rebuild and warns any who oppose either the rebuilding or the law of God that they will face the judgment of the King of Persia. Obviously, once again, this was written in Aramaic for the sake of the enemies of the Jews, so that they may read, easily understand, and fear the King, and, so, leave the Jews alone to finish their work. When the language once again switches back to Hebrew in Ezra 7:27, it is about great praise given to God from Ezra's grateful heart.

The Jews were not about to abandon their heart language for a heathen language. Therefore, I believe Jesus spoke Hebrew as He conducted His life and ministry. It should also be noted, that Aramaic was spoken in Palestine and influenced Hebrew. There were place names and other Aramaic words that became part of the Hebrew spoken in Israel. This is typical of any language. Consider how many French and Spanish words have become English words. Some of the French words are café, garage, route, chauffer, encore, ensemble, rule, chemise, á propos, and purée. Spanish words in English include adobe, rodeo, fiesta, lasso, patio, and tomato.

What is the point of all this? In the Old Testament we have conversations conducted in Egyptian. In the New Testament, Jesus preached and taught in Hebrew. Yet, when God inspired Moses and the Gospel writers to record these histories, He inspired them in a different language than that used in the real events. God inspired Moses to take the Egyptian words of Pharaoh, the baker, the butler, and Joseph and write them down in Hebrew. God inspired Matthew to write the Hebrew words of Jesus in Greek. The act of inspiration was itself an act of translation. God, who knows all languages, translated the Egyptian words into Hebrew and inspired the Scriptures in Hebrew. He translated Jesus' Hebrew words into Greek and inspired the writing in Greek.

God, Himself, is the first Bible Translator.

I'm quite certain someone will point out that the words of Moses, for example, were not Scripture when they were spoken. They did not become Scripture until they were inspired and written down. Therefore, God may have been translating, but He was not translating Scripture. An argument can perhaps be made about Moses and Pharaoh, but the same cannot be said of the words of Jesus.

Jesus is God (1 Tim. 3:16) and when He speaks it is from the mouth of God. Notice Galatians 3:8 again, "And the scripture, foreseeing that God would justify the heathen through faith, preached before the gospel unto Abraham, saying, In thee shall all nations be blessed." There was no written Scripture when Abraham received this message, yet it is said "the Scripture ... preached." It was God who did the preaching, according to Genesis 12:1-2. When God opens His mouth to communicate truth to mankind, it is Scripture. When Jesus spoke and preached, He being God, it was Scripture. When Jesus spoke, it was in Hebrew, but when God was ready for the words to be written, He inspired the exact same words Jesus spoke in Hebrew into Greek. It was a *perfect translation*. God did not stop there. He has gone beyond that and led His people to translate the Bible into many languages through 2000 years of history after the cross. This proves that a translation can be perfect. We will look at that more later.

Chapter Four

The Great Commission And the Plan of God

19 Go ye therefore, and teach all nations, baptizing them in the name of the Father, and of the Son, and of the Holy Ghost:
20 Teaching them to observe all things whatsoever I have commanded you: and, lo, I am with you alway, even unto the end of the world. Amen. (Matt. 28:19-20).

In 1793, William Carey sailed for India under the banner of the English Baptist Missionary Society. He was to go on to become known as the "Father of Modern Missions." However, before he was able to go forth as a missionary, he had to convince his fellow Baptists in England that it was scriptural to use means for the conversion of the nations. They, being filled with a strong Calvinism, had no burden to preach the Gospel to the entire world. It is reported that Doctor Ryland said to him, "Sit down young man; when the Lord gets ready to convert the heathen He will do it without your help or mine." [24] In the hope of convincing them he wrote a book called *An Enquirey into the Obligation of Christians to Use Means for the Conversion of the Heathen*.

Later he spoke to a group of ministers at a Baptist Association meeting in Nottingham. He preached from Is. 54:2,3, *"Enlarge the place of thy tent, and let them stretch forth the curtains of thine habitations: spare not, lengthen thy cords, and strengthen thy stakes; For thou shalt break forth on the right hand and on the left; and thy seed shall inherit the Gentiles, and make the desolate cities to be inhabited."* In this sermon Carey issued the challenge, "Expect great things from God; attempt great things for God."[25]

Under his ministry, the Bible was translated into 40 different languages and dialects before his death. He, himself, did much of this work. Of these translations some two hundred and twelve thousand copies were issued during his lifetime. [26]

William Carey felt that Bible translation was a necessary part of preaching the gospel and establishing churches among an unreached group of people. The need for Bible translation could not be clearer. But today, as in Carey's time, it seems that some need to be convinced.

Are you a Bible believer? Then what could be more convincing than the Word of God itself? What could be clearer than to see God's plan from the scriptures? The Word of God is sent to every nation and to every language. It will be preached to those who speak every language and there will be converts out of every nation. In this chapter, we are going to look at a few key passages that show that every language figures in the plan of God and that the Word of God should be translated into these many languages.

Only One Bible

> Translation it is that openeth the window, to let in the light; that breaketh the shell, that we may eat the kernel; that putteth aside the curtain, that we may look into the most Holy place; that removeth the cover of the well, that we may come by the water, even as Jacob rolled away the stone from the mouth of the well, by which means the flocks of Laban were watered [Gen 29:10]. Indeed, without translation into the vulgar tongue, the unlearned are but like children at Jacob's well (which was deep) [John 4:11] without a bucket or something to draw with; or as that person mentioned by Isaiah, to whom when a sealed book was delivered, with this motion, Read this, I pray thee, he was fain to make this answer, I cannot, for it is sealed. [Isa 29:11]. [27]

At the time of this writing, there are 4011 languages that do not have any known published Scripture, according to Wycliffe. [28] The nations who speak these languages vary from six individuals to over fourteen million.[29] This is bad enough, but it is worse when you take into account the many poorly done translations. As we travel world-wide, we often find translations that are, at least partially, badly done and are in need of revision or replacement.

Regardless, there are many who are totally unaware of the need of Bible translating. There are also those who seem to think Bible translating is an unnecessary effort. One idea that some hold was expressed by a well-known evangelist in answer to a question: does there have to be a perfect translation in languages other than English? After answering, *no*, he gave this explanation.

> ***God has always given His word to one people in one language to do one job; convert the world.*** The supposition that there must be a perfect translation in every language is erroneous and inconsistent with God's proven practice ...
>
> (1) The Old Testament:
> It is an accepted fact that, with the exception of some portions of Ezra and Daniel, the Old Testament was written in Hebrew. It is also accepted that it was divinely given to the Jews.
> Thus God initiates His pattern of operation. ***He gave His words to one people in only one language*** ... The Old Testament was given **exclusively** to the Jews.
>
> (2) New Testament:
> It is also an accepted fact that the New Testament was written in Greek. Koine Greek to be exact. Again, the Lord apparently saw no reason to inspire a perfect original in all of the languages of the world extant at that time. Only this time, instead of giving His Book to a nation, such as Israel, He simply gave it to the Christians who were told to go out and convert the world. (Matthew 28:19) ...
>
> (3) The Entire Bible:
> It is obvious that God now needed to get both His Old Testament and His New Testament welded together in a language that was common to the

world. Only English can be considered such a language.

The English language had been developing for many centuries until the late sixteenth century. About that time it finally reached a state of excellence that no language on earth has ever attained. It would seem that God did the rest. He chose this perfect language for the consummation of his perfect Book ... Today nations who do not speak English must still teach English to many of their citizens. Even nations antagonistic to the West such as Russia and Red China must teach English to their business and military personnel.

Thus in choosing English in which to combine His two Testaments, God chose the only language which the world would know. Just as He has shown in His choosing only **one** language for the Old Testament and only **one** language for the New Testament, He continued that practice by combining those two testaments in only **one** language. (Emphasis-SC) [30]

The Case for Perfect Translations

In common with those who agree with this idea, I believe the King James Bible is the inerrant Word of God in the English language; a complete, accurate, true, faithful, and mature translation; and a standard for all other translations. That is, after all, what the English word "perfect" means in regard to a translation: complete and inerrant.

> PERFECT means: "being entirely without fault or defect : flawless ... satisfying all requirements : accurate ... faithfully reproducing the original ... lacking in no essential detail : complete" [31]

The first use of the word *perfect* in the Bible is Genesis 6:9 and applies to Noah, who is described as a just and perfect man. It is also used of the Scriptures in Psalms 19:7. The Hebrew word, *tamiym*, means blameless or complete. It is translated without blemish, without Spot, upright, whole, full (as in a full year), sound, undefiled, and sincerity. The word perfect is not some mysterious word that carries a meaning that we can't quite fathom. It is quite an ordinary term. In regard to the Bible, whether in the original languages or a translation, *perfect* means *complete and inerrant*. I see **no Scriptural reason** *why any translation in any language cannot be complete and inerrant.*

Many prefer to use the words *accurate and faithful*. What exactly does that mean?

> ACCURATE means: "free from error especially as the result of care ... conforming exactly to truth or to a standard : exact"[32]
>
> FAITHFUL means: true to the facts, to a standard, or to an original [33]

In looking at these definitions, it is evident that when we say a translation is *accurate,* it means that *it is inerrant, without error.* This is intrinsic in the meaning of the term. If we say a translation is also faithful, we should understand that means it is *true to the original.* If it is true to the original, it is complete and without error. *Therefore, any translation that is accurate and faithful is without error and complete; it is perfect.* A complete and accurate Bible is perfect. As we shall see, in order to fulfill Matthew 4:4, every people must have a complete and accurate (inerrant, faithful, perfect) Bible in their own language or a language they *easily* understand.

There are some weaknesses to the above "only one language" argument that should be noted. I find **nothing in Scripture** to back up the idea that God combined the Old and New Testaments into only one language, English, and that all other Bibles in other languages cannot be perfect. I find **nothing in history** to back it up and we will look at history later.

That view is an opinion only.

The argument says in part that in these days English is a universal language and nations which don't speak English must teach English to many of their citizens, such as the military and business people. However, this is true in only some countries, not all. Perhaps these countries teach English to the more educated and politically connected, but what about the less educated? What about the common laborer? What about the uneducated farmer? What about the naked tribesman sitting on a log by the Amazon River? What about the millions, yes, the billions, who are not included in this English training? In my travels in West Africa, I have learned something about the nine countries of West Africa, whose official language is French. Many speak fluent French, all know their tribal language, but *very few* speak or read English.

For over two centuries we have known that we cannot evangelize the world by teaching them English or with an English Bible. We expect ... no, we require that a missionary who goes to a foreign country learn the language of the people and communicate with them in that language. Yet, somehow, some think they can be evangelized with an inerrant Bible only in English? How would you like to be told you can never have an inerrant Bible in your mother tongue? Wouldn't you want to have a Bible, an inerrant Bible, in your mother tongue? There is nothing in the Bible to back up the opinion that you *cannot* have a complete accurate (perfect) Bible in anything, but English.

In a 2004 article titled *Writing Global English*, Dennis List had this assessment of how "global" English really is.

> The British Council estimates that the world has about 375 million people who speak English as a first language, another 375 million who speak it regularly as a second language in a country where English has some semi-official status (such as India), and about 750 million more people who speak English as a foreign language. For more details, see Barbara Wallraff's article What Global Language? from The Atlantic Monthly for November 2000. The implication I drew from this article was that at least half the people who know English don't know it perfectly. When writing pages for this website, I (DL) think of my own skill-or to be more precise, lack of skill - in French. I studied French at school for 5 years, and can read simple French - though slowly... As for

spoken French, I can't keep up with it: watching TV5 (the French satellite channel) is very frustrating. If only the French wouldn't speak so fast! And if only they would pause between words![34]

This assessment of English usage amounts to 1 billion 500 million people who perhaps could *possibly* be evangelized with an English Bible. In double checking these numbers, I found that Dennis List was more generous in his numbers than the current information on the web site "English Language All About the English Language." They list 400 million mother tongue users and 700 million foreign language users of English. [35] Wikipedia lists 400 million mother tongue users, 750 million second language users, and 700 million users of English as a foreign language. [36]

There were about 7.5 billion people on earth. If the numbers and assessment in the largest estimate above are correct, it amounts to a total 1 billion 550 million. That leaves 6 billion people (at least), who know little or nothing about English, and who could *not* be evangelized or trained in discipleship with an English Bible.

In the light of Matthew 4:4, "**Man** *shall not live by bread alone, but by* **every word** *that proceedeth out of the mouth of God*", the whole notion of a completely faithful and accurate Bible in only one language is ridiculous. The very idea flies in the face of what God has *actually said*. God *has* said that *every person* in the world shall live by *every one* of His words. Not only that, but it also flouts what God did at Babel in confusing the world's languages (Genesis 11). God doesn't *want* the world to communicate in only one language and He doesn't communicate with the world in only one language. God separated the nations in their own languages, so they could more easily seek God (Acts 17:26-27; e.g. Gen. 10:20). The diversity of language is God's idea, God's plan, God's will. *So, if all of us of every nation are to live by every one of God's Words, it is God's will and plan that we have every one of His words in our own language.* That sounds, to me, like it requires a perfect (complete and accurate) Bible in many languages.

God did limit the number of languages in which He *gave* the Word, but that was a matter of *inspiration* not translation. That is, God limited the Word to three languages *when He first gave the Word* (1 Tim. 3:16). But, that was only the beginning. There is not one word in Scripture that says God limited the number of languages into which His Word could be perfectly translated. Inspiration and translation are two entirely different things. Translation is the process by which the original words of God are transferred from the original languages or another accurate translation to a new language. God is involved in the process of translation, but it is *fundamentally different from inspiration.* When God originally gave His Word, it is obvious that he needed to limit the number of languages used. He inspired it in Hebrew, Aramaic, and Greek. However, there is no word from God that limits the process of accurate, even perfect, translation to only a few languages or to only one language. It can encompass all languages. There can be an accurate translation in every language. Man is limited and fallible, but God is not.

The only conclusion we can come to is that God actually *wants* all His words to be completely and accurately (perfectly) translated into every language. Once again, I turn to Matthew 4:4. We must have all God's Words if we are to live by every word that proceeds out of His mouth. That means we must have them, every Word of God, in our own language or a language we easily understand. *Therefore, it is God's will that His words be translated accurately and completely.* A faithful and accurate (i.e. perfect) translation *can* exist in *every language.*

The Great Commission

The logical place to look in examining God's plan for the evangelization of the world and the translating of the Scriptures is the great commission. Is Bible translating included in the Great Commission? To answer that question, I will quote each of the five instances where the commission is given.

> *Go ye therefore, and teach all nations, baptizing them in the name of the Father, and of the Son, and of the Holy Ghost: Teaching them to observe all things whatsoever I have commanded you: and, lo, I am with you alway, even unto the end of the world. Amen. (Matt. 28:19-20)*
>
> *And he said unto them, Go ye into all the world, and preach the gospel to every creature. (Mark 16:15)*

> *And said unto them, Thus it is written, and thus it behoved Christ to suffer, and to rise from the dead the third day: And that repentance and remission of sins should be preached in his name among all nations, beginning at Jerusalem. And ye are witnesses of these things. (Luke 24:46-48)*
>
> *Then said Jesus to them again, Peace be unto you: as my Father hath sent me, even so send I you. (John 20:21)*
>
> *But ye shall receive power, after that the Holy Ghost is come upon you: and ye shall be witnesses unto me both in Jerusalem, and in all Judaea, and in Samaria, and unto the uttermost part of the earth. (Acts 1:8)*

I invite you to carefully examine all these verses. Do you find any specific mention of Bible translation work? You say, no? You cannot find the word "translating" anywhere? So, Bible translating is not in the Great Commission?

Well, then. Tell me, do you find the words "church planting" anywhere in the Great Commission? No, you do not. They are not there. So, are we to come to the conclusion that "church planting" is not in the Great Commission, just because the words are not there? That would come as a surprise to a great many churches and missionaries.

However, it's obvious that church planting is definitely included in the Great Commission, even though it is not explicitly mentioned. The example in the Book of Acts is that evangelism leads to the formation of churches. The Great Commission commands "teaching" twice. Once you have taught people the gospel, it is necessary to gather the converts into groups for further training in discipleship. If you have evangelized a few people, baptized them, gathered them into a group, have them meet regularly for preaching and teaching, and appointed leadership, you have a church. The activities of the Great Commission will naturally lead to starting churches as surely as buying food leads to eating.

The same is true for Bible translation. It is impossible to carry out the teaching functions of the Great Commission without Bible translation. What are we going to teach? The will of God doesn't

The Great Commission and the Plan of God

float in the air. It is written down in a book. We learn all the plan and truth of God from a book. When Paul preached in Berea, the people searched the Scriptures to find out if he was telling the truth (Acts 17:11). What if they had not had the Scriptures? They couldn't be sure if Paul was telling the truth. Why is it when we witness that we often show the sinner verses of Scripture? It is because we want them to see for themselves what God says.

It is a fact that we cannot train believers in discipleship and the truths of God without the Scriptures. If we translate the Scriptures into their language, we can teach them, and they can also search the Scriptures for themselves. Without the Scriptures, we cannot fulfill the Great Commission. It is impossible.

Suppose a missionary goes to a people who have no Bible. He cannot win them to Christ or train them to live for Christ without audibly or in writing telling them what God says. If he does this, he is translating (if he is faithful to correctly quote God), because he is telling them what God said in their language. He may only tell them what God says audibly, but he is still translating. So, he must become a translator. What if a missionary goes to a people who have a Bible, but he finds the Bible they have is full of errors and is a generally bad translation? He will still have to tell the people what God truly says in those mistranslated places and, therefore, he still becomes a translator. If he leaves and the people are still without a Bible or still have a bad Bible, we will see in Acts 20 that he leaves them vulnerable for the attack of Satan. *It is impossible to fulfill the great commission without Bible translating.*

We are born again by the Word of God (1 Peter 1:23). Without the Word, we cannot win souls or even preach the gospel of Jesus Christ. This requires that the gospel be translated into every language. Furthermore, it requires that the gospel be translated *perfectly* into all languages. Since the Word of God is *perfect*, because it came from a perfect God, then only the *perfect* Word of God can give the new birth. Therefore, the *perfect* gospel must exist in every language.

The words of God were given to "live by." The word gives us milk so that we can become healthy and grow as babies in Christ (1 Peter 2:2). It is meat for those who are mature (Heb. 5:14). It is compared to bread (Mt. 4:4). It is honey (Ps. 19:10) and its wisdom is fruitful (Prov. 8:19). Those who gaze at it are transformed into the image of Christ (2 Cor. 3:17-18; James. 1:22-25). The Scriptures give spiritual strength and muscle and give us *"an inheritance among all them which are sanctified"* (Acts 20:32) Is it any wonder why we must live by *"every word that proceedeth out of the mouth of God"*? The Word of God is absolutely necessary to growth and godliness. Errant words will not accomplish this. For life and growth, we must give them inerrant words; that is, the perfect Words of God.

The Word of God was given for training in discipleship and service: *"That the man of God may be perfect, throughly furnished unto all good works"* (2 Tim. 3:17). In the Great Commission, the Lord Jesus commanded, *"Teaching them to observe all things whatsoever I have commanded you."* This second command to teach in Matthew 28:19-20 involves training for discipleship and service. Once again, this cannot be done unless the Word of God is in their language. The perfect Word is called upon so that *"the man of God may be **perfect**."* Therefore, if an Ewe speaking Togolese, for example, is to become perfect, *he needs the perfect Word.*

In Revelation 1:3, we find the statement, *"Blessed is he that **readeth**."* These words were written for every human being on earth since man (mankind) shall live by every word that proceeds out of the mouth of God. Think of that. The naked tribesman in the jungle is told, *"Blessed is he that readeth."* How can he do this if he does not have the Word of God written in his language? Furthermore, the Bible is *"a lamp unto my feet and a light unto my path"* (Ps. 119:105) for that naked uncivilized man just as much as it is for the well dressed Englishman or American or German. If that naked man, sitting on his log by the Amazon river, must live by every word that proceeds out of the mouth of God, then he is to obey this verse also: *"**Study** to shew thyself approved unto God, a workman that needeth not to be ashamed, rightly dividing the word of truth"* (2 Tim. 2:15). He is also told, *"This book of the law shall not depart out of thy mouth; but thou shalt **meditate** therein day and night, that thou mayest observe to do according to all that is written therein: for then thou shalt make thy way prosperous, and then thou shalt have good success"* (Joshua 1:8). How, I ask again, can he do this unless he has the Word of God in his language? God has left us with the responsibility to enable him to fulfill the commands of the Word by translating the Word and, if need be, to reduce his language to writing and to teach him to read.

God's Plan of Ministry

When Paul was traveling to Jerusalem at the end of his third missionary journey, he determined to stop near Ephesus to bid farewell to the elders there. In the eighteen verses of his speech in Acts 20, he referred to the Word of God or to the preaching of the Word of God in nine verses. In this passage, Paul commended the future of the church which he had built to the God who was able to preserve it and to the Word of God.

> *25 And now, behold, I know that ye all, among whom I have gone preaching the kingdom of God, **shall see my face no more.***
> *26 Wherefore I take you to record this day, that I am pure from the blood of all men.*
> *27 For I have not shunned to declare unto you **all the counsel of God.***
> *28 Take heed therefore unto yourselves, and to all the flock, over the which the Holy Ghost hath made you overseers, to feed the church of God, which he hath purchased with his own blood.*
> *29 For I know this, that after my departing shall grievous wolves enter in among you, not sparing the flock.*
> *30 Also of your own selves shall men arise, speaking perverse things, to draw away disciples after them.*
> *31 Therefore watch, and remember, that by the space of three years I ceased not to warn every one night and day with tears.*
> *32 And now, brethren, **I commend you to God, and to the word of his grace**, which is able to build you 'up, and to give you an inheritance among all them which are sanctified. (Acts 20:26-32)*

Paul had spent many years writing inspired letters to various churches. The gospels and other Scripture had been inspired since the resurrection, with still more to come. It was to these scriptures that he was commending the churches (2 Peter 3:16) as well as those of the Old Testament. He trusted God's ability to use the scriptures to continue the church growth and expansion that he began. He did not trust Timothy or Titus or Silas to do this, because they too would soon be passing from the scene. But, He knew that God's Word would always remain.

Two Phases of Ministry

The passage in Acts 20 reveals two phases of ministry that every missionary goes through. Like Paul, he first travels to a strange area filled with strange people. Unless the new Country speaks His own language, he will need to learn their language before he can begin his ministry to them.

Every new such mission ministry always begins with the missionary as an example. *"Ye know, from the first day that I came into Asia, after what manner I have been with you at all seasons, Serving the Lord with all humility of mind, and with many tears, and temptations, which befell me by the lying in wait of the Jews"* (Acts 20:18-19). Paul also mentioned this in 1 Thess. 1:5, *"For our gospel came not unto you in word only, but also in power, and in the Holy Ghost, and in much assurance; as ye know what manner of men we were among you for your sake."* And Paul told Timothy to look to his example, *"But thou hast fully known my doctrine, manner of life, purpose, faith, longsuffering, charity, patience, Persecutions, afflictions, which came unto me at Antioch, at Iconium, at Lystra; what persecutions I endured: but out of them all the Lord delivered me"* (2 Timothy 3:10-11). Long before a missionary is able to speak fluently enough to clearly preach the Gospel, the people will know him well. They may not understand his message. They may not know why he is among them. But, they will know *what he* is. They will be able to see his character through his behavior. They will be able to see his heart and his compassion. This will help prepare the way for the verbal ministry to come.

The content of the missionary's verbal ministry is described in Acts 20:20, 21, and 27. Paul kept back *"nothing that was profitable"* to them. What he preached and taught is described first in verse 21 as *"repentance toward God, and faith toward our Lord Jesus Christ."* Later (in verse 27), he says that he taught them *"the whole counsel of God."*

Eventually he wins his first converts. Other converts follow, and his ministry begins to take root. He is busy preaching the gospel, teaching converts, comforting the hurting, and helping the saints. Also, as Paul, he goes through many hard times. Satan attacks in numerous ways, and other difficulties arise. There may be persecution, as Paul experienced on many occasions. There may be sickness or other trouble of various kinds. Nevertheless, through it all, the missionary is among the people to whom he is ministering. He is in constant contact with them. He is very aware of their spiritual condition.

However, in the end all of this must change. The missionary may stay with the people of his ministry for many years, but eventually there comes a time when he must leave. A missionary cannot stay forever. We are not thinking here of only a short-term furlough. We are looking at his final departure. When that happens, most missionaries never see that particular group of people again. When the missionary is gone, the people are on their own. He can no longer preach to them or teach them. He can no longer comfort them. He can no longer protect them from false teachers or, as Paul called them, "wolves." He no longer knows their spiritual condition except through correspondence and then the best he can do for them may be to pray. Otherwise any further ministry is very limited or stopped altogether.

Paul was past the stage where he had left them in presence. Now he could see that in the near future he would leave them permanently through death. He seemed to consider this his last chance to minister to them face to face and his concern was for their future. How would they be able to carry on? Paul would no longer be around to help them and protect them with his teaching.

The Continuing Safety of the Churches

Now that Paul had returned for a short visit, his eyes were on the future of the church in Ephesus. To what did Paul entrust the future of the Ephesian church? Did he depend on them always keeping in remembrance what he had verbally taught? He certainly did not. He assured them that there would be a time when grievous wolves would teach falsehoods and that some would seek to draw away disciples for themselves. These wolves would not come from outside but would arise from among the elders of the church itself. If a church only has the verbal ministry of a missionary, who is no longer there to help, the wolves will get them. Memories fade and it will be easy for the wolves to deceive them. When the leaders of the church begin to teach things contrary to the missionary's doctrine, it doesn't take long for the church to become confused about what is true. Early in Paul's ministry the Galatian churches were confused on doctrine because of false teachers who came to them shortly after Paul left (Gal.3:1). It didn't take long for them to be deceived in the absence of written teaching from Paul. Therefore, he wrote the book of Galatians to straighten them out.

In every culture, every new church that is planted has to fight a battle with the "grievous wolves" sooner or later. What will keep them doctrinally straight? It won't be a remembrance of the doctrinal truths taught by a missionary who has long since departed, no matter how eloquently or creatively presented. Safety can come from only one source, the source Paul trusted. *"And now, brethren, I commend you to **God**, and to the **word of his grace**, which is able to build you up, and to give you an inheritance among all them which are sanctified"* (Acts 20:32). Paul entrusted them to God first and the Word of God second. The only standard that can withstand the ravages of time, false teaching, and failing memory is a permanent standard, the written Word of God. For that, the people need the Bible in their own language. If they have the written Word of God then they can go on even without any further help from a missionary, because the word is able to build them up.

The Word of God will do its job according to its nature (2 Timothy 3:16, 17). The Scriptures in the language of the people will teach them what the right doctrines are and the right way to walk with God (doctrine). The Scriptures will perfect the saints and enable them to fulfill all the will of God for their lives. The word is able to *"build you up"* (verse 32). The Word of God is to the spirit what food is to the body. It is compared to meat (Heb. 5:12), to milk (Heb.5:12), to bread (Luke 4:4), to honey (Ps. 119:103), to apples (Prov. 25:11), and to water (Eph.5:26). The Scriptures will put spiritual muscle on those who make it their regular diet. Those who do not do that will become weak and vulnerable to Satanic attack.

With the translated Scriptures, the written Word of God, in their hands, the national church has a chance to survive and flourish.

Without the Scriptures the national church will eventually sink into false doctrine and moral error. It will eventually cease to be a New Testament church.

Transformation by the Word

The ultimate goal of the Christian life is to be conformed to the image of the Son of God (Rom. 8:28-30). That transformation begins in this life. Rom. 12:1-2 tells us that we are transformed by the renewing of our minds. Our minds are renewed by the Spirit and the Word of God. 2 Cor. 3:18 says:

> *But we all, with open face beholding as in a glass the glory of the Lord, are changed into the same image from glory to glory, even as by the Spirit of the Lord. (2 Cor. 3:18)*

The glass in this verse is the Word of God (James 1:23). The glory of God is found in the face of Jesus Christ (2 Cor. 4:6). As we gaze into the glass (the Word) we are changed from glory to glory into the image we see (Christ). When we look into the mirror of the Word of God, the image we see is Jesus Christ. Jesus said, *"Search the scriptures; for in them ye think ye have eternal life: and they are they which testify of me"* (John 5:39). As we look regularly into the Scriptures, the Spirit of God transforms us step by step into the image of Jesus Christ. *"Let the word of Christ dwell in you richly in all wisdom"* (Col. 3:16).

The Sufficiency of God's Words

One of the most important doctrines about the Bible is *the sufficiency of Scripture*. The word *sufficiency* means *it is enough*. The Word of God is totally, 100 percent sufficient to accomplish the purpose for which God sent it. Without the Bible in our own language we lack this sufficiency.

What is the purpose for which God sent the Word? Once again, Matthew 4:4 lays it out. The Word of God gives us all we need to live a life that pleases both God and ourselves. It gives us all we need to have holy character and behavior. It supplies all we need to be transformed into the image of Christ.

> *3 According as his divine power hath given unto us all things that pertain unto life and godliness, through the knowledge of him that hath called us to glory and virtue:*
> *4 Whereby are given unto us exceeding great and precious promises: that by these ye might be partakers of the divine nature, having escaped the corruption that is in the world through lust. (2 Peter 1:3-4)*

Life and godliness come through knowledge of the Lord Jesus. Christians escape the corruption of the world and partake of the divine nature through God's promises. Where do Christians find this knowledge and these promises? They find them in the Word of God of course. God wants people of all nations and languages to have these things.

If we *cannot* give them perfect translations, how imperfect should we allow their translations to be? Perhaps, we should be content to let the United Bible Societies and Wycliffe Bible Translators provide corrupt translations (see chapter twelve). That's all they need isn't it? No, what they really need is translations in their own languages that accurately contain *"every word that proceedeth out of the mouth of God."*

Nothing in the sciences or philosophies of mankind can make you complete and mature, spiritually, mentally, and emotionally. A life-time of psychological studies is not sufficient for it. The wisdom of man is not sufficient for successful living. Paul explains, *"Howbeit we speak wisdom among them that are perfect: yet **not the wisdom of this world**, nor of the princes of this world, that come to nought: But we speak **the wisdom of God** in a mystery, even the hidden wisdom, which God ordained before the world unto our glory"* (1 Cor. 2:6-7). *"But of him are ye in Christ Jesus, **who of God is made unto us wisdom**, and **righteousness,** and **sanctification**, and **redemption**: That, according **as it is written**, He that glorieth, let him glory in the Lord"* (1 Cor. 1:30-31).

There are many places in the Scriptures that speak to this subject, but one of the best is Psalms 19:7-14.

7 The law of the LORD is perfect, converting the soul: the testimony of the LORD is sure, making wise the simple.
8 The statutes of the LORD are right, rejoicing the heart: the commandment of the LORD is pure, enlightening the eyes.
9 The fear of the LORD is clean, enduring for ever: the judgments of the LORD are true and righteous altogether.
10 More to be desired are they than gold, yea, than much fine gold: sweeter also than honey and the honeycomb.
11 Moreover by them is thy servant warned: and in keeping of them there is great reward.
12 Who can understand his errors? cleanse thou me from secret faults.
13 Keep back thy servant also from presumptuous sins; let them not have dominion over me: then shall I be upright, and I shall be innocent from the great transgression.
14 Let the words of my mouth, and the meditation of my heart, be acceptable in thy sight, O LORD, my strength, and my redeemer.

Verses seven through nine describe the Word. They present *six lines of thought*, with *three elements each*: a title for the Word, a Characteristic of the Word, and a benefit of the Word.

Vs	Title	Characteristic	Benefit
7	Law	Perfect	Converts soul
	Testimonies	Sure	makes wise
8	Statutes	Right	rejoices heart
	Commandments	Pure	enlightenment
9	Fear	Clean	endures forever
	Judgments	True and Righteous	Righteousness

Fig. 6

Verses ten through fourteen show the Scriptures to be the sufficient source of life's true benefits.

1) The Words of God are the greatest source of wealth (10)
2) The Words of God give life's greatest pleasures (10)
3) The Words of God provide the greatest protection (11)
4) The Words of God give life's greatest profits (11)
5) The Words of God gives the greatest purification (12-13)
6) Finally, the Words of God give life's greatest joy.

Thy words were found, and I did eat them; and **thy word was unto me the joy and rejoicing of mine heart**: *for I am called by thy name, O LORD God of hosts. (Jeremiah 15:16)*

Conclusion

God created the plan to give the world a large variety of languages. In spite of the difficulty that causes in communication, the scattered nations have to be reached with the gospel. After the resurrection, the Lord Jesus Christ sent His church to take the gospel to them. Christians are to preach the gospel and teach the converts how to walk with the Lord as disciples. The only way that can be done is to teach them the Word of God. That requires translating the Bible into their languages.

A missionary enters his ministry to win the people to Christ and to plant churches and to make disciples. He may stay many years ministering to them and preaching the Word of God. However, the time will come when he must leave. After he is gone the churches he has planted will face many dangers, one of which is false teachers who will arise from inside and from outside the church. If the only thing they have to protect themselves from false teachers is the memory of what the missionary taught, they are on shaky ground. The churches need something they can trust, that will be firm and true-something that will not change according to the whims of men. The only thing that fulfills this need is the perfect written Word of God; translated into their language. Therefore, it is imperative that the missionary see to it that the word is translated into the languages of the national churches as perfectly as possible. If they have a Bible that is not accurate or complete in many places, he has an obligation to give them an accurate and true translation. When he leaves he will then be able to entrust them to God and His word. If this is done, God can protect the future of those churches and multiply them throughout the people group.

The Words of God are precious words. These words are part of His heart, His being, His character. They are the words GOD chose to use to communicate about Himself and His will and His plans to all of mankind. God knew what He was doing when He chose these words. Therefore, a translator must handle them reverently and carefully. It is these Words of God that he must translate, not substitute other words of his own choosing. The meaning of the Scriptures depends on the words God chose. If a translator changes the words, he changes the meaning. He should take care that he not be found a liar. Do not tamper with God's Words.

The Words of God are sufficient for our lives to become perfect in Christ Jesus. It is only God's Words that can accomplish this. These words are the source of truth that makes us successful in life; that enable us to successfully face all life's issues; that make us able to fulfill God's will for our lives. The sufficient source of truth Is the Bible **alone.** It is not the Bible PLUS something. It is not the Bible plus philosophy. It is not the Bible plus psychology. It is not the Bible plus science. It is not the Bible plus ANYTHING. It is the Bible, the Words of God, **ALONE.**

Chapter Five

The Scriptural Definition Of Bible Translating

And at the ninth hour Jesus cried with a loud voice, saying, Eloi, Eloi, lama sabachthani? which is, being interpreted, My God, my God, why hast thou forsaken me? (Mark 15:34)

What does it mean to translate? People involved in or concerned about translation work answer that question in different ways. Some would say that translating is moving each word of a document from one language to another *literally*. Others would say that it is moving the *meaning* of words and phrases from one language to another, without regard for the specific words used.

There are differences in views of the definition of *meaning* also. Some see meaning as intrinsic in the words themselves. If we use words that mean the same in both languages, we will be translating word-for-word. This view is called *Formal Equivalence translating*. These would say that the meaning of the words is what the words mean in the mind of the author of the Bible, God.

However, others think that meaning depends on what the readers think and how the readers react to the words. The theory of *Dynamic Equivalence* says that the new translation should cause the readers to react the same way that the original readers reacted. Who is to determine how the first readers reacted to Scripture? Why, the translator, of course. When one reduces Dynamic Equivalence to its simplest elements, the meaning does not depend on an objective standard, such as a dictionary. Meaning depends on what the translator *thinks* it is. Here are definitions of Bible translating some give.

The Scriptural Definition of Translating

Biblical translation, the art and practice of rendering the Bible into languages other than those in which it was originally written. [37]

Until recently there have been two competing theories of Bible translation: formal equivalence and functional equivalence (*also called Dynamic Equivalence-Author*). Formal equivalence, which underlies most of the so called literal English Bible translations, strives to attain word-for-word correspondence between the source text and the translated text. In other words, it seeks wherever possible to transfer the grammatical structure of the source text directly into the receptor language. Due to the work of scholars like Nida (1964), Nida and Taber (1969), and Beekman and Callow (1974), functional equivalence has superseded formal equivalence as the dominant approach to Bible translation over the past 35 years. Rather than word-for-word correspondence, it strives to identify the meaning of the original and transfer that meaning into a natural translation that is easy to understand.[38]

Does the Bible define "Bible Translating?" Every good and perfect gift is from above (Jms. 1:17). An accurate and true Bible translation is a good gift. Therefore, it is God who determines what translating is and how it is to be done. The New Testament uses the word "translation" once in Heb. 11:5, regarding the removing of Enoch from earth. The Greek word there is *metatithēmi,* and it means to transfer from one place to another or to change. [39]

However, the Bible uses the word *interpretation* in regard to language. In the Bible, the word "interpretation" is used when someone is explaining the meaning of something, such as a dream (Gen. 41:12). At other times, it is used in the sense of "translating" or moving words from one language into another. The Greek word is *methermeneuo,* one meaning of which is "to change over." [40] That is, in this case, to change over from one language to another. Let's look at a number of the places where the Bible uses this word.

Interpretation in the Bible

Matthew 1:23-Behold, a virgin shall be with child, and shall bring forth a son, and they shall call his name Emmanuel, which being interpreted is, God with us.

In this case, the Hebrew word *Emmanuel* is translated into Greek. The Hebrew word means *God with us.* This is the exact and precise meaning of the Hebrew word. The Hebrew language has one word which expresses this meaning, but the Greek language does not. Therefore, to express this in Greek requires the use of four words, *meth hemon ho theos* or *the God with us*. Regardless of the fact that four words are needed to express "Emmanuel" in Greek, "God with us" is the exact literal and necessary translation of the Hebrew word. It is a precise meaning of a specific word in Hebrew translated into the precise meaning in Greek with the specific words needed to express that exact meaning.

Mark 5:41-And he took the damsel by the hand, and said unto her, Talitha cumi; which is, being interpreted, Damsel, I say unto thee, arise.

Some say that "Talitha cumi" are both Aramaic words.[41] *The* word Talitha is apparently from Aramaic, but the Hebrew word for "arise" is *cum* or *cumi* (e.g. Gen. 13:17; 21:18 in Heb). Greek has one particular word that means *rise* or *arise*. However, here we seem to have additional inserted words, "I say unto thee." Why is that? A translation sometimes needs inserted words to bring out the meaning. The KJB (and every translation) does that. But, the KJB, as a rule, puts those words in italics, so you will know that they were inserted to help the meaning. In this case, the words are implied in the command, but they are inserted to emphasize *who* was saying, arise. Only God can give life Rom. 4:17). The command was given by Jesus and life came to the little girl. Therefore, Jesus must be God in the flesh.

Once again, the words and their exact meaning were transferred into another language (Greek), using the precise words necessary to express that exact meaning. In this case, the command

The Scriptural Definition of Translating

form in one language (Hebrew) is transferred into another language (Greek) as a command. Even the grammar matches.

> Mark 15:22-And they bring him unto the place Golgotha, which is, being interpreted, The place of a skull.

Golgotha is a transliteration of the word Γολγοθᾶ into English letters. In Luke 23:33, it is called Calvary, which is *kranion* (a skull) in Greek. Golgotha has been described as an Aramaic word. [42] However, in John 19:17, the word is said to be Hebrew. Golgotha also means "a skull." The expression "the place" in the interpretation (the target language) is not properly part of the translation, but comes from *"the place* Golgotha" in the source quote. This is an exact literal translation.

> *Mark 15:34-And at the ninth hour Jesus cried with a loud voice, saying, Eloi, Eloi, lama sabachthani? which is, being interpreted, My God, my God, why hast thou forsaken me?*

This also is a literal translation. *Eloi* means "my God." The Hebrew word *lama* means "why." Finally, the word *sabachthani* means "have you forsaken me." Remember, these "interpretations" represent translation work done by the Holy Spirit, since it is all inspired of God (2 Tim. 3:16). God seems to like translating things very precisely and exact.

> *John 1:38-Then Jesus turned, and saw them following, and saith unto them, What seek ye? They said unto him, Rabbi, (which is to say, being interpreted, Master,) where dwellest thou?*

Again, this is a literal translation of a single Hebrew Word, *Rabbi*. It is translated into the Greek word, *didaskalos*. *Rabbi* means "teacher." *Didaskalos* means "teacher." *Didaskalos* is translated into English with the word *master*. An old meaning of the English word *master* is "teacher," as in *schoolmaster*.

John 1:41-He first findeth his own brother Simon, and saith unto him, We have found the Messias, which is, being interpreted, the Christ.

The same is true in this verse. The direct exact and precise translation of the Hebrew Messiah (*Messias*) into Greek is Christos (the English spelling is Christ). Both words carry the meaning "the anointed one."

John 1:42-And he brought him to Jesus. And when Jesus beheld him, he said, Thou art Simon the son of Jona: thou shalt be called Cephas, which is by interpretation, A stone.

The facts of the previous verse also apply to this translation from Aramaic (*Cephas*) into Greek (*Petros*-a stone). So, in Greek this man was called Peter. In Aramaic, he was called Cephas. Both words mean "a stone."

John 9:7-And said unto him, Go, wash in the pool of Siloam, (which is by interpretation, Sent.) He went his way therefore, and washed, and came seeing.

In this verse, we start with the Hebrew word "siloam," which means "sent." The interpretation in Greek is "apestalmenos," which (wonder of wonders) means "sent."

Acts 4:36-And Joses, who by the apostles was surnamed Barnabas, (which is, being interpreted, The son of consolation,) a Levite, and of the country of Cyprus ...

As we have seen, names often have a meaning. The name Barnabas means "son of consolation" in Aramaic. The interpretation here is a literal translation. As in many places, the single word in Hebrew or Aramaic requires a multiple word translation in Greek. There is no single word in Greek that means "son of consolation," so the interpretation uses the words *uios parakleseos*, son of consolation. The translation is an exact word-for-word translation, except that the word "the" is added in English for clarity. Sometimes it is necessary to add or subtract a conjunction to make the translation in another language smooth or proper grammatically. For example, the Spanish language uses definite articles that would not be correct in English. *El senior Clark* literally becomes *the Mr. Clark* in English, but in English the definite article is incorrect syntax, so it should be left out in a translation.

> *Acts 9:36 - Now there was at Joppa a certain disciple named Tabitha, which by interpretation is called Dorcas: this woman was full of good works and almsdeeds which she did.*
>
> *Acts 13:6 - And when they had gone through the isle unto Paphos, they found a certain sorcerer, a false prophet, a Jew, whose name was Barjesus:*
> *Acts 13:8-But Elymas the sorcerer (for so is his name by interpretation) withstood them, seeking to turn away the deputy from the faith.*

The examples of Tabitha and Elymas are the same principle, although Luke didn't tell us the precise meanings of the names Dorcas and Tabitha. Nevertheless, both the Aramaic Tabitha and the Greek Dorcas mean *Gazelle*. The name Elymas is something of a mystery. There is little information available, but what there is gives a bit of a different scenario. Elymas is apparently a Hebrew word, so the interpretation is not between Elymas and Bar-Jesus. Both are Hebrew names. The name, Elymas, means *sorcerer, magician, or corrupter*. So, in Acts 13:8 the name *Elymas* is translated as *sorcerer*. Therefore, once again, these are translations between words in different languages that are exactly equivalent with one another in meaning.

> *Hebrews 7:1, 2 - For this Melchisedec, king of Salem ... To whom also Abraham gave a tenth part of all; first being by interpretation King of righteousness, and after that also King of Salem, which is, King of peace;*

There are two interpretations or translations in these verses. Melchisedec is a compound name that has special meanings. The

Hebrew *Melech* translates to *King*. *Zedech* is a Hebrew word meaning righteousness. When the two are combined it means *king of righteousness*. Melchisedec was the King of Salem (later to be called Jerusalem). He word *Salem* means *peace*. So, combining *Melech* with *Salem* equals *king of peace*. No one has to wonder about the meaning of these words. Their meanings are dictionary clear.

These final verses are all in the same category as John 1:42 regarding the translation of names. In every instance, a name in the source language has a specific meaning. The translator chose a word in the target language that is the exact meaning of the same name in the source language. It is the same name in both languages.

This exhausts the use of the word *interpretation* in the New Testament in regard to transferring words from one language to another. Basically, the words in the source language, with their exact objective meaning, are directly translated into words that have the same exact objective meaning in the target language. Every example shows that each word is translated and that every word is important to God, even to an exact translation of names. These are all examples of formal equivalent translating.

All of this also explodes another myth; that words in one language do not correspond exactly in meaning with words in another language that mean the exact same thing. The idea is that words in one language are slightly different in meaning with the corresponding words in another language. That is not *always* true, because people in each language deal with the exact same objects, the exact same feelings, the exact same problems and issues, the exact same challenges, the exact same feelings, wishes, wants, ambitions, etc. Each people group with its own language speaks words that express these common things. An Aramaic speaking person may say "Cephas," and a Greek speaking person may reply "Petros," but it is still the *same* stone! One may cry "Eloi, Eloi!" Another will scream "O Theos mou, o theos mou!" Nevertheless, it expresses the exact same feeling with "My God, My God!"

A Biblical Definition of Translating (Interpretation)

Now, we are able to formulate a definition of translating based on the statements of the Bible itself. That definition is as follows.

The Scriptural Definition of Translating

Translating is transferring the words, grammar, and idiom along with their meaning from one language (the source language) into the nearest equivalent words, grammar, and idiom of another language (the target language) with equivalent meaning.

Chapter Six

The Scriptural Method of Translating

Ἐν ἀρχῇ ἦν ὁ λόγος, καὶ ὁ λόγος ἦν πρὸς τὸν Θεόν, καὶ Θεὸς ἦν ὁ λόγος. (John 1:1)

In the beginning was the Word, and the Word was with God, and the Word was God. (John 1:1)

The study we have just finished on the definition of translating can give us some insight into the proper method of translation. God has not left us to our own wisdom when it comes to the method to use to translate His Word. God has a preference as to how it is to be done.

There is a great deal of disagreement over the proper method to be used in Bible translating. In their book, *Translating the Word of God,* John Beekman and John Callow explain two sides of the spectrum, which they call *literal* and *idiomatic.* Within these they divide available translation methods into four types: 1) highly literal, 2) modified literal, 3) idiomatic, and 4) unduly free. These represent the entire spectrum of translation methods from one extreme to another. Beekman and Callow further classify them in two other categories: acceptable methods and unacceptable methods. They produced the following chart.

	Unacceptable	Types		
	Acceptable	Types		
Highly Literal	Modified Literal	Idiomatic		Unduly Free

Fig. 7 [43]

The *Highly literal* method translates the Scriptures with the exact words and grammar of the source text into the target language. An example can be given from Matthew 1:23. If we translate the verse in a highly literal fashion, we get, "Behold, a virgin shall in stomach have, and shall bear a son." Clearly, is not good English and will not work as a finished translation. So, the KJV translated it, "Behold, a virgin shall be with child, and shall bring forth a son ... " We will discuss the KJV translation in this verse again in the next chapter.

A modified literal method takes care to translate so that the target language translation is natural according to the words and grammar of that language. Again, Matthew 1:23 in the KJB is an example of that. The translation comes from Greek and it sticks as close as possible to Greek, but it must read clearly and accurately in English. A modified literal approach recognizes the importance of both the words and grammar of the source text as well as the necessity to reproduce the meaning of the source text in the target text. So, the translator realizes that "shall in stomach have" is really an idiom that means she is pregnant. Therefore, the KJV translators made the English say just that. More will be explained about this method later.

The unduly free translation considers the words and grammar of the source text to be of no importance at all. The only importance is to make the message as understandable and relevant to the audience as possible. The translator is free to use any words he chooses, as long as he communicates what he thinks the message is or should be. It is open to considerable distortion of the message God intended to communicate with the words that He chose.

The idiomatic translation seeks to reproduce the meaning of the source text as nearly as possible in the target text using the normal words and grammar of the target language. The emphasis is on transferring the meaning. The idiomatic translator feels perfectly free to change the words, grammar, and style of the source text at any time, if he thinks it communicates the message better. The translator feels that the choice of words and grammar used in the source text may be unsuitable to communicate the message in the target language. Nevertheless, he sticks closer to the source text than the unduly free translator, but less than modified literal.

Since Beekman and Callow published their book in 1974, the field of translating has focused on two basic ways to find "equivalence" between the source text and the target text. Currently the discussion is centered on two opposing equivalencies: Dynamic Equivalence and Formal Equivalence. The diagram created by

Beekman and Callow can be expanded thusly in current theory. The question marks are to indicate that only one is Scriptural.

Formal	Equivalence	Dynamic	Equivalence
	Unacceptable	Types	
	Acceptable	Types ???	
Highly Literal	Modified Literal	Freely Idiomatic	Unduly Free

Fig. 8

Dynamic Equivalence

Dynamic Equivalence (sometimes called Functional Equivalence) is a translation method that was made popular by a linguist named Eugene Nida (1914-2011). He defined Dynamic equivalence as the "quality of a translation in which the message of the original text has been so transported into the receptor language that the *response* of the *receptor* is essentially like that of the original receptors." [44] The focus of this method is on the "response" of the audience and how the audience perceives meaning. Dynamic Equivalence makes "meaning" the primary determinate of a good translation. The goal of Dynamic Equivalence is to make the translation in the target language create the same reaction and have the same effect on the target readers as the text in the source language had on its readers. Leland Ryken, professor of English emeritus at Wheaton College and a member of the ESV translation committee, defined it this way.

> Briefly stated, the theory of dynamic equivalence in Bible translation emphasizes the reaction of the reader to the translated text, rather than the translation of the words and phrases themselves. In simplest terms, dynamic equivalence is often referred to as "thought for thought" translation as compared to "essentially literal" [45]

Dynamic Equivalent: A meaning in the receptor language that corresponds to (is "equivalent" to) a meaning in a native-language text (for example, the "heart" as the modern way of denoting the essence of a person, especially the emotions, which for the ancients was situated in the kidneys).

Functional equivalence: a theory of translation that favors replacing a statement in the original text with a functional equivalent whenever the original phraseology or reference is obscure for a modern reader in the receptor language. [46]

Dr. Ryken is against dynamic equivalence. He prefers "essentially literal" methodology, which he defines very similarly to the definition we give to "formal equivalence." I consider them to be the same. In his book, he used various approaches to show the weaknesses of the dynamic equivalence theory. One of these is to compare it to how famous literature is quoted or translated. He described the dynamic equivalent method this way.

> More specifically, consider how you would feel if a transcriber decided to do the following things to something that you had painstakingly and consciously composed:
>
> • reduced the level of vocabulary from what you had written to what the translator regarded as a seventh-grade vocabulary level;
>
> • cut your sentences down into a series of shorter sentences;
>
> • dropped metaphors because he decided that a target audience did not know how to handle figurative language; changed words that he thought to be old-fashioned;

- eliminated words that he thought to be technical;

- changed words to match what he thought you had intended to say. [47]

    This is what dynamic equivalence does to the Word of God. Dynamic Equivalence will sacrifice the words and grammar of the source text to transfer the perceived meaning to the target language. "Meaning" and "effect", however, are not *objective* in nature, such as definitions one would find in a dictionary. The meaning depends entirely on the understanding and imagination of the translator. This makes it easy for the translator to allow personal prejudice to enter the translation and to ignore cross referenced passages that explain the text and define words. Dynamic Equivalence can easily result in an unacceptably free translation or paraphrase, such as the Message or the Living Bible. When the translator changes the words of the source language to make the message more understandable to the readers, what he ends up with is no longer God's Word, but it has become the words of the translator. Such a method hides the real words of God. There have been times when these failures have produced a translation of a passage that turns it into a lie.

    Dynamic Equivalence theory tends toward a pure idiomatic translation. We would not say that one may never translate idiomatically. That is an issue very different from this. We will look at that closer later. However, dynamic equivalence is not averse to such things as translating "white as snow' into "white as fungus" for a jungle culture that has never seen snow; or, perhaps, translating "the lamb of God" into "the pig of God" if it fits the culture of a tribe in Papua New Guinea. Historically English Bible translating has been done using a Formal Equivalency method. Today, nearly every translation effort uses Dynamic Equivalence. Some translations are a mix between the two.

Formal Equivalence

    This refers to a translation approach which attempts to retain the language forms of the original as much as possible in the translation and still keep correct usage and grammar in the target language. It is sometimes called word-for-word translating. The Bible translator must accurately translate the words of the source texts in the clearest manner. However, the translation into the target language must be done according to the grammar and word usage of the target language, and read and flow naturally as in the standard spoken or written target language. To ensure accuracy and clarity, the translator should generally translate idiomatic expressions (that cannot be understood literally in the target language-we will look at this more later) according to idiomatic usage in the target language. (This is what we found in Matthew 1:23. The literal "shall in stomach have" was translated idiomatically as "shall be with child.") Therefore, a formal equivalent translation is defined as *a **word** translated into its nearest equivalent word, **grammar** is translated into the nearest equivalent grammar (which may not be the same as the source language), and **idiom** to the nearest equivalent idiom, while maintaining the same meaning as the original.*

The Bible Method

So, what does the Bible say about the proper method? There is no possibility that God would leave us without guidance in this very important area. Which, if any, of the above methods are closest to God's method?

To answer these questions we will have to go over some ground we have covered before and make an application of what we have observed in the several places the Bible talks about "interpretation." These are the examples we looked at in chapter six. Below is a chart of the verses on "interpretation" with the method they match.

Verse Ref.	Hebrew or Aramaic	Interpretation (Translation)	Method Used
Mt. 1:23	Emmanuel	God with us	Formal Equivalent
Mk. 5:41	Talitha cumi	Damsel, ... arise	Formal Equivalent
Mk. 15:22	Golgatha	place of a skull	Formal Equivalent
Mk. 15:34	Eloi, Eloi, lama sabachthani?	My God, My God, why hast thou forsaken me?	Formal Equivalent

Verse Ref.	Hebrew or Aramaic	Interpretation (Translation)	Method Used
John 1:38	Rabbi	Master (teacher)	Formal Equivalent-
John 1:41	Messias	Christ	Formal Equivalent-
John 1:42	Cephas	a stone	Formal Equivalent-
John 9:7	Siloam	Sent	Formal Equivalent-
Acts 4:36	Barnabas	Son of consolation	Formal Equivalent-
Heb. 7:1-2	Melchisedec	King of Righteousness	Formal Equivalent-
	King of Salem	King of Peace	Formal Equivalent

Fig. 9

These examples, given by inspiration, are examples of the interpretive (translation) work of the Holy Spirit. In the above examples, the method used by the Holy Spirit matched the formal equivalence method described above. The Bible also gives us a number of other reasons why we should use a formal equivalent method for translating the Bible.

Hiding the Words of God

*Turn you at my reproof: behold, I will pour out my spirit unto you, **I will make known my words unto you**. (Prov. 1:23)*

*And in that day shall the deaf hear **the words of the book**, and the eyes of the blind shall see out of obscurity, and out of darkness. (Is. 29:18)*

When I was a teen in school, I had to learn the Gettysburg Address and deliver the speech in front of the class. The Gettysburg Address of President Abraham Lincoln is a classic piece of historic literature. Before I gave the speech, I carried it on a piece of paper in my pocket for several days so I could learn it word-perfect. One day

The Scriptural Method of Translating

when I pulled it out, my teacher told me it looked like it had gone through the war. When I gave the speech, I gave it with the same words Abraham Lincoln had written and spoken.

What if I had decided that the speech had out-of-date words and no longer spoke to people the way it had in 1863? After all, the current culture is much different than it was then. The attitudes of many people are much different than they were then. What if I had decided to make some small changes to help give it the same impact it had in 1863?

I would have flunked my assignment. That's what would have happened. *When people want to read the Gettysburg Address, they want to read the words of President Abraham Lincoln.* They want to know what he said, not what I say.

The same is true with any classic piece of literature. *Tom Sawyer*, by Mark Twain, is an example. An editor may decide that *Tom Sawyer* had to be changed, because no one walks the streets of St. Petersburg, Missouri in bare feet any more. No one has to deal with slaves along the Mississippi anymore. Does anyone whitewash fences anymore? *Tom Sawyer*, as written by Twain, is out of date and out of touch, says the editor. If an editor tried to update the book, it would no longer be Twain's work. When people pick up *Tom Sawyer*, they want to read Twain's words, not the words of an editor.

The same principle stands true when translating these works into foreign languages. People expect a Mark Twain book to be translated into the exact words that Twain would have used had he written in that language; words corresponding to his English words.

Modern secular translation services know the value of approaching translation with a formal equivalent method. The industry that translates technical information has set quality standards called "ISO 9001:2000 process and the SAE J2450 Translation Quality Standard." On its web site, the company, One Word, says it checks these categories for errors: wrong term, wrong meaning, omission, structural error, misspelling error, punctuation error, and miscellaneous error.[48] Professionals know that an exact and accurate translation is important, especially with technical, medical, government, and legal documents. They know that the exact accuracy of such translating can mean the difference in whether you get a lawsuit or start a war.

A Practical Theology of Bible Translating

A translator can "express the meaning of (the writer or speaker or something written or spoken) using different words, especially to achieve greater clarity." However, when the translator does this, *it is called paraphrasing.*[49] A paraphrase happens when someone changes an author's words into words of his own. That is what dynamic equivalence does to the Words of God in the Bible. Dr. Ryken explains this further.

> Scholars who deal in a serious way with literary texts have a name for texts that do not correspond to the actual words of an author. Such a text is called a corrupt text. It is defined as a text that has been changed from its original and reliable form to something different from that standard. Technically the term is usually reserved for accidental errors made in the process of copying or transcription, but I am extending the concept to cover anything that produces the effect of such accidents-namely, a text that has been altered from the original, intentionally or unintentionally. Even deviations in punctuation and spelling are considered forms of corruption, though it is possible for a reliable edition of a text from the past to have its punctuation and spelling modernized. What is never considered appropriate is to change the words themselves.[50]

Let's look at a few examples of these two methods. Below are some comparisons between the KJV translation (which is a formal equivalent to literal translation), the New International Version (NIV), the Contemporary English Version (CEV), and the Message.

Example 1:

KJV	***Psalms 1:3** And he shall be like a tree planted by the rivers of water, that bringeth forth his fruit in his season; his leaf also shall not wither; and **whatsoever he doeth shall prosper.***
NIV	**Ps. 1:3** That person is like a tree planted by streams of water, which yields its fruit in season and whose leaf does not wither—**whatever they do prospers**

The Scriptural Method of Translating

Message	**Ps. 1:2-3** Instead you thrill to God's Word, you chew on Scripture day and night. You're a tree replanted in Eden, bearing fresh fruit every month, **Never dropping a leaf, always in blossom**

Do these versions say the same? No, they do not. The NIV puts "prosper" in present tense. The KJV is future. To say that one *shall* prosper is not the same to say that one is currently prospering. The meaning is not the same. The Message leaves out prospering altogether and adds many words that are not in the Hebrew text. You are "replanted" in Eden instead of "by the rivers of water" (water is a type of the Word of God). You bear fruit "every month" instead of in your "season." You blossom instead of prosper.

Example 2:

KJV	*1 Thessalonians 1:3 Remembering without ceasing your work of faith, and labour of love, and patience of hope in our Lord Jesus Christ, in the sight of God and our Father;*
NIV	We remember before our God and Father your work produced by faith, your labor prompted by love, and your endurance inspired by hope in our Lord Jesus Christ.
Message	... as we call to mind your work of faith, your labor of love, and your patience of hope in following our Master, Jesus Christ, before God our Father.

The KJV is a literal translation of the Greek TR. The NIV adds the words "produced by," "prompted by," and "inspired by." None of these are in the Greek text. The NIV left out "in the sight of." The NIV leaves out "without ceasing." To "remember before our God" does not mean the same as "remembering without ceasing." The NIV misplaces "God and Father," which words are not in the Greek text at this point.

The Message is a very free translation that carries some resemblance to the Greek text, but is obviously a paraphrase. The Greek text does not speak of following the Lord in this verse. The Message changes the word "Lord" to "Master," which does not mean the same, since the term "Lord" refers not only to His authority, but also to His deity. "Remembering" and "call to mind" does not mean the same. One does not have to call to his mind to remember something or someone. Memory can be stimulated by many things, including the Holy Spirit.

Example 3:

KJV	**Ps. 31:1** *1 In thee, O Lord, do I put my trust; let me never be ashamed: deliver me in thy righteousness.*
CEV (Contemporary English Version)	1 I come to you, Lord, for protection. Don't let me be ashamed. Do as you have promised and rescue me
Message	1 I run to you, God; I run for dear life. Don't let me down! Take me seriously this time!

The differences in wording in this example can be clearly seen. The different words cause subtle changes in meaning. The three translations don't even sound like the same verse. These are merely three of hundreds of examples that could be given. If the Word of God can be translated with such radical differences, is it any wonder the world is confused and has lost its confidence in the Bible?

In the Middle Ages (500-1500 AD approximately), the Catholic Church controlled most religion and religious teaching in Europe. One of their great endeavors was to attempt to keep the Word of God from the common people. They did this by 1) declaring the Latin version to be the official "Bible" of the Church, 2) teaching Latin only to the clergy, 3) forbidding the Bible to be translated into the languages of the people, and 4) forbidding the common people to read and interpret the Bible. Nowadays, the "cat is out of the bag," so to speak. There are so many versions available to the general public that this strategy does not and cannot work. However, dynamic equivalence works, because it substitutes the words of men in place of the words of God. That effectively hides the words of God from mankind.

It is God's will to make known His words to us (Prov. 1:23), and it is His will that we are able to read the words of His Book (Is.

29:18). However, when the Words of God are handled in the manner I have just shown, *the true Words of God are as effectively hidden from people, as they were in the Middle Ages.* Other words are substituted for or added to the words of God. Sometimes His words are removed. Other times the meaning of His words is twisted. All in all, *the words of men have been substituted for the words of God.*

> *he that hath my word, let him speak my word faithfully. What is the chaff to the wheat? saith the LORD. (Jer. 23:28)*
>
> *Therefore, behold, I am against the prophets, saith the LORD, that steal my words every one from his neighbour. (Jer. 23:30)*
>
> *Behold, ye trust in lying words, that cannot profit. (Jer. 7:8)*

The Words of God are Unique and Special

> ***Ye shall not add unto the word*** *which I command you,* ***neither shall ye diminish ought from it****, that ye may keep the commandments of the LORD your God which I command you. (Deut. 4:2)*
>
> ***Add thou not unto his words****, lest he reprove thee, and thou be found a liar. (Prov. 30:6)*
>
> *For I testify unto every man that heareth the words of the prophecy of this book,* ***If any man shall add unto these things, God shall add unto him the plagues that are written in this book****: And if any man shall* ***take away from the words of the book of this prophecy, God shall take away his part out of the book of life****, and out of the holy city, and from the things which are written in this book. (Rev. 22:18-19)*

If we feel that we must be so careful when translating the words of a famous author, a legal team, or a government document, why are we so loose when translating the Words of Almighty God? His words make the difference of whether you go to Heaven or Hell.

His words are the ultimate legal document. Why do we feel that we are free to substitute the words of men for the words of God?

God is the highest and the greatest Author in the universe. We know that He should be feared and revered. What we sometimes forget is that **His Words** should also be feared and revered. He has, after all, exalted His Word above His name (Ps. 138:2). The high regard that man should feel for God's Word is expressed in the verses above. When one contemplates translating God's Word, he should approach the words with awe and fear. It should make us determined that we will translate His Word faithfully and accurately, praying that we not add to or take away from His words. *These loose translators presume too much.*

> 33 ¶O the depth of the riches both of the wisdom and knowledge of God! how unsearchable are his judgments, and his ways past finding out!
> 34 For **who hath known the mind of the Lord? or who hath been his counsellor**?
> 35 Or who hath first given to him, and it shall be recompensed unto him again?
> 36 For of him, and through him, and to him, are all things: to whom be glory for ever. Amen.
> (Rom. 11:33-36)

The Words of God are Perfect

*He is the Rock, **his work is perfect**: for all his ways are judgment: **a God of truth** and without iniquity, just and right is he. (Deut. 32:4)*

*As for God, **his way is perfect**; the **word of the LORD is tried:** he is a buckler to all them that trust in him. (2 Sam. 22:31)*

***The law of the LORD is perfect**, converting the soul: the testimony of the LORD is sure, making wise the simple. (Ps. 19:7)*

***Be ye therefore perfect**, even as your Father which is in heaven is perfect. (Mt. 5:48)*

The Scriptural Method of Translating

Let your heart therefore be perfect *with the LORD our God, to* ***walk in his statutes****, and to* ***keep his commandments****, as at this day.* (1 Kings 8:61)

Those who embrace dynamic equivalence, in effect, are ignoring the implications of the doctrine of inspiration. If it is true (and it is) that God inspired every word of Scripture, then those *specific words* are words God has *specifically chosen* to give mankind. He chose those words and no others. He inspired those specific words and He preserved those words through all the centuries until now.

God has never given permission to anyone to change His words. In fact, he has specifically forbidden changing the words (Deut. 4:2; Prov. 30:6; Rev. 22:19-19). Therefore, a translator is under an obligation to God to carefully translate His words into the closest most accurate words that he can find.

All "*his* **work is perfect**" (Deut. 32:4). Everything God has done and will do is perfect. Whether it is creation, His judgments, His covenants, His dispensations; they are all perfect. His provision of salvation is perfect. When He saved your soul, His work was perfect. His perfect works necessarily includes the inspiration of Scripture. Every word of Scripture is perfect. God's preservation of those words is perfect. How can any translator even *think* he could improve on perfection? No one can say what God has said better than God said it. No one can use words that are better than the words God has used. He is a "God of truth" (Deut. 32:4). A translator had better take heed how he translates the words of God, because they are words of truth. If a translator uses other words, he may find that he has lied against God and hidden the words of God from the world.

"*As for God, his* **way is perfect**; *the word of the LORD is tried*" (2 Sam. 22:31). God has a plan for His actions in history and in each of our lives. He prescribes the way in which we should walk. He guides us with His eye (Ps. 32:8). All His way is perfect and it has been revealed in His Word. "*The word of the Lord is tried.*" What God has said has been tested in the fire of life. What God has said works in the reality of practical everyday living. Following God's way, revealed in God's Word, gives success in living. How *dare* a translator to substitute His own words instead of God's *tried* words. How *dare* a translator to take away our light!

For thou art my lamp, O LORD: and the LORD will lighten my darkness (2 Samuel 22:29).
Thy word is a lamp unto my feet, and a light unto my path (Ps 119:105).

The Word of God, as God inspired it, converts our souls and gives us wisdom (Ps. 19:7). Peter further explains this: *"Being born again, not of corruptible seed, but of incorruptible, by the Word of God, which liveth and abideth for ever"* (1 Peter 1:23). The Lord Jesus Christ is *"made unto us wisdom"* (1 Cor. 1:30). Take note, that Jesus Christ is *"the word"* (John 1:1). He is the author of the word. Therefore, His Words are wisdom. It is ONLY the words God inspired that are *"incorruptible seed."* The words of a translator are only human words, if they do not exactly match God's Words. When the translator substitutes his own words for the words of God, he has substituted man's words for God's wisdom. He has substituted corruptible seed in place of incorruptible.

Because God's work and way are perfect, we must be perfect (Mt. 5:48; 1 Kings 8:61). The only way to do this is to trust and love Him: "He that hath my commandments, and keepeth them, he it is that loveth me" (John 14:21). How can we do this if his commandments are changed by translators? God's commands are HIS. We must walk as He directs in His word. That requires that we have HIS words, not the fallible words of some translator who thinks he knows more than God.

God Knows All Cultures for All Time

10 Declaring the end from the beginning, and from ancient times the things that are not yet done, saying, My counsel shall stand, and I will do all my pleasure:
11 Calling a ravenous bird from the east, the man that executeth my counsel from a far country: yea, I have spoken it, I will also bring it to pass; I have purposed it, I will also do it. (Isaiah 46:10-11)

Know therefore this day, and consider it in thine heart, that the LORD he is God in heaven above, and upon the earth beneath: there is none else. (Deut. 4:39)

The Scriptural Method of Translating

Know therefore that the LORD thy God, he is God, the faithful God, which keepeth covenant and mercy with them that love him and keep his commandments to a thousand generations;
(Deut 7:9)

Some, who agree with dynamic equivalence theory, tend to think that the cultures of today are so different from the cultures of Biblical times that a new approach is needed. In chapter six of his book, Dr. Ryken listed eight false beliefs about modern readers that affect translation efforts. These are characteristics about readers in the Western world, but the general belief is that translation is guided by the culture for which translation is being done. While it is true that translators need to know the target culture, it is for the purpose of choosing the exact right words to translate the specific Words of God. We are not changing those words to accommodate the culture. The false views of modern readers are listed below.

> FALLACY #1: CONTEMPORARY BIBLE READERS HAVE Low INTELLECTUAL AND LINGUISTIC ABILITIES
> FALLACY #2: THE BIBLE Is READ MAINLY BY PEOPLE UNFAMILIAR WITH IT
> FALLACY #3: BIBLE READERS CANNOT HANDLE THEOLOGICAL OR TECHNICAL TERMINOLOGY
> FALLACY #4: FIGURATIVE LANGUAGE IS BEYOND THE GRASP OF BIBLE READERS
> FALLACY #5: MODERN READERS REQUIRE SHORT SENTENCES
> FALLACY #6: BIBLE READERS CANNOT BE EDUCATED BEYOND THEIR PRESENT LEVEL OF ABILITY
> FALLACY #7: THE BIBLE IS MORE DIFFICULT FOR MODERN READERS THAN FOR THE ORIGINAL READERS
> FALLACY #8: READERS, NOT AUTHORS, DETERMINE MEANING [51]

The general view is that the Bible, as it is, does not speak to current world cultures as it spoke to the culture when it was written. To do that, it must be put into new words that will affect the culture where it is being translated. In other words, it should be translated to accommodate the culture.

It seems there is also a failure to realize that the God who created the universe is also the *God of time*. He is *all-knowing* and, therefore, he fully knows all cultures everywhere anytime in history. When He inspired His words, it makes sense that He inspired words that would speak to any and every culture everywhere, when accurately and precisely translated into their language. The Word of God was given to human beings to deal with human nature. The customs and background may change, but human nature never changes. Forests are cut down, technology grows, buildings get bigger and more comfortable, and a million other changes may take place over time, yet *human beings remain the same*. Human nature is constant. Therefore, God's Words remain constant. There are no better words to deal with human nature.

The Words ARE the Meaning

A wise man will hear, and will increase learning; and a man of understanding shall attain unto wise counsels: To understand a proverb, and the interpretation; the words of the wise, and their dark sayings. (Prov. 1:5-6)

For the LORD giveth wisdom: out of his mouth cometh knowledge and understanding. (Prov. 2:6)

Dynamic equivalence focuses on meaning. It tries to reproduce the meaning of the source text in the target language. It produces a thought for thought, meaning for meaning translation. The words themselves are secondary. The translation can use different words chosen by the translator, as long as the meaning is the same. The judge of whether the meaning is the same is the translator himself. That meaning can be a purely subjective meaning determined based on the theological perspective and experience of the translator.

The Bible is the expression of God's wisdom (Prov. 2:6), because His wisdom, knowledge, and understanding came out of His mouth (see Mt. 4:4). We have studied this before as a statement of

Biblical inspiration. When people seek wisdom, they know they have to listen to the *words* of the wise (Prov. 1:5-6). The wise choose words that specifically express the meaning of their wise sayings. God also chose words that communicate His wisdom, understanding, and knowledge.

For a translator, who is finite and limited in wisdom, to think that he can express the wisdom of God, whose wisdom is infinite, in human words other than those God chose is the height of human arrogance. No man can fully understand all the mind and wisdom of God. He can seek to know how each of God's individual words are defined and how they are used in context. Then he can seek to transfer that understanding into another language as accurately as possible. But, to rethink God's thoughts and express them in other words chosen by the translator himself is beyond his ability.

No translator is capable of translating the meaning of God's Words in other words chosen by men. Why? It is because the meaning is in the words themselves. Words have meaning. God chose the words He did to express the meaning He intended to express. There is no such thing as disembodied meaning or disembodied thought. Meaning and thought are embedded in words. When a wise man chooses certain words, he chooses those words to express specific meaning. Using other words runs the risk of distorting or loosing that meaning.

The translator should strive to translate each word of the source text into an equivalent word in the target language, while maintaining an equivalent meaning for each word and creating a grammatically correct translation in the target language.

Chapter Seven

The Scriptural Method Applied

16 Take heed to yourselves, that your heart be not deceived, and ye turn aside, and serve other gods, and worship them;
18 Therefore shall ye lay up these my words in your heart and in your soul, and bind them for a sign upon your hand, that they may be as frontlets between your eyes.(Deut. 11:16, 18)

Let me briefly remind the reader of the definition of Formal equivalence: *this method translates the words, grammar, and idioms of the source language into the nearest equivalent words, grammar, and idioms of the target language.*

To illustrate this method of translating, we will look at the King James Bible translation. The source text of the King James Bible was the Hebrew Masoretic text edited by Jacob Ben Chayim and the 1598 Beza Edition of the Greek Received Text. The target language, of course, was English.

Every language is different. Each has its own way to express specific ideas and thoughts. Some languages differ a little and others differ greatly. In some ways Greek is very different from English, but in other ways the Greek use of words is similar. This simply recognizes the work of God in dividing the languages of the world. All translators must recognize these facts.

A 100% Word-for-word literal translation is not possible between any two languages, if you are to retain the same meaning in both languages. The Bible translator must accurately translate all of the words of the source text in the clearest manner possible according to the grammar and usage of the target language, and at the same time make the target language read and flow naturally as in the standard spoken language. The translator must strive for each word being translated into the **nearest equivalent word**. He must strive that the grammar of the source language be translated into the **nearest equivalent grammar** of the target language, which grammar may differ from the source language. Each idiom of the source language must be translated into the **nearest equivalent idiom** of the target language. We will look at examples of each of these categories. If this is done well, the result will be God's Words in the target language.

Word to the Nearest Equivalent Word

If a literal word-for word translation works in the target language, it should be followed. However, the usage and syntax of the target language must prevail. The target language translation must read clearly, smoothly, and naturally. For example, languages differ in their use of articles and conjunctions. Some languages freely add these items; others limit their use; some languages don't even use "a" or "an." When literal translating works well in the target language, use it.

Example 1: John 1:1

> **Greek: 1** Ἐν ἀρχῇ ἦν ὁ λόγος, καὶ ὁ λόγος ἦν πρὸς τὸν Θεόν, καὶ Θεὸς ἦν ὁ λόγος. (in arche en o logos kai o logos en pros ton theon kai theos en o logos)
>
> **Literal translation from Greek:** In beginning was the word and the word was with the God and God was the word.
>
> **English KJV:** In the beginning was the Word, and the Word was with God, and the Word was God.

The English is a word-for-word literal translation except for adding one necessary definite article (*the* beginning) and leaving out one definite article (with *the* God). These changes were necessary to ensure a clear natural flow according to the syntax of the target language, English. The KJB also reverses the word order in the last phrase. However, this is consistent with the grammar of the Greek. Both words, "word" and "God," are in the nominative case indicating that one is the subject and one is a predicate nominative. This means that each word refers to the same person. Word order in Greek is normally subject-verb-object, but this is not rigid. The word order can vary if the writer wants to emphasize certain words.

Example 2: 1 Thessalonians 4:3

Greek 1 Thess. 4:3 - τοῦτο γάρ ἐστι θέλημα τοῦ Θεοῦ, ὁ ἁγιασμὸς ὑμῶν, ἀπέχεσθαι ὑμᾶς ἀπὸ τῆς πορνείας

Literal translations from Greek – this for is will of the God, the sanctification of you, to abstain you from the fornication

English KJB - For this is the will of God, *even* your sanctification, that ye should abstain from fornication

This is a translation that follows the Greek text in a very literal fashion, but shows the necessity of adjusting the translation to make complete sense in English. It should be clear that the 100% literal translation is often awkward in English. Therefore, the word "even" was added and placed in italics, so that the reader would know it is not in Greek. The infinitive "to abstain" expresses an intent that one should abstain from fornication. So, it was translated as "that ye should abstain." Finally, "the God" and "the sanctification" and "the fornication" are improper in English, so the articles were not translated. However, each word, except for the articles, is given an exact translation in English.

Example 3: 1 Thessalonians 4:2

Greek 1 Thess. 4:2 - οἴδατε γὰρ τίνας παραγγελίας ἐδώκαμεν ὑμῖν διὰ τοῦ Κυρίου Ἰησοῦ.

Literal translation from Greek - you know for what commandments we gave to you by the Lord Jesus.

KJB - For ye know what commandments we gave you by the Lord Jesus.

This example is a literal translation from Greek. The only adjustments made to accommodate the demands of English was to move the word "for" to the beginning of the sentence and translate ὑμῖν as "you" rather than "to you." The word "to" is understood in English. In Greek, the word γὰρ (gar-for) is never the first word in the sentence. It comes second or third. Regardless of this, the thought expressed by it is often the first thought of the sentence. When this is true, it comes first in the English translation. It's just a matter of grammatical rules. The same is true with the word δε (de-but, and, now).

Example 4: 1 John 1:4

> **Greek 1 John 1:4** καὶ ταῦτα γράφομεν ὑμῖν, ἵνα ἡ χαρὰ ἡμῶν ᾖ πεπληρωμένη.
>
> **Literal translation from Greek** – and these things we write to you, that the joy of you may be full.
>
> **English KJB** - And these things write we unto you, that your joy may be full.

There are no issues with articles or conjunctions in this verse. It is a word-for-word translation.

Grammar to Nearest Equivalent Grammar

The distinctions between languages are from God. Every language has its own grammatical requirements and rules of syntax. Two languages may be very different in how they use grammar and syntax. They also may be very similar. A grammatical structure in the source language may require the translator to use either the same or a different grammatical structure in the target language to maintain the same meaning. Sometimes the same grammatical structure used in two languages causes a different meaning or creates an unnatural construction.

Example 5: Matthew 2:8

Matthew 2:8 is an example of how it is sometimes not good translating to transfer the exact grammar from the source language into the target language.

> **Greek:** καὶ **πέμψας αὐτοὺς** εἰς Βηθλέεμ εἶπε, **Πορευθέντες** ἀκριβῶς ἐξετάσατε περὶ τοῦ παιδίου· ἐπὰν δὲ εὕρητε, ἀπαγγείλατέ μοι, ὅπως κἀγὼ **ἐλθὼν** προσκυνήσω αὐτῷ.

> **Literal Translation from Greek: And having sent them** to Bethlehem, he said, **When you have gone**, diligently search for the young child. And when you have found, bring word to me, that I also, **having come,** may worship him.
>
> **English KJB:** And **he sent them** to Bethlehem, and said, **Go** and search diligently for the young child; and when ye have found him, bring me word again, **that I may come** and worship him also.

The Greek verse has three participles. To translate this with the same grammar in English is understandable, but awkward and unnatural for English. It is better to translate the participles as indicative (a simple statement of fact) in the English translation. The KJB uses an indicative in all three places. The meaning between the Greek and the English is exactly the same. Notice how the translators sought to use the same words in English that God used in Greek. It may seem that "when you have gone" translated into "go" leaves out some words. On the contrary, "when you have gone" is only one word in Greek and the English word "go" expresses the meaning.

Example 6: Galatians 2:20

> **Greek Gal. 2:20-** Χριστῳ συνεσταύρωμαι
>
> **Literal translation from Greek:** I am crucified with Christ ...
>
> **KJB Gal. 2:20-** I am crucified with Christ ...

On the surface, there seems to be no difference between Greek and English here. However, the agreement is on the surface only. The English is in *present* tense. The Greek is not. The Greek verb is in *perfect* tense.

There is no perfect tense in English that matches the Greek perfect tense. There is no exact equivalent. There are three Perfect tenses in English. They show action that has been completed in the past or will be done in the future: I have done it, I had done it, or I will have done it. Although the Greek perfect tense has to do with action completed in the past, it carries an idea that the English does not. The Greek perfect tense is action done in the past which has present effects. If I say, "God saved me," it is an English past tense. However, I can say the same thing in Greek perfect tense and it means "God saved me in the past and I am currently in a saved condition and one of God's saints."

So, the continual problem has been how to translate the Greek perfect tense in English. If, in the Greek perfect tense. I say, "I am crucified with Christ," I am saying that I was crucified and my old man is still dead (see Romans 6 for the explanation). If I translate it into past tense in English, it is a simple past action and the present results are lost. However, if I use present tense there is a greater chance that both aspects will be understood. This would be similar to saying in English present tense, "The bed is made." This statement *implies* that the bed was made by someone in the past and it is still made. So, the KJB translators usually translated the Greek perfect as an English present tense.

Example 7: Acts 7:44

Greek Acts 7:44 – ὁ λαλῶν τῷ Μωσῇ
Literal translation from Greek: speaking unto Moses
KJB Acts 7:44 - as he had appointed, speaking unto Moses, that he should make ...

This is also an example of a participle. λαλῶν (lalon) is a present participle and is translated as an English present participle: "speaking." Previously, the example of Matthew 2:8 showed how a participle is better translated by a plain statement. That is, a different grammar was more correct in the target language. However, in this case, the same grammar that is in the source language is also appropriate for the target language. This is something that can only be decided by careful and prayerful thought given to each verse.

Idiom to Nearest Equivalent idiom

An idiom "an expression in the usage of a language that is peculiar to itself either grammatically (such as *no, it wasn't me*) or in having a meaning that cannot be derived from the conjoined meanings of its elements (such as *ride herd on* for "supervise")." [52] Words, grammar, and idioms should be translated literally into the target language as a foundational principle. However, sometimes, a completely literal translation will *not* communicate the same meaning in the target language text.

Sometimes an idiom is translated by modifying the words or grammar of the source text. You may not be able to understand an idiom by looking at the words involved, but it always has a specific objective meaning. The meaning does not depend on a translator's opinion or interpretation. Often, an idiom, if translated literally, will give the reader a wrong understanding of its meaning. In these cases, it is best to translate the idiom according to its meaning. For example, the meaning of the English idiom, "The cat is out of the bag," has nothing to do with a cat or a bag. It means, "The secret is revealed." In an instance like that, the idiom should be translated phrase for phrase.

Some idioms are the normal way ideas and thoughts are expressed in a language. Below are some examples from German. First is the literal translation of the German expression and then the normal English expression.

GERMAN	ENGLISH
My car goes not.	My car doesn't work.
That do I for my life with pleasure	I adore doing that
That is not looked to with pleasure.	that is not liked -or- That is unacceptable.
He has it with pleasure, when one to him compliments.	He likes it, when someone compliments him.

Fig. 10

This is not the same as dynamic equivalence for several reasons. First, a true idiom has a definite specific objective meaning in the source language as in the examples above. Also, sometimes, the real meaning of an idiom has little to do with the literal meaning of the words involved. Another English example is "he was sold a pig in a poke." Again, the meaning has nothing to do with a pig, a poke, or a sale. It means, "He was cheated." That is, the idiom has a clear and objective meaning. Therefore, it is not subject to interpretation by the translator. Its meaning is not flexible. Second, a formal equivalent translator does not feel free to translate idiomatically except where absolutely necessary. The dynamic equivalent translator feels free to translate idiomatically anywhere and anytime.

Example 8: Matthew 1:23

> **Mat 1:23** Ἰδοὺ, ἡ παρθένος ἐν γαστρὶ ἕξει καὶ τέξεται υἱόν,
>
> **Literal Translation:** Behold, the virgin in stomach shall have and shall produce a son...
>
> **KJV Mat 1:23:** Behold, a virgin shall be with child, and shall bring forth a son...

The Greek idiom "in stomach" is translated in the KJV as "be with child." This is an example of phrase for phrase translating and should only be used when necessary. The Greek phrase is one way the Greeks express the condition of pregnancy. The two phrases have exactly the same meaning.

Example 9: Romans 3:4

> **Greek:** μὴ γένοιτο
>
> **Literal Translation:** May it not be!
>
> **English KJV** For what if some did not believe? shall their unbelief make the faith of God without effect? **God forbid**

The KJV used an English idiom to translate the Greek idiom. The Greek does not use the word "God." The English idiom means the same as the Greek idiom. The English phrase, "God forbid," means, "May it not be."

Example 10: John 10:35

An idiom may be translated literally if the translator does not know the meaning of a particular idiom or when the literal translation is not seriously difficult to understand. In which case, he may translate the words of the idiom just as they stand in the source text.

> **Greek:** εἰ ἐκείνους εἶπε θεοὺς, πρὸς οὓς ὁ λόγος τοῦ Θεοῦ ἐγένετο, (καὶ **οὐ δύναται λυθῆναι** ἡ γραφή);
>
> **Literal translation of Greek:** and the Scriptures **cannot be broken.**
>
> **English KJV:** If he called them gods, unto whom the Word of God came, and the scripture **cannot be broken** …

The Greek word for broken is lethenai. It comes from the word luo, which means to loose, break, dissolve, or destroy anything that is bound together. "Cannot be broken" is a Jewish idiom that means "cannot be refuted." The phrase was often used by Jewish debaters to refer to any argument they believed to be irrefutable. When a debater would make a point, he would cry, "it cannot be broken." The phrase "cannot be broken" is clear enough that it can be translated literally.

Example 11: Philemon 1:7

An idiom may be translated literally if it is explained in the greater context.

> **Greek:** ὅτι τὰ **σπλάγχνα** τῶν ἁγίων ἀναπέπαυται διὰ σοῦ, ἀδελφέ.
> **Greek** = bowels
> **English KJV:** For we have great joy and consolation in thy love, because the **bowels** of the saints are refreshed by thee, brother.

The Greek term "bowels" refers to the seat of the emotions and attitudes of a person. It is used in the sense we may use the word "heart." (The Greeks also used "heart" this way.) However, the meaning is not clear from this verse.

It is clear, however, from Colossians 3:12.

> **Colossians 3:12** Put on therefore, as the elect of God, holy and beloved, **bowels of** mercies, kindness, humbleness of mind, meekness, longsuffering;

Example 12: 1 John 3:17

An idiom may be translated literally by adding an explanation (even if that explanation is in the greater context). The added explanation for **Bowels** is found in 1 John 3:17

The Scriptural Method Applied

> **1 John 3:17** But whoso hath this world's good, and seeth his brother have need, and shutteth up his **bowels *of compassion*** from him, how dwelleth the love of God in him?

The words "of compassion" are in italics in the KJB showing that they are not in the original languages, but were added by the translators to increase understanding.

Example 13: 2 Corinthians 2:17

> **Greek:** 2 Cor. 2:17 οὐ γάρ ἐσμεν ὡς οἱ πολλοὶ **καπηλεύοντες τὸν λόγον τοῦ Θεοῦ,**
>
> **Literal translation:** not for we are as the many **who corrupt the Word of God**
>
> **KJB:** For we are not as many, **which corrupt the Word of God:**

Once again it appears there is no problem with this Greek word for "corrupt," but in reality there is a big problem. The problem can be seen in how other translations translate the word, *kapelevontes*.

> **New KJV:** 2 Cor. 2:17 For we are not, as so many, **peddling the Word of God**
>
> **NIV:** Unlike so many, we do not **peddle the Word of God for profit.**
>
> **ESV:** For we are not, like so many, **peddlers of God's Word**
>
> **NASB:** For we are not like many, **peddling the Word of God**

Why peddling instead of corrupting? This is an instance where the translator must be very careful. Some words present possible pitfalls where one can make a colossal mistake.

The Greek word in question is only used one time in the New Testament, so it cannot be compared to other contexts. We have to look at Greek Lexicons. Those dictionaries reveal to us that the word *kapeleuontes* does indeed mean a trader or peddler, but can mean corrupter (figuratively). [53] However, it is a word that referred to legitimate retailers at first, but came to mean something else as they "watered down" or adulterated their goods. Therefore, it became an *idiom* denoting someone who corrupts things. It is similar to our "snake oil salesman," which became an idiom for one who cheats another by selling corrupt goods. It is very comparable to our "pig in a poke."

> The majority of modern versions render this as "peddle" or "sell the Word of God for profit" instead of "corrupt the Word of God." The Greek word *kapeleuontes* does carry the meaning of a *peddler* or *retailer*. However, it connotes one who sells with *deceit*, a *corrupter*. Dr. Walter Bauer states that the word came to mean "to adulterate."[54] Dr. Joseph Thayer agrees, noting, "But as peddlers were in the habit of adulterating their commodities for the sake of gain . . . (the word) was also used as synonymous with to corrupt, to adulterate."[55] Likewise, Dr. Gerhard Kittle states that *kapeleuontes*, "also means 2. to falsify the word (as the *kapelos* purchases pure wine and then adulterates it with water) by making additions . . . This refers to the false Gospel of the Judaizers."[56]
>
> The early church fathers understood the verse to refer to those who corrupt God's Word. Athanasius (373 AD) wrote, "Let them therefore be anathema to you, because they have 'corrupted the word of truth'."[57] Gregory of Nazianzus (390 AD) alludes to 2 Corinthians 2:17, Isaiah 1:22 and Psalm 54:15, using the word "corrupt":
>
> And who is sufficient for these things? For we are not as the many, able to corrupt the word of truth, and mix the wine, which maketh glad the heart of man, with water, mix, that is, our doctrine with what is common and cheap, and debased, and stale, and tasteless, in order to turn the adulteration to our profit . . .[58]

It's interesting that Gregory Nazianzus exactly described the activity of the modern dynamic equivalent translators. They change and water down the Word of God in order to make profit for the publishers. In America, English Bible translating is *big* business.

The Scriptural Method Applied

Sometimes, it is especially difficult to translate idioms. An idiom has a specific and clear meaning. Sometimes they can have more than one meaning. It can be difficult to determine whether to translate an idiom literally or according to its meaning. It can be helpful to see how the English KJB translated the verse. Translate idioms with much prayer and study.

Conclusion

These days, in the world of Bible translating, there is much tension between the two major methods of Bible translating: dynamic equivalence and formal equivalence. Dynamic equivalence can be called a thought for thought or meaning for meaning translation. This book defines formal equivalence as a method that seeks to translate every word in the target text for the nearest equivalent word in the source language, the source grammar into the nearest equivalent grammar of the target, and the idioms of the source into the nearest equivalent idioms of the target. It does this while maintaining the same meaning between the two and maintaining correct grammar and usage in the target language. Other names for this method are *word-for-word* and *essentially literal*.

The Bible gives us several examples of translation in the New Testament. It calls these "interpretation." The examples all show a literal-formal equivalent translation method. Seeing these examples it would be good for the translator to take heed to them and conclude that the Biblical method most closely matches formal equivalence. We have given examples of how dynamic equivalence can drastically change the Bible.

We do not have God's permission to take away from His Words or to add to them or to change them. God's Words are perfect. God knows every culture throughout history and He has chosen words that will communicate to all of them. We do not do any of the cultures of earth a favor by changing the words God inspired. The meaning that God wishes to communicate to the world is intrinsic in the words themselves. The words ARE the meaning. Thought and meaning do not exist in a vacuum by themselves. Thought and meaning are carried by words. God's Words carry the meaning he wants the world to know. To change the words is to change the meaning.

Chapter Eight

Translating, Bible Study, and Bible Teachers

When wisdom entereth into thine heart, and knowledge is pleasant unto thy soul; Discretion shall preserve thee, understanding shall keep thee (Prov. 2:10-11)

Blessed is he that readeth (Rev. 1:3)

Hermeneutics is a theological term about the principles of studying and understanding the Bible. What does Bible study have to do with Bible translating, you ask? Hermeneutics and Bible translating are actually closely related in at least two ways.

The first way has to do with the translator's understanding of Scripture. It is harder to translate a portion of the Bible when you do not understand it. Understanding helps the translator to keep his translation consistent with the Scriptural context. Of course, it's likely that none of us will understand everything in the Bible. What does a translator do when he doesn't understand the passage he is translating? He makes sure that he knows the definition of each word in the context and translates it as literally as he can. It will be up to the Holy Spirit to guide and illuminate teachers, who will make it clear to Bible students.

The second way Bible study is related to Bible translating has to do with the limitations of translating. Translations are not supposed to be commentaries. The process of translating is not supposed to result in a text that explains everything. The translation in the target language is only supposed to reproduce the words in the source text, not explain them. Explaining the words of God is the job of teachers, not the translator. However, to translate words accurately and literally as possible requires that the translator seek to understand those words.

Translating, Bible Study, and Bible Teachers

Basic Systems of Hermeneutics

There is a lot taught about Bible Hermeneutics. Some of it is Scriptural and some isn't. This chapter is about the theology of hermeneutics and how to apply those principles to the biblical text. We are not interested in human theory. However, a basic look at the two most major theories will help put it in context. There are two basic systems: 1) the allegorical method and 2) the historical-grammatical method.

The ***allegorical method*** assumes that there are several levels of interpretation, but it focuses first on the symbolical or spiritual interpretation.

> Perhaps the most famous instance of allegorical interpretation is Origen's explanation of the Parable of the Good Samaritan in Luke 10. In the allegorical view, the man who is robbed is Adam, Jerusalem is paradise, and Jericho is the world. The priest is the Law, and the Levites are the Prophets. The Samaritan is Christ. The donkey is Christ's physical body, which bears the burden of the wounded man (the wounds are his sins), and the inn is the Church. The Samaritan's promise to return is a promise of the second coming of Christ. [59]

The allegorical method has a severe weakness. It seeks to understand every passage of Scripture allegorically or symbolically. If one approaches the Bible like that, he can make any passage mean anything he wants it to mean. It leaves little objective way to understand the Bible.

"***Historical-grammatical interpretation***" is a five dollar phrase that simply says *let words mean what words mean in their Biblical, grammatical, and historical context.* It does not deny that there can be various spiritual *applications* of Scripture, but true understanding is based on the normal meaning of words and grammar. That is, the Bible is to be understood literally. Everyone recognizes that some Scripture is meant symbolically, especially some prophecies. Usually, however, the Bible makes it clear when a passage is not to be taken literally. An example of such a place is

Isaiah 55:12. However, notice that even in passages such as this, the words mean what they normally mean: *mountains* means *mountains*, *hills* means *hills*, *trees* means *trees*, and *hands* means *hands*. But, the *application* is to people. Allusions, symbolism, Illustrations, and metaphors should be translated literally.

> *For ye shall go out with joy, and be led forth with peace: the mountains and the hills shall break forth before you into singing, and all the trees of the field shall clap their hands.*

The real question is: what does *the Bible* teach about finding the meaning of Scripture? Does the Bible give us any guidance? It seems inconceivable that God would not give us such guidance.

Start with the Right Attitudes

Your attitude toward the Bible is the first key to understanding. Your attitude toward the Bible will determine the quality of your translation. Your attitude toward the Bible determines whether it is effectively working in you or not.

> *For this cause also thank we God without ceasing, because, when ye received the Word of God which ye heard of us, ye received it not as the word of men, but as it is in truth, the Word of God, which effectually worketh also in you that believe. (1 Thess. 2:13)*

The first attitude is to accept the Bible, the whole Bible, as the Word of God. You must understand the truth about inspiration and preservation. You have to come to the place where you KNOW you have the Word of God in your hand.

Second, you must believe what the Word of God says. Many times, the difficulty with understanding the Bible is not that it is unclear. The problem is a failure to *believe* what it says. That's one thing that makes the doctrine of verbal plenary preservation so important. It guarantees that God has preserved all Scripture word-perfect. Knowing that, you can have confidence that the Bible is true and is available for you and will work in you effectively. If you want to know which Greek text and translation is the right one, you will find some answer to that in chapter ten through twelve and the appendices.

The Cry of Your Heart

> *1 My son, if thou wilt receive my words, and hide my commandments with thee;*
> *2 So that thou incline thine ear unto wisdom, and apply thine heart to understanding;*
> *3 Yea, if thou criest after knowledge, and liftest up thy voice for understanding;*
> *4 If thou seekest her as silver, and searchest for her as for hid treasures;*
> *5 Then shalt thou understand the fear of the LORD, and find the knowledge of God.*
> *6 For the LORD giveth wisdom: out of his mouth cometh knowledge and understanding.*
> *7 He layeth up sound wisdom for the righteous: he is a buckler to them that walk uprightly.*
> *8 He keepeth the paths of judgment, and preserveth the way of his saints.*
> *9 Then shalt thou understand righteousness, and judgment, and equity; yea, every good path.* (Prov. 2:1-9)

Do you want to "receive His words?" Do you want to know His Word so that His commandments are hidden with you? Is knowledge of the Bible the desire of your heart? You can have understanding and wisdom if you seek it in the right place. "For the Lord giveth wisdom: out of his mouth cometh knowledge and understanding." As you know, what He gave and what came out of His mouth are the Scriptures.

You must *"incline thine ear unto wisdom, and apply thine heart to understanding"* (Prov. 2:2). We would say, "open your ears and listen." However, it's more than listening. We also have to hear what's being said. "He that hath ears to hear, let him hear" (Mt. 11:15). Then again, it is more than hearing. You have to apply your heart. Give it earnest interest, commitment, attention, and effort.

You must pray for the knowledge of God's Word (Prov. 2:3). *"If any of you lack wisdom, let him ask of God, that giveth to all men liberally, and upbraideth not; and it shall be given him. But let him ask in faith, nothing wavering. For he that wavereth is like a wave of the sea driven with the wind and tossed. For let not that man think that he shall receive any thing of the Lord"* (James 1:5-7).

Seek wisdom, knowledge, and understanding as silver, and as hid treasures *(v. 4).* How hard do you work for money? How much of your time does it take? How focused is your mind and effort to earn money? That is how you are to seek the hidden treasures of God's knowledge, understanding and wisdom. It is not that you give searching the Bible the same amount of *time* you give a job. It is that you give it the same *intensity of effort*.

The Bible says, *"Study to shew thyself approved unto God"* (2 Tim. 2:15). We do this by *"rightly dividing the word of truth"* (2 Tim. 2:15). Some object by telling us that the Greek word for "study" does not mean "study." It means *be diligent.* According the Word Study Dictionary, the word means, "To make every effort to do one's best, to be eager." [60] There are two things you need to know. The English word, *study*, means "an application of mind" and *application* is "intenseness of thought" and "the employment of means."[61] Listen! If one is to make every effort and does his diligent best to rightly divide the word of truth, there is only one way to do it. He must intensely apply his mind and employ methods to learn the truth. *In other words, he must **study**!*

The word, *study,* is a highly appropriate translation in this verse.

The result of all this intensity and effort is that you will *"understand the fear of the Lord, and find the knowledge of God"* (v. 5).

> These verses do not suggest a careless reading or cursory examination of the Scriptures. The soul is exhorted to "receive" these words. The sayings of God must be received into the heart where they are to be stored. The ear must be inclined to wisdom; the heart applied to understanding; the mouth crying after knowledge; and the voice lifted up for spiritual intelligence. The whole being is thus devoted to the

search for the truth. The earnest seeker must dig into the Word of God as a man searching for silver or hidden treasure. He will not be content with surface findings. When God's Words are valued more than our necessary food, the result is certain: "Then shalt thou understand the fear of the Lord, and find the knowledge of God". Diligent Bible study is on the decline even among those who value precious truth. Reading books about the Bible is very different from searching the Word for oneself. Notes and expositions may be helpful. But these works of uninspired men must not be permitted to take the place of the sure Word of God. Such one-sided study will cause men to draw their thoughts from one another instead of from God. This will result in dry intellectuality rather than fresh, vigorous spirituality.[62]

The Employment of Means

*When **wisdom** entereth into thine heart, and **knowledge** is pleasant unto thy soul; Discretion shall preserve thee, **understanding** shall keep thee (Prov. 2:10-11).*

Three words are repeated frequently in the Book of Proverbs. These three words are knowledge, understanding, and wisdom. They outline three aspects of Bible Study. Very often Bible study starts and ends in the wrong place. We read a chapter and ask ourselves, "What does that mean?" Then, after we have understood it to our satisfaction, we quit. We have sought understanding, but we have left off knowledge and wisdom. We must begin with knowledge, obtain understanding, and end by receiving wisdom.

Some of those who teach "how to do Bible study" use three additional words that help us understand these concepts. Those words are *observation, interpretation,* and *application.* Observation corresponds to Knowledge. It is when we look at a passage of Scripture and ask, "What does this passage *say*?" Interpretation is a word that helps define understanding. Interpretation leads us to ask,

"What does this passage mean?" Finally, after we know what it says and are reasonably sure what it means, we are ready to make an application of Scripture to our hearts, lives, and circumstances. When that is done and we know what we should do as a result of knowledge and understanding, we must do it. At that point, we will have gained wisdom.

Seeking for Knowledge

Knowledge is "A clear and certain perception of that which exists, or of truth and fact."[63] Observation is the Bible study method by which we gain knowledge of the Scriptures. It is the process of observing just what the Bible *SAYS.* This is the beginning point of Bible study. You cannot discover *what a passage means* until you know *what the passage says*. If you don't take words to mean what words normally mean in their context, you'll never get past this point. You cannot tell what Scripture says unless you take it according to the normal definition of words. Allegory will never give you clear observation. We need to pay attention to the details of a passage.

1. Ask the who, what, where, when, and why questions. Who is speaking or doing the action? To whom is he speaking? Where are they? Why are they there? Why are they doing that? Is anything repeated or emphasized? Are there causes and effects or comparisons and contrasts? Are there any key words or phrases? [64]
2. Look up the definitions of words you don't know in a dictionary. For this purpose, the 1828 Webster dictionary is probably the best dictionary for the King James Bible. There are also fair Bible dictionaries available that can be a help, such as Smith's Bible Dictionary, or Easton's Bible Dictionary.
3, The Bible is generally a self-defining book. Do not ignore the value of cross-references. If the word you want defined is not defined in the immediate context, use a concordance like *Strong's Exhaustive Concordance* to look up other places in the Bible where the word is used. Teachers often speak of the

law of first mention. Sometimes the first mention of a word defines it.
4. Consulting the Greek language *can* help to define the words. E-sword is a free download Bible study program that makes this easy. Be sure to download the KJC (King James Concordance) module. It lists every Greek word in the New Testament and all the ways the KJB translated them.
5. Write down any questions that occur to you in this step that your observations did not answer.
6. In some cases, knowledge of the background of a Bible book can be a help, such, as the author, the date of writing, the historical background. This information can be found in outside sources, like commentaries. However, most of the information you need is found in the greater context of the Bible itself. A concordance can be of great help for this.

Obtaining Understanding

The step in Bible study which teachers call *Interpretation* is the step that gives you *understanding* of Scripture. Once we have made all the factual observations that we can about a portion of Scripture, it is time to ask. "What does this Scripture mean?" We will have already gained some understanding from the first step, but understanding takes us much deeper.

1. You start by looking at the questions you wrote down in the previous step. Write any further questions that come to mind. Now it's time to start a diligent search for the answers.
2. Some of those answers may be found in the immediate context of the passage.
3. Answers may also be found in Scripture from other parts of the Bible. The Bible is a great commentary on itself. The Bible both defines its own terms and explains itself.

4. To find these other places in the Bible you could use a concordance of the Bible or Bible software with good search capabilities, such as E-sword or Theophilus.
5. Finally, you may have to ask a respected teacher or check a trusted commentary or Bible Dictionary.

Gaining Wisdom

Finally, after you have gained knowledge and understanding, it is time to make *application* of Scripture. This is where you ask the question, "How does this passage apply to my life" or "What difference does this passage make to me?" What action do you need to take to obey the Word? How can you put the Word into practice today? What habit must I change? What thoughts must I keep out of my mind? What attitudes do I need to change? In these and other ways you can apply the Word of God to your life. This is how you gain *wisdom*.

> 22 But be ye doers of the word, and not hearers only, deceiving your own selves.
> 23 For if any be a hearer of the word, and not a doer, he is like unto a man beholding his natural face in a glass:
> 24 For he beholdeth himself, and goeth his way, and straightway forgetteth what manner of man he was.
> (James 1:22-24)

An Illustration

Knowledge, understanding, and wisdom can be illustrated by the gospel. When I hear the gospel or read it, I *observe the facts* that Jesus is the Son of God, and He died for our sins including my own, and that God raised Him from the dead. I *understand* that He paid for all our sins so we can be forgiven and He rose from the dead so that He can give us eternal life. I have knowledge and understanding, but, I am not yet wise. I become wise when I apply these truths to *myself*. I am *wise* when I embrace the truth that I have sinned and He died for

MY sins and offers ME life and forgiveness; therefore, I will trust Him as MY Savior.

So, do not begin and end Bible study in the wrong place; by asking first, "what does it mean?" Go the whole circle. Start with knowledge, proceed to understanding, and end with gaining wisdom.

Rightly Dividing the Word

Study to shew thyself approved unto God, a workman that needeth not to be ashamed, **rightly dividing the word of truth**. *(2 Tim. 2:15)*

There are natural divisions in the Word of God. It is very important that we are aware of and accept these divisions. It would be impossible to fully explain all these divisions in a volume of this size and focus. So, I will list many of them below. The reader who wants to know more should consult *Dispensational Truth* or *Rightly Dividing the Word,* by Clarence Larkin. These are wonderful books with a lot of good knowledge, but, as a caveat, I would caution the reader, when looking at them, to remember the Scriptural statement about the Bereans, who were "more noble than those in Thessalonica, in that they received the word with all readiness of mind, and searched the scriptures daily, whether those things were so" (Acts 17:11). These books are available in e-book format from preservedwords.com or Amazon.com. The print books are also available from Amazon.

I. **Old Testament/New Testament:** This is the clearest division in the entire Bible. The new Testament has further revelation beyond the Old Testament.

II. **Jew, Gentile, and Church:** (1 Cor. 10:31-32)
The Jews are the special chosen race. The Gentiles are all other races. The Church of God consists of saved Jews and Gentiles. There are parts of the Bible written to each.

III. **The Seven Covenants:**
1. The Edenic Covenant (Gen. 3)

The Edenic Covenant involves the rules God laid down as a result of the fall of man.
2. The Noahic Covenant (Gen. 9:11-13)
After the flood, God made a covenant with all mankind. We are still under the provisions of this covenant.
3. The Abrahamic Covenant (Gen. 12:1-3; 15:18; 17:1-21)
The Abrahamic Covenant was an everlasting covenant between God and Abraham's descendants through Isaac and Jacob. It guaranteed them an Inheritance in Palestine. It involved all mankind, because it foretold the coming of the seed, Jesus Christ, and promised blessing on all those who bless Abraham.
4. The Law or Mosaic Covenant (Ex. 19:5)
The Covenant of the Law involved the giving of God's law to Israel. However, it also described God's moral law by which all mankind is judged.
5. Palestinian Covenant (Deut. 28 :1-68 ; 29 :1)
The Palestinian Covenant between God and Israel defines the terms under which God will let Israel live in their land. If they violate the terms, He will remove them, but when they repent, He will bring them back.
6. Davidic Covenant (2 Sam. 23:5; 7:1-17).
God has promised David a sure house and a sure throne with a King on his throne forever.
7. New Covenant (Jer. 31:31-33)
The New covenant is when God writes his laws in our hearts and all know him personally. It is the conditions under which Christians currently live. The Jews, as a whole, get it in the Millenium.

IV. **The Seven Dispensations**
1. Dispensation of Innocence (Gen.1-3)

Adam and Eve were created in innocence. They had to pass the obedience test to be righteous. There was one prohibition. They failed and had to leave the garden.

2. Dispensation of Conscience (Gen. 4-6)

Following the fall, there were no direct commandments from God. However, God had given man a conscience (Rom. 2:15). In general, mankind failed to live according to his conscience and God drowned them out in a flood.

3. Dispensation of Government

After the Flood God gave people to the right to rule themselves. He gave certain responsibilities that required it, such as capital punishment (Gen. 9). This responsibility is continuing across dispensations. In Shinar, they set up a government independent of God with a determination to remain together instead of scatter like God had commanded them. They were judged by the dividing of tongues (Gen. 7-11; 9: 1, 2; Gen. 11: 1-4; Gen. 11:5-8).

4. Dispensation of Promise

After the dispersal of the nations, God called Abram (Abraham) to leave his home in Ur and travel in Canaan. God promised the land to Abram, Isaac, Jacob and Jacob's descendants. Genesis ends with Jacob's family descending into Egypt, a land where they were eventually put into slavery (Gen. 12:1-3; Gen. 13:14-17; Gen. 15:5; Gen. 26:3; Gen. 28:12-13; Exod. 1: 13-14).

5. Dispensation of Law

God delivered Israel out of Egypt through Moses and Aaron. He gave them the Law at Mount Sinai in Arabia. The entire history of Israel until the Babylonian captivity was of one failure after another with short times of recovery and revival. The best times in the history of Israel were the reigns of David and Solomon (Exod. 19:1-8; 20; 2 Kings 17:1-18; 2 Kings 25: 1 -11; Acts 2:22-23; Acts 7:51-52; Rom. 3:19-20; Rom. 10:5; Gal. 3: 10).

6. Dispensation of Grace
When the Lord Jesus Christ died on the cross and rose from the dead he instituted the New Covenant and the dispensation of Grace. Having paid for the sins of mankind, we can now be fully forgiven and cleansed from all sin (Hebrews 9). We are justified by faith in the blood of Jesus Christ and given the Holy Spirit to dwell in us permanently. In spite of this and many other blessings, the dispensation ends in apostasy and a lukewarm condition (Rev. 3:14-22). The dispensation will end with the coming of Christ to take the church out of the world. After the church is taken out, God will pour out His wrath on the world for seven years (1 Thess. 4:16-17; Jer. 30:5-7; Dan. 12:1; Zeph. 1:15-18; Matt. 24:21-22; Matt. 25:31-46; Matt. 24:29-30.)

7. Dispensation of the Kingdom
After the seven years of tribulation, the Lord will return to earth and reign over it for one thousand years (Isa. 2:1-4; Isa. 11; Acts 15:14-17; Rev. 19:11-21; Rev. 20:1-6).

8. This is followed with the destruction of earth and the universe. God will judge the rest of the dead at the Great White Throne Judgment and He will make a new perfect heaven and earth (Rev. 20-21).

V. **The Five Judgments**
1, The Judgment of Sin at the cross (Mt 27)
2. The Judgment of Sin in the Believer
(1 Cor. 11:31-32)
3. The Judgment Seat of Christ

     (1 Cor. 3:11- 17; 5:8-9)
  4. Judgment of the Nations (Mt. 25:31-32)
  5. Great White Throne (Rev. 20:11-15)
VI. **The Two Advents of Christ:**
The first coming and the second. The second coming consists of the rapture (1 Thess. 4:13-18) and the Revelation (Rev. 19).

Scripture with Scripture

12 Now we have received, not the spirit of the world, but the spirit which is of God; that we might know the things that are freely given to us of God.
13 Which things also we speak, not in the words which man's wisdom teacheth, but which the Holy Ghost teacheth; **comparing spiritual things with spiritual.** (1 Cor. 2:12-13)

  The best interpreter of the Bible is the Bible itself. It is tempting to turn first to a commentary or some other book. These can be a help, but not as much help as you will find in other passages of Scripture. The previous section recommended a very good way to get an overall picture of Scripture and God's plan for the ages, the divisions of Scripture. But, the Bible interprets the details also. A good concordance like Strong's is important for doing this, because it helps you track the usage of concepts and words through the Bible. If you use a computer or phone Bible, the search function serves this purpose.
  The Bible illuminates itself. For example, if you wanted to see what the Bible says about marriage, you can find many places in Scripture that explain it. You could look up what the Bible says about the term marriage, wife, husband, family, etc. It doesn't matter where you start. With the "law of first mention," often the facts expressed the first time a concept or term is mentioned follow the same pattern in subsequent mentions. The first mention of the term *marriage* is in Exodus 21:10, where we learn that a wife is a "her" not a "him." We also learn there are duties to marriage. To learn more one should read the surrounding verses. Then we could turn to the first marriage in Genesis 2:18-25. There we find the definition of marriage and much more. "Therefore shall a man leave his father and

his mother, and shall cleave unto his wife: and they shall be one flesh" (Gen. 2:24).

The Bible often defines its own terms. A good case in point is the word "adoption." The usual teaching seems to be that when we first trusted in Christ, God adopted us. Is this true? First, look up the word in a concordance or in the search function of a computer Bible program. You will find the word is used five times in the KJB New Testament. You might first go first to Ephesians 1:5, "Having predestinated us unto the adoption of children." You might notice Romans 8:15 and learn that we have received the Spirit of adoption. Then you will probably find Romans 8:23, *where adoption is defined* as "the redemption of the body." After that, you are likely to launch into a study of the redemption of the body. All in all you will learn a great deal and you looked nowhere but into the Bible alone.

Translators Verse Teachers

While it is important for a translator to know and understand as much of the Scriptures as he can, he is not to turn his translation into a running commentary. It is not the job of a translator to teach through his translation. It is his job to understand the words of God and then transfer those words into a new language as carefully and accurately as he can; no more and no less. If a portion of Scripture is ambiguous, it is not his job to explain the ambiguity. If God inspired any of His words with ambiguous meanings, then the translator needs to leave the ambiguity in the translation just as God had it. Perhaps, God wants that passage to be taken more than one way. If the translator decides which way it should be taken and translates it that way, then he may be hiding a profound truth from God's people.

God is a God of great wisdom and depth. "O the depth of the riches both of the wisdom and knowledge of God! how unsearchable are his judgments, and his ways past finding out!" (Rom. 11:33). It is impossible for a translator to bring out all the many angles of God's wisdom. That's why he needs to stick to God's Words and not to change them. God has inspired the words that can bring out all the wisdom that He wants mankind to know. God is unlimited. He has unlimited depth in His understanding and wisdom and He has embedded that kind of depth into His Word. No man, be he translator or teacher, can reach the bottom of God's wisdom, knowledge, and understanding.

It is the calling of teachers, not translators, to explain God's Words. *"For Ezra had prepared his heart to seek the law of the LORD, and to do it, and to teach in Israel statutes and judgments"* (Ezra 7:10). *"And Ezra opened the book in the sight of all the people … So they read in the book in the law of God distinctly, and gave the sense, and caused them to understand the reading"* (Neh. 8:4, 8).

Is there anything hard to understand in the Book of God? Then translate the words and leave it hard to understand. God will give the teacher the ability to "give the sense."

Chapter Nine

The Qualifications of a Translator

19 We have also a more sure word of prophecy; whereunto ye do well that ye take heed, as unto a light that shineth in a dark place, until the day dawn, and the day star arise in your hearts:
20 Knowing this first, that no prophecy of the scripture is of any private interpretation.
*21 For the prophecy came not in old time by the will of man: but **holy men of God** spake as they were moved by the Holy Ghost. (1 Peter 1:19-21)*

What are the qualifications for a person who wishes to become a translator? The Bible talks about Bishops, Elders, and Pastors. It gives their qualifications in 1 Timothy 3. The Bible talks about deacons and gives their qualifications in 1 Timothy 3. Where are the qualifications for a translator? The word *translator* isn't even used in Scripture. So, how are we to know what the qualifications are?

In chapter three, we established the fact that Bible translating is a need and a valid ministry under the Great Commission of the Lord Jesus Christ. In some ways the qualifications of a translator are the same as the qualifications of anyone who wants to help fulfill the Great Commission. Although, they are not listed in any one place, there *are* qualifications to fulfill the Great Commission.

19 Nevertheless the foundation of God standeth sure, having this seal, The Lord knoweth them that are his. And, Let every one that nameth the name of Christ depart from iniquity.
20 But in a great house there are not only vessels of gold and of silver, but also of wood and of earth; and some to honour, and some to dishonour.
21 If a man therefore purge himself from these, he shall be a vessel unto honour, sanctified, and meet for

the master's use, and prepared unto every good work. (2 Timothy 2:19-21)

The most basic qualification of all is that a translator must be saved. "*The Lord knoweth them that are His.*" A person cannot translate the Word of God well, when he does not know God. "But the natural man receiveth not the things of the Spirit of God: for they are foolishness unto him: neither can he know them, because they are spiritually discerned" (1 Cor. 2:14). How can a person who is dead in sin (Eph. 2:1-3) understand God and His Word? How can a person who is carnal, dominated by the flesh (Eph. 2:1-3), understand the spiritual words of God? A saved person can. "But ye are not in the flesh, but in the Spirit, if so be that the Spirit of God dwell in you. Now if any man have not the Spirit of Christ, he is none of his … For as many as are led by the Spirit of God, they are the sons of God" Rom. 8:9, 14}.

The second basic qualification for a translator is to depart from iniquity. There are a number of ways to express this idea. A translator needs to be living a life in obedience to the Lord. Jesus said, "He that hath my commandments, and keepeth them, he it is that loveth me" (John 14:21). None of us is perfect. That is not the issue. However, a translator should be taking steps in his life to separate from sin and stay separated from sin. We all inevitably fail in some way, but there is a solution. "If we confess our sins, he is faithful and just to forgive us our sins, and to cleanse us from all unrighteousness" (1 John 1:9). "For a just man falleth seven times, and riseth up again" (Prov. 24:16). If we fail, we confess and get back up and go on … over and over until we get to Heaven.

The same concept of departing from iniquity is also found in 2 Peter 1:21, "*holy men of God spake as they were moved by the Holy Ghost.*" God chose holy men as His instruments of inspiration when He gave His Word. It only stands to reason that translators should also be holy persons. Holiness is expected of us all. "*As obedient children, not fashioning yourselves according to the former lusts in your ignorance: But as he which hath called you is holy, so be ye holy in all manner of conversation*" (1 Peter 1:14-15). The basic idea of holiness is separation from sin.

Separation also involves departing from associations and relationships that hinder the work: "*If a man therefore purge himself from these …*" (2 Tim. 2:20). The Scripture also explains, "*Be ye not unequally yoked together with unbelievers: for what fellowship hath righteousness with unrighteousness? and what communion hath light with darkness? And what concord hath Christ with Belial? or what part hath he that believeth with an infidel?"* (2 Cor. 2:14-15) There are some associations that are distractions from living in a godly way or from fulfilling God's plan. Close associations with ungodly people can lead to ungodliness in you. Also, translation work requires time, a lot of time. Some activities are necessary in life, such as caring for one's family. On the other hand, there are activities, associations, and commitments that take up time that would be better spent fulfilling the calling of God on your life.

We have seen the following verse before, but we will look at it again. It includes three qualifications of a translator.

> *For this cause also thank we God without ceasing, because, when ye received the Word of God which ye heard of us, ye received it not as the word of men, but as it is in truth, the Word of God, which effectually worketh also in you that believe. (1 Thess. 2:13)*

A Bible translator must believe that all Scripture is given by inspiration of God. This is a necessity for a Bible translator. There is no other option. As we have said before, this makes a vast difference in how you translate. If you believe the Scriptures came from God, you will revere His words. If you do not believe it, it will not make any difference how you handle God's Word.

A translator must believe it is the individual words that are inspired, not just the message. Do you believe that God inspired His Word only in the sense that it was His message that was inspired? If so, then you will probably only seek to translate the message without regard to the actual words used.

A Bible translator must believe in verbal plenary providential preservation of the Words of God. If you believe that all God's Words were given by inspiration, do you also believe that He kept them perfectly? If you do not, then you cannot have full confidence that the Bible you hold in your hand is truly the Word of God in all its parts. There will be doubt about some parts of the Bible. A translator needs to be sure in his own heart that what he is translating is truly the Word of God, in each word as well as the whole.

The Qualifications of a Bible Translator

Some say that God only preserved the message of His Word. The message is true, but some of the words may be in error. Once again, that kind of "faith" will allow you to translate *your own private perception* of the "message" in whatever words you choose. No. As we have clearly seen, God promised to preserve all the words that He inspired. Every word of the Bible and the entire Bible has been preserved and is the Word of God. That must be the faith of the translator.

A translator must know where he can find an actual copy of God's Word. So, if God preserved His Word, where is it? Is it in the United Bible Societies Greek Text? Is it in the Textus Receptus, the Received Text? Is it in the King James Bible or the myriad of other translations available? A translator needs to have convictions about these things. We will look at this subject further in the next chapter.

Our previous examples of "interpretation" in the New Testament also reveal some qualifications of the translator.

A translator must be educated enough to know both the source language and target language well. In every example of interpretation, it is clear that the Biblical writer was very familiar with Hebrew, Aramaic and Greek. In the Biblical examples, Hebrew and Aramaic were the source languages, and the target language was Greek.

These three languages are also the languages in which the Bible was written. Therefore, they are the primary source languages in Bible translating. A translator should know these languages. He also will need to learn the target language well.

Translators who know Greek and Hebrew are few these days. Some translation teams are translating from the KJB. The situation is challenging. In a translation project in Togo, West Africa, we have found this to be true. Togo is a French speaking country. The entire translation team is Togolese. Two people on the team know Greek and the same two know English. They all know French and the tribal target language. The two who know English and Greek are translating the New Testament from the Greek Received Text, while referring to the KJB and a new revision of the French Ostervald Bible, revised by Pastor Mario Monette, in Canada, based on the KJB. The other translators are using the French Bible. The translations from French are being checked from the Greek Received Text by one of the men who knows Greek. We check the accuracy of the translation based on the Greek Received text and the KJB.

A translator must be educated in Bible theology. Biblically, this is supposed to be a characteristic of every Christian. We all need to know the Word of Truth. But, for a translator it is an especially important need. A teacher who speaks the Word must know the Word. A person who translates the Word must know the Word.

A translator must reject the concept of ownership. It is easy for a translator or group of translators to feel that the translation belongs to them. It does not. Such a concept must be rejected. The translation, if it is truly an accurate translation of the Scriptures, produces the Words of God in another language. Those Words belong to only one person, the Lord God Himself. No man can claim or should feel he owns any part of them. When the KJB translators did their work, they committed it to God who is able to use and preserve it. God has done just that through more than four centuries. A translator need not worry about the fate of the translation when it is done accurately and for the glory of God. The Almighty is in control.

Finally, a translator must understand and be committed to the Biblical method of translating. The translator must be committed to a formal-equivalent translation method, because that is the method God uses in the examples of "interpreting" He gave us.

Although, many more "qualifications" could be added to this brief list, these few, immensely important items are required by Biblical statement and example. I have tried to draw the qualifications from the Scriptures.

Chapter Ten

The Septuagint and the Hebrew Old Testament

Behold, ye trust in lying words, that cannot profit. (Jeremiah 7:8)

Because they have committed villany in Israel, and have committed adultery with their neighbours' wives, and have spoken lying words in my name, which I have not commanded them; even I know, and am a witness, saith the LORD. (Jeremiah 29:23)

In this chapter and the next two, we will apply some of the truths about translating that we have studied to the Biblical text itself. There are several Scriptural principles contained in the previous chapters that we will apply to the Bible text. Two of these are inspiration and preservation, which we *must* apply to the history of the Biblical Text. It is important that you go beyond simply *believing* that God inspired and preserved the Bible. It is necessary that all Christians in general and translators in particular be certain of the *exact identity* of the true inspired Greek and Hebrew texts and their copies.

Furthermore, one of the qualifications of a translator is. *"A translator must know where he can find an actual copy of God's Word."* Bible translating is spiritual work; a cooperation between the translator and God. God works effectively in those who believe the Bible they hold in their hand (1 Thess. 2:13). To this end, we will summarize the history of some of the important Hebrew and Greek Bible documents:

    1) The Hebrew Text of the Old Testament,
    2) The Traditional Greek hand-written text that existed from the beginning, and
    3) The printed Greek Received Text and its use by the King James translators,
    4) The Septuagint, and
    5) The United Bible Societies Greek Text.

As you know, the Old Testament was written in Hebrew with small parts in Aramaic. However, the general scholarly teaching is that the early Christians did not use the Hebrew text. They say Christians used a Greek translation of the Old Testament called the "Septuagint." We will look at that first.

The "Septuagint" is very popular with evangelical scholars and it is supported by both the Roman Catholic Church and the Greek Orthodox Church. The "Septuagint" includes the Apocrypha, but many protestant scholars accept it anyway. The Catholic and Orthodox leadership believe that the Lord Jesus approved of the "Septuagint" and, therefore, the apocrypha. The "Septuagint" is a loose translation that supports dynamic equivalence translating. It promotes the idea that preservation is only the message, not the words. Finally, scholars tell us that the "Septuagint" is witness to a different tradition of the Hebrew text, thereby causing us to doubt the text we have.

You may notice that I have put the word "Septuagint" in quotes. I do this because it is the name given by the scholars to several Greek Old Testaments that currently exist. It is my contention that the "Septuagint" per se never existed and the current Greek Old Testaments are edited and constructed texts.

The Septuagint

The so-called Septuagint is designated LXX. It seems to be the darling of the scholars. They often refer to it. I dispute the claim that Jesus and the Apostles quoted it and that it was the Old Testament of the early Christians. The Septuagint is an Old Testament in Greek, supposedly translated from Hebrew by seventy Jewish elders in Alexandria Egypt about 250 BC.

The entire tradition of a whole Old Testament translated into Greek in the time of Ptolemy II Philadelphus (circa 250 BC) rests on a document called the *Letter of Aristeas* and the testimony of several ancient people who repeated the Aristeas story.

> 1. **The Letter of Aristeas:** This is a letter scholars have dated in the second century BC (100-200 BC,) but the author of the Letter claims to have been a courtier of Ptolemy II Philadelphus (Reign 283-246 BC). The only copies of the

The Septuagint and the Hebrew Old Testament

Letter now existing are dated 11-16th centuries AD. It tells how the *Hebrew Law*, on the advice of Demetrius Phalereus the chief librarian, came to be translated into Greek during the reign of Ptolemy II Philadelphus for inclusion in the library at Alexandria, Egypt. Most scholars today believe the letter to be a forgery. [65] Therefore, they have dated the Letter in the second century BC (rather than third century BC) and have called it *Pseudo-Aristeas*, because he wasn't who he said he was. Bruce Metzger, the famous scholar of Princeton University and the United Bible Societies Greek New Testament, had this to say about the letter.

Most scholars who have analyzed the letter have concluded that the author cannot have been the man he represented himself to be but was a Jew who wrote a fictitious account in order to enhance the importance of the Hebrew Scriptures by suggesting that a pagan king had recognized their significance and therefore arranged for their translation into Greek. [66]

Furthermore, the Jewish Encyclopedia has a list of errors in the letter.

Errors in the Letter.
The author of this letter declares himself (§ 16) a heathen; as such, in §§ 128, 129, he asks Eleazar concerning the purport of the Jewish dietary laws; and in § 306 consults the translators about the meaning of the ceremony of washing the hands before prayer (see Schürer, ii. 444, note 57). But it is universally recognized that in point of fact his panegyrizing tendency toward Judaism throughout shows him to be a Jew (Kautzsch, "Die Apokryphen," i. 16); it is also certain that he cannot have lived in the time of Philadelphus. However important and reliable his general information may be concerning Egyptian affairs, government, and court-ceremonial in the times of the Ptolemies (Wilcken, in

"Philologus," iii. 111), his historical statements about the time of Philadelphus are unreliable. In § 180 he changes Philadelphus' defeat at Cos into a victory; he does not know that Demetrius was banished on the accession of Philadelphus, or that the latter's marriage with his sister was childless (§§ 41, 185); he transplants the philosopher Menedemus arbitrarily to the court of the Ptolemies (§ 201), and lets the historian Theopompus and the tragedian Theodektes relate incredible stories to Demetrius (§§ 314, 315). Of Theodektes, who died before 333 B.C., Demetrius can scarcely have had cognizance. [67]

2. **Aristobulus of Alexandria:** He was a Jewish philosopher, who lived circa 150 BC, possibly c. 181-124 BC (second century BC). He sought to reconcile the Jewish law with Greek Philosophy. He interpreted the Scriptures allegorically. He supposedly testified that *the Jewish Law* had been translated into Greek and completed during the reign of Ptolemy II Philadelphus. I say supposedly, because we only have the testimony of others, such as, Clement of Alexandria (c. 150 to 215 AD) and Eusebius (c. 265-340 AD), as to what Aristobulus said. [68]

3. **Philo:** The dates of this man's life were about 20 BC to 50 AD. So, he was a contemporary of Josephus. He was a Hellenistic Jewish philosopher (an apostate Jew), who sought to reconcile the Jewish faith with Greek philosophy, as did Aristobulus. He, too, mentioned the Letter of Aristeas and repeated the story of the translation of the Jewish law under Ptolemy Philadelphus. [69]

4. **Josephus:** The Jewish historian repeated the story that *the Jewish Law* was translated into Greek around 250 BC and gave information about the letter of Aristeas. [70] Josephus lived about 37-100 AD.

5. **Clement of Alexandria (150-215 AD):** Clement was head of the catechetical school of Alexandria, Egypt. Although he mentioned the "Septuagint," he did not add anything new to the story.

6. **Origen:** Origen Adamantius (184-253 AD) was a scholar of Alexandria who put the "Septuagint" into a six column parallel Old Testament. We will look at this later.

7. **Justin Martyr:** He lived from about 110-165 AD, also repeated the story. However, he didn't say that the translation was of the law, nor did he say it was the whole Old Testament. He went beyond most other writers and told a story about the accuracy of the translation that was pure fantasy. He said the seventy scholars from Jerusalem were separated and each privately translated the entire thing. When their translations were compared they were all the same without any difference, even in one word (Philo told a similar story). He knew this was true, because someone showed him little beds where they supposedly slept (over 350 years before). What a gullible creature! [71]

8. There were others later who mentioned the Septuagint. However, by their time and the time of Origen, there were several translations of the Old Testament into Greek, all of which were done long after the lives of the Apostles. Among these translations were those of Theodotion, Symmachus, and Aquila. Two of the later individuals who wrote of the Septuagint were Jerome and Eusebius, of whom I will speak later.

In all of these, there is no first-hand or manuscript evidence presented to back up the stories. Some of the stories themselves rest on the weakest concepts, like "I know the story is true, because I saw the beds they slept on." The Hope of Israel organization has presented information supporting the Septuagint. They said:

> Notice! Now we have two ancient authorities (Aristeas and Philo – SC) who confirm the essential story of the translation of the Pentateuch into Greek during the reign of Ptolemy Philadelphus. "In the mouth of two or three witnesses shall every word be established," God says. The fact that Josephus' account differs slightly -- has "variations" -- from the letter of Aristeas is proof that he did not just copy the letter or get his information from the letter itself,

> entirely, but had other sources at his disposal. These slight "variations" add further weight to the evidence that the story is true, in its important aspects. [72]

This is a severe fallacy. A "witness" is someone who has seen or heard something (1 John 1:1-3). The only one who was supposedly in a position to be a witness of the translation was Aristeas. He is the only one who said he lived at the time. However, his testimony is generally dismissed as a forgery, due to numerous errors of verifiable facts. It cannot be trusted. Therefore, there are actually NO witnesses to the Law or an entire Old Testament which was translated in the third century before Christ's birth. You could quote 50,000 people who *say* it happened and still have NO *witnesses*. If you accept as witnesses those who lived 100 to 800 years after the events, you may as well name as "witnesses" all the *modern* scholars who declare there was a BC Greek Old Testament called "Septuagint."

Notice also that the testimony is that **the Law only** was translated before Christ, not the entire Old Testament. The term *law* could refer to the whole Pentateuch (Genesis-Deuteronomy) or it could refer to only the Book of Deuteronomy. There are a few fragments of the Jewish Law in Greek that scholars have dated before Christ. However, that is the extent of the actual evidence. Even that is uncertain. Scholars have been wrong in their dating before.

Actually, when scholars want to point out an actual Septuagint manuscript, they point to the Old Testament copies found in the manuscripts Vaticanus (4th Century AD according to most textual scholars), Sinaiticus (4th Century AD according to most textual scholars), or Alexandrinus (5th Century AD). All of these were written 600 or more years after the Old Testament was supposedly translated in Alexandria, Egypt.

However, the dates of both the Codices Vaticanus and Sinaiticus have been called into question. The Scholar, Erasmus, who gave us the first edition of the Received Text in 1516, believed Vaticanus was both inferior and the text was recent, rather than ancient. He believed that parts of Vaticanus were back translated from the Latin Vulgate, after a Papal Bull issued at the Council of Florence about 1435. For that reason and the fact that Vaticanus did not follow the quotes of the orthodox Greek "fathers," Erasmus considered Vaticanus to be an untrustworthy text. He refused to use it. [73]

Regarding Codex Sinaiticus, Dr. Jack Moorman has written a book entitled *Was Codex Sinaiticus Written in 1840!* Also, David W. Daniels wrote *Is the "World's Oldest Bible" a Fake?* These books raise serious questions about the authenticity of the Sinaiticus manuscript and present extremely strong evidence showing that Sinaiticus was written in 1839-40, and that it was artificially aged and corrected by Tischendorf himself (the man who found it and took it away from the Monastery of St. Catherine at the traditional site of Mt. Sinai in 1859).

> Would God have withheld the truth for 1800 years, only to have it show up in an Orthodox monastery in the desert? And then would God arrange for it to be stolen, first 43 leaves of it in 1844, then the rest of it, with Russian help, in 1859? And then would He have it only "released" to the public in 1862 —but not directly, only as an altered, printed copy? Would He have His people see only a typeset text that covers up thousands of erasures, write-overs, marginal notes and optional readings? Would it be missing over 1/3 of the Old Testament? And after that, would it be mixed with fairytales like Tobit and Judith, Bel and the Dragon, Susanna, and 4th Maccabees, the non-historical, fanciful writings of men? [74]

As indicated in the above quote, the "Septuagint" contains the Apocrypha: books such as Tobit, Song of Susanna, I and II Maccabees. These books are included as part of the Greek Old Testament. However, orthodox Jews rejected them. They were never part of the Hebrew Old Testament. These books were included between the Testaments in the first edition of the King James Bible, not as part of the inspired Scripture. The Preface of the KJB made It clear that the translators did not consider the Apocrypha to be inspired.

Aristobulus of Alexandria

There is more going on in all of this than honest men writing true history. Remember, Satan opposes and imitates God (2 Cor. 11). Do not forget that Satan is a liar and the father of lies (John 8:44) and that he calls and sends his own ministers (2 Cor. 11:13-15). Think about the fact that Satan is present in the world today and has been throughout history since the Garden of Eden (Gen, 3). God has a plan that he has been working out in history. Satan also has a plan that he has been doing his best to work out in history. I believe, the Septuagint is one of Satan's tools to lead men astray from the true Word of God. This strategy has been centuries in the making. It is entirely possible that Aristobulus of Alexandria was a part of the enemy's plan.

The dates of Aristobulus' life are uncertain. Most scholars place him in the second century BC., possibly about 181-124 BC. There is a lot of uncertainty about his life since what we know about him comes from others much later in history: Clement of Alexandria, Anatolius of Laodicea, and Eusebius of Caesarea. Clement (150-215 AD) was a professing Christian, the head of the catechetical school in Alexandria, Egypt. Anatolius (early third century-283 AD) was the Bishop of Laodicea in Roman Syria. He was also a scholar of the physical sciences and Aristotelian philosophy. Eusebius (c. 265-340 AD) was Bishop of Caesarea and a church historian. Eusebius was supposed to have had two fair-sized fragments of Aristobulus' writing.

If 2 Maccabees 1:10 refers to this Aristobulus, he was said to belong to a priestly family and was a teacher of Ptolemy (presumed to be Philometer VI 181-146 BC). [75] Many years before the more famous Philo, Aristobulus, a Hellenistic Jew, is said to have endeavored to reconcile the Jewish law with Greek philosophy. He proposed (and sought to prove) that Greek philosophy came from Jewish wisdom and sources. The quotations of Clement and Eusebius are from a document apparently titled *Commentaries on the Writings of Moses.* That would be the first five books of the Bible, the Jewish Torah or Law.

If we take Aristobulus to be a real historical person and what was said above to be true in regard to his philosophy and writing, Aristobulus would need a copy of the Jewish Law in Greek. His commentary was on the Law and his audience was Greek speaking. It is interesting that he is supposed to have repeated the story of the translation of the Law into Greek between 283-246 BC and of the Letter of Aristeas. It is also interesting that today's scholars, for the most part, reject the genuineness of the Letter of Aristeas. They do not believe it was written by a third century BC person who was a courtier in the reign of Ptolemy II Philadelphus. Instead a date of the second century BC is assigned to the letter, putting it in or near the life of Aristobulus. It is also said that the author of the Letter was a Jew, who was seeking to defend the Jews of Egypt, as Aristobulus was. Was Aristobulus himself the author of the Letter of Aristeas? Did Aristobulus himself translate the Jewish Law into Greek and attempt to pass both off as more ancient documents?

That's certainly more reasonable than the attitude of the scholarly world. Their idea is that, although the Letter of Aristeas is a fictional forgery and a lie, at the same time it tells a historical truth about the translation of the Old Testament into Greek. We cannot trust the Letter, we know it's a lie, but let's believe it anyway. That's rather faulty thinking, to say the least.

Philo of Alexandria

Philo of Alexandria (c. 20 BC-50 AD) was the next ancient witness of the Septuagint outside the false letter of Aristeas and Aristobulus. Philo was a Jew who had turned to Greek philosophy. His goal was to reconcile the law of Moses with Greek philosophy. He studied the theories of Pythagoras, Plato, Aristotle, and the Stoics. He also taught the allegorical method of Bible interpretation. To him, the Bible cannot be understood literally. His teachings were the beginning of what we call "Jewish Gnosticism."

> **GNOSTICISM**, designates the beliefs held by a number of nonorthodox Christian sects flourishing in the first to second centuries C.E., which developed mystical systems of philosophy based on the *gnosis* (Gr. "knowledge") of God. These systems were syncretic, i.e., mixtures of pagan magic and beliefs from the Babylonian and Greek world as well as from the Jewish. Judaism made an important contribution to the conceptions and the developments of Gnosticism. [76]

The Source of the Greek Old Testament Law

Of all the people of whom we have certain or semi-certain record, Aristobulus and Philo are the only two who could possibly have started the legend of the "Septuagint." From all we know about them, we can start to form a picture. They were men deceived by Greek philosophy. They did not believe the Hebrew Old Testament and were, at the same time proud to be a Jews. However, they were Hellenistic Jews or what the Bible called "Grecians." That is, they were apostate Jews. Here is what we know.

> 1. *They had the motive.* The desire was to infuse and reconcile Greek philosophy with Jewish law and thought. In order to do this they needed the Old Testament Law in a form that they could use and communicate to those within their potential influence. The desire seemed to be to affect the Greek world, so they needed the Old Testament or at least the Pentateuch *in Greek*. It is probable that one of them was responsible for the first translation of the Law from Hebrew into Greek. We will see that this is plausible when we look at the actual manuscript evidence of the "Septuagint." The fragments of the law in Greek that have been found can easily date within either Aristobulus' or Philo's lifetime. We will look further at this later.
> 2. *They had the means.* Aristobulus had connections with the priestly line and the household of Ptolemy. Philo was born into a noble, wealthy, and honorable family. His family had connections with the Ptolemies, the Hasmonean rulers in Palestine, the Herodians, and the Julio-Claudian dynasty of Rome. Both were well educated, being taught Greek culture, ancient Egyptian Culture, Jewish culture, and Philo was taught Roman culture. They were educated In Judaism and in Greek philosophy. [77]
> 3. *They had the Opportunity.* Philo had freedom of travel. He was at the temple in Jerusalem at least once. He traveled to Rome to see Emperor Caligula as a representative of the Alexandrian Jewish community. Both had plenty of time and plenty of resources in Alexandria.

The letter of Aristeas is a fictional forgery and even its date is uncertain. It is unreliable, but it did exist. Before Philo, the only one who wrote of the "Septuagint" was Aristobulus. Before Aristobulus, *no one* wrote of a "Septuagint." However, after Aristobulus and

Philo, many wrote about it. It appears that one of these men is the fulcrum on which the see-saw rocks. The legend of the Letter of Aristeas began with Aristobulus and could very well have been written in his lifetime or even by him. As we shall see, the manuscript evidence we have (that is dated before Christ) is dated within his reach.

Pieces ... Pieces ... What About the Pieces?

Pieces and fragments of the Law of Moses (Gen.-Deut.) in Greek have been found, labeled "Septuagint," and dated before Christ. Some of these have been found in Egypt. Others were found among the Dead Sea Scrolls. The following chart lists those Greek fragments of the Old Testament that are dated before Christ.

Symbol	Name	Date	Content
801	4Q119	1st cent BC or 1st AD	fragments of Leviticus 26:2-16
802	4Q120	1st cent BC or 1st AD	fragments of Leviticus 1:11, 2:3-6:5
803	4Q121	1st cent BC	fragments of Numbers 3:39-4:16
805	7Q1	1st cent BC	fragments of Exodus 28:4-7
819	4Q122	2nd cent BC	fragments of Deut 11:4
847	Papyrus Fouad 266	2nd/1st cent BC	Deuteronomy 10:22; 11:1.10,11.16; 31:26-19; 32:2,4; 33:14-19.22-23.26-27
848	Papyrus Fouad 266	2nd/1st cent BC	Deuteronomy 17:14 to 33:29 (with gaps)
942	Papyrus Fouad 266	2nd/1st cent BC	Genesis 3:10-12; 4:5-7.23; 7:17-20; 37:34-38:1; 38:10-12
957	Papyrus Rylands 458	2nd cent BC	Deut 23:24(26)-24:3; 25:1-3; 26:12; 26:17-19; 28:31-33; 27:15; 28:2

Fig. 11 [78]

Of these ten items, the last four were found in Fayyum, Egypt, south of Cairo. The first six were found among the Dead Sea Scrolls. The Dead Sea Scrolls were ancient documents found in a

A Practical Theology of Bible Translating

series of caves on the northwest of the Dead Sea, an area called Qumran, starting in 1947. Hundreds of fragments and larger pieces have been recovered. [79] Notice that the pieces listed here are all of the **Pentateuch only.** There was one other, but it was of the apocryphal book, Baruch.

About the Dates of the Pieces

At first glance, this seems to indicate that some sort of Greek translation existed before Christ. Of course, any piece of the Greek OT that scholars think was written before Christ will be called "Septuagint" because of their personal beliefs, not the evidence. Please, notice several things about these items.

First, the dates are anything but certain or exact. As one can see from the chart, all of these pieces have been assigned a date before Christ. "Assigned a date" means that paleographers and/or other scholars have examined the fragmentary remains along with elements around the site, such as, the pottery nearby, and they have made an *educated guess* at a date. They use such things as carbon 14 dating, inscriptions on pottery found at the site, writing style, and other things to help them do this. They often make a great attempt to be accurate. Nevertheless, the dates frequently cannot be determined with certainty. Also, it is often impossible to determine exact dates. Sometimes, the dates are determined based on preferences or pre-conceived prejudices, as I will demonstrate. No one can be absolutely certain that the assigned dates are correct.

Notice the dates assigned to the fragments. The first one was said to be *either* first century AD or first century BC. That's quite precise, huh? It's a two hundred year span. Some are assigned to the first century BC, a one hundred year span. Some are dated to *either* first century or second century BC. That's 200 BC to 1 BC, another two hundred year span. A couple of them are assigned to second century BC. If that's true, it covers 200 BC to 101 BC, another one hundred year span. Fragments found in the same cave (cave 4) at Qumran were assigned different dates at least a century apart; 4Q122 is second century, while 4Q121 is first century. When one glances over some of these pieces, the printed Greek letters seem little different than those in Vaticanus four or five hundred years later. See the example on the next page.

The Septuagint and the Hebrew Old Testament

The document dates fall within a confined period. The Qumran area was occupied by either Essenes or a Saducean group from about 140 BC until 68 AD when the Romans occupied the area. If the Greek fragments were written there, it almost certainly was sometime during that period. However, they could have been written *anytime* during that period. In point of fact, many of the scrolls could have been brought there rather than written there.

The dating methods used are not precise. Hundreds of pieces were recovered from cave 4. Some were obtained by purchase from Bedouins and others by sifting the dust on the floor. Out of that one cave among many mixed pieces came many varied dates from the first century AD to the fourth century BC (a fragment of Samuel in Hebrew-4QSam).

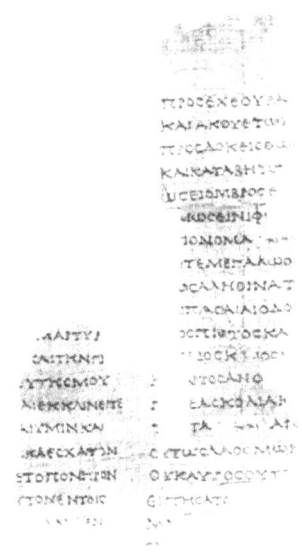

Papyrus Fouad 266 [80]   Vaticanus [81]
Fig. 12

There were several methods used to date the finds of the Dead Sea Scrolls. Let's look at some of them as described by Norman L. Geisler and William E. Nix in their book, *A General Introduction to the Bible*. Their point is to assure students of the reliability of the dates. However, they have also created some doubt about the dates.

Carbon 14, radiometric dating, is sometimes used. This method is not used much, because it destroys some of the material itself. Geisler and Nix do give us one example.

> This was applied to half of a two-ounce piece of linen wrapping from one of the scrolls in cave 1 by Dr. W. F. Libby of the University of Chicago in 1950. Results indicated an age of 1,917 years with a two-hundred-year (10 percent) variant, which left the date somewhere between 168 B.C. and A.D. 233. [82]

Carbon 14 yielded a date somewhere in a 401 year period! That's not very precise dating, is it? The date yielded by carbon 14 had to be corrected for a 200 year variant in both directions.

Paleography (Writing Forms) and Orthography (Spelling) is next. Geisler and Nix describe the action of John Trevor in mailing photographs of the Isaiah scroll to W. F. Albright and they quote Albright's conclusions.

> There is no doubt **in my mind** that the script is more archaic than the Nash Papyrus ... **I should prefer** a date around 100 B.C. ... What an absolutely incredible find! (Author's emphasis) [83]

This quote itself is incredible. Regardless of how much expertise an examiner has, his conclusion is an *opinion* that is based on *his mind and attitudes* and *on his preference*. Date setting based on these methods is highly subjective. That's why the dates given are so imprecise, giving spans of hundreds of years at times.

Another example of this has to do with the Codex Sinaiticus manuscript. Constantin von Tischendorf (1815-1874) is credited with discovering Codex Sinaiticus in St. Catherine's Monastery at the traditional site of Mt. Sinai in 1859. After examining the manuscript, he announced that it should be dated in the fourth century AD. However, David Daniels presented contrary evidence in his book, *Is the "World's Oldest Bible" a Fake?* One part of that evidence has to do with Paleography.

The Septuagint and the Hebrew Old Testament

> Uspensky further states that Euthalius the deacon of Alexandria came up with that way of writing in columns like you see in Sinaiticus and Vaticanus, but it was only done for a short time. And this change in formatting didn't start till at least 446 AD. In his simple, detailed analysis, Uspensky gave evidence that Sinaiticus was no earlier than the middle 5th century! That's 100 years too late to be one of Constantine's 50 Bibles decreed in 330, or to qualify as the "the oldest and best." At 450 AD, that puts it at the same age that people date the only other possibly ancient Alexandrian codex, Alexandrinus. So now we know the Sinaiticus can be no older than 450 AD. But wait. Vaticanus was also made like that, with three columns instead of 4, and lots of empty space. That means Vaticanus can't be older than 450 AD, either! So neither Sinaiticus nor Vaticanus could have been one of Constantine's 50 Bibles. [84]

This proves that the so-called "expert," Tischendorf, was at least 100 years off in his dating estimate! Tischendorf and others may have been convinced *in their own minds* and they may have *preferred* a date of 325-350 AD, but they were wrong by at least a century based on this evidence.

Another example concerns the Syriac Peshitta translation. Dr. Edward F. Hills explained.

> Of the Syriac versions the most important is the Peshitta, the historic Bible of the whole Syrian Church, of which 350 manuscripts are now extant. The Peshitta was long regarded as one of the most ancient New Testament versions, being accorded a 2nd-century date. In more recent times, however, Burkitt (1904) and other naturalistic critics have assigned a 5th-century date to the Peshitta. But Burkitt's hypothesis is contrary to the evidence, and today it is being abandoned even by naturalistic scholars. All the sects into which the Syrian Church is divided are loyal to the Peshitta. In order to account

for this it is necessary to believe that the Peshitta was in existence long before the 5th century, for it was in the 5th century that these divisions occurred. [85]

Brooke Foss Westcott (1825-1901) and Fenton John Anthony Hort (1828-1892) were Anglican scholars and textual critics who created a Greek New Testament to replace the Received Text. It was based on the manuscripts, Vaticanus and Sinaiticus. They persuaded the Revised Version translation committee to adopt the new text. Their theory was that the text of the traditional Greek New Testament, which are the basis of the Textus Receptus (see the next chapter), was created by editors in Syria in the fifth century AD. Burkitt was committed to this theory. Since the Peshitta is of the Traditional text type, Burkitt tried to make it fit Westcott and Hort's theory by declaring it to be a fifth century translation. His **preference** of the fifth century was based on **bias not science**.

Third, there is evidence for dating found in archaeology. This indicated dates from 150 BC to 135 AD. Geisler and Nix describe the evidence.

> The accompanying pottery was analyzed as Late Hellenistic (c. 150-63 B.C), and Early Roman (c. 63 B.C. to A.D. 100). The coins found in the monastery ruins proved by their inscriptions to extend from 135 B.C. to A.D. 135. The cloth was analyzed as to type and pattern, and it, too, supported the early date. [86]

What is our conclusion, then, about the assigned dates? All of the dates arrived at in these processes are general dates, not specific dates. They are so general that they apply to the entire era in which Qumran was occupied. If this is so, the fragments assigned to the first century BC *could* actually be first century AD. That would put them in or near Philo's life. The few that are assigned by the scholars to the second century BC could also be later. On the other hand, the dates as they are also fit very well into the possibility that Aristobulus is the source of both the legend and the translation of the Law. In which case, the translation was not made for the general use of the Jews and Greeks. It was made for Aristobulus. Nevertheless, a few copies of it could have been made.

The Septuagint and the Hebrew Old Testament

At any rate, these fragments do not constitute any sort of *proof* that there was a Greek Pentateuch translated in the time of Ptolemy II Philadelphus (third century BC). Nor does it prove there was a whole Old Testament translated into Greek at *any time before Christ*. It does not provide *any* evidence that the Jews of Palestine and Christians of Jesus' lifetime and the early church typically used any Greek Old Testament. The only thing it shows is that the cult of the Essenes or the Sadducees (as has been suggested) at Quran had some of the Pentateuch in Greek. However, they do not appear to have had much Greek writings. There is very little evidence of Greek, but there are hundreds of Hebrew fragments. All of this supports the concept that what we *now* call the "Septuagint" has no connection with any Greek Old Testament translated before Christ.

Origen's Hexapla and the Septuagint

There is a direct line of philosophical succession from Philo through Clement of Alexandria to Origen Adamantius of Alexandria (184-253 AD). Sometime shortly before 240 AD, the scholar, Origen Adamantius compiled a book in six columns called the Hexapla. This was an edition of the Old Testament. It only survives in a few fragments. Scholars who have studied it say that the column lay-out was as follows:

Column 1. The Hebrew Text
Column 2. The Hebrew Text in Greek letters
Column 3. The translation of Aquila of Sinope into Greek (2nd Century AD)
Column 4. The translation of Symmachus the Ebionite into Greek (late 2nd Century AD)
Column 5. A revised edition of the Septuagint (Origen's own eclectic revision of the "Septuagint")
Column 6. The translation of Theodotian into Greek (middle 2nd century AD) [87]

Although, the Hexapla was written in the third century AD, it is still no proof or evidence that a "Septuagint" existed before Christ. Origen is said to have denied that the fifth column was his own translation, but many still believe it was. The fifth column was certainly his own *revision*, at the very least. To *revise* a text means to *change* the text. Origen created the fifth column by revising Theodotian, Symmachus, Aquila, and (according to Jerome) three other unknown editions of Greek Old Testament. [88] No one knows where he got all his material.

Since we do not have Origen's Hexapla, let me point out certain facts of history. Origen was a professing Christian, who lived from about 184 AD to 253 AD. He was in Alexandria for many years, but eventually relocated to Caesarea Maritima, where he taught in the theological school there and he established a well-known library. Later, the Presbyter, Pamphilus, added to it. The library contained about 30,000 scrolls. Without a doubt, Origen's Hexapla and many other Biblical materials he worked on were there.

Later, three major events occurred. First, is the fact that Eusebius (c. 265–340 AD) became the Bishop of Caesarea about 313 AD. Among Eusebius' many other endeavors, he and Pamphilus occupied themselves with a revision of the "Septuagint." [89] They got this "Septuagint" from Origen.

The second major event was the profession of Christian faith by the Emperor Constantine in 306 AD. In 313 AD, he issued the Edit of Milan, which granted toleration to the Christian religion.

The third event was the request Emperor Constantine made to Eusebius for 50 Bibles in 331 AD. Eusebius was accustomed to using the library of Origen in Caesarea and, no doubt, got his material for these Bibles there.

Scholars have dated Codex Vaticanus at about 350 AD, but as we have seen it is no earlier than 450 AD. Nevertheless, the Vaticanus Old Testament is declared by scholars to be the "Septuagint." Vaticanus' Old Testament and Apocrypha doubtless came from Origen's Hexapla. The translator of the Latin Vulgate, Jerome (c. 347-420 AD), said that the "Septuagint" in his days came from Origen.

> Jerome understood that the Septuagint of his day was developed by Origen. He believed that Origen used several different Greek manuscripts and that all of them had been corrupted! He disputed Augustine's assertion that the apostles usually quoted from the Septuagint! He pointed out that their quotations

often don't match any version of the Septuagint or any other Greek New Testament.

It is clear that what is called the Septuagint today has nothing to do with the story of "The Letter to Aristeas." What is called the Septuagint today is the work of Origen (almost 200 years after the time of Christ). [90]

Whatever the original sources were for the fifth column of the Hexapla, it has been called "eclectic." [91] Eclectic means that it came from various sources, rather than just one. Whatever those sources were, they included the other Greek versions of columns 3, 4 and 6, especially Theodotian. It may also have included material from Philo. Origen revised these sources himself to produce the fifth column, which he called "Septuagint." The fifth column was further revised by Eusebius and Pamphilus. Doubtless, the Old Testament of the fifty Bibles came from Eusebius' own revision of the fifth column of Origen's Hexapla. So, their "Septuagint" had been changed at least twice and, according to Jerome, came from corrupt sources.

So, before the fifty Bibles with their "Septuagint" Old Testament ever reached Constantine, the OT had been revised a minimum of two times. Since scholars consider the Old Testament of Vaticanus to be the "Septuagint," the matter is further complicated. The Vaticanus manuscript itself, according to those who have examined it, was written by two or three scribes, but there were also two others who worked on it making "corrections." One was contemporary with the original scribes and the other did his work in the tenth or eleventh centuries. Dr. Eugene Scott, in *Codex Vaticanus* (1996), says it was also corrected in the 8th and 15th centuries for a total of four correctors. [92] Therefore, the original contents have been changed and marred to a considerable extent. So, the "Septuagint" Old Testament in Vaticanus has been removed at least six revisions from the sources Origen used with possibly parts back translated from Latin (as Erasmus thought). My conclusion is that even if there was a BC Septuagint (which cannot be proven by the evidence), we have *no idea what the original content was*. [93] Therefore, the whole attempt of the scholarly world to exalt the "Septuagint" is given to a document that could not possibly be original, even if there was a "Septuagint."

In 1588 (23 years before the release of the King James Bible) William Whitaker wrote: "Learned men question, whether the Greek version of the Scriptures now extant be or be not the version of the seventy elders. The sounder opinion seems to be that of those who determine that the true Septuagint is wholly lost, and that the Greek text as we have it, is a mixed and miserably corrupted document. Aristeas says that the Septuagint version was exactly conformable to the Hebrew originals, so that when read and diligently examined by skillful judges, it was highly approved by the general suffrage of them all. But this of ours differs amazingly from the Hebrew, as well in other places and books, as specially in the Psalms of David." (William Whitaker, *Disputations on Holy Scripture*, 1588, p. 121; Soli Deo Gloria edition 2000) [94]

As we have noted, it is now clear that the "Letter of Aristeas" is a fraudulent piece of fiction, there is no reason to believe an original pure Septuagint ever existed. It is also very evident that what now exists is highly corrupt and faulty. Dr. Stringer further said:

In Ira Price's, *The Ancestry of Our English Bible,* he mentions several important manuscripts of the Septuagint, p. 52-80. Everyone (except the John Rylands fragment) is the Origen version of the Septuagint - produced long after the New Testament. Every manuscript was produced at least two hundred years after the New Testament that "scholars" claim that it quotes. "But the earliest extent manuscript of this version (the Septuagint) is dated around 350 A.D..." (H. S. Miller, *General Biblical Introduction, p.* 120) ... Professor Paul Kahle (1875-1964) challenged the conventional wisdom of the Septuagint theory. He was not a King James Only advocate. He was a German professor of Oriental Studies. He was a recognized scholar of Mideastern languages.

Professor Kahle simply refused to accept the legend of "The Letter of Aristeas." He called it "propaganda." He refused to follow the conventional wisdom that treats "The Letter of Aristeas" as fictional but authoritative history at the same time. Kahle's theory states that what we call the Septuagint today is actually the result of an attempt to standardize a Greek translation of the Old Testament. [95]

Who Quoted Whom?

The claim is made that the Greek Old Testament was the Bible of the Jews and Christians of the first century. This is highly questionable in light of the fact that the Old Testament forbids adding to or taking away from God's Words (Deut. 4:2; Prov. 30:6). The "Septuagint" does both many times. The Sadducees of the first century may have accepted this. They were Jewish heretics who embraced Greek culture, anyway. However, the Pharisees would not have accepted it, because they were very strict about the Law of Moses. Paul would not have accepted it either, because he was a Pharisee and he took the Scriptures very seriously and literally. The church would have rejected such a text at the beginning, also, having been taught by the Apostles.

The Lord Jesus Christ believed every word of the Hebrew Old Testament and He would not have endorsed a version that adds to and takes away from it. The Lord Jesus was completely committed to the Hebrew Old Testament. We will see the proof of that later in this chapter. Dr. Donald Waite assures us of this and quotes Matthew 4:4, Matthew 5:17-18, and Luke 24:27, 44.

> The Old Testament Hebrew Text Was Authorized by Jesus. Not only was the Scripture accumulated by Jews, but it was authorized by Jesus. Jesus Christ authorized the traditional Masoretic Hebrew Old Testament text. Though we have looked at some of these verses under the subject of Bible preservation, we will look at them once more from a slightly different aspect. [96]

Sometimes the "Septuagint" matches the Hebrew text and sometimes it doesn't. Sometimes it matches the New Testament and sometimes it doesn't. Again, there is *no* direct evidence that the early Christians made regular use of any kind of "Septuagint."

One of the passages often quoted to prove Christian use of the "Septuagint" is Luke 4:18-19, where Jesus turned to Isaiah 61:1-2 in the Synagogue. Notice the comparison below. If you look at these verses closely, you will notice that none of the three versions match. Jesus was not reading either the Hebrew or the Septuagint, even though He had indeed turned to Isaiah 61:1-2 in the scroll, when He was in the Synagogue that day. I will explain this, but first look at the comparison.

> **KJB:** *18 The Spirit of the Lord is upon me, because he hath anointed me to preach the gospel to the poor; he hath sent me to heal the brokenhearted, to preach deliverance to the captives, and recovering of sight to the blind, to set at liberty them that are bruised 19 To preach the acceptable year of the Lord. (Luke 4:18-19)*

> Septuagint: The Spirit of the Lord is upon me, because he has anointed me; he has sent me to preach glad tidings to the poor, to heal the broken in heart, to proclaim liberty to the captives, and recovery of sight to the blind; to declare the acceptable year of the Lord, and the day of recompence; to comfort all that mourn; (Is. 61:1-2)

> Hebrew (represented by the KJB)*: The Spirit of the Lord GOD is upon me; because the LORD hath anointed me to preach good tidings unto the meek; he hath sent me to bind up the brokenhearted, to proclaim liberty to the captives, and the opening of the prison to them that are bound; To proclaim the acceptable year of the LORD, and the day of vengeance of our God; to comfort all that mourn;*
> *(Is. 61:1-2)*

The Septuagint and the Hebrew Old Testament

The following chart breaks this down phrase by phrase.

Phrase	Source	Statement
1	LUKE	The Spirit of the Lord is upon me
	LXX	The Spirit of the Lord is upon me
	ISAIAH	The Spirit of the Lord GOD is upon me
2	LUKE	because he hath anointed me to preach the gospel to the poor;
	LXX	because he has anointed me; he has sent me to preach glad tidings to the poor
	ISAIAH	because the LORD hath anointed me to preach good tidings unto the meek;
3	LUKE	he hath sent me to heal the brokenhearted
	LXX	to heal the broken in heart,
	ISAIAH	he hath sent me to bind up the brokenhearted
4	LUKE	to preach deliverance to the captives,
	LXX	to proclaim liberty to the captives
	ISAIAH	to proclaim liberty to the captives,
5	LUKE	and recovering of sight to the blind,
	LXX	and recovery of sight to the blind
	ISAIAH	----
6	LUKE	to set at liberty them that are bruised
	LXX	----
	ISAIAH	and the opening of the prison to them that are bound
7	LUKE	To preach the acceptable year of the Lord
	LXX	to declare the acceptable year of the Lord,
	ISAIAH	To proclaim the acceptable year of the LORD,
8	LUKE	----
	LXX	and the day of recompense
	ISAIAH	and the day of vengeance of our God;
9	LUKE	----
	LXX	to comfort all that mourn
	ISAIAH	to comfort all that mourn

Fig. 13

So, what was going on here, since the quotes do not completely match? First, Jesus is clearly NOT quoting the "Septuagint" or any Greek Old Testament, because his statements do not match it. Second, Jesus turned to the "place where it was written" (Lk. 4:17), which was apparently a section that included Is. 42-61. Part of Jesus' statement was from Is. 42. What we find in Luke 4:18-19 is not Jesus *reading* from Isaiah. *It is what He said after He read.* Notice that when He spoke, he avoided using the words "GOD" and "LORD," because in Hebrew both are "Jehovah." It was not acceptable to use the great name of God in the Synagogue. The Lord Jesus did not mention the parts in the Hebrew about "vengeance" and comforting those that mourn, because these apply to His second coming. This is Jesus making application of the prophecies of Isaiah 42-61 to Himself. This is explained by New Testament scholar Craig A. Evans.

> Jesus cites in a synagogue (4:18-19) what appears to be a passage from Isaiah 61, but it turns out to be a mixture of several passages or themes from the book of Isaiah. Among them is Isaiah 42, which in the Targum (42:3, 7) especially refers to the poor, the blind, and prisoners, who are pointedly mentioned in Jesus' "citation." [97]

A Word About the OT Quotes in the NT

There are many places in the Septuagint where it does not match either the Hebrew text or the New Testament.   In many places the New Testament more closely matches the Hebrew than it does the Septuagint. So, the Lord and the apostles did not quote from the Septuagint. Yet, in those places where the New Testament matches the Septuagint, who quoted from whom?

More than one Septuagint edition has been printed in English. One of the most famous is the one by Sir Lancelot Charles Lee Brenton published in 1844 (which was used in Fig. 12 and Is. 61:1-2 LXX). His primary source was Codex Vaticanus written 350 to 450 years (or more) *after* Christ. Another English-Greek Septuagint, *Septuaginta: A Readers Edition Hardcover (English and Greek Edition),was* edited by Gregory R Lanier and William A Ross in 2018. There is also a Greek edition by Alfred Rahlfs, edited by Robert Hanhart (2007 edition) which is based on Vaticanus, Sinaiticus, and Codex Alexandrinus (5th century AD).

The Septuagint and the Hebrew Old Testament

The Vaticanus, Sinaiticus, and Alexandrinus manuscripts, being written in the fifth century at the earliest, came too late for the Lord and His apostles to quote from, but the manuscripts were just in time to quote the New Testament. Is. 61:1-2 in the Septuagint is an example of that. There are readings in the Septuagint that are not in the Hebrew or vice versa, so it is not likely to be a true translation of the Hebrew Masoretic Text. Yet, some of those readings match the Greek New Testament in Luke 4:18-19. It is my contention that the New Testament came first and the Greek manuscripts copied it along with an attempt to translate the Hebrew. Therefore, the manuscripts are a hybrid of the two, the Hebrew OT and the Greek NT.

The New Testament quotes or refers to hundreds of verses from the Old Testament. Unfortunately, there is a lot of confusion and ignorance among Christians as to the nature of these quotes. That is perhaps one reason why they are generally dismissed by simply saying that they were quotes from the "Septuagint." They were not.

The Nature of New Testament Quotes

There are many direct and indirect quotes. By *indirect quote*, I mean a quote that is merely a *paraphrase* of the teaching of one or more Old Testament verses or a teaching which *appeals* to one or more Old Testament passages for confirmation or proof.

There are *allusions* and *possible allusions*. An allusion is "a passing or casual reference; an incidental mention of something, either directly or by implication." [98] One example of allusion is Matthew 12:42, *"The queen of the south shall rise up in the judgment with this generation, and shall condemn it: for she came from the uttermost parts of the earth to hear the wisdom of Solomon; and, behold, a greater than Solomon is here."* The Scripture alluded to is 1 Kings 10:1, *"And when the queen of Sheba heard of the fame of Solomon concerning the name of the LORD, she came to prove him with hard questions."* Matthew 12:42 is not intended to be a real quote. It is intended to be an *application* of 1 Kings 10 to the present situation in the Lord's life. There are many allusions in the New Testament.

Another type of quote is similar to an allusion. It is a teaching which appeals to Old Testament Scripture for support. Of course, we do this all the time in teaching and preaching. We make a statement and then refer to what is written for proof. Many times, we don't quote the actual Scripture, but, rather, we paraphrase it. The Scripture says...then we put it in our own words. The New Testament does something similar. For example, Romans 2:24 says, *"For the name of God is blasphemed among the Gentiles through you, as it is written.* " Here it says, *"as it is written,"* but you will not find this statement, as it is, anywhere in the Old Testament. Instead, you will find Ezekiel 36:20, *"And when they entered unto the heathen, whither they went, they profaned my holy name, when they said to them, These are the people of the LORD."* You will also find Isaiah 52:5, *"Now therefore, what have I here, saith the LORD, that my people is taken away for nought? they that rule over them make them to howl, saith the LORD; and my name continually every day is blasphemed."* This is one of the New Testament equivalents of proof-text teaching.

On the other hand, there are also direct and true quotes from the Hebrew Old Testament. To illustrate, We will turn again to the quote in Matthew 1:23, *"Behold, a virgin shall be with child, and shall bring forth a son, and they shall call his name Emmanuel, which being interpreted is, God with us."* This verse is quoted from Isaiah 7:14, *"Therefore the Lord himself shall give you a sign; Behold, a virgin shall conceive, and bear a son, and shall call his name Immanuel.* " One can readily notice that Matthew 1:23 is not an exact quote in every detail. There are differences. Matthew 1:23 says *"shall be with child"* and Isaiah 7:14 says *"shall conceive."* Matthew 1:23 says *"shall bring forth a son"* and Isaiah 7:14 says *"bear a son."* This is typical of many of the Old Testament verses that are quoted in the New Testament. How do we explain this? Well, that's actually quite easy.

This is not just a quote; it is a Bible translation. Whenever anyone, even the original author, takes something written in one language and puts it into another language, it is translation. If I write something in English and then write it in German, I have translated my own words. In this case, God has translated his Old Testament Hebrew words into Greek. However, it gets more complicated than that. Men have entered the picture and translated God's Words into English. So, you have three languages involved: Hebrew, Greek, and English. The Hebrew Old Testament was translated into Greek. The Hebrew was translated into English and the Greek was translated into English. Now, we are comparing English with English. Any translation between two languages can cause minor word differences or differences in grammar or differences in word order, as we have seen. However, the meaning remains the same if the job has been done right. So, in Matthew 1:23, we have *"with child"* instead of *"conceive,"* but the meaning is the same. We also have *"bring forth a son"* instead of *"bear a son,"* but the meaning is the same.

Hopefully, this is enough information to help the reader understand that the Old Testament quotes in the New Testament cannot be explained by appealing to the "Septuagint." If the reader wants to learn more about the Septuagint, he should read *The Septuagint (LXX)* by Dr. H. D. Williams, MD, PhD, available on the web site for The Old Paths Publications.

Why Does It Matter?

Why does it matter whether the New Testament quoted the Septuagint or not? What difference does it make whether there *was* a Septuagint or not? I have spent a great deal of space on this subject, because it is of great importance for at least three reasons. First, if the Apostles and the Lord quoted this Greek Old Testament, then it justifies the work of the modern revisers, text correctors, and dynamic equivalence translators. If the Lord and the Apostles quoted the Septuagint, then they placed their approval on it. The Septuagint adds to the Hebrew text (God's inspired Word) and subtracts from the Hebrew Text and is generally a bad translation. That being the case and if the Lord approved it anyway, then, it is ok to translate the Bible with whatever words you think make sense. You are not restricted to the words of the Hebrew text. You may add, subtract, paraphrase, and reword as much as you want.

Second, scholars tell us that the "Septuagint" is witness to a different Hebrew textual tradition that is older than the Masoretic Text. The Hebrew text you have may not be correct. That being the case, you, as a translator, cannot afford to ignore the "Septuagint" as a translation source. The correct reading may be in the "Septuagint." This actually creates doubt about the Hebrew Masoretic Text. Which is right? Should I choose the "Septuagint" reading in a particular verse or the Hebrew reading? You make that choice yourself and you become the judge of what is the Word of God and what isn't.

The fact is, those who say this do not believe in the providential preservation of Scripture. They do not believe in the sovereignty of God. They do not believe that the Hebrew text we have is the right one, so God did not preserve the right Hebrew text. He must have been too weak to keep it. The facts are, the "Septuagint" is a corrupt Old Testament and you, as a translator, should steer clear of it.

Third, if the Lord Jesus quoted the "Septuagint," he approved of a text that includes the apocrypha. Therefore, the Catholics are justified in using the Apocrypha. In addition, the Protestants are wrong to reject the Apocrypha. They should accept it and, while they are at it, they should return to the Catholic Church. However, the real truth is that the Apocrypha was never a part of the Hebrew Old Testament. There are some strange things the Apocrypha speaks well of: praying or paying for the dead, purgatory, committing suicide, an angel of God lying, sorcery and magic. [99] Is this of God?

The Hebrew Masoretic Text

The Masoretic Hebrew text is the traditional Hebrew text of the Old Testament. When the translators, in the time of King James, started translating in 1604, the current Masoretic text of the Hebrew Old Testament was the Second Rabbinic Bible edited by Jacob Ben Chayim.   This was the primary source for the KJB Old Testament translation. Where did this Hebrew OT come from? Can it be relied on as the preserved Word of God in the Old Testament?

I believe the Lord Jesus Christ is a good and reliable witness about these matters, don't you? After all, He is the Word (John 1:1) and He is God (1 Tim. 3:16). From a study of the Gospels, it is evident that the Lord Jesus knew the Hebrew text of the Old Testament. He quoted from it and clearly approved of it. From Him, we can establish that the Hebrew text in use in His time was an accurate and faithful copy of the originals. Several times, He commented on the Hebrew text that was current in His day.

> *17 Think not that I am come to destroy the law, or the prophets: I am not come to destroy, but to fulfil.*

The Septuagint and the Hebrew Old Testament

18 For verily I say unto you, Till heaven and earth pass, one jot or one tittle shall in no wise pass from the law, till all be fulfilled. (Mt. 5:17-18)

The "jot" and the "tittle" refer to Hebrew letters. Therefore, Jesus was clearly referring to the Hebrew Old Testament that was readily available in His time. The Lord mentions the Law and the prophets specifically here, and if He was concerned about the preservation and fulfillment of the Law (verse 18), certainly He was just as concerned about the preservation and fulfillment of the rest of the Old Testament. Verse seventeen is proof of that. The mention of the Law and the Prophets is proof that the Lord Jesus was referring to the Hebrew text of His day, not the so-called Greek "Septuagint." The Hebrew Old Testament was and is divided into three parts: The Law, the prophets, and the Writings. The "Septuagint" is not divided that way. According to this statement, the copy of the Hebrew OT in circulation at that time was a perfectly preserved copy of the original words, even to the "jot" and "title."

The Lord Jesus Christ had complete confidence in the perfect preservation of every word in the Hebrew Old Testament.

> *And beginning at **Moses** and all the **prophets**, He expounded unto them the things concerning Himself. (Lk. 24:27)*
>
> *And He said unto them, These are the words which I spake unto you, while I was yet with you, that all things must be fulfilled, which were written in the **law of Moses**, and in **the prophets**, and in **the Psalms**, concerning Me. (Lk. 24:44)*

Again, the Lord Jesus is quoting and teaching from the Hebrew Bible. He mentioned all three divisions of the Hebrew Old Testament in these verses: Law, Prophets, and Writings (the Psalms were part of the Writings). The Lord Jesus affirms the accuracy of the then current Hebrew OT by these comments.

Therefore, we have established that during the life of the Lord Jesus Christ there was an exact copy of God's original Hebrew and Aramaic words in circulation. So, this accurate Hebrew Old Testament had been preserved word-perfect from the time that

Moses started writing the Law in about 1450 BC. If God preserved His Hebrew Old Testament Words that long, about 1500 years, why couldn't He preserve them another 2000 years? Did He suddenly lose His mind? Did He lose His power? What happened to the Word of God after the death and resurrection of the Lord Jesus Christ?

According to the Talmud, there was a standard copy of the Hebrew OT kept in the temple at Jerusalem for copyists to use. After the period of the gospels the Rabbis helped to preserve the text. However, in 70 AD, the Roman General, Titus, crushed a rebellion of the Jews, destroyed the temple, and destroyed Jerusalem. Many Scripture manuscripts perished in the violence. This increased Jewish urgency to accurately preserve the text. It must be understood that from the time of the return from Babylonian exile to the time of Jesus Christ, the Old Testament had been thoroughly taught to the people. By the Lord's time on earth, the Hebrew text was firmly established in the Jewish heart and mind. After the 70 AD destruction, the urgency to preserve the text was very strong.

So, after the temple was destroyed, the Hebrew text was preserved by groups of Jewish scribes. The first of these, *the Tannaim* in the Holy Land, kept the text until about 250 AD. The second group was called the *Amoraim.* and they copied the text, carrying on the written text and the oral tradition of the pronunciation until about 500 AD. They were concentrated in the land of Israel and in Babylonia.

The Amoraim were followed in the 500's AD by the *Masoretes*, Jewish scholars located mainly in Tiberias, Jerusalem, and Babylonia. The text preserved by the Masoretes became known as the *Masoretic Text*. They preserved the Old Testament through extremely careful copying throughout the Middle Ages. Finally, the Hebrew Old Testament was printed on the newly invented moveable type printing press in 1488. Since then, preserving the Masoretic text has been easier. The Ben Chayim edition was printed by Daniel Bomberg in Venice in 1524-25. This edition, in effect, became the Received text of the Hebrew Old Testament.

> The Ben Chayyim Masoretic text was the standard text, in fact, the only text in use for over 400 years. As such, it bears the stamp of approval from God's people and is obviously the text which God

The Septuagint and the Hebrew Old Testament

preserved. This text follows the vast majority of the Hebrew manuscripts which have been discovered.

The Kittel text is also commonly called the Ben Asher text. This text was based on a corrupted Hebrew manuscript called the Leningrad manuscript. It was published in 1937 and contains what is estimated to be about 20,000 changes from the Ben Chayyim Masoretic text. Many of the differences between the two Hebrew texts are based upon vowel points. The vowel points were inserted into the Hebrew manuscripts by the Masoretes around the fifth century A.D. The vowel points for the Ben Chayyim text leads to the pronunciation of the name of God as "Jehovah". The Ben Asher text does not support that pronunciation in most of the places where the name is found. Admittedly, most of these changes are minor. Nevertheless, some of them are not. And, since we stand on the verbal plenary inspiration of the Scriptures, even the minor changes should not have been done.

One example where your choice of Hebrew manuscripts will affect your translation can be shown from Joshua 21:36-37 … The New Jewish Publication Society and other modern Hebrew Bibles do not contain these two verses. There are a few other places where the differences between the two manuscripts will affect your translation … Thus, the two Hebrew texts are similar but not quite the same. Obviously, this will affect your translation work. If your goal is to produce a translation that is as good as the King James Version, then you must use the same Hebrew manuscript that the King James translators used. And the King James translators used the Ben Chayyim text. [100]

David Christian Ginsberg published an edition of the Ben Chayim text in 1894. That edition is now the standard text issued by the Trinitarian Bible Society. The greatly touted Dead Sea Scrolls, found in the Qumran caves, support our Masoretic text. God has preserved the Old Testament in the Masoretic Hebrew Text of the

Ben Chayim tradition and the Ginsberg edition. God has preserved the Old Testament in the Hebrew Text that underlies the King James Bible.

Chapter Eleven

The Traditional Greek Text of the New Testament

8 The words of the LORD are pure words: as silver tried in a furnace of earth, purified seven times.

7 Thou shalt keep them, O LORD, thou shalt preserve them from this generation for ever. (Ps. 12:6-7)

The Received Text (or Textus Receptus in Latin) is a printed Greek New Testament that is based on the vast majority of ancient hand-written New Testament manuscripts.

The Traditional New Testament Text

Unfortunately, due to lack of space, we will have to summarize these things, but I have included some further sources in the *Introduction to the Appendices* for the reader who wishes to look deeper.

The last New Testament book, the Book of Revelation, was written by the Apostle John under the inspiration of God in about 98 AD. In the following centuries the New Testament books were copied and recopied many times. They were also translated into a number of languages. Now, we have over 5,700 existing manuscripts copied at various times over the centuries from 150 AD to 1600+ AD. These pieces of evidence are all hand written and range from fragments to nearly complete copies of the New Testament. They include ancient lectionaries (guides used in church services that contain Scripture). In addition, there are ancient translations and Scripture quotations of early church "fathers." About 94% of the evidence agrees and the manuscripts in this category are called the *Traditional Text* or the *Byzantine Text or the Majority Text.* It is called the Traditional text because it can be traced back to about 150 AD in the early writers, lectionaries, fragments found (150 AD), and in ancient versions, such as the Syriac Peshitta Version (150 AD) and the Old Latin (120-150 AD). These ancient documents trace the existence of the Traditional Text continuously to within about fifty years of the lives of the Apostles. Since there are translations from the Traditional Greek Text dated at 150 AD, the text must have existed a considerable time before that. This strongly indicates that the traditional Greek text is the true text penned by the Apostles and their associates.

Currently we are in the midst of a great conflict between two major textual traditions. One is the Traditional text, which is our subject in this section. The other opposing tradition is the Alexandrian Text, which represents the minority of ancient manuscripts. The outstanding examples of the Alexandrian Text are Codex Vaticanus and Codex Sinaiticus. Codex Alexandrinus is of a mixed type, having readings from both the traditional Text and from the Alexandrian. Vaticanus and Sinaiticus have been dated about 350 AD. It is said they are the oldest manuscripts and, therefore, they are closest to the originals and that makes them the best. In reality, they are not the oldest witnesses to the New Testament text, as I pointed out in the previous paragraph.

One of the greatest champions of the Traditional Text was John W. Burgon (1813-1888), Dean of Chichester Cathedral in England. When Dean Burgon died in 1888, he left a certain amount of his work unfinished. His associate, Edward Miller, gathered his materials and edited them to produce the book, *The Traditional Text of the Holy Gospels Vindicated and Established.* He espoused certain principles for the examination of ancient documents of the Bible. These were Bible believing principles. They sharply contrasted with the principles of his contemporaries, Westcott and Hort, who thought that older is better and treated the Bible like it is any other ordinary book. The list of the principles is as follows:

    1. Antiquity;
    2. Consent of Witnesses, or Number;
    3. Variety of Evidence;
    4. Respectability of Witnesses, or Weight;
    5. Continuity, or Unbroken Tradition;
    6. Evidence of the Entire Passage, or Context;
    7. Internal Considerations, or Reasonableness. [101]

The Traditional Text and Its Antiquity

Antiquity has to do with how far back in history a particular text can be traced. This is an important consideration, but it is not the only one and, alone, it does not settle the matter. We can't depend on age alone. However, there are other factors and, when they are taken along with age, they can settle the issue.

The reason age alone is not sufficient is because of 2 Corinthians 2:17, *"For we are not as many, which corrupt the word of God."* Manuscripts bearing severe heretical corruptions appeared early in Church history. Therefore, the oldest manuscript in existence may not be the best. In addition, the true New Testament text would be available to Christians all through the church age. It would not show up magically 1800 years after the birth of Christ. As we have seen, God inspired the New Testament to win people to Him and teach us how to live. Therefore, we must have it in every stage of history. As Jesus promised to be with us every day until the end of the world (Mt. 28:19-20), we need His Word every day to know His will. Remember, God has preserved every word, every day, all the way through history. And, He preserved them for our use. They have been available all along, not left lying in some hidden, dusty, moldy manuscript recently brought to light. So, a massive and widespread testimony of agreeing manuscripts stretching over a span of centuries and showing up in a variety of sources all displaying consistency is a powerful testimony to authenticity.

Nevertheless, antiquity is the first consideration. Scholars have divided ancient manuscripts into several "types." The main divisions are Alexandrian (the source is Egypt), Western (used in Rome), and Traditional (also called Byzantine or Majority Text). Generally, scholars say the Alexandrian text is best (this idea originated with liberals and evangelicals learned it from them-see Appendix 2). These types are based on distinctive and different words and phrases (readings) in various verses. For example, the Traditional Text manuscript says "only begotten son" in John 1:18 and another text says "only begotten god." It must also be noted that many manuscripts are of a "mixed" type. Many of these "mixed" manuscripts are placed in the Alexandrian category by scholars (due to their personal prejudice that the Alexandrian is best).

One of those mixed manuscripts is Codex W of the Gospels, which is dated in the 4th or early 5th century. The Book of Matthew and the last two-thirds of Luke are of the Traditional type. This is significant because Westcott and Hort popularized the theory that a group in Antioch constructed the Traditional text in the 4th century.

> The discovery of W tends to disprove the thesis of Westcott and Hort that the Traditional Text is a fabricated text which was put together in the 4th century by a group of scholars residing at Antioch. For Codex W is a very ancient manuscript. B. P. Grenfell regarded it as "probably fourth century." (3) Other scholars have dated it in the 5th century. Hence W is one of the oldest complete manuscripts of the Gospels in existence, possibly of the same age as Aleph (Sinaiticus-SC). Moreover, W seems to have been written in Egypt, since during the first centuries of its existence it seems to have been the property of the Monastery of the Vinedresser, which was located near the third pyramid. If the Traditional Text had been invented at Antioch in the 4th century, how would it have found its way into Egypt and thence into Codex W so soon thereafter? Why would the scribe of W, writing in the 4th or early 5th century, have adopted this newly fabricated text in Matthew and Luke in preference to other texts which (according to Hort's hypothesis) were older and more familiar to him? Thus the presence of the Traditional Text in W indicates that this text is a very ancient text and that it was known in Egypt before the 4th century. [102]

Antiquity and the Papyri

Other evidence also supports the existence of the Traditional type of text early in church history. Another mixed text is the Chester Beatty Papyri (200-250 AD). Dr. Hills said, "When the Chester Beatty Papyri were published (1933-37), it was found that these early 3rd century fragments agree surprisingly often with the Traditional (Byzantine) Text against all other types of text." [103]

The Traditional Greek Text of the New Testament

Even the Codex Alexandrinus (Codex A) is a witness to the Traditional Text in the Gospels. It is dated in the 5th century and was written in Egypt. So, the text witnesses to the fact that the Traditional Text was in Egypt at an early date.

Another example of a mixed text is Papyrus 90, dated 2nd century AD, somewhere between 100 and 200 AD. The scholars have classified P 90 as Alexandrian, but it is as much Traditional as it is Alexandrian. [104]

Then there is the Magdalen Papyrus 64, fragments of Matthew 26. P 64 consists of three small fragments acquired in 1901, in Luxor Egypt, by Egyptologist Charles Bousfield Huleatt. He presented them to the Magdalen College, Oxford. The fragments contain part of Matthew 26:7, 8, 10, 14, 15. **The fragments are dated 50 AD.** I am sure these fragments are categorized as Alexandrian. It is said, "Without any variant of the text Eberhard Nestle and Kurt Aland." [105] However, I have examined the fragments and made comparison to the Received Text. ***P 64, 50 AD, is a perfect match to the Textus Receptus!***

Next, let's take a look at Papyrus 52 from the John Rylands Library. P52 is a piece of the Gospel of John written on front and back containing John 18:31-33 and John 18:37-38. Once again, P 52 was found in Egypt. There is a disagreement among scholars as to what date to assign P52. Some say it is dated 100-150 AD. Others think it should be 125-175 AD. In either case, it is assigned to the second century.

So what do we find with P 52? My conclusions here are based on my own comparison of P 52 with the Received Text. I will start with a base conclusion that there are differences between P 52 and the Received Text. Does that mean P 52 is a different kind of text? No, but the scholars have left P52 uncategorized. The three differences are as follows.

Verse	P 52	Received Text
1-18:31	Emein	Emin
2-18:32	iselthein	Eiselthen
3-18:33	O P (following prait**orion**)	praitorion palin o pilatos

Fig. 14

The first two differences are clearly different spelling, but they are the same words. The third instance is unclear. The scholars think the "O P" are part of "o pilatos." This would mean P 52 left out or the TR added "palin." However, the simplest conclusion is that O P was for "o palin," not "o pilatos." That would mean, the scribe misplaced the "O." This would not be unusual in handwritten manuscripts. That sort of thing obviously happens. In the space of this small paragraph, I have made several errors and had to correct them. 1800 years ago, when one was writing with pen and ink on papyrus, corrections were not easy to do. **My conclusion is that P 52 matches the Traditional Text except for the two spelling differences.**

I will give you one more example of the Papyri. **Papyrus 32** is also in the John Rylands University Library. It contains Titus 1:11-15 and 2:3-8. It is classified as Alexandrian. The scholars think it shows agreement with Sinaiticus. I also checked P32 against the Received Text. Except for one spelling difference *the two are exactly the same*. The spelling difference consists of one letter, a nu (N) instead of a Rho (P), which could easily be a scribal error. **In other words, there is as much reason, maybe more, to believe P 32 is Traditional Text as there is to think it is Alexandrian.** P32 is dated 200 AD.

Other Evidence of Antiquity

We have also seen that evidence from ancient translations also supports the Traditional Text. The Peshitta Syriac is dated about 150 AD and has a Traditional type text. The Sinaitic Syriac is traditional in type and is dated in the 3rd century. The Gothic version was based on the Traditional Text and translated about 350 AD. All of this proves that the Traditional Text is a very early text.

Dr. Edward Hills, who graduated from Yale University, Westminster Theological Seminary, Columbia University, and Harvard University (under the supervision of the famous textual scholar, Kirsopp Lake), studied the textual criticism of the New Testament and came to this conclusion.

> The making of these two texts (Western and Alexandrian-SC) proceeded, for the most part, according to two entirely different plans. The scribes that produced the Western text regarded themselves

more as interpreters than as mere copyists. Therefore they made bold alterations in the text and added many interpolations. The makers of the Alexandrian text, on the other hand, conceived of themselves as grammarians. Their chief aim was to improve the style of the sacred text. They made few additions to it. Indeed, their fear of interpolation was so great that they often went to the opposite extreme of wrongly removing genuine readings from the text ...

As all scholars agree, the Western text was the text of the Christian Church at Rome and the Alexandrian text that of the Christian scribes and scholars of Alexandria. For this reason these two texts were prestige-texts, much sought after by the wealthier and more scholarly members of the Christian community. The True Text, on the other hand, continued in use among the poorer and less learned Christian brethren. These humble believers would be less sensitive to matters of prestige and would no doubt prefer the familiar wording of the True Text to the changes introduced by the new prestige-texts ... And since they were poor, they would be unable to buy new manuscripts containing these prestige-texts.

For all these reasons, therefore the True Text would continue to circulate among these lowly Christian folk virtually undisturbed by the influence of other texts. Moreover, because it was difficult for these less prosperous Christians to obtain new manuscripts, they put the ones they had to maximum use. Thus all these early manuscripts of the True Text were eventually worn out ... None of them seems to be extant today. The papyri which do survive seem for the most part to be prestige-texts which were preserved in the libraries of ancient Christian schools. According to Aland (1963), both the Chester Beatty and the Bodmer Papyri may have been kept at such an institution. But the papyri with the True Text were read to pieces by the believing Bible students of antiquity. In the providence of God they were used by the Church. They survived long enough, however, to preserve the True (Traditional) New Testament Text during this early period and to bring it into the period of triumph that followed. [106]

The Traditional Text and the Number of Manuscripts

The modern textual critics, who learned their profession from Westcott and Hort, belittle the importance of the number of manuscripts that support the Traditional Text. They have often said that manuscript witnesses must be "weighed" not counted. However, we would expect the text that was most used to be the majority text. We would expect the text that was preserved and promoted by the Spirit of God to be the one that is most often copied.

An example of this principle is the KJB, first published in 1611. We believe it is the correct English Bible coming from the Traditional Text and the Received Text. Every year for about 400 years it has been a best seller. Even now, without any special marketing strategies, it is still a best seller. This is in spite of the fact that its competitors (NIV, NKJV, NASV, CEV, ESV, etc.) have been all promoted with modern mass media marketing techniques. This is a significant thing. The KJB has nothing like their marketing efforts, yet it is still a best seller. It is promoted by the Spirit of God.

Also, number is a key ingredient to finding the truth according to the Scriptures. A factual testimony can only be established with two or three witnesses. One will not do.

> *But if he will not hear thee, then take with thee one or two more, that in the mouth of two or three witnesses every word may be established. (Matthew 18:16)*
> *This is the third time I am coming to you. In the mouth of two or three witnesses shall every word be established. (2 Corinthians 13:1)*
> *Against an elder receive not an accusation, but before two or three witnesses. (1 Timothy 5:19)*

The Traditional Greek Text of the New Testament

He that despised Moses' law died without mercy under two or three witness (Hebrews 10:28)

Dr. Jim Taylor investigated the overall evidence and what it suggested in his book, *In Defense of the Textus Receptus.*

> As you can see from what we have just discussed, the majority of all the existing manuscript evidence is in agreement with the Textus Receptus. Only a very small fraction of manuscripts disagree. It is often said that the remaining manuscripts fall into another "family" or grouping, but in actuality, the differences between them are so radical that each manuscript would have to be in a family of its own! Let's try to summarize this a bit. If we include the lectionaries, we have a total of 5,773 extant manuscripts. 5,369 support the Textus Receptus in full or in part. 207 manuscripts support the Critical text (Alexandrian-UBS text-see chapter 12-Author) in full or in part. Another 226 manuscripts are either mixed texts which have been thrown in to other so-called "families" or else unclassified for one reason or another. 5369 Byzantine manuscripts versus 207 Alexandrian manuscripts. It's pretty clear which one was favored. [107]

Dean Burgon presented this reasonable view of the number of textual witnesses.

> There exists no reason for supposing that the Divine Agent, who in the first instance thus gave to mankind the Scriptures of Truth, straightway abdicated His office; took no further care of His work; abandoned those precious writings to their fate ... I am utterly disinclined to believe—so grossly improbable does it seem—that at the end of 1800 years 995 copies out of every thousand, suppose, will prove untrustworthy; and that the one, two, three, four or five which remain, whose contents were till yesterday as good as unknown, will be found to have retained

the secret of what the Holy Spirit originally inspired. I am utterly unable to believe, in short, that God's promise has so entirely failed, that at the end of 1800 years much of the text of the Gospel had in point of fact to be picked by a German critic (Tischendorf-Author) out of a waste-paper basket in the convent of St. Catherine; and that the entire text had to be remodelled after the pattern set by a couple of copies which had remained in neglect during fifteen centuries, and had probably owed their survival to that neglect; whilst hundreds of others had been thumbed to pieces, and had bequeathed their witness to copies made from them. [108]

Strange as it may appear, it is undeniably true, that the whole of the controversy may be reduced to the following narrow issue: Does the truth of the Text of Scripture dwell with the vast multitude of copies, uncial and cursive, concerning which nothing is more remarkable than the marvellous agreement which subsists between them? Or is it rather to be supposed that the truth abides exclusively with a very little handful of manuscripts, which at once differ from the great bulk of the witnesses, and—strange to say—also amongst themselves? [109]

The Traditional Text and the Variety of Evidence

This important consideration focuses on the fact that Traditional Text manuscripts were scattered geographically all over the Christian world from 100 to 1600 AD. Few can say it better than Dean Burgon.

> Now those many MSS. were executed demonstrably at different times in different countries. They bear signs in their many hundreds of representing the entire area of the Church, except where versions were used instead of copies in the original Greek. Many of them were written in monasteries where a special room was set aside for such copying. Those

who were in trust endeavoured with the utmost pains and jealousy to secure accuracy in the transcription. Copying was a sacred art. And yet, of multitudes of them that survive, hardly any have been copied from any of the rest. [110]

Speaking generally, the consentient testimony of two, four, six, or more witnesses, coming to us from widely sundered regions is weightier by far than the same number of witnesses proceeding from one and the same locality, between whom there probably exists some sort of sympathy, and possibly some degree of collusion. [111]

No one can doubt, for it stands to reason, that Variety distinguishing witnesses massed together must needs constitute a most powerful argument for believing such Evidence to be true. Witnesses of different kinds; from different countries; speaking different tongues:—witnesses who can never have met, and between whom it is incredible that there should exist collusion of any kind:—such witnesses deserve to be listened to most respectfully. Indeed, when witnesses of so varied a sort agree in large numbers, they must needs be accounted worthy of even implicit confidence. Accordingly, the essential feature of the proposed Test will be, that the Evidence of which "Variety" is to be predicated shall be derived from a variety of sources. Readings which are witnessed to by MSS. only; or by ancient Versions only: or by one or more of the Fathers only:— [112]

The Traditional Text and Respectability

Dean Burgon speaks of "respectability" as a part of the weight a manuscript is given. He said:

In the first place, the witnesses in favour of any given reading should be respectable. "Respectability" is of course a relative term ... Some critics will claim, not respectability only, but absolute and oracular authority for a certain set of ancient witnesses,— which others will hold in suspicion ... We listen to any one whose character has won our respect: [113]

The thousands of manuscripts of the New Testament and NT quotes from the early church "fathers" and lectionaries date from the second century to the 1600's. They are all witnesses to the text of the original inspired New Testament. If witnesses are called to court they have credibility or respectability only if they agree. Two or three witnesses may establish the facts, but the witnesses must agree. This is illustrated from the trial of the Lord Jesus.

> *55 And the chief priests and all the council sought for witness against Jesus to put him to death; and found none.*
> *56 For many bare false witness against him, but their witness agreed not together.*
> *57 And there arose certain, and bare false witness against him, saying,*
> *58 We heard him say, I will destroy this temple that is made with hands, and within three days I will build another made without hands.*
> *59 But neither so did their witness agree together.*
> (Mark 14:55)

When Dean Burgon said, "Some critics will claim, not respectability only, but absolute and oracular authority for a certain set of ancient witnesses," he was writing about Vaticanus and Sinaiticus and certain other Alexandrian manuscripts like them, all of which were promoted by Westcott and Hort and most modern scholars today. This group of manuscripts generally opposes the Traditional text. However, like the witnesses in Jesus' day, "Their witness agreed not together." They do not represent a single unified text, but they greatly disagree with one another. Dr. D. A. Waite summarized the agreement of these manuscripts.

> Any witnesses, such as "B" (Vatican) and "Aleph" (Sinai), which disagree one with the other in over 3,000 substantial places in the Gospels alone would certainly not be respectable witnesses. Certainly such

false witnesses cannot be "respectable" by objective standards.[114]

On the other hand, the Traditional Text is recognized as one unified text. Most of its manuscripts have not been copied from any of the other manuscripts. They each stand alone as thousands of independent witnesses. According to Dean Burgon this is not true with the Alexandrian manuscripts.

> If one Codex (z) is demonstrably the mere transcript of another Codex (f), these may no longer be reckoned as two Codexes, but as one Codex. It is hard therefore to understand how Tischendorf constantly adduces the evidence of "E of Paul" although he was perfectly well aware that E is "a mere transcript of the Cod. Claromontanus" or D of Paul. Or again, how he quotes the cursive Evan. 102; because the readings of that unknown seventeenth-century copy of the Gospels are ascertained to have been derived from Cod. B itself.[115]

However, it has often been proclaimed that no two Traditional Text manuscripts agree 100%. How this is known as a fact by those who say it is a mystery to me. I seriously doubt that those who say this have any proof of it beyond having heard it from someone else. Furthermore, I seriously doubt that any of those who say this have examined all the 5200+ plus manuscripts of the Traditional Text.

The collation efforts of Wilbur Pickering demonstrated evidence of that it is not true that every Traditional manuscript has errors. The Traditional Text is categorized into families. Pickering collated the manuscripts in Family 35. He had some amazing results.

> Notice that of twenty-one MSS, eleven of their exemplars (over half) were 'perfect', and another five were off by only one variant (the worst was only off by six, for two books) … I conclude that all twenty-one MSS were independent in their generation, and I see no evidence to indicate a different conclusion for their exemplars … I now invite attention to location and date. The MSS come from all over the

Mediterranean world. The six Mt. Athos MSS were certainly produced in their respective monasteries (five). Ecclesiastical politics tending to be what it tends to be, there is little likelihood that there would be collusion between the monasteries on the transmission of the NT writings—I regard the six as representing independent lines of transmission (five of the exemplars were not identical). MSS from Trikala, Patmos, Jerusalem and Sinai were presumably produced there; 18 was certainly produced in Constantinople; 35 was acquired in the Aegean area. The MSS at the Vatican and Grottaferrata may very well have been produced there … The implications of finding a perfect representative of any archetypal text are rather powerful. All the 'canons' of textual criticism become irrelevant to any point subsequent to the creation of that text (they could still come into play when studying the creation of the text). For MS 18 to be perfect, all the generations in between had to be perfect as well. Now I call this incredibly careful transmission. Nothing that I was taught in Seminary about New Testament textual criticism prepared me for this discovery! Nor anything that I had read, for that matter. But MS 18 is not an isolated case; all the twenty-one MSS in the chart above reflect an incredibly careful transmission—even the worst of the lot, minuscule 201 with its 6 variants [the 'singulars' in 1893 and 1248 are careless mistakes (unhappy monks), is really quite good, considering all the intervening generations. [116]

Nevertheless, I concede that there are some disagreements among many of these copies. Scribal mistakes do occur. The kind and volume of disagreement among them is different than the disagreement between Vaticanus and Sinaiticus. Many of the various kinds of disagreements in the Traditional text are minor. I have illustrated some of them in the following chart. They are true scribal mistakes. This chart does not show actual variances, but is illustrative only and are based on Mark 7:23.

MSS	TEXT	ERROR TYPE
1	All these evil things from within **come**, and defile the man.	Wrong word order
2	These evil things come from within, and defile the man.	Omit word
3	All **of** these evil things come from within, and defile the man.	Add word
4	All these evil things come from **without**, and defile the man.	change word
5	All these evil things come from within, and **defl** the man.	Misspelling
6	All these evil things come **form** within, and defile the man.	Misspelling
7	All these evil things come from within	Accidentally leave out phrase

Fig. 15

The importance of these types of errors is not that they occur. The importance is that the correct readings are easily seen when all six copies are compared. The first manuscript has the wrong word order, but the other five have it correct, so the right word order is evident. Two of the manuscripts have misspellings, but the other manuscripts reveal the true spelling. Even if a word or phrase is omitted in one of them, the others reveal that fact. The same is true for a word added or changed.

The Traditional Text and Continuity

If the manuscripts of a textual tradition could be traced all the way back to the second century, it would be a powerful testimony to its genuineness. The Traditional Text has just this history and is found present in all the stages of church history. Tracing the Traditional text back to the fifth century (400-500 AD) is easy. The fifth century manuscript Alexandrinus is considered to be a Traditional Text manuscript in the Gospels. Let's trace some of the Traditional text manuscripts.

A Practical Theology of Bible Translating

Sign	Name	Date
P64 *	Magdalen Papyrus 64	50 AD
P52 *	Papyrus 52	100-175 AD
P66	Papyrus Bodmer II P66 (see below)	125 AD
P32 *	Papyrus 32	200 AD
A (02)	Codex Alexandrinus	5th
C (04)	Codex Ephraemi Rescriptus	5th
W (032)	Codex Washingtonianus	5th
Q (026)	Codex Guelferbytanus B	5th
061	Uncial 061	5th
N 022	Codex Petropolitanus Purpureus	6th
0103	Uncial 0103	7th
E^e (07)	Codex Basilensis	8th
F^e (09)	Codex Boreelianus	9th
G^e (011)	Codex Seidelianus I	9th
H^e (013)	Codex Seidelianus II	9th
L (020)	Codex Angelicus	9th
V (031)	Codex Mosquensis II	9th
Y (034)	Codex Macedoniensis	9th
Θ (038)	Codex Koridethi	9th
0142	Uncial 0142	10th
8	Minuscule 8	11th
1241	Minuscule 1241	12th
6	Minuscule 6	13th
11	Minuscule 11	14th
30	Minuscule 30	15th
90	Minuscule 90	16th

Fig. 16 [117] * Included based on my own comparisons

There are, of course, many more manuscripts than these. These manuscripts are testimony of the fact that the Traditional text type has existed throughout church history since the first century. The high number of these manuscripts is a testimony that they not only **existed**, but that they were **used**.

Is there evidence to show the existence of the Traditional Text before the fifth century? We have already shown that there is. However, to make it clear I will reiterate and add to that information here.

The Traditional Greek Text of the New Testament

There is evidence in the Papyri for an early Traditional Text date. Papyrus was like a cheap paper made from the Papyrus plant. It decayed easily. It fell apart quickly. There is not much New Testament written on papyrus that is evidence for the Traditional Text, but there is some. In addition to P64, P52, and P32, this was confirmed by the discovery of Papyrus Bodmer II P66. It is the Gospel of John consisting of 75 leaves and 39 unidentified fragments. It was dated 200 AD, but many now are dating it at 125 AD. It is usually classified as Alexandrian. In reality it is a mixed text. Dr. David Brown commented on Bodmer II and shared the examples in the following chart.

> Further, I find it very encouraging that more recently discovered papyrus fragments have confirmed the Majority Text. "Nineteenth-century biblical scholars claimed that much of the first fourteen chapters of the Gospel of John was corrupted by scribes in the later Byzantine Era. This claim was shown to be utterly false by the discovery of Papyrus Bodmer II (also called P66). Dated about A.D. 200, (now by many at 125 A.D.) prior to the commencement of the Byzantine Era, this Papyrus verified many of the disputed passages attributed to late Byzantine copyists and demonstrated that these passages were present in very early manuscripts." (Modern Bible Translations Unmasked by Russell & Colin Standish; p.37-38). Dr. Gordon Fee has shown that in John chapter 4, P66 agrees with the Traditional Text (and thus the King James Bible) 60.6% of the time when there are textual variations (Studies in the Text and Method of New Testament Textual Criticism, by Epp and Fee). While P66 is a mixed text it does demonstrate so called "Byzantine readings well before that era. [118]

In the places listed in the table below and others P66 sides with the Traditional Text.

Ref.	P66/Traditional	Vs. Alexandrian
John 4:1	κυριος (Lord)	Ιεσους (Jesus)
John 5:9	και ευτηεος (and immediately)	omitted
John 5:17	δε Ιεσοθς (but Jesus)	δε Ιεσους Κυριος (but Jesus Christ)
John 6:36	με (me)	omitted
John 6:46	και την μετερα (and the mother)	omitted
John 6:69	ο Χριστος (the Christ)	omitted
John 7:10	αλλ ος (but as)	αλλ (but)
John 7:39	πνευμα αγιον (Holy Spirit)	πνευμα (Spirit)

Fig. 17

An early date for the Traditional Text is supported by the early church "fathers." The early writers who left writings behind (so-called church fathers) often quoted the Traditional text. The table below has a few specific examples of fathers who quoted the Traditional Text and where. This information comes from the same source as the quote above, Dr. David Brown and also Dr. Thomas Strouse. In these, the Traditional Text reading which was quoted by the writers is designated (T) and the Alexandrian reading is designated by (A).

This list could go on and on. There are many of these writers who quoted specific Traditional Text readings. When I put in the chart "quoted (T) but omitted (A)," I mean that the verse, word, or phrase shown is quoted by at least one church father (but not limited to one), and it is omitted in the Alexandrian text.

Name and Dates	Ref.	Quote
Irenaeus (130-202)	Mark 1:2	"prophets"(T) - "prophet" (A)
Irenaeus	Mark 16:19	quoted (T) but omitted (A)
Justin (100-165)	Luke 22:44	quoted (T) but omitted (A)
Ireneaus	John 1:18	"begotten son"(T) "god" (A)
Hyppolytus (170-236)	John 3:13	"the Son of man which is in heaven" (T) – omitted (A)
Tertullian (160-221)	John 5:3-4	quoted (T) but omitted (A)
Cyprian (200-258)	1 John 5:7-8	quoted (T) but omitted (A)

Fig. 18

Several excellent summary charts are included in *The Traditional Text of the Gospels*, dividing the fathers by the era in which they lived. See below for a reproduction of some of this information giving the name, date, how many times the Traditional Text was quoted, and how many times another type text was quoted. It looks at the places where there are differences between the Traditional Text and the Alexandrian, Western, or something else, and it is confined to the gospels only.

The Early Church "Fathers" 100-250 AD (The Apostolic Fathers)

Name	Date	Traditional	Other
Didachè (document)	50-100	11	4
Epistle to Diognetus	c. 50-200	1	0
Papias	c. 60-160	1	0
Hegesippus	c. 110-180	2	0
Justin Martyr	100-165	17	20
Athenagoras	133-190	3	1
Gospel of Peter	100-150 (?)	2	0
Irenaeus	130-202	63	41
Clement of Rome *	died in 99	18	7
Hippolytus	170-236	26	11

Fig. 19 [119] (*Clementine Homilies)

Later Ante-Nicene and Nicene Fathers 200-400 AD

Name	Date	Traditional	Other
Gregory Thaumaturgus	c. 213-270	11	3
Cornelius	Died 253	4	1
Gregory of Nazianzus	c. 329-390	18	4
Methodius	Died c. 311	14	8
Titus of Bostra	Died c. 378	44	24
Basil	c. 329-379	272	105
Eusebius of Caesarea	c. 260-339	315	214
Cyril of Jerusalem	313-386	54	32
Ambrose of Milan	c. 337-397	169	77
Lucifer of Cagliari	Died c. 370	17	20

Fig. 20 [120]

Alexandrian and African Fathers 100-400 AD

Name	Date	Traditional	Other
Cyprian	c. 200-258	100	96
Tertullian	c. 155-240	74	65
Novatian	c. 200-258	6	4
Didymus	c. 313-398	81	36
Clement of Alexandria	c. 150-215	82	72
Dionysius	Died 264	12	5
Origen Adamantius	c. 184-253	460	491
Alexander of Alexandria	Died c. 328	4	0
Athanasius of Alexandria	c. 296-373	179	119

Fig. 21 [121]

The information in the examples listed here are similar for the "church fathers" not listed. There are a total of 76 listings in *The Traditional Text,* similar to those in these charts. These statistics give us some strong implications about the existence and location of the Traditional text from the earliest of times.

*The first and foremost thing we learn is that the Traditional text **existed** in the first century.* It was predominantly quoted by the Didache in the first century. This shows that the Traditional Text existed in the days of the Apostles. There is also Clement of Rome who died in 99 AD, who quoted the Traditional text 18 times out of 25.

Corruptions of the Word of God were insinuating themselves into copies in the first century. We learn this from Clement, who quoted some other text 7 times. The corruptions of the Word of God Paul talked about (2 Cor. 2:17) were making their way around the Mediterranean area.

The charts also indicate the early dominance of the Traditional text. The early church writers used the Traditional text far more often than they used anything else. Even though corruptions were present in the early days and grew stronger later, the traditional Text was dominant. The traditional Text continued to be the most used text all the way to 400 AD. There is absolutely no indication that an official revision was done in Palestine in the fourth century. The witness to the Traditional text was continuous.

The Traditional Greek Text of the New Testament

The corruption of the text was worst in Alexandria. As you can see, those who were in Alexandria or elsewhere in Africa (such as Carthage) used the Alexandrian text more than most of the others. However, they were all mixed, because they also used the Traditional Text. That shows that the Traditional Text was also in Egypt from an early time. The Traditional was both present and frequently used. That shows that it existed, was strong, and popular.

Origen moved from Alexandria to Caesarea in Palestine, being strongly welcomed by the Bishops in Palestine. As you might recall, he started the library at Caesarea. His influence among the Bishops in Palestine was powerful. He brought his Alexandrian Scripture scrolls with him when he came from Alexandria. There followed later many who were influenced by him. These included Eusebius, Bishop of Caesarea, Basil, Cyril of Jerusalem, and probably Titus of Bostra. These used Origen's Bible material and quoted often from the Alexandrian Text. Apparently, in Palestine of that time, the Traditional Text and the Alexandrian Text were in stiff competition (just as they are today).

Rome and at least part of Italy was also strongly affected by the Alexandrian Text. Justin Martyr lived there and Ambrose lived in Milan, not far from Rome.

An early date for the Traditional Text is supported by the ancient translations. We have gone over this information about ancient translations before. Here, I have provided a table for you showing some of these translations and their dates.

Date	Translation
150 AD	The Old Syriac Peshitta
120-150 AD	The Old Latin or Itala
350 AD	The Gothic
300 AD	The Ethiopic

Fig. 22

The Bible of the entire Greek Church, and the later Greek Orthodox Church, was the Traditional Greek Text. The Traditional Text prevailed in the Eastern half of the Roman Empire and continued to be the Bible of the Greek churches throughout the Middle Ages. The Greek Bible of the Greek Orthodox Church published in 1904 has 1 John 5:7, which is strenuously rejected by those who believe in the

Alexandrian Text. On the other hand, the Latin Vulgate, translated about 382 by Jerome, became the Bible of the West. Rome nearly abandoned the Greek Bible altogether. Previously, in the early centuries, the Alexandrian text prevailed in Africa and influenced Rome. Hence, the Latin Vulgate has a distinct Alexandrian flavor.

This continuity did not exist with the Alexandrian Text. Part of Jerome's basis for translating his Latin Version in 382 AD was the Alexandrian Text. The Roman Catholic Church quit using the Greek manuscripts and embraced the Latin Vulgate as its official Bible. It took several hundred years before the people also embraced it. So, the Alexandrian Greek Text had very little influence in the Middle Ages and the Renaissance/Reformation period. It was a little used text. That is probably why Vaticanus survived. It was closed up in the library. God did not use it or its sister manuscripts very much, if any.

Where is the 2nd 3rd and 4th Centuries Greek Manuscript Support?

There are definite historical reasons why there are so few purely Traditional Text papyri. There are reasons why so many manuscripts from that time are mixed texts or missing altogether.

Heresy is one of the greatest reasons for the presence of mixed and alternative texts. Remember the statement of the Apostle Paul that the Word of God was being corrupted in his time. Many of the heresies were built around the Greek philosophies, heresies such as Gnosticism, and were centered in Alexandria, Egypt.

> *For we are not as many, which corrupt the word of God:* (2 Cor. 2:17)

See chapter seven for a discussion of the word "corrupt." Paul said *many* were busy corrupting the Word of God in his day. There is no reason to suppose that the corrupting activity stopped with Paul's death. Chances are it increased. Remember, how Paul told the Ephesian elders …

> *For I know this, that after my departing shall grievous wolves enter in among you, not sparing the flock. Also*

of your own selves shall men arise, speaking perverse things, to draw away disciples after them.
(Acts 20:29-30)

You don't suppose they stopped with simply *speaking* perverse things, do you; especially since many were already busy corrupting God's word? Paul was speaking of corrupting influence in *Ephesus*. The corruption was not confined to Alexandria, although it was strong there.

> It is no less true to fact than paradoxical in sound, that the worst corruptions to which the New Testament has ever been subjected, originated within a hundred years after it was composed; that Irenaeus and the African Fathers and the whole Western, with a portion of the Syriac Church, used far inferior manuscripts to those employed by Stunica, or Erasmus, or Stephen, thirteen centuries after, when moulding the Textus Receptus. [122]

Numerous heresies were dealt with in the New Testament. 1 John 4:2 seems to point directly at Docetism (Jesus did not have a real physical body, so he did not die on the cross and the resurrection was not real). The denial of the deity of Christ taught by Marcion in the 2nd Century is answered in 1 Timothy 3:16. That verse was probably changed in the Alexandrian text by Marcion or someone who thought like him. The heresy that salvation is by works is debunked in Romans. The influence of the Judaizers, who wanted to put Christians under the law, is fought in Galatians. Antinomianism, the denial that Christians have any moral obligations is taught against everywhere in the New Testament. Finally, Gnosticism is dealt with in Colossians and 1, 2 John.

Another reason papyri are hard to find in the Roman Empire is climate. The northern coast of the Mediterranean, Syria, Turkey, Greece, and Italy is very moist. Papyrus is such a fragile material that it just does not last. Most Papyri are found in southern Palestine and Egypt, where the Alexandrian text prevailed early. Egypt and Southern Palestine are dry. Everywhere in the Roman Empire Christians lived from 100 to 300 AD had a climate that made papyrus rot and disintegrate quickly, except Africa and Southern Palestine.

A further reason for the scarcity of Tradition manuscripts is that parchment, or vellum, tended to be reused. Parchment was a more expensive writing material and sometimes it was hard to get. Their solution was to scrape the used parchment and gently wash off the ink. Then they would write over the old text. The old writing would usually become faint, but it would still be there. A reused piece of parchment is called a palimpsest. Below is Codex Nitriensis, a 6th Century palimpsest manuscript, with Syriac text.

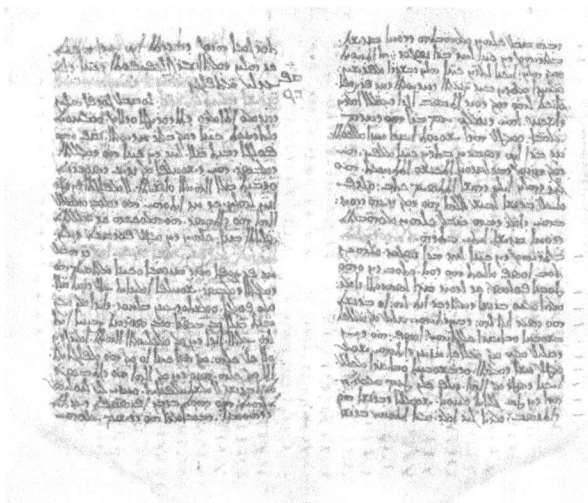

Fig. 23

The Traditional Text had the most frequently used manuscripts by common Christians and copies simply wore out from use. I have worn out some Bibles in my lifetime. Today, the most well made Bible will not last a hundred years of constant use. It is the least used Bible that lasts the longest. In the first and second centuries, Bibles had to be copied by hand. That was a long painstaking process. It was no doubt done carefully and when finished the Bibles were cared for. Nevertheless, they were well used. At first, Bibles were written on cheap papyrus, so the oldest fragments are papyrus. Much later parchment (called vellum) was used. That was a much longer lasting material, but even that got old, worn, and torn. Due to use and quality of materials, the Traditional Text had few first and second Century papyrus New Testament fragments survive.

The Traditional Greek Text of the New Testament

Few Traditional Text copies exist from that time period because of Roman persecution. In particular, the tenth imperial persecution on the church, carried out by Roman Emperor Diocletian and his Co-Emperor, Galerius, was especially devastating. It began in 303 AD.

> The fatal day fixed upon to commence the bloody work, was the 23d of February, A. D. 303, that being the day in which the Terminalia were celebrated, and on which, as the cruel pagans boasted, they hoped to put a termination to Christianity. On the appointed day, the persecution began in Nicomedia, on the morning of which the prefect of that city repaired, with a great number of officers and assistants, to the church of the Christians, where, having forced open the doors, they seized upon all the sacred books, and committed them to the flames … This was followed by a severe edict, commanding the destruction of all other Christian churches and books; and an order soon succeeded, to render Christians of all denominations outlaws … A general sacrifice was commenced, which occasioned various martyrdoms. No distinction was made of age or sex; the name of Christian was so obnoxious to the pagans, that all indiscriminately fell sacrifices to their opinions. Many houses were set on fire, and whole Christian families perished in the flames; and others had stones fastened about their necks, and being tied together were driven into the sea. The persecution became general in all the Roman provinces, but more particularly in the east; and as it lasted ten years, it is impossible to ascertain the numbers martyred, or to enumerate the various modes of martyrdom. [123]

Part of this great general persecution was the burning of Christian books, including the Bible. The persecution took place in all parts of the empire, but particularly in the eastern provinces, which is where most of the Traditional Text copies were being made. Many pure manuscripts perished during that time. Since the persecution arose at the beginning of the fourth century, it was first, second, and third century manuscripts that were destroyed. Copies then were few compared to now.

> Christian leaders and Christian Scriptures were especially targeted. Embedded in a text from AD 320 called the *Gesta Apud Zenophilum,* there is an account of Roman persecution of Christians that occurred on May 19, 303, in Cirta, a city in Numidia. (The History of Information website also has some data about it.)
>
> How many manuscripts were seized by the Romans in Cirta, Numidia, in one day, in 303? Under Roman interrogation, Catullinus the Deacon initially handed over just one very large codex. But as the interrogation continued, more codices were surrendered: a man named Eugenius was confronted at his house, and he handed over four codices. Felix the Lector handed over five codices. Victorinus, another lector, was also confronted at his house, and he handed over eight codices. Next, Projectus the Lector handed over five large codices and two small codices. Victor the Grammarian was confronted at his house, and he handed over two codices, and four quinions (that is, loose book-sections consisting of five parchment sheets folded together). The Romans also confronted Euticius of Caesarea, who denied having any manuscripts. The Romans went on to the house of Coddeo, who, it seems, was not at home, but his wife was present, and she handed over six codices.
>
> The total: **33 codices, and four segments of codices**. Needless to say, if we had those manuscripts from 303, our textual apparatuses would look very different. And that's just one city in Numidia. Nicomedia (an early target of the Diocletian persecution, in what is now Turkey) had many more manuscripts than that, and so, I suspect, did the churches in Corinth, Ephesus, Rome, Athens, Philippi,

Berea, Smyrna, Pergamum, and throughout Turkey (Asia, Bithynia, Lydia, Galatia, Pamphylia, Cilicia, Cappadocia, etc.). My point here is not that those 34 manuscripts (and the multitudes of other manuscripts destroyed during the Diocletian Persecution) **must** have had the Byzantine Text written on their pages, but simply that the repetition of similar scenes throughout the Roman Empire explains, to a large extent, our lack of New Testament manuscript-evidence from large swaths of Roman territory. [124]

Following this tenth and last imperial Roman persecution, there was a short period of ascendency of the Alexandrian Greek text in the Western Roman Empire. Constantine the Great became the emperor in Rome in 306 AD and professed Christianity. He finally defeated his last rival for the throne in 324. In the meantime, he issued the edict of Milan in 313, which ended Roman persecution of the Church and elevated it to a status of "tolerated religion." He asked Bishop Eusebius of Caesarea for fifty Greek Bibles in 331. Eusebius got his material for these Bibles from the Library in Caesarea where Origen of Alexandria had left all his Biblical materials (the library suffered in the persecution, but was able to be repaired by the Caesarean bishops). Origen's biblical materials as judged by his writings were Alexandrian or mixed in nature. This hindered the Traditional text in the Western Empire in the fourth century. However, Traditional Text copies were growing in number and by the fifth century, they completely dominated the Christian world.

The Traditional Text and Context

Context has to do with how a verse or phrase or word fit with the words before and after it. Context also includes the larger teaching of Scripture. Does a manuscript have a reading which is out of place with the context closest to it or is it out of harmony with the teaching of the Bible in general? Dean Burgon explained it this way.

> A word,—a phrase,—a clause,—or even a sentence or a paragraph,—must have some relation to the rest of

the entire passage which precedes or comes after it. Therefore it will often be necessary, in order to reach all the evidence that bears upon a disputed question, to examine both the meaning and the language lying on both sides of the point in dispute. [125]

Examples would be helpful to understand this. For that purpose, I will give two.

1. **1 Corinthians 13:5**
    <u>Vaticanus</u>: "Charity does not seek what does not belong to it." In Greek –"to me eautes"
    <u>Trad. Text</u>: "Charity does not seek her own"-"ta eautes."
    The sentiment of Vaticanus is directly opposite the sentiment of 1 Corinthians 13, as a whole. The context is teaching that charity seeks the good of others. That is what is meant by the Traditional Text reading, "Charity does not seek its own." It does not seek its own good, but it seeks the good of others. However, the way it is put in Vaticanus states, "I only seek the good of what belongs to me."

2. **The rich young ruler:** Matthew 19:16-17; Mark 10:17-18; Luke 18:18-19.
    The young man came to Jesus and called Him, "Good Master." Vaticanus and the Traditional Text record two different responses of Jesus to what the young man called Him.
<u>Trad. Text</u>: "Why do you call me good?"
<u>Vaticanus</u>: "Why do you ask me concerning the good?"
    The rich young ruler's full question was, *"Good Master, what shall I do that I may inherit eternal life?"* It should be obvious that an inquiry about "the good" has nothing to do with the question Jesus was asked. Apparently, it isn't so obvious, because in Matthew 19:16-17 the United Bible Societies Greek Text has the answer as it is in Vaticanus. The UBS Text, just as Vaticanus did, even leaves out "good" in "Good Master." That puts it further out of context, because it takes away *any* reference to *anything* the young man said regarding *anything* "good." Also, in the UBS the two other references to this story (Mt. 19:16; Luke 18:18) have Jesus' statement as it is in the Traditional Text. This creates a serious conflict when the reader is comparing different Gospel accounts of the incident. There is also a

cultural context to this. The concept of "the good" was a subject of Greek philosophical discussions. Remember, there were those in Alexandria who wanted to reconcile Christianity with Greek Philosophy. This is one such attempt.

The Traditional Text and Internal Evidence

There are many differences between the Traditional Text and the Alexandrian and Western texts. Some whole verses are missing in the Alexandrian. Others consist of phrases, single words, incorrect geographical references, or even spelling. However, never think that these are minor. Every word of God is indispensable. So, we want to know that we have every word. Internal considerations deal with these detailed items, like spelling and grammar and wrong use of words. Below are some examples of these issues.

1. **Luke 19:37**
Alexandrian, Vaticanus: Panton on eidon dinameon
Trad. Text: Pason on eidon dinameon

As you can see, the only difference is *panton* and *pason*. Both are the same word. In English it means "all," but they are different grammatical parts of speech. *Pason* matches *dinameon* grammatically. *Panton* does not. Therefore, it is impossible for *panton* to be correct, and it must be rejected.

2. **1 John 5:7-8**
The previous example does not affect doctrine, but that is not always the case. This one affects the doctrine of the trinity. The Alexandrian Text, the UBS Text, and most modern versions leave out the phrase, "in heaven, the Father, the Word, and the Holy Ghost: and these three are one. And there are three that bear witness in earth." This leaves the two verses to simply say, "For there are three that bear record the Spirit, and the water, and the blood: and these three agree in one." The trinity is left out. In English, the verse after the objectionable words are removed is proper grammatically, but not in Greek. The Received Text has this right. I will let Dr. Edward F. Hills explain it to you.

> In the third place, the omission of the *Johannine* comma involves a grammatical difficulty. The words

spirit, water, and *blood* are neuter in gender, but in 1 John 5:8 they are treated as masculine. If the Johannine *comma is* rejected, it is hard to explain this irregularity. It is usually said that in 1 John 5:8 *the spirit, the water, and the blood* are personalized and that this is the reason for the adoption of the masculine gender. But it is hard to see how such personalization would involve the change from the neuter to the masculine. For in verse 6 the word Spirit plainly refers to the Holy Spirit, the Third *Person* of the Trinity. Surely in this verse the word *Spirit* is "personalized," and yet the neuter gender is used. Therefore since personalization did not bring about a change of gender in verse 6, it cannot fairly be pleaded as the reason for such a change in verse 8. If, however, the *Johannine comma* is retained, a reason for placing the neuter nouns *spirit, water,* and *blood* in the masculine gender becomes readily apparent. It was due to the influence of the nouns *Father* and *Word,* which are masculine. [126]

3. **Mark 1:2-3**
   <u>Vaticanus, UBS, Alexandrian</u>: Isaiah the prophet
   Traditional: prophets
   KJB: *As it is written in the prophets*
   NIV: as it is written in Isaiah the prophet

The difference in these verses is obvious. The Alexandrian text, Vaticanus, Sinaiticus, the UBS text, the Nestle-Aland Text, and nearly every English translation put it like the NIV. They have all incorporated a lie into the Scriptures.

What follow the word "prophet" in the Alexandrian text is an Old Testament quote. However, the quote is only partly from Isaiah. The rest of it is from Malachi. That's *TWO* prophets, not one.

Malachi 3:1 *Behold, I will send my messenger, and he shall prepare the way before me*

Isaiah 40:3 *The voice of him that crieth in the wilderness, Prepare ye the way of the LORD, make straight in the desert a highway for our God.*
Mark 1:2-3 *As it is written in the prophets, Behold, I send my messenger before thy face, which shall prepare thy way before thee. The voice of one crying in the wilderness, Prepare ye the way of the Lord, make his paths straight.*

Someone, in early church history changed the text from "prophets" to Isaiah the prophet." Whoever it was no doubt did not understand that the source of part of the statement was Malachi and thought it was an error. However, it happened, a lie was introduced in the Alexandrian copies. It was embraced by today's Alexandrian scholars.

These are in the same scholarly group who thought Elhanan killed Goliath the Gitite (see 2 Sam. 21:19 in the NASB, RSV, NRSV, ESV, ASV, CSB, CEV, God's Word Translation, the Message, and others) in spite of the story in 1 Samuel 17.

Verifying there was a Traditional "Text" and an Alexandrian "Text"

A young man used to live in my garage. His name was Bob; no last name, simply Bob. I used to go to the garage at various times and *beat the living day lights* out of "Bob." I didn't need a provocation, but I could beat on "Bob" anytime I wanted. Bob was a punching dummy. My son put him there so we could "use" him anytime we wanted. Bob is like some of the arguments given against the Traditional text – just dummy arguments. We call them "straw-man" arguments.

One of these straw man arguments goes like this: You keep talking about "readings" (words, phrases, and verses), but you don't show us a "text." Where is the text? There is no "text." This is a true straw man argument. First, what are texts, if not a collection of words, phrases, and sentences? Nearly all scholars recognize that there is a difference between Traditional and Alexandrian readings and texts. All these readings that are available had to be copied from somewhere. In the earliest times the Bible books of the New Testament were not collected together in one book, but were copied individually. A writer may have the four gospels in the Traditional Text on his desk and the rest of the NT books in the Alexandrian Text at the same time. When he copied them and bound them in a codex, he just produced Codex Alexandrinus. If he writes a letter, his letter may have Traditional quotes from Mark and John, but Alexandrian quotes from Romans, because those are the types of manuscripts he has. Have you not seen how writers today will quote several different versions in one chapter of one book? Does that mean there is no "text" to back them up? They are just "readings?"

If we say there is no actual Traditional Text, we may as well say there was no Alexandrian Text, either. Scholars are fond of classifying manuscripts as "Alexandrian," but many "Alexandrian" manuscripts of the first four centuries are actually *mixed*. We see that also with the church "fathers."

The surest proof that there were and are both a Traditional Text and an Alexandrian Text is the result of their transmission through history-our present day "texts." Two primary streams of Bibles have come down to us and have resulted in the creation of two competing printed Greek New Testaments that are different in about 8,000 places: The Textus Receptus or Received Text (TR) and the United Bible Societies Greek (UBS) Text, which grew out of the Westcott and Hort text of the 1880's. There is also the Nestle-Aland Greek Text, but it has the exact same text as the UBS. The character of the TR is recognized to be the Traditional Text. The UBS is clearly Alexandrian in character and scholars recognize it so.

The Majority Text

Finally, I will mention and *dismiss* the more minor printed Greek text called The Majority Text. Actually there are two *different* "majority texts:" 1) *The Greek New Testament According to the Majority Text*, by Zane Hodges and Arthur Farstad, and 2) *The New Testament in the Original Greek According to the Byzantine / Majority Textform*, by Maurice Robinson and William Pierpont. First off, neither of these is "according to the majority text." None of them collated *all* the manuscripts of the Traditional Text to produce a "majority" text. They got their text from a man named Von Soden, who had collated about 400 manuscripts. These texts differ from one another and they differ from the Received text about 1,000-1,500 times. Furthermore, until Baptist Mid-missions started using the "majority text" for translation, they remained barely alive in the library. God wasn't using them much (if any). I wonder. Would God wait until the church was nearly 2,000 years old before giving it a pure New Testament? Let's hear from Robinson and Pierpont.

> It is an awesome task to attempt to present the Greek New Testament in its greatest possible integrity. **Faithful scribes** through the centuries have labored to preserve and transmit the written Word as originally given by inspiration of God. Building upon this tradition, the **textual critic** seeks not to produce a merely "good" text, nor even an "adequate" text, but instead to establish as nearly as possible the precise form of the written Word as originally revealed. [127]

The credit for preserving the New Testament text is given to "faithful scribes" and to "textual critics." It doesn't go to God Almighty? He is the one who promised to preserve it, and He is the one who takes the responsibility. Well, maybe that's not what they meant? Nevertheless, how have the scribes and textual critics been doing?

> For over four-fifths of the New Testament, the Greek text is considered 100% certain, regardless of which text type might be favored by any critic. [128]

Almost One-fifth of the New Testament remains less than certain? One-fifth of the New Testament equals 5.4 *whole books* or 1,594.4 *whole verses*! The scribes and textual critics don't seem to be doing very well do they? Well, apparently they don't think God has done very well either. What unbelief!

The fact remains that it was the Received Text that was put together from Traditional Text manuscripts. It was the Received Text God used to start the Reformation and to accomplish every major move of the Holy Spirit up to beyond the mid 1900's. It was the Received Text that was blessed and approved by God almighty for the last 500 years. It still is. We will see that in the next chapter.

Chapter Twelve

The Received Text, the KJB, and the UBS

Now go, write it before them in a table, and note it in a book, that it may be for the time to come for ever and ever (Is. 30:8)

Seek ye out of the book of the LORD, and read: no one of these shall fail, none shall want her mate: for my mouth it hath commanded, and his spirit it hath gathered them. (Is. 34:16)

The Received Greek Text was based on the Traditional Greek Text that existed from the days of the Apostles. The received text is the printed version of the Traditional text. They are one and the same. It is fundamentally a different text than the UBS Text.

According to Dr. Edward Hills, the origin and development of the Received Text was guided by the common faith in the 14- 1500's. He described the common faith this way:

> This common view remained a faith rather than a well articulated theory. No one at that time drew the logical but unpalatable conclusion that the Greek Church rather than the Roman Church had been the providentially appointed guardian of the New Testament text. But this view, though vaguely apprehended, was widely held, so much so that it may justly be called the common view. Before the Council of Trent (1546) it was favored by some of the highest officials of the Roman Church, notably, it seems, by Leo X, who was pope from 1513 to 1521 and to whom Erasmus dedicated his New Testament. Erasmus' close friends also, John Colet, for example, and Thomas More and Jacques Lefevre, all of whom like Erasmus sought to reform the Roman Catholic Church from within, likewise adhered to this common

view. Even the scholastic theologian Martin Dorp was finally persuaded by Thomas More to adopt it. [129]

There were textual errors and printing errors in the Received Text when it was first printed. These and other readings were corrected in subsequent editions of the printed text. The history of the text from 1516 through 1894 is a history of purification and each edition of the Received text brought it closer to perfection. These editions represented steps in the process of God's preservation of His pure words.

Some may object to the previous statement on the grounds that if God preserves His words He did not need to purify or perfect them. His words in Greek are pure and perfect, already. However, it was not the words He was perfecting, but rather a printed Greek text that brought all the words of God in the New Testament together into one place. This is something that had never before existed. Printing was a new thing. Hand-written copies of the New Testament were often incomplete and sometimes had errors. All of this had to be looked at carefully and decisions made as to what was the correct reading. This is not the same as the process of textual criticism going on today among doubting and unbelieving scholars. This all took place in a context of faith in God's preservation of His words.

The conquests of the Muslims in Turkey had caused many eastern scholars and churchmen to move into Central and Western Europe. With them, they brought many manuscripts and the knowledge of Greek by those who spoke it. Some became teachers. Europeans learned Greek from those who knew it as a living language. One who learned Greek well was the scholar, Erasmus.

Desiderius Erasmus (1466-1536)

Desiderius Erasmus (1466-1536) was one of the most famous scholars of the Renaissance and Reformation. He traveled widely in Europe during his lifetime and collected a number of New Testament manuscripts. Among these were the following with their designations on the Gregory-Aland list:

1) 1-an 11th century manuscript of the Gospels, Acts, and the Epistles. (Still designated 1)

2) 2^e-an 11th or 12th century manuscript of the Gosples. (Now designated 2)
3) 2^{ap}-a 12th century manuscript of Acts and the Epistles. (Now designated 2815)
4) 4^{ap}-a 15th century manuscript of Acts and the Epistles. (Now designated 2816)
5) 1^{rk}-a 12th century manuscript of Revelation. (Now designated 2814)
6) 7-a 12th century manuscript of the Gospels. (Still designated 7)
7) 817-a 15th century manuscript of the gospels. (Still designated 817)
8) 3-a 12th century manuscript of the entire New Testament except Revelation (Still designated 3). This was used in Eramus' second edition.
9) The Complutensian Polyglot in his later editions.

Erasmus had access to many more manuscripts than this. He traveled Europe and devoured libraries. The Papal Librarian, Paulus Bombasius, gave him many variant readings and offered the entire Vaticanus manuscript to him to use. Erasmus rejected it.

Erasmus issued five editions of the Greek text: 1516, 1519, 1522, 1527, and 1535.

The Complutensian Polyglot

While Erasmus was laboring in Central Europe, a group of scholars in Spain was working on an edition of the whole Bible. The effort was led by Cardinal Francisco Jiménez de Cisneros (1436–1517), called Cardinal Ximenes. The Complutensian Polyglot was a Bible in Greek, Latin, Aramaic, and Hebrew. Cardinal Ximenes collected a number of Greek manuscripts. The work went on from 1502 to 1517. The Greek New Testament was printed in 1514, but not issued. However, Erasmus' Greek New Testament was published and issued first. The Complutensian Polyglot was not in circulation until 1522.

It is clear that many of the Greek copies Ximenes gathered were of the Traditional Greek type, which was the same type of manuscripts that produced the Received Text. So, this group had some very good source material. They also had some corrupt sources as well, seeing they used Jerome's Latin Vulgate (400 AD), the official Bible of the Roman Catholic Church. However, according to F.F. Bruce, it does not appear that the manuscript *Vaticanus* was a source for the Polyglot. Regardless, it was good enough to become a resource for the coming editions of the Received Text and, as we will see, for the King James translation.

God is the God of History.

We should take a close look at what God was doing at this time. God wasn't just sitting in Heaven watching the antics of some men who styled themselves as scholars. No, He was making preparation for a major change in history. Some have said that Erasmus was in competition with Ximenes to get his New Testament published first. I see it differently. It was God who was in competition with Ximenes, because He wanted Erasmus' text published first, so that it would be available to be used in the upcoming Reformation, when Europe rebelled against the Catholic Church. If a text produced by a Catholic Cardinal won first place, the Reformation may never have happened. Erasmus was forced to become a priest, but he never performed in the priesthood. Erasmus' first edition was published in 1516. The Reformation began the following year, 1517, when Martin Luther posted his ninety-five theses to the door of the church in Wittenberg, Germany. Erasmus' second edition in 1519 became the basis of Martin Luther's German translation. God made a deliberate choice of the Received Text over the Complutensian Polyglot. Nevertheless, the Polyglot became an important source for the further purification of the Received Text.

The Complutensian Greek text became the basis for the Greek New Testament of the polyglot printed in Antwerp in 1568-72 by **Christopher Plantin**.

A minor edition of the TR and the Old Testament was printed by **Aldus Manutius' press** in 1518 (Manutius himself died in 1515). The Old Testament was based on the Complutensian Polyglot, and the New Testament was almost entirely a reprint of the Erasmus 1516 edition. One source said even the printing errors were reproduced. Another source said the KJV translators consulted it.

Robert Stephanus (1503-1559) and Simon Colinaeus

Robert Stephanus (1503-1559) and his step-father, Simon Colinaeus, were the next editors of the Received Text. They were French printers in Paris. Colinaeus issued an edition of the TR in 1534. The editions of Robert Stephanus (Estienne in French) were issued in 1546, 1549, 1550, and 1551. His editions of the Received Text aroused the opposition of the Catholic Church so much that he had to flee Paris in 1550 and settle in Geneva, Switzerland. His last edition was from Geneva and was the first to be divided into chapters and verses. The third edition was known as the "royal edition" or "editio regia," and it was the first to use a critical apparatus, referring to manuscript sources. Stephanus used the Complutensian Polyglot and had manuscript evidence beyond that listed above as used by Erasmus. This included:

1) Codex Bezae-a 5th century manuscript including most of the four Gospels and Acts and a small fragment of 3 John. (Now designated D^{ea} or 05)
2) Codex Regius-an 8th century manuscript containing most of the four Gospels. (Now designated Le or 019)
3) 4-a 13th century manuscript with an almost complete copy of the four.
4) 5-a 13th century manuscript of the entire New Testament except Revelation.
5) 6-a 13th century manuscript of most of the New Testament except Revelation.
6) 7^{pk}-a 12th century manuscript of nearly all of Paul's epistles (now designated 2817).
7) 8-an 11th century manuscript of the entire four Gospels.
8) 9-a 12th century manuscript of the entire four Gospels.

Theodore Beza (1519–1605)

Theodore Beza (1519–1605), of Geneva, started with the third edition of Stephanus (1550) and published editions nine times from 1565-1604. A tenth edition was published after his death. In his

1582 edition, Beza listed some additional materials he used. Some of these were not Greek New Testaments. They included a Syriac version, an Arabic version translated into Latin, D (Codex Bezae), and D2 (Codex Claromontanus). However, he rarely changed anything from the fourth edition of Stephanus. God was always in control.

None of these editors differed with one another more than about 250 times and many of these were spelling, accent marks, breathing marks, word order, and other minor differences.

The Authorized Version (KJB)

The King James Bible translators used more than one edition of the Received Text for their translation. In 1603, the Received text was still developing, so the translators were open to the possibility that the text may still need to be edited. According to Frederick Scrivener (1813-1891), it is reasonable to determine that their primary source text was Beza 1598, because the KJV is almost an exact match for it.

> In considering what text had the best right to be regarded as "the text presumed to underlie the 'Authorized Version,'" was necessary to take into account the composite nature of the Authorized Version, as due to successive revisions of Tyndale's translation. Tyndale himself followed the second and third editions of Erasmus' Greek text (1519, 1522). In the revisions of his translation previous to 1611 a partial use was made of other texts; of which ultimately the most influential were the various editions of Beza from 1560 to 1598 ... Between 1598 and 1611 no important edition appeared; so that Beza's fifth and last text was more likely than any other to be in the hands of King James's revisers, and to be accepted by them as the best standard within their reach. It is moreover found on comparison to agree more closely with the Authorized Version than any other Greek text ... [130]

Dr. Scrivener compared every verse of the KJB New Testament with Beza's 1598 text. He found about 190 differences (variances). All these are listed in the above referenced book.

How did the KJV translators decide what edits to make to the TR? They certainly arrived at their conclusions by divine guidance. They started with Beza 1598, but they also used the other editions of the TR, the Complutensian Polyglot, and other language translations, such as Martin Luther's German, the Reina-Valera Spanish, and the Erasmus and Beza Latin translations. Nevertheless, the adjustments they made were **the pinnacle of the edits made to the TR text**. However, the edits of the KJB translators to the Received Text of Beza were made in English, not Greek. Their edits to the Received Text of Beza were incorporated into the Greek Text by Scrivener. The KJV translation and its suggested changes to Beza's 1598 text was an important step toward a completely pure Greek text.

The Elzevir Editions

The Elzevir Editions were published after the publication of the King James Version. The Elzevirs were a Dutch family of printers. They published two editions in 1624 and 1633. There was a statement in the preface of the 1633 edition that declared this text was now the Greek text received by all. Hence, the name Received Text or, in Latin, Textus Receptus, is applied to the entire Greek text tradition starting in 1516 with Erasmus' first edition up the 1881 edition of Frederick Scrivener.

The 1689 Baptist Confession of Faith

The 1689 Baptist Confession of Faith confirmed the general attitude toward the Received Text. The 1646 Westminster Confession of Faith agreed with it.

> The Old Testament in Hebrew (which was the native language of the people of God of old), and the New Testament in Greek (which at the time of the writing of it was most generally known to the nations), **being**

immediately inspired by God, and by his singular care and providence kept pure in all ages, are therefore authentic; so as in all controversies of religion, the church is finally to appeal to them. But because these original tongues are not known to all the people of God, who have a right unto, and interest in the Scriptures, and are commanded in the fear of God to read and search them, therefore they are to be translated into the vulgar language of every nation unto which they come, that the Word of God dwelling plentifully in all, they may worship him in an acceptable manner, and through patience and comfort of the Scriptures may have hope. [131] (Emphasis mine-Author)

This is the true Bible-believing attitude.

The Scrivener edition

Frederick H. A. Scrivener (1813-1891) issued an edition of the Received Text in 1881, which is usually ignored by liberal and liberal leaning scholars. Even some KJB Bible believers ignore it. However, it is a valid edition of the text and a further purification. It is entirely based on the Beza 1598 edition with the edits made by the King James translators. When it was published in 1881, it was said to be "According to the text followed in the Authorized Version." Scrivener used a process to find and adjust the differences between Beza's text and the KJV.

1) First, Scrivener compared each verse of the KJB New Testament with Beza 1598 to see if they matched.
2) He found about 190 places where they were different.
3) For each difference, he looked for the Greek manuscript evidence or Greek text that had the necessary reading. He would not make a change in Beza without Greek authority.
4) He made changes in the 190 places based on what he found in the Greek evidence.

5) He corrected printer errors in the Beza text.
6) He corrected Beza for inconsistent and incorrect Greek spelling.
7) He adjusted the paragraphs and punctuation.

Scrivener's labors were comparable to those of any other TR editor. Erasmus may have labored more because he put the text together in the first place. Stephanus may have labored more because he divided the text into verses and chapters in his fourth edition. However, the labors of Scrivener rise to their level of scholarship and intensity.

A Specific Example of the Scrivener Edits

A Specific Example of the Scrivener Edits is Revelation 7:14.

Revelation 7:14- (KJV) And I said unto him, Sir, thou knowest. And he said to me, These are they which came out of great tribulation, and have washed their robes, and made **them** white in the blood of the Lamb.

(Beza) And I said unto him, Sir, you know. And he said to me, These are they which came out of great tribulation, and have washed their robes, and made **their robes** white in the blood of the Lamb.

(Scrivener) And I said unto him, Sir, you know. And he said to me, These are they which came out of great tribulation, and have washed their robes, and made **them** white in the blood of the Lamb.

Scrivener found the correct reading in the Greek text of the Complutensian Polyglot. Therefore, the Scrivener Edition of the TR has the right reading.

A Perspective

The KJV translators helped to make an excellent text better, by choosing alternative readings that already existed in the historic Traditional Greek Text that the Biblical church had used since the first century. God has preserved all His inspired Greek words. They were already pure (Prov. 30:5) and are available.

So, on the one hand, the men of the KJB translated God's Words that had been in existence since the days of the Apostles. On the other hand, the King James translators were also editors of the Received Text. Their edits were made in English, rather than Greek. It was Dr. Scrivener, who placed those edits into the Greek Received Text after searching for the Greek source of the edits. Then, he produced the "Greek text that underlay the KJV." It should be noted that the edits in the Received Text made by the translators of the King James Bible **were the final edits made to the Received Text.** Elzevir's edits did not flow into the Scrivener text. The KJV translators' edits did. God, who is sovereign in history, did not make a mistake here. The God of history led the work that was done on the TR by Dr. Scrivener. His edition was the final edition of the TR.

Other Reasons to Believe the Received Text is the Word of God

We can see the choices God has made, when we examine history. When we see, we are given a chance to walk in harmony with Him. The Received Text is a continuation of Traditional Text history. It has a consistent history from the first century. But, there are other reasons to believe it to be the Word of God.

For example, God could have chosen to base the entire Reformation on the Complutensian Polyglot, produced by a Roman Catholic Cardinal, but He did not. God deliberately chose the Received Text and the Hebrew Ben Chayim Masoretic Text to be the foundation and power of the Reformation. The cry of the Pope rejecting Reformers was, "Sola Scriptura!" ("Only Scripture!") And, the Scripture they embraced was the Received Text and the Masoretic Text. They were clearly led by God in this. Many modern scholars and historians recognize that the Reformation was from God, but they will not acknowledge the Bible of the Reformers. The God, who did not make a mistake when He began to free His church from the overbearing hand of Rome, certainly did not make a mistake when He chose which Bible to give them.

The Received text that God chose was based on manuscripts of the Traditional Text. That text is the type of text found in over 90% of all the available ancient manuscript evidence. That is concrete evidence that goes back to 150 AD in Greek manuscripts. It goes back at least as far in the ancient translations into Syriac and Latin. It goes back to the first century in the quotes of the church "fathers." It has been the New Testament of the Greek churches for many centuries. The Traditional text rests upon solid evidence greater than that of the UBS text. The Traditional text has been available from the days of the apostles to now.

As I have pointed out, corrupters of the Scriptures were at work in the days of the apostle Paul. It is no wonder, because the Devil has attempted to imitate everything God has done (2 Cor. 11). Some of those corrupt manuscripts are still around. Two of them are Vaticanus and Sinaiticus. The UBS text is based on weak corrupt sources and was edited by men who were unbelievers in the inspiration, preservation, and authority of the Word of God; blind leaders of the blind.

The following are some further reasons to embrace the Masoretic text of Ben Chayim and the Greek Received Text.

The Received Greek and Hebrew Texts were the cause of the evangelistic movements that took place in Europe from 1500 to 1900. It began with the 1516 publication of the Received Text, and Martin Luther's translation into German from the TR and Hebrew. A flurry of new translations from the same sources followed over the next century. These translations started a movement of evangelism and teaching that lasted into the 1900's. We are still going on the momentum of that movement. As you can learn in Appendix 2, throughout this period, the liberals and textual critics were on the outside of that movement.

The Received Greek and Hebrew Texts and the translations they produced started the greatest foreign missions movement in history. This began with the Moravian mission movement in the 1600's and 1700's. It finally broke forth in the 1790's with the world wide mission movement led by William Carey, who went to India from England. He was convinced from the Scriptures that we must commit ourselves to foreign missions. This movement is still going on. It began and was carried on under the Word of God in the form of the Received text and translations from it.

The Received Greek and Hebrew Texts and their translations have been responsible for the Reformation and every great revival since. There have been numerous revivals acknowledged by historians since the Reformation: the Great Awakening, the Cumberland Valley Revival, almost continual revival in

1800's America, and revival under evangelists like Dwight Moody, Billy Sunday, Mordecai Ham, and a host of others. Even Billy Graham "typically used the King James Version when preaching." [132]

On the other hand, the new versions of the English Bible, not translated from the Received Texts, have slowly taken over the Christian landscape since the 1950's. In doing so, they have presided over decay in the churches, weakness in our influence on our culture, general unbelief in the Bible as the Word of God and rejection of the Bible in our culture, and over a society that has progressively become more and more rebellious against God and filled with ungodliness. Look at the downward fall in Romans 1:21-32. The United States has exactly followed that course since the mid 20th century.

The Greek and Hebrew Texts the King James Bible was translated from are like the Jews. The children of Israel, the Jews, have survived for centuries no matter what has been thrown against them. They have survived, because God wanted them to survive. He has a plan of greatness and prosperity for them. Nothing can destroy the Jews. Likewise, in spite of over one hundred new English translations and the modern marketing techniques that have been used to promote them, they still have not destroyed the King James Bible. The KJB continues to survive and be a best seller, without the special marketing techniques. The KJB continues to enjoy a large popularity that can only be attributed to God. Not only that, but it has been reported by the Trinitarian Bible Society that the Scrivener edition of the TR is the most popular edition.

The United Bible Societies Text and Its Forebears

Of course, it is not the Devil's nature to sit still while God is inspiring a New Testament and preserving both Testaments. Paul explained the work of the Devil in 2 Corinthians 11:3-4, 13-14.

> *3 But I fear, lest by any means, as the serpent beguiled Eve through his subtilty, so your minds should be **corrupted from the simplicity** that is in Christ.*
> *4 For if he that cometh preacheth **another Jesus**, whom we have not preached, or if ye receive **another spirit**, which ye have not received, or **another gospel**,*

which ye have not accepted, ye might well bear with him.
*13 For such are **false apostles, deceitful workers**, transforming themselves into the apostles of Christ.*
*14 And no marvel; for **Satan himself is transformed into an angel of light.***
*15 Therefore it is no great thing if **his ministers also be transformed as the ministers of righteousness**; whose end shall be according to their works.*

Satan is revealed in these verses as having his own false ministers, false apostles, and false workers who present another Jesus, impart another spirit, and preach another gospel. Certainly, then, Satan will create another Bible, maybe many other Bibles. That is exactly what he has done and he began to do it in the days of Paul (2 Cor. 2:17).

In the 21st century, there are primarily two competing *printed* Greek New Testaments. One is the Received Text (TR), which is based on the Traditional Greek Text manuscripts. The second, is the United Bible Societies Greek Text (UBS). They cannot both be the true text, because they differ in about 8,000 places. The UBS text is based on about 6% of the ancient evidence, but primarily on two manuscripts that contain most of the New Testament: Vaticanus and Sinaiticus.

The United Bible Societies is an association of over 150 Bible Societies scattered around the globe. Its headquarters is in London. It began in 1946 with the British and Foreign Bible Society (1804) and the American Bible Society (1816) among its founding members. The UBS coordinates the work of its member societies. They are involved in Bible translation and distributing Bibles and other literature. The United Bible Societies is an apostate organization. Let me show you why I say that.

The United Bible Societies and Apostasy

These societies have been characterized by apostasy from the very beginning. This includes the British and Foreign Bible Society (BFBS) before it helped found the UBS. When the BFBS started, it immediately began to cooperate with Catholic priests including helping a priest in his translation of a new German New Testament. It would be well to note that the Catholic Church has always promoted its own version of the Bible, which is different from the protestant Bibles (based on the Received Text) in thousands of places. They have always condemned purely protestant versions translated from the Received Text.

> The policy of the United Bible Societies regarding the Apocrypha and interconfessional co-operation with Roman Catholic scholars on Bible translations was outlined in a booklet published by the American Bible Society in 1970 ... Referring to the interdenominational character of the Bible societies, [the booklet] states that Roman Catholics participated in the founding of some Bible societies in Europe, and that "the British and Foreign Bible Society from the beginning co-operated with Roman Catholic groups." It is also acknowledged that Roman Catholic churchmen were invited to participate in the founding of the American Bible Society in 1816. [133]

> The work of joint Bible translation and distribution between Protestants and Catholics was encouraged by the Driebergen conference of Bible societies in June 1964, which was attended also by Roman Catholics. The chief recommendations of the conference were: to prepare a "common text" of the Bible in the original languages, acceptable to all Churches, including Roman Catholics; and to explore the possibility of preparing a "common translation" in certain languages, which could be used by Protestants and Roman Catholics alike. It was further recommended that the Bible societies should consider translating and publishing the Apocrypha when Churches specifically requested it. [134]

In addition to cooperating with the Roman Catholic Church, the BFBS also included Unitarians, who deny the deity of Jesus Christ.

When the constitution of the British and Foreign Bible Society was first formulated, it was understandably not foreseen that the question of Unitarianism would have much relevance to the society's work. Before long, however, Unitarians gained substantial influence upon the affairs of The Bible Society, particularly in Europe, where some auxiliary societies were run almost exclusively by persons of Unitarians beliefs. [135]

This precipitated an argument so intense that it finally resulted in a split in the BFBS. In 1831, a large number of delegates broke away and formed the Trinitarian Bible Society which is faithful to the Trinity, as well as the KJB and the Received Text, to this day.

The UBS Greek Text was produced by liberal heretics. Both the Nestle-Aland Text in Germany and the United Bible Societies Greek Text were originally based on the Westcott and Hort Text, which was used to translate the Revised Version in England (1881).

> The international committee that produced the United Bible Societies Greek New Testament, not only adopted the Westcott and Hort edition as its basic text, but followed their methodology in giving attention to both external and internal consideration.[136]

B. F. Westcott and J. F. A. Hort, the Anglican scholars of the nineteenth century, learned liberal beliefs and thinking from a century of liberal thought coming from Germany. They hated the Textus Receptus (on which the KJV was based). They sought to turn the examination of the Biblical text (which was called "textual criticism") into a purely scientific thing that treated the Bible as if it was the same as any other book and dismissed inspiration and the providential preservation of the text altogether.

> Eighteenth century German textual scholars, Johann Griesbach and Johann Bengel, spurred the modern textual critical theory of re-examining the Textus Receptus and introduced a number of "scientific"

criteria for determining authentic New Testament readings. In the late nineteenth century, English Churchmen Brooke Westcott and Fenton Hort adopted many of these criteria ... The establishment of these "scientific" criteria for textual criticism caused the divine work of biblical preservation to become a merely naturalistic enterprise. If the only criteria to determine the authentic readings are to determine what manuscripts are the oldest and what readings are supposedly less "improved" and "smooth", then where does one's faith fit in? [137]

This kind of approach to choosing what reading should go into the New Testament text actually led to a methodology that boiled down to little more than mere educated guesses! Should you trust a text that was put together based on the educated guesses of a bunch of theological liberals? Westcott and Hort described this approach.

The first impulse in dealing with a variation is usually to lean on Intrinsic Probability, that is, to consider which of two readings makes the best sense, and to decide between them accordingly. The decision may be made either by an immediate and as it were intuitive judgment, or by weighing cautiously various elements which go to make up what is called sense, such as conformity to grammar and congruity to the purport of the rest of the sentence and of the larger context; to which may rightly be added congruity to the usual style of the author and to his matter in other passages. (intrinsic probability and intuitive judgment = make your best guess-Author) [138]

The first edition of the UBS Text was published in 1966. The text is in its fifth edition, which was published in 2014. The third edition (1975) introduced more than 500 changes in the text of the New Testament. This third edition and the 26th edition of the Nestle-Aland Greek New Testament established a single text for them both. The fourth Edition (1993) and the fifth edition extensively revised the included critical apparatus, but did not change the text. The UBS Greek New Testament and the Nestle-Aland continue to share an identical text.

The Editors of the UBS Text

The first, second and third editions were edited by Kurt Aland, Matthew Black, Carlo M. Martini, Bruce M. Metzger, and Allen Wikgren. The fourth and fifth editions were edited by Barbara Aland, Kurt Aland, Johannes Karavidopoulos, Carlo Martini, and Bruce Metzger. Among these names are individuals who deny that the Bible is verbally inspired and infallible. I will take special note of some of them below.

Bruce Metzger (1914-2007) was George L. Collard Professor of New Testament Language and Literature at the theologically liberal Princeton Theological Seminary. He was the head of the continuing Revised Standard Version translation committee, was the lead catalyst in the translation of the New Revised Standard Version, and was involved in the production of the condensed Reader's Digest Bible. Bruce Metzger was an unbeliever in the literal inspiration, preservation, and inerrancy of the Bible. [139] He denied the Mosaic authorship of the Pentateuch (the first five books of the Bible), he believed the Book of Daniel was written after the events the book prophesies, he denied Paul's authorship of some of his New Testament Epistles, and questioned the authenticity of other New Testament books. [140] He believed that much of the Old Testament was drawn out of a matrix of myth and legend.[141] He did not believe the story of the Genesis flood. Job was a folktale. Jonah was a legend. Peter did not write 2 Peter and the opening chapters of the Old Testament are not history. [142] Jesus said, "For had ye believed Moses, ye would have believed me: for he wrote of me. But if ye believe not his writings, how shall ye believe my words?" (John 5:46-47)

Kurt Aland was also editor of the Nestle-Aland Text which, as we have said, now matches the UBS text exactly. He rejected verbal inspiration and he did not believe in an authoritative, settled canon of Scripture. He rejected the traditional authorship of the four gospels. Everything is to be questioned and doubted. Dr. Kurt Aland did not believe in the inspiration and infallibility of Scripture. He did not believe in the inerrant preservation of the scriptures.

Finally, Carlo Martini is a Roman Catholic Cardinal. He was Archbishop of Milan and Professor of New Testament Textual Criticism at the Pontifical Biblical Institute in Rome.

The UBS text has been a completely modernist pro-Catholic production from start to finish. In the Introduction to the Nestle-Aland: Novum Testamentum Graece, 27th edition, page 45, the editors say this about the relationship of the UBS to the Roman Catholic Church.

> The text shared by these two editions was adopted internationally by Bible Societies, and following an agreement between the Vatican and the United Bible Societies it has served as the basis for new translations and for revisions made under their supervision. This marks a significant step with regard to interconfessional relationships. [143]

Those who follow this text are following blind leaders who deny the verbal inspiration of Scripture, the veracity of Scripture, and the verbal plenary preservation of the Scriptures. These editors are blind spiritually and those who follow them often do it out of ignorance. If the blind follow the blind ...?

The UBS Text differs greatly from the Received Text. There are thousands of word differences between the two. Everett W. Fowler evaluated the third edition of the UBS Greek Text compared to the Received Text, which, as mentioned before, is the same text as the fourth and fifth editions. He published the results in *Evaluating Versions of the New Testament*. [144] Figure 10 enumerates the whole verses and partial verses missing from the UBS text as compared to the TR.

Number of whole verses missing in UBS	17
Omissions of whole and partial verses	1309

Fig. 24

The total word differences were categorized as follows. These do not include differences in spelling of proper nouns. The category of "words classed as different words" does not include "spelling variations shown in Greek lexicons as accepted ways of spelling words which have identical meanings but which are not listed as different words (for example: labor=labour)."

Words in the Received Text omitted from UBS	3602
Words classed as different words	3146
Words in UBS not in the Received Text	976
Words spelled different, but not different words	950
Total word differences	8674

Fig. 25

Why do we have such concern over individual words, even if some of them do not materially affect the translation? There are a total of 8,674 word differences between the Received Greek Text and the UBS Greek Text. The New Testament was inspired in Greek and every Word of God is important. As we have abundantly seen, God, Himself, emphasizes the importance of every word.

The United Bible Societies Greek text was produced by spiritually blind men. Those who follow the work of these men have blind spots, as well. "If the blind follow the blind ..."

Why the Received Greek Text and the Received Hebrew Masoretic Text? The answer is quite simple. The Received Texts have always been God's choice and He is certainly a lot smarter than you and I. I'd rather be on the side of what God has chosen than on the side of modernistic scholarship.

Chapter Thirteen

A Short History of Bible Translating

Remember the former things of old: for I am God, and there is none else; I am God, and there is none like me
(Isaiah 46:9-10)

*Thus saith the LORD, Stand ye in the ways, and see, and **ask for the old paths, where is the good way,** and walk therein, and ye shall find rest for your souls. But they said, We will not walk therein. (Jeremiah 6:16)*

God is the God of history. He has determined the ultimate end of history and has outlined the course the world will take to get there. God is intimately involved with the activities of history. Throughout the Old Testament we can see how He intervened in history on behalf of His people and in dealing with man in general. God was not silent in the New Testament either. The most monumental involvement of God in the history of man took place in the New Testament. This was the coming of the Lord Jesus Christ into the world along with His work, crucifixion, and resurrection. After His ascension, the power He gave his apostles and servants was remarkable. The great promise of His involvement is found in the Great Commission: "lo, I am with you alway, even unto the end of the world" (Mt. 28:20). God desires world evangelism and is involved with efforts to reach mankind with the gospel.

The tone was set for God's involvement in history after the close of the New Testament period. With some spiritual discernment, it is possible to trace the footsteps of God. Jesus said, "Without me ye can do nothing" (Jn. 15:5). So, when God's work is done, it is God who has done it through man as His instrument. All labor for the Lord is done by His grace and sufficiency (1 Cor. 15:10; 2 Cor. 3:5).

So what do the footprints of God in history tell us about His attitude toward translating His word into all languages? The answer to this question is abundantly seen throughout the church age. From the close of the apostolic age (about A.D. 100) new translations appeared in abundance up until the time of the first pope (about A.D. 500). There was little translation done while the Catholic Church dominated the European scene for about 1000 years. However, as soon as the reformation dawned with the posting of the 95 theses by Martin Luther, Bible translation literally exploded. The true church had broken its chains to the great oppressive whore (Rev. 17).

The Post Apostolic Age

After the death of the Apostle John (about A.D. 100) there was a flurry of Bible translation efforts that carried through beyond 450 AD. By about 150 AD the Bible had been translated into Syriac (the Peshitta version) and Latin (generally called the Old Latin version or the Itala). Around 170 a man named Tatian published a harmony of the gospels known as the Diatessaron. This was also translated into Syriac. Egyptian versions, known as Coptic, began to appear in several dialects by about the middle of the third century (250 AD). Ulfilas, the great missionary to the Goths, translated the Bible into Gothic about 350 AD. The Bible was translated into Armenian after 400 AD. The Georgian Version was translated for the people in the mountainous region between the Black and Caspian Seas in the middle of the fifth century. The Nestorians were a group of missionary Christians who migrated eastward from the Mediterranean region. As they traveled from Syria to central and east Asia in the fifth century and later, they translated the Bible into several languages. [145] Most of these translations are clearly from the Traditional type Greek text (which gave us the Received Text and the KJB) and a few others are from the Alexandrian.

The Middle Ages

The Middle Ages began about A.D. 500 with the first Pope and ended with the Reformation about 1500. The period was called the "Dark Ages" at one time and a dark time it was. The Roman Catholic Church held sway in Europe the whole time. The Popes and the Roman Church kept the population of Europe captive to doctrines of salvation by faith plus works rather than by God's grace. They brought Kings into subjection by threats of excommunication, while many times working political intrigue behind the scenes. If anyone dared oppose the church they ran the risk of death by burning, torture, or other means. The church even sent armies against whole populations of "heretics." [146] Richard Bennett, a former Roman Catholic Priest says:

> Citing tradition and her own authority, the Church of Rome claims to have "divine and catholic faith". When people believe this they are enslaved because once external religion is accepted as genuine, truth and the Gospel of salvation are no longer understood as flowing from the Bible. Nevertheless, the Roman Catholic Church claims she controls the means of salvation for everyone. She then imposes a system of works upon them for their entire lives. Her priests affirm their convictions by means of their sovereign Pope and a salvation conveyed by means of sacraments. [147]

Nevertheless, even in the face of terrible Catholic persecution, true believers held firm. Though they sometimes suffered and even died for rejecting the authority of the Pope, preaching salvation by grace through faith in Christ alone (Eph. 2:8, 9), and the authority of the Bible alone, they continued preaching the Gospel throughout the middle ages.

Some translation work was accomplished in the Middle Ages. The Gospel of John was translated by the Venerable Bede about 735. The Old High German version appeared in 748. The Old Slavonic was started in 843 by Cyril and Methodius.

One Bible believing missionary movement was started on the beginning edge of the middle ages by a former slave. A man named Patricius was born about 389 in England. This is the same Patrick who is remembered each year on "Saint Patrick's Day." He was not a good Catholic. He was a Bible believing hell-fire-and-damnation preacher who was claimed by the Catholics probably because the Irish people loved his memory so dearly and the Pope wanted the loyalty of the Irish.

Patrick was taken captive by a band of Irish plunderers when he was in his teens. He was held for 6 years until he was able to escape. However, God sent him back to the Irish to evangelize his former captors. He arrived back in Ireland in 432. He convinced King Loigaire to tolerate Christians and soon afterwards the king's brother became a convert and gave Patrick land to start a church. His method was to start a church and move on to a new area. After fifteen years of labor much of Ireland was evangelized. He continued on for more than another fifteen years preaching the gospel of the Lord Jesus Christ.

Patrick's evangelistic zeal spawned a movement that resulted in missionaries going from the British Isles to many places throughout central Europe and as far north as Iceland. Britain actually became their first "foreign" field. Ruth Tucker, in her book From Jerusalem to Irian Jaya, explains their methods (quoting E.H. Broadbent).

> Their method was to visit a country and...found a missionary village...Groups of twelve monks would go out, each under the leadership of an abbot, to open up fresh fields for the gospel. Those who remained taught in the school, and as they had sufficiently learned the language of the people among whom they were, translated and wrote out portions of Scripture, and also hymns, which they taught to their scholars. [148]

Here, then, was one of the first great missionary movements of the middle ages, carried on under the nose of the rising Roman Catholic beast, and it included the ministry of translating the Scriptures.

As has been mentioned above a Christian movement called the "Nestorians" had spread eastward from Asia Minor. It continued to spread through much of the middle ages. Wherever the movement went it established churches and won many converts. The Nestorian movement expanded into Persia, the Arabian Peninsula, then into central Asia, India, Afghanistan, and Tibet. These areas became great centers of Christian activity. By the ninth century Nestorians had moved into China. From there they went on to Korea, Japan, and South East Asia. They started churches, established schools, trained young men in Bible institutes, and sent out full-time ministers. Their influence grew more and more. By the thirteenth century it is estimated that they had at least twenty-seven metropolitan patriarchs and two hundred bishops in China and surrounding areas. However, the church eventually declined under the onslaught of Islamic armies and the armies of Genghis Khan, Tamerlane, and other barbarian leaders which destroyed cities where the Nestorians had strong influence. No doubt many of their members and their leaders were put to the sword. [149] Finally, as they traveled they translated the Scriptures into several languages. [150]

Here again in the midst of a missionary movement we find the translating of the Bible as an integral part of the mission ministry.

Numerous evangelical groups remained faithful in Europe during the middle ages. Prominent among these were the churches of northern Italy, which date back to apostolic times and later called the Vaudois or the Waldenses. They continued to propagate the gospel during this dark time. The Vaudois were not translators of the word, but they held true to their Bible, which in turn became a great influence on some of the translations that were made early in the Reformation period 1500-1700. Their Bible was the Old Latin version called the "Itala," translated about 150 AD. [151] This Bible influenced the translation of the French Olivetan, the Luther German, and the Geneva English Bible. [152] Later, they also used a translation in the Romaunt language, which was a common language in much of Europe from the 8th to the 14th centuries.

The Reformation and After

Martin Luther, a Catholic Monk in Wittenberg, Germany had gotten saved reading the Bible. When he read Rom 1:15, "The just shall live by faith," he realized that salvation is a free gift of God. Christ had done the work to obtain salvation when he died on the cross and rose from the dead, and, so, there was nothing further for Martin Luther to do except rest on Christ's work as his hope for eternal life. [153]

Shortly after he got saved, Martin also became very disgusted with the preaching he heard that offered "indulges," that is, the forgiveness of sins if you contributed money to the church. He was so appalled that on October 31, 1517 he posted ninety-five theses

A Practical Theology of Bible Translating

against indulgences on the door of the Wittenberg church building. So the battle was on and the Reformation was launched!

In the two centuries that followed there would be millions who would break away from the Roman Catholic Church and there would be much bloodshed from persecution, because the great beast does not give up its children easily. This movement away from the Catholic Church would result in the development of the great reformed denominations; the Lutheran, the Presbyterian, and the Anglican, etc. Later the pietist churches would arise and the other denominations which continue to develop to the present day. Through it all the evangelical churches of the middle ages continued and some of them finally showed up in the 1600's as Baptist churches. [154]

The Reformation was a movement started, empowered, and continued by God. When Christians knew that they were free of the chains that had bound them to the Catholic Church for centuries, they immediately began to desire the Word of God in their own language. The Catholic Church had only allowed their version of the Latin Bible (the Latin Vulgate) to be read in churches. Believers wanted a new pure Bible in their own language. Following the posting of the 95 theses there was a veritable explosion of translations into the common language of the people. The following has been compiled of *some* of these translations from 1517 to 1900, so you can have an idea of what a great amount of translation work was completed.

Date	Translation/ Translator	Language
1517-19	Old Belarusian	Belarusian
1522/34	Luther Bible	German
1526	Tyndale Bible	English
1526	Jacob van Liesvelt	Dutch
1526	Olaus Petri New Testament	Swedish
1529	Zurich Bible	Swiss German
1530	Lefèvre Bible	French
1530	Brucioli Bible	Italian
1540	Gottskalksson New Testament	Icelandic
1541	Hungarian New Testament	Hungarian
1541	Laurentius Petri Bible	Swedish
1548	Nicholas Vinck Bible	Flemish

A Short History of Bible Translating

Date	Translation/ Translator	Language
1548	Agricola	Finnish
1550	Christian III	Danish
1562	Croatian New Testament	Croatian
1563	Brest Bible	Polish
1569	Reina-Valera	Spanish
1581	Russian Gutenberg	Cyrillic
1582	Primus Truber Bible	Slovenian
1584	Gunbrandar Bible	Icelandic
1588	Salesbury/Morgan	Welsh
1593	Kralitz Bible	Czech
1602	William Daniel New Testament	Irish
1607	Diodati Bible	Italian
1611	The King James Version	English
1648	New Testament	Romanian
c. 1659	Chyliński	Lithuanian
1661	John Elliot Bible	Natlick-Algonquin
1679	Bible	Romansch
1690	Bible	Irish
1715	Portions	Mohawk
1718	Bible	Romansch
1793-1832	William Carey and Associates: From 1793-1832 Carey's team translated over 40 Asian & Middle Eastern languages.	Various
1830	Jones and Griffith	Malagasy
1833	Edwin James New Testament	Ojibwa
1835	Adoniram Judson	Burmese
c. 1857	Van Dyke	Arabic
1890	Rodolphe Petter New Testament	Cheyenne

Fig. 26

These are only a few of the translations. Why was it in the hearts of God's people to make these translations unless the Spirit of God put it there? Why did God lead His people to go to such an effort to disseminate the Word of God around the world? It must be for only one reason. God wants His word to be spread around the world, and He wants it not only in a world-wide language (English) that only the well educated can understand (outside an English speaking country), but He wants His word to be available to common poorly educated people in a language that those people can understand: their heart language and mother tongue.

The People of the Book

This chapter on tracing God's footsteps would not be complete without a reference to "the people of the book." In the book Eternity in Their Hearts, Don Richardson included an entire chapter (chapter two) devoted to what he calls "The Peoples of the Lost Book." Below I have summarized most of the peoples he lists.
155

The Karen People

The Karen tribe is a people scattered through Burma. In 1828, George Boardman, the missionary associate of Adoniram Judson, baptized the first Karen convert. The Karen had resisted efforts by the Buddhists to convert them for centuries because they themselves were already devoted to a supreme god they knew as Y-wa. They saw Y-wa as a god with many of the same characteristics as Jehovah, all powerful, all knowing, everywhere present, eternal, creator of all things, and not entirely pleased with their performance. They also had another traditional belief. They believed that someday Y-wa would send to them a *white brother* who would bring them the *book of Y-wa*. This fact helped prepare them to hear the gospel and, when the white brother, George Boardman, did show up with the book, it led to the conversion of hundreds of thousands of them and made them missionaries to their own villages and to surrounding peoples.

The Kachin People

The Kachin people lived far to the north of Burma. Their folk religion had taught them to believe in a great creator called Karai Kasang. He was similar in characteristics to Y-wa. They felt that Karai Kasang was a kind deity, but they felt distant from him. The Kachin believed that Karai Kasang had once given a book to their forefathers and that they had lost it. They did not have a clear tradition of how

Karai Kasang would bring the book back to them, but they were open to its return.

The Lahu People

The Lahu live southeast of the Kachin and north of the Karen. Their tradition was that Guisha, creator of all things had given their forefathers his law written on rice cakes. The people of that time ate the rice cakes because of a famine. It would be impossible to obey the creator precisely until they regained his written laws. The Lahu had prophets of Guisha whose job was to keep alive the hope of their law being restored. In the course of time, God brought missionaries and the Book of God to them.

The Wa People

Sandwiched between the Kachin and the Lahu were the Wa. These people were head hunters. From time to time prophets of the one they believed to be the true god, Siyeh, would arise to condemn headhunting and spirit appeasement. One of these prophets was called Pu Chan by the nearby Shan people. His Wa name is unknown. He persuaded thousands of the tribesmen to quit headhunting on the basis that Siyeh was about to send a white brother with a copy of the lost book.

The Kui People

The Kui people live along the Thai-Burma border. Some of these people have been known to build houses of worship for the true God in anticipation of the time when a messenger of the true God would come with the lost book in his hand and enter the house.

The Lisu People

In the early 1800's there lived several hundred thousand people in the Yunnan Province of China called the Lisu. These people were looking forward to the coming of a white brother who would bring them a book of the true God written in the Lisu language. This is very interesting because at the time the Lisu language did not have an alphabet and, therefore, there was no Lisu written language!

The Naga People

The Naga people are on Burma's northern border. Their supreme God was known as Chepo-Thuru or Gwang depending on the dialect of their language. According to their tradition, their forefathers had received the law of God written on animal skins, but dogs had eaten them up.

The Mizo People

There is another people of India living some 300 miles southwest of the Naga. They also have a tradition of a lost book.

In the century following the coming of Adoniram Judson to Burma each of these people were reached with the gospel. Multiplied thousands were saved and the New Testament was translated. It would be worth the expense to buy the book, *Eternity in Their Hearts*, to read the thrilling story of the impact of the gospel on these peoples.

The Current Day

Bible translation work has continued to the present day. It is carried on by a number of mission organizations. Nearly all of the current day mission organizations doing translating are following the leadership of the United Bible Societies. Now, with the foregoing history as a background, we can launch into our review of the major agencies involved in today's translation efforts. Let me say, though, in the interest of balance, that I am glad that some effort is being made. I am also not evaluating the salvation or spirituality of anyone involved in these organizations, except to examine some of their beliefs and obvious doctrinal preferences. We are looking at methods and principles and practices that have developed since the Received text was abandoned in favor of the UBS Text. This happened gradually from approximately 1900 to 1980.

A Short History of Bible Translating

Major Agencies

Some of the major agencies making this effort today are:

1. Lutheran Bible Translators
2. Pioneer Bible Translators
3. New Tribes Mission
4. Evangel Bible Translators
5. Bible League International
6. The Seed Company
7. The International Mission Board (Southern Baptist)
8. Baptist Mid-Missions/ Bibles International
9. SIL and Wycliffe Bible Translators
10. United Bible Societies

When one examines the web sites of these organizations he finds some interesting and somewhat disturbing things when evaluated in the light of loyalty to the Received Greek and Hebrew Texts.

Lutheran Bible Translators

Lutheran Bible Translators was founded in 1964. It is, as the name suggests, affiliated with Lutheran Churches. They serve on five continents in over fifty language groups. On their partner sites page they list Pioneer Bible Translators, Wycliffe Bible Translators, and United Bible Societies. [156] So, it is clear that they are very ecumenical and there is UBS influence in their translation efforts.

Pioneer Bible Translators

Pioneer Bible Translators is a "Church of Christ" related organization. Pioneer Bible Translators began in 1976. They serve in 73 language projects in 17 countries. In their statement of faith they say, "Baptism is the pledge of a good conscience to God that clothes us in Christ" and we are "baptized into Christ." Also, they quote from the NIV, a UBS Text based translation. Therefore, they follow the corrupt UBS Greek text. [157]

New Tribes

New Tribes has changed its name to Ethnos360. In the UK it is still called New Tribes. It's still dedicated to planting churches as well as translating the Bible. In this way they are similar to the missionaries of the 1700's and 1800's. They are not, however, committed to the King James Bible or to the Received Text. NTM was founded in 1942. Today they have over 3000 missionaries serving in various parts of the world. They strive to serve where no one has yet gone. [158] However, they are infected with the same virus of modern scholarship that has so permeated much of Christianity. Charles Turner of The Baptist Bible Translators Institute was with New Tribes for 20 years. "He was a missionary to New Guinea with New Tribes Mission for twenty years, but left that mission in 1982 to protest its ecumenism and refusal to use the Received Text as the basis for its translation work." [159] Therefore, most of NTM's translation work will show the influence of the UBS Text.

Evangel Bible Translators

This is an organization headquartered in Rockwall, Texas. EBT was founded in 1976 through the encouragement of Cameron Townsend of Wycliffe Bible Translators. Once again it is clear from their web site that there is no commitment to either the KJB or the Received Text. It appears they are committed to the UBS Text. [160]

Bible League International

The Bible League International exists to train churches in discipleship, literacy programs, church planting, translating, and distribution of the Bible. Again there is no commitment to the KJB or the Received Text. Instead their commitment is to something called the Easy to Read Version, which is a typical modern version. For example the ERV in English leaves out the "blood" in Col. 1:14 and "begotten" in John 3:16. They seem to be busy spreading the ERV in languages that already have other translations such as, Bengali, Bulgarian, Portuguese, Russian, Spanish, Serbian, Thai, Vietnamese, Ukrainian, and Chinese. So, it appears there is no new ground being broken here. [161]

A Short History of Bible Translating

The Seed Company

The Seed Company partners with other organizations to help in Bible translation projects. In the past they have partnered with organizations such as the International Mission Board, YWAM, The JESUS Film Project, Scripture Gift Mission, World Teach, and Wycliffe Bible Translators. These organizations encourage the use of the UBS text. To be involved in a translation project using the UBS text shows an obvious lack of commitment to the Received Text. [162]

The International Mission Board

The International Mission Board of the Southern Baptist Convention was started in 1845 along with the establishment of the Convention itself. The first commissioning was held in 1846. The IMB has gone into partnership with Wycliffe Bible Translators. The SBC itself has no commitment of any kind to the KJB or the Received Text. Some individual ministers are committed, however. Many are not. [163]

Baptist Mid Missions/ Bibles International

Baptist Mid Missions, a distinctively Baptist independent mission agency, was started in 1920. Today they serve in many areas of ministry in over 50 countries. [164] In 1981 Baptist Mid Missions organized a division dedicated to translating the Bible. This branch, Bibles International, is one of the few players in the field that makes a commitment as to what Greek and Hebrew source texts its missionaries should use for translation purposes. They tell us that their translators use the Hebrew Masoretic Text and the Greek Majority Text. They do not commit themselves to use the Received Text. [165]

SIL and Wycliffe Bible Translators

We are taking these two together because both Wycliffe and SIL (originally The Summer Institute of Linguistics) were started by Cameron Townsend. SIL was the training arm of Wycliffe. Wycliffe is the premier Bible translating organization in the world. They have been involved in hundreds of translation projects. There are many working with Wycliffe who are good hearted people with a burden for the unsaved and a vision for unreached people groups. Unfortunately, though the work appears great on the outside, all may not be well within. Charles Turner wrote an article, entitled Wycliffe Bible Translators, in which he revealed some serious compromises. First, he shows by specific examples how that, under Townsend, SIL trained Roman Catholic priests and that Wycliffe helped priests in their efforts to translate the Bible and teach tribal people. There was also some effort to translate some passages in a neutral way that would not offend Roman Catholics. Townsend, himself, went beyond this and said, "Since we are non-sectarian and non-ecclesiastical, we get help from Catholics, Protestants, Jews, Moslems, Buddhists, and even atheists." Brother Turner also documents that Wycliffe and SIL are pro-charismatic and that many of those involved in the mission are charismatic in actuality. Finally, he shows that Wycliffe is new-evangelical. He shows many characteristics that the two have in common. This was documented for a period of about twenty years while Cam Townsend was still alive. [166] Wycliffe has over 5000 missionaries from 70 denominations so it would be impossible to pigeon hole all of them in these categories. But, these general characteristics were apparently built into the organization by its founder. Finally, as a general rule Wycliffe missionaries use the UBS type text. [167]

The United Bible Societies

Other than this brief mention, I will not spend time on the United Bible Societies here. I have discussed it in a previous chapter.

The Other Side

When I was earning a master's degree I wrote a thesis on "Seven Reasons why we must translate the Word of God." in 2005, there was very little going on regarding translating of the Bible from the Received Text or from the KJV. I made an extensive search for such translation projects. I came across a few.

A Short History of Bible Translating

Since then some additional work has developed and some new organizations have been started. This is the good news. The bad news is that very few Bible believing churches know of these efforts and very few have committed themselves to help.

Now, there are some mission organizations that are involved in the general area of Bible translating and are faithful to the Received Text. Some of these organizations are primarily involved in translation projects, but other are primarily involved in publishing, distribution, and training. Therefore, all the infra-structure is in place for a mighty future push.

Baptist Bible Translators Institute

> The idea for a Baptist missionary training school was born as a result of an initial missionary trip into the Tlapaneco Indian area of Guerrero, Mexico, made by Missionary George Anderson and Pastor Paul Henderson. When Brother Anderson tried to live among the Indians and teach them, he discovered that their understanding of Spanish was very limited. He also realized that he had no idea how to learn their unwritten language. He wrote to his Bible college and to several other Baptist schools asking this question: 'Do you teach missionaries how to learn languages?' They all replied, 'No.' George and his wife, Sharon, left the field and enrolled in a linguistic training program with the purpose of starting a similar school for Baptists. Thus, in 1973, the Baptist Bible Translators Institute began in Ft. Worth, Texas. The following year the school was moved to its present location near Bowie, Texas. [168]

Since then graduates have gone to more than 20 countries. The current executive director is Rex Cobb, a veteran missionary and Bible translator. BBTI is the only organization that I could find on the internet that has an active explicit strategy to recruit potential translators and has a firm public commitment to the KJB and the Received text. However, BBTI is not a mission agency, although it has helped students in reaching the field in any way it can. It is a training institution. It trains missionaries in linguistics, Greek, Church planting, Bible translation and other important aspects of cross-cultural ministry. It is an important training organization for the churches.

Trinitarian Bible Society

The Trinitarian Bible Society was formed in December 1831. Its purpose is to distribute faithful translations in many languages. They have been very successful in this. They have also supported translation projects in a number of African, Asian, and European languages. They are not a missionary recruiting organization, however. So, even though the TBS has been vastly effective in distributing the Word of God and standing firm for the TR and the KJV, they have had less involvement in translation projects. Nevertheless, they and the BBTI are two of the few mission organizations that have an active plan to increase the number of translations from the TR. [169]

Graceway Bible Society

Graceway is a Canadian organization that was created with a dedication to the TR and the KJV. Their ministry is primarily the distribution of the Word of God in as many languages as they can. In their own words: "GRACEWAY BIBLE SOCIETY came into being 1968, and operates as a independent charitable organization incorporated in 1977 under Canadian Law … GRACEWAY BIBLE SOCIETY desires to ensure that believers may have a reliable Bible … The basis of our Society affirms that the Holy Scriptures are given by inspiration of God and are to be received as the "sole, supreme, and infallible rule of faith and practice". These are vital issues and matters of important principle which make it impossible to integrate the work of the GRACEWAY BIBLE SOCIETY with the "United Bible Societies" or with any liberal ecumenical movement. Christian workers in many countries look to GRACEWAY BIBLE SOCIETY for regular supplies of Scriptures which are now available in many foreign languages, and there are constantly increasing opportunities for the worldwide distribution of the Word. Complete Bibles, New Testaments, Gospels, Scripture Booklets, Leaflets, Text Cards, etc are made available by the GRACEWAY BIBLE SOCIETY and contain the Word of God alone without doctrinal notes or comments." [170]

A Short History of Bible Translating

Bearing Precious Seed

The Bearing Precious Seed ministries are local church Bible publishing and distribution ministries. Bearing Precious Seed is a generic ministry name that operates in several churches in the USA. Each ministry is independent of the others and operates under the authority of a local church. Bearing Precious Seed prints Bibles and Bible portions in numerous languages. Their goal is to print Received Text based Scripture.

First Bible International

The work of firstBible International began in 2003 under the direction of Dr. Charles Keen. After 35 years as pastor and leading First Baptist Church of Milford, Ohio to be one of the great mission sending churches of our generation, the Lord gave Dr. Keen a vision for the unreached people groups of the world. FirstBible International is a Bible Translating and Publishing Ministry with a Three-Fold Goal: Bible publishing, national training, and church planting." They "contend that neither church planting nor national training can be done effectively until we have a Bible in the heart language of the people we are trying to reach." First Bible International has raised a large amount of money to support translation projects started by Trinitarian Bible Society and others. First Bible International also sponsored a new KJV equivalent translation into Mongolian. Currently First Bible operates as a Bible translating and publishing ministry that is part of Bearing Precious Seed at First Baptist Church in Milford, Ohio. [171]

Worldview Ministries

Worldview ministries was started by Dr. Ken Fielder, former pastor for sixteen years at Westside Baptist Church in Mansfield, Ohio. Dr. Fielder was the Assistant Director of First Bible. Later, he departed and started Worldview. He says, "I am convinced that the translation of the Bible into the heart languages of the unreached is the key to completing the Great Commission. No other work can have such thorough and eternal impact on a culture." They seek to realize the goal of spreading the Word of God through church planting, national training, Bible translating, and a focus on unreached people groups. As a translation philosophy they are "committed to the accurate translation of Scriptures. We accept the Bible as the very Word of God, given to us by plenary-verbal inspiration and preserved for us by God. Therefore, we are committed to formal equivalence or essentially literal translation of the words of God. We seek the guidance and help of God in achieving accuracy in this sacred work." Worldview operates Worldview Institute in India to train translators. They have a translation project in Mbarara, Uganda and a second one planned in Arua. Another project is underway in Tibet and a project in China is targeting a people group with no written language and a project is underway in Myanmar. A further translation project is planned for Liangmai. [172]

Bearing Precious Seed Global/ Global Bible Translators

BPS Global began in June 2007. In 2005-2006, I was mailing copies of my master's thesis (then published as "Must We Translate?") to a number of churches, schools, and mission agencies. One of those copies went to the Bible school at First Baptist Church in Milford, Ohio. It was subsequently given to Dr. Steve Zeinner, who was then the Director of Bearing Precious Seed-Milford. He contacted me and over the next several months we found that we had a similar burden for the translation of the Word of God into the World's languages. In 2007, we agreed to start a Bible translation ministry. Dr. Zeinner joined Plantation Baptist Church in Plantation, Florida and became the General Director. BPS Global became a ministry of Plantation Baptist Church.

The purpose of BPS Global is to increase the number of Received Text based, KJV equivalent, translations of the Word of God, to have those translations printed globally in the best way available, and to advance church planting and translating among unreached people groups. BPS Global starts new translation projects, trains translators on-site in-country, partners with the Baptist Bible Translators Institute, provides translation advisory services, raises funds to print new translations, and arranges the printing. BPS Global is committed 100% to the belief that the correct foundation of Bible translating is the Greek Received Text, the Hebrew Masoretic Text, and the KJV. To date, by the grace of God, we have been involved in translation efforts in Korea, Thailand (in the Isan language), China (in the Mandarin language), India (in the Telugu language), Togo, West Africa (in the Ewe language), Paraguay (in the Guarani language), and in German. In addition, our ministry has extended to Ghana, the Philippines, Myanmar, Ecuador, and French Canada. The Isan New Testament in Thailand was finished in 2016. The 22 million Isan people have never before had any Scripture in their mother tongue until this project started under the leadership of Ron Myers, an associate translator.[173]

Conclusion

It's hard to imagine how that anyone could miss the point of such a mountain of evidence. We have been looking for the footprints of God in history and we have found them! There is a consistent history of Bible translation effort among believers from the time just after the Apostles until now. The efforts summarized above are still going on.

It is an unavoidable fact that God's people have in their hearts a desire to see God's Word spread abroad. Many Christians desire to see the Scripture translated into the world's languages. Why is this interest and desire there? The answer is obvious. God put it there. Why do you suppose God put this in the hearts of His children? Once again there can only be one answer. God wants all people to have His word in an understandable language. God has led many of His ministers to translate the Scriptures. Why has He done this? Again the answer is the same. God wants His word to be easily heard and known by everyone in a language they can easily understand! We must commit ourselves to the effort of Bible translation like never before!

Chapter Fourteen

The Future:
Bible Translating and Prophecy

---

9 And they sung a new song, saying, Thou art worthy to take the book, and to open the seals thereof: for thou wast slain, and hast redeemed us to God by thy blood out of every kindred, and tongue, and people, and nation;
10 And hast made us unto our God kings and priests: and we shall reign on the earth. (Rev. 5:9-10)

This chapter deals with prophetic events. Therefore, it may be prudent to address a topic that is generating quite a bit of controversy these days. I take the position that the rapture described in 1 Thessalonians 4:13-18 will occur before the seven-year Tribulation. There are several reasons for this.

    1.   The very purpose of the tribulation excludes the church. The tribulation period of seven years is also known as the seventieth week of Daniel's people, the Jews. In Daniel 9:25-27 God outlines the final history of Israel up to the second coming of Christ when they will accept Him as their Messiah.

    2.   The weeks are years. They cannot be weeks of days or the prophecy would make no sense at all. Several have made calculations as to when the first 69 weeks began and when they ended. The first 69 weeks go to "Messiah the Prince." Suffice it to say that the calculations show that the first 69 weeks come to the end of the earthly life of the Lord Jesus Christ. We know from history that the final week did not immediately follow the resurrection. The church came next and is a period between the 69th and 70th weeks.

    3.   The seventieth week is the final fulfillment of God's plan for Israel. It is called the "time of Jacob's trouble" (Jer. 30:7). It is a Jewish period of history after the church age is finished.

    4.   The Church was not present during the first 69 weeks and it will not be in the last week.

5. All the prophecies of the Old Testament regarding the tribulation period are completely focused on Israel and the pouring out of God's wrath on a rebellious earth. They deal with God's program for Israel.

6. The nature of the Church is that of a "mystery" (Eph. 1, 3). It was an unrevealed, unusual, not understood mystery in the Old Testament. It is a particularly spiritual entity, the body and bride of Christ, consisting of both Jew and Gentile together in one body. This is revealed in the New Testament as a new thing, a new creation of God. It is fundamentally, by nature different than Israel. It is something that did not exist in the Old Testament. It will not exist on earth in the tribulation, because the tribulation is the final fulfillment of Old Testament history before the second coming.

Revelation 4:1 says, "After this I looked, and, behold, a door was opened in heaven: and the first voice which I heard was as it were of a trumpet talking with me; which said, Come up hither...." Here is a beautiful picture of the rapture. Revelation 1-3 is filled with messages to the churches, then a door opens in Heaven and the church departs. When Jesus comes down from Heaven part way to earth, we will hear the sound of a trumpet and a voice saying, "Come up hither." How beautiful and wonderful that will be! Then the scene that will break upon our eyes is given in Revelation 4:2-5.

> *2 And immediately I was in the spirit: and, behold, a throne was set in heaven, and one sat on the throne.*
> *3 And he that sat was to look upon like a jasper and a sardine stone: and there was a rainbow round about the throne, in sight like unto an emerald.*
> *4 And round about the throne were four and twenty seats: and upon the seats I saw four and twenty elders sitting, clothed in white raiment; and they had on their heads crowns of gold.*
> *5 And out of the throne proceeded lightnings and thunderings and voices: and there were seven lamps of fire burning before the throne, which are the seven Spirits of God. (Rev. 4:2-5)*

The Purpose of God

> *8 And when he had taken the book, the four beasts and four and twenty elders fell down before the Lamb, having every one of them harps, and golden vials full of odours, which are the prayers of saints.*
> *9 And they sung a new song, saying, Thou art worthy to take the book, and to open the seals thereof: for thou wast slain, and hast redeemed us to God by thy blood out of every kindred, and tongue, and people, and nation;*
> *10 And hast made us unto our God kings and priests: and we shall reign on the earth. (Rev. 5:8-10)*

Not everyone agrees on the identity of the elders. It is important that we have some idea of their identity, though. The twenty-four elders were introduced in chapter four, but not much is said about them there.

There are many clues as to their identity in chapter five, however. They sing a *new song.* It is a song that the angels cannot sing because it is about redemption and the angels were never redeemed. The elders say that they were redeemed. This shows that they are human beings. They were redeemed by the blood of Christ. Although the redemption of the blood extends for all saved in all ages, this group is found in heaven immediately following the rapture (4:1) and they are crowned in accordance with the promise to the Church of reigning with Christ (2 Tim. 2:12). They are not Israel, but rather they are gentiles and Jews since they are redeemed out of all nations, the gentile nations and Israel (Ephesians 1-3). They are not the tribulation saints because this takes place at the beginning of the tribulation. The Old Testament saints are not raised until the beginning of the Millennium (Rev. 20:1-6) for all except the unsaved are raised by then. Furthermore, these are said to "elders," which indicates they are representatives of a larger group.

Why the number twenty-four? It seems to be an enigma. The number twenty-four is not used in Scripture except in the Book of Revelation. However, there is a clue there. The number twelve is found throughout Scripture and it is associated with Israel, all the way to the New Jerusalem. Revelation 21:12 says, "And had a wall great

The Future: Bible Translating and Prophecy

and high, and had twelve gates, and at the gates twelve angels, and names written thereon, which are the names of the twelve tribes of the children of Israel." Israel is represented in Heaven by the twelve gates. Revelation 21:14 says, "And the wall of the city had twelve foundations, and in them the names of the twelve apostles of the Lamb." The Church is represented in Heaven by the twelve foundations. Obviously twelve plus twelve equals twenty-four. This is significant, because the church is a combination of Jews and Gentiles in Christ. This is what seems to be the significance of the number twenty-four. The twenty-four elders represent the church.

How does this help us understand the purpose of God in history and the New Testament church? If the elders of Revelation four and five represent the church, then Revelation 5:8-10 tells us a great deal about what God plans to accomplish in this age. When we reach heaven we will find there people from every nation and people and kindred. We will also find people who speak every language on earth. God doesn't say "many" here. He says "every." When God means "many," he says "many" (Rev. 10:11). I take it that Revelation 5:8-10 includes all the languages of earth.

Revelation 5:8-10 tells us that one day heaven will be populated by people who speak each of the languages in the above paragraph. There will be people from "every" tongue. Heaven will enjoy the presence of people who, on earth, spoke Dariganga (Mongolia), Irula (India), Mandailing Batak (Indonesia), Phuan (Laos), Khamti (Myanmar), Divehi (Malidives Islands), Tangchangya (Bangladesh), Firozkohi (Afghanistan), Tjam (Cambodia), Bonan (China), Banjar (Malaysia), and all others. These peoples and many others need to have two things well established within their cultures and languages. They need strong indigenous reproducing churches and they need the Bible. Much work remains to be done. Shouldn't independent Baptists commit themselves to such a work as this?

The Prophecy of God

> 9 After this I beheld, and, lo, a great multitude, which no man could number, of all nations, and kindreds, and people, and tongues, stood before the throne, and before the Lamb, clothed with white robes, and palms in their hands;

> 10 And cried with a loud voice, saying, Salvation to our God which sitteth upon the throne, and unto the Lamb.
> 11 And all the angels stood round about the throne, and about the elders and the four beasts, and fell before the throne on their faces, and worshipped God,
> 12 Saying, Amen: Blessing, and glory, and wisdom, and thanksgiving, and honour, and power, and might, be unto our God for ever and ever. Amen.
> 13 And one of the elders answered, saying unto me, What are these which are arrayed in white robes? and whence came they?
> 14 And I said unto him, Sir, thou knowest. And he said to me, These are they which came out of great tribulation, and have washed their robes, and made them white in the blood of the Lamb.
> 15 Therefore are they before the throne of God, and serve him day and night in his temple: and he that sitteth on the throne shall dwell among them.
> 16 They shall hunger no more, neither thirst any more; neither shall the sun light on them, nor any heat.
> 17 For the Lamb which is in the midst of the throne shall feed them, and shall lead them unto living fountains of waters: and God shall wipe away all tears from their eyes. (Revelation 7:9-17)

The above verses are a prophecy about conversions which take place during the Tribulation....not the church age. So, it in no way relates to the church age. Does it? Or, is there something here that is brought about partially by what Christians do now?

Remember the spiritual situation when the Tribulation opens. The rapture will have just taken place and every saved person on earth will be gone. Get that. There will be no saved people on earth at that time. No one will be there to preach the gospel or witness for Christ.

Yet, Revelation 7 speaks of 144,000 Jewish converts (7:1-8) and a great multitude of Gentiles (7:9-17). The number of this multitude of Gentiles is said to be so great that no one could number it. It will doubtless be millions upon millions. All of these will be saved during the tribulation and they will come from everywhere.

The Future: Bible Translating and Prophecy

The Gentiles are once again said to be "of all nations, and kindreds, and people, and tongues." The same goal to win all nations that has been given to the Church is also given to the Tribulation saints. "And this gospel of the kingdom shall be preached in all the world for a witness unto all nations; and then shall the end come" (Mt. 24:14). The Church Age saints started from 120 followers of Christ, but the Tribulation saints will start from 0. The difference is that we have had twenty centuries, 2000 years, to accomplish this goal. They will only have about 7 years!

Where do these saints come from? The tribulation will open with no saints and no preachers. The Bible says, "For whosoever shall call upon the name of the Lord shall be saved. How then shall they call on him in whom they have not believed? and how shall they believe in him of whom they have not heard? and how shall they hear without a preacher?" (Romans 10:14) How will the first Tribulation saints be saved when they need a preacher?

There are angels which make general announcements in the Tribulation. Do they preach the gospel? In Revelation 10 an angel shows up. But his announcement is that "time shall be no more." This is not quite what you would call "preaching the gospel."

However, there are three other angels that show up in Revelation 14. The first will come preaching the "everlasting gospel."

> *6 And I saw another angel fly in the midst of heaven, having the everlasting gospel to preach unto them that dwell on the earth, and to every nation, and kindred, and tongue, and people,*
> *7 Saying with a loud voice, Fear God, and give glory to him; for the hour of his judgment is come: and worship him that made heaven, and earth, and the sea, and the fountains of waters.*
> *8 And there followed another angel, saying, Babylon is fallen, is fallen, that great city, because she made all nations drink of the wine of the wrath of her fornication.*
> *9 And the third angel followed them, saying with a loud voice, If any man worship the beast and his image, and receive his mark in his forehead, or in his hand,*

> *10 The same shall drink of the wine of the wrath of God, which is poured out without mixture into the cup of his indignation; and he shall be tormented with fire and brimstone in the presence of the holy angels, and in the presence of the Lamb:*
> *11 And the smoke of their torment ascendeth up for ever and ever: and they have no rest day nor night, who worship the beast and his image, and whosoever receiveth the mark of his name.*
> *12 Here is the patience of the saints: here are they that keep the commandments of God, and the faith of Jesus.*
> *13 And I heard a voice from heaven saying unto me, Write, Blessed are the dead which die in the Lord from henceforth: Yea, saith the Spirit, that they may rest from their labours; and their works do follow them. (Rev. 14:6-13)*

The first angel preaches the everlasting gospel saying, "fear God give glory to Him and worship Him." The second angel announces that Babylon is fallen. The third declares God's judgment on those who take the mark of the beast. They preach to the world, all nations, kindred, tongues, and peoples.

These angels do not preach the gospel of the grace of God. They preach judgment. This could lead to conversions. However, the timing seems to present a question. Chapter thirteen ends with the ministry of the Antichrist and chapter fourteen opens with the 144,000 servants of God from chapter 7 now in Heaven. It seems some time has passed since chapter 13 and these servants have been martyred. The ministry of the angels is followed by the appearance of Christ reaping the earth. He is preparing to return. The passage indicates that not only has some time passed, but most of the conversions have already occurred, because the 144,000 have already been killed and are now in heaven.

In chapter fifteen the last plagues are quickly poured out and the way is made for the gathering at Armageddon (15:12). At the beginning of chapter fifteen there is a reference to the saints, now in heaven, worshiping God at the Crystal Sea before the throne. The timing of this passage seems to be at the end of the tribulation. If so,

The Future: Bible Translating and Prophecy

the preaching of the angels is not the reason for the conversions of chapter 7. C. I. Scofield said this about Rev. 14:6-13 about the "everlasting gospel:"

> This is to be preached to the earth-dwellers at the very end of the great tribulation and immediately preceding the judgment of the nations (Mt 25:31, refs.). It is neither the gospel of the kingdom, nor of grace. Though its burden is judgment, not salvation, it is good news to Israel and to those who, during the tribulation, have been saved (Rev. 7:9-14; Lk. 21:28; Psa. 96:11-13; Isa. 35:4-10). [174]

We must look elsewhere for an explanation of the bulk of the conversions in the Tribulation, including the conversion of the 144,000.

It has been speculated by some that the 144,000 are worldwide evangelists. This is probably true since they are called the "servants of God" and the conversion of the Gentiles is shown immediately following the sealing of the "servants." Laying aside the question of how the 144,000 are to be converted, consider the task that they would have to accomplish. They would have to reach every people group in the remotest places on earth. They would have to accomplish in less than seven years, what the Christian Church has not done in 2000 years! How, then, could this task be accomplished?

I will not say that I know the answer for certain. But, the simple truth is that, although all saved people will be gone after the rapture, God will not have left Himself without a witness. One of the greatest pushes going on among evangelical Christians right now is to translate the Bible (albeit from inferior texts in most cases) into every language on earth. We must join that effort (using the right texts) as we never have before, so that, when the rapture takes place, every nation, people, kindred, and tongue will still have the witness of the Gospel in a Bible they can read in their own language (every tongue). These Bibles will still be there when all the Christians are gone. They will be read by some and conversions will take place. It won't be necessary for the 144,000 to preach to all of them. The conversions will come from reading God's Word. Even though we repudiate such versions as the NIV and any other translation that comes from the

UBS Greek text, there is still enough Gospel correctly translated in many of these translations and versions to lead people to a saving knowledge of Christ. The answer for the conversions of Revelation 7 may be a very simple one: the presence of a Bible in their language. When you help or are involved in Bible translation, you are helping to evangelize those left behind after the Rapture.

Conclusion

God's plan includes the translation of the Word of God into the languages of the world. It is true that there is not a direct command to translate the Bible, but there is a command to preach the gospel and to teach all nations and that necessarily involves breaking the language barrier. But, preaching the gospel is not enough to establish new believers in their faith. This requires the written and/or recorded Word of God; read, listened to, studied, memorized, preached, taught and lived. We are not shy about letting Christians in the United States and Western Europe know how important this is. But, we are not nearly as concerned about translating and providing the Word of God to those who have never had it or have poor translations. They also need the word in order to be established in the faith. They will, in fact, be reached. Heaven will someday be populated by representatives of every language from both the Church Age and the Tribulation. That job will be accomplished. The only question is: will you be involved? God will get someone to help. Will it be you?

Chapter Fifteen

Unto the Uttermost Part of the Earth

9 Remember the former things of old: for I am God, and there is none else; I am God, and there is none like me,
*11 **Calling a ravenous bird from the east, the man that executeth my counsel from a far country** ... (Isaiah 46:9,11)*
*8 But ye shall receive power, after that the Holy Ghost is come upon you: and ye shall be witnesses unto me both in Jerusalem, and in all Judaea, and in Samaria, **and unto the uttermost part of the earth**. (Acts 1:8)*
17 Therefore to him that knoweth to do good, and doeth it not, to him it is sin. (James 4:17)
34 Awake to righteousness, and sin not; for some have not the knowledge of God: I speak this to your shame. (1 Cor. 15:34)

I hope that by now you are beginning to see the need to translate the Word of God into the languages that still have no Bible and into languages that only have an inadequate or corrupt Bible. In fact, I hope you have begun to get burdened about the issue, perhaps even feel an urgency about it. Millions have still never heard the name of Jesus Christ. Millions are still without the gospel and without the Word of God.

One question remains. Where do we go from here? Or, what must we do in response to this urgent need? The answer is one which can include everyone.

However, before we go on to suggest some answers to this question, let's face certain realities. First, much of the world is closed to missionaries from the USA and in some places Americans are hated or are restricted from mission work even if they are allowed in the country. This applies, for example, to China and Moslem countries. Even though this is true, much of the world is still open to American missionaries. This includes Papua New Guinea and other places in the Far East, much of Africa, South America, Central America, and North

America. UBS and SIL (Wycliffe) or one of the other organizations listed in Chapter 8 are already working in most of the largest people groups, but that doesn't mean we cannot start our own translation projects in those languages, if needed. There are also still thousands of languages, ranging from a few hundred to over a million speakers, where the Word of God has not been translated yet. As we pursue translation projects in Bibleless languages, there will be many opportunities to revise some of the work done by UBS and others using a corrupt Greek Text.

Many missionaries and pastors have long recognized that the Lord Jesus gave us a plan for missions in Acts 1:8. First, evangelize Jerusalem and Judea, then reach out to Samaria, and finally reach the uttermost part of the earth. Historically, this is exactly the process that took place in the Book of Acts. However, it applies to more than history. It should be the plan for every church. When a new church is established, it begins to evangelize the city where it is located. Then, it should reach out to other cities and to its entire region. Finally, it should go beyond and help evangelize the world. It does this by recruiting missionaries, sending missionaries, and supporting missionaries.

The same plan applies to Bible translation work. For many years, many American and European missionaries have gone to other countries and translated the Bible. Missionaries have gone to African and Asian countries since the nineteenth century and their work has borne much fruit. In the last several decades, African and Asian Christians have joined the ranks of the translators. In many cases, American or European missionaries have still been the leaders. African and Asian Christians have already begun to move into leadership in this need for Bible translation. This movement needs to continue and be helped along by missionaries from the West.

Perhaps an example would help in understanding this. It is a simple concept. Many missionaries have gone to Togo, West Africa and Christianity is widespread there. We encountered a large group of believers in Togo who were looking at creating a more faithful Bible translation in the Ewe language. A Bible translation project was started. It is led and carried out entirely by Togolese. Most of the translation team is in the city of Lomè, the capital. As of November, 2018, the country of Togo had ten other people groups with absolutely NO published scripture, as far as is known. The largest of these has a population of over 790,000, and the smallest has 5,600. The members of the Ewe translation team are learning a lot about doing this work. As time goes on, they will be able to train new translators and send them to these other tribes. They won't have to stop there. Ghana, a next door country to the west, has twenty-seven more people groups with no published Scripture. Benin, east of Togo, has nineteen more. Trainers from the west can come to Togo on temporary assignment to help with the training, if they are needed at first. Later, they will not be needed.

What Can the Churches Do?

The operative word here is *strategy*. Strategy means the plans and methods used to accomplish the evangelization of the world. For the churches, it is the methods we employ to decide where and on whom we bestow our missions support, prayer, and effort. Maybe the idea of a church making strategy for the effective application of its missions program is a strange concept to you. That may be because very few churches invest much time making strategy.

It's clear that Paul made strategy in his approach to missions. He had three basic strategies. First, he intended to establish a church in many major cities of the Empire, from which the gospel could spread. This was like an army establishing a beachhead during an invasion of an island in wartime.

His second strategy is illustrated in his entrance into Thessalonica. "Now when they had passed through Amphipolis and Apollonia, they came to Thessalonica, where was a synagogue of the Jews: And Paul, as his manner was, went in unto them, and three sabbath days reasoned with them out of the scripture" (Acts 17:1, 2). Notice that he went first to the synagogue and that this was his *manner*. That is, it was *his typical plan*. His strategy was to approach the Jews first. This was not just because they were God's chosen people in the Old Testament. It was also because they were a readymade audience for the gospel. They were familiar with Biblical terminology, history, and the promises of God. They were already prepared to understand the gospel in distinction from the majority of Greeks who thought in terms of secular philosophy and myths of the gods. Also, attached to the synagogue were many Greeks (called "God Fearers") who were seeking knowledge of the God of Israel.

They too were prepared to understand the Gospel. The synagogues, therefore, gave Paul an immediate audience and he had access because he was a Rabbi.

Paul's third strategy was to recruit and train new workers. He recruited Timothy (Acts 16:1-3) and Titus (2 Cor. 8:23). "And there accompanied him into Asia Sopater of Berea; and of the Thessalonians, Aristarchus and Secundus; and Gaius of Derbe, and Timotheus; and of Asia, Tychicus and Trophimus" (Acts 20:4). Of Timothy Paul said, "For this cause have I sent unto you Timotheus, who is my beloved son, and faithful in the Lord, who shall bring you into remembrance of my ways which be in Christ, as I teach every where in every church" (1 Cor. 4:17). Paul summarized some of Timothy's training, "But thou hast fully known my doctrine, manner of life, purpose, faith, longsuffering, charity, patience, persecutions, afflictions (2 Tim. 3:10-11). He trained these men through teaching, discussions, showing an example, and on the job; just as Jesus trained his disciples.

Finally, it was his strategy to build strong, well-taught, and well-led churches. He did this by teaching, writing letters, sending men to check up on them, and by example. A well-translated Bible is indispensable to the churches.

Paul's strategy in approaching the synagogues clearly would not work today. It worked well with Paul, because his background as a Pharisee and Rabbi gave him easy access to speak there. In our day there is no such access to most of us, because we are gentiles. Therefore, even though the gospel we bring is unchangeable, there is maximum flexibility in the strategies we employ. Although some of the strategies we have used in the past have become tradition, there are many circumstances in which they will not work. Except for teaching, preaching, fellowship, prayer, and living a godly example, all other methods and strategies are flexible. Think outside the box.

To make a clear and appropriate strategy requires prayer, study of the Word, and thought. It may seem unspiritual to believe that one must use his mind in seeking appropriate ways to approach people with the Gospel or in considering whom to support, but let me remind you of the Word of God through the writer of Proverbs, "He that handleth a matter wisely shall find good" (Prov. 16:20). So, here are some suggestions on how to make strategy.

1. Approach missions support prayerfully.
2. Become informed about world needs.
3. Decide which world needs should have priority in your support.
4. Divide your available mission support among your priorities by percentage.
5. Seek missionaries and mission organizations that fulfill the chosen priorities.
6. Be flexible.

Bible translation ministry is a highly neglected ministry among independent Baptist churches. Therefore, it would be wise for churches to set aside a certain portion of their mission budget for Bible translation and printing.

What Can Mission Agencies Do?

In this section, I am not thinking about the three organizations listed earlier that have formed in the past few years to further Bible translation efforts. I am thinking about mission agencies that existed before these, such as Maranatha Baptist Missions, or Word for the World Baptist Missions, or Worldwide New Testament Baptist Missions and others, all of whom stand positively on the KJV as the Word of God.

1. Every Bible believing mission agency should consider opening a division dedicated to Bible translating as did Baptist Mid Missions (Bibles International), but using correct texts and methods.
2. Every mission agency should consider starting efforts to educate the churches regarding the needs of unreached peoples and the need for translating the Bible. History shows that missionary movements were not wide spread until mission organizations were formed and led the way. One of the reasons for this is that agencies educate the churches. Our churches are woefully ignorant of the need of unreached people groups and for Bible translating.

3. Every Bible believing mission agency should consider putting goals in place to plant churches and translate the Bible in unreached people groups. This does not mean that I think the agencies have no goals or strategies. I think they do. However, it should be a goal to recruit missionaries for specific areas, people groups, and projects.
4. Bible believing mission agencies should implement immediate active steps to recruit and train missionary translators.

What Can the Bible Schools Do?

Many churches are developing training institutions run and controlled by the churches. This is a very good trend. In researching some of these schools it appears that an effort is being made to take the task seriously and to do a good job in preparing the next generation of church leaders and missionaries. However, I noticed certain weaknesses. In many of these schools there was a lack of teaching on mission concepts and thorough training on how to do missions. Also, there is very little study in Hebrew and Greek and how to learn languages.

Some missions teaching is present in many of these schools, but, if we are ever going to meet the needs around the world, there should be a great increase in the emphasis on missions. Regardless of whether a graduate plans to be a Pastor, evangelist, deacon, Sunday school teacher, or a church worker they all need to have a strong vision for and understanding of missions. Else how can the churches remain strong in their mission vision and understanding? The students need to have a thorough knowledge of the theology of missions and the conditions in today's world. They especially need to know what and where the greatest mission needs are. The schools, then, need to impart to their students a full understanding of the current missions needs in the world including the need for Bible translation. Some of our schools need to establish specific courses to train translators for pioneer missions, as well.

Some of the specialized training necessary to prepare a missionary in Bible translation and pioneer church planting among unreached people groups are these.

1. Theology and Bible Studies
2. Biblical Counseling
3. Hebrew and Greek
4. Missions Theology and Survey
5. Principles of Cross-Cultural Communication
6. Biblical Cultural Anthropology
7. All Aspects of Linguistics
8. Principles of Language Acquisition with Practical Application
9. Creating a Written Language and Teaching Adults to Read
10. Church Planting Techniques
11. Principles of Disciplemaking: the Lord's Method
12. Field Medicine/ Tropical Medicine
13. Survival in the Wild
14. Carpentry, Electrical, and Other Practical Skills

The Baptist Bible Translator's Institute in Bowie, Texas includes much of this, but why should not other schools include some of these things as well?

What Can Individual Christians Do?

As I see it, there are three things that a believer must, not should, but must do.

Every believer must become informed about missions and the needs in the world. It may surprise some that the first obligation is not prayer. However, the command of Jesus is to first *look* on the fields (Jn. 4:35). This indicates that our prayers should be informed prayers. We should know the condition of the fields so we can pray for them intelligently. For this purpose I recommend the book Operation World (amazon.com) and the information at www.operationworld.org/ wrld.

Every believer should pray that God will raise up multitudes of laborers (Mt. 9:37, 38). Believers should pray for the unreached nations and for God to raise up missionaries who are also translators.

Every believer should decide to do something to further the cause of missions, especially unreached nations. It may be to pray, give, to spread information, to volunteer, or to go. But you can do something.

Four Strategies

Recruiting American missionaries, training them, and sending them are our traditional approaches to missions. This is a Scriptural focus. We are told to pray for laborers. That is a focus we must not lose. However, we need to expand that strategy. I would like to suggest four further strategies to increase the number of translators.

We need to commit ourselves to recruiting nationals to become translators. When an American commits to become a translator, it can be as much as ten years or more before he can begin translating. There is four years of college, three years of deputation, and one to three years language training and experience. Nationals already know the language and the culture. The gospel has been going around the globe for a long time. Churches have been established in many parts of the world. There are many trained and mature nationals who are able to lead their own translation teams. They can get to work on translating much faster than a new missionary from elsewhere. They will need training in translation principles, though. It would be easy for the United States to send translation consultants to train them and check the accuracy of their translations.

We need to take the training to them. In the past many foreign Christians have sought to come to the US to be trained in theology. Missionaries have also started numerous training institutions on the field to train them in theology. However, there is little training in linguistics and translation available. We have neglected that in both the US and on the foreign fields. This is a situation we can no longer tolerate. In the US, the Baptist Bible Translators Institute teaches linguistics and Bible translation, but very few other institutions do that. There are almost no schools that teach these things anywhere in the countries that used to be called third world. Very few foreign nationals can afford to come to the United States for training. As nationals gain experience in Bible translating, we can guide them to start such schools and expand translation efforts. In the meantime, we can send teams to various places and encourage the nationals to do the work.

We need to send teams of translation consultants to various parts of the world to hold translation conferences. The purpose of these conferences is stir the national church leaders with a burden to translate the Bible and give them initial training. They need to get their own burden to accomplish this ministry.

In the US we need to concentrate on recruiting translation consultants who can carry out this work. We should always be open to Americans becoming translators in a language. However, a great deal more can be accomplished by sending a team to start a project with nationals in one language and then sending them to another language and another and so on.

We've covered a lot of ground in this study. In the last chapter, I have asked the question, "Where do we go from here?" In the final analysis, I can't answer this question for you, because I don't know the will of God for you specifically. I can only answer it for me. I can also say this. The information contained in this book should move the heart of every believer. When Jesus looked at the multitudes, He was moved with compassion, because they seemed to him to be sheep scattered without a shepherd. Should we be any less moved, seeing that the Spirit of Christ lives in us? If you have read all this up to this point you have begun to comply with the Lord's command for all believers (Mt. 9:35-38; Luke 10:2; John 4:35. He commands you to look on the fields and pray that God will send laborers into the harvest.

Proverbs 24:11 If thou forbear to deliver them that are drawn unto death, and those that are ready to be slain;
12 If thou sayest, Behold, we knew it not; doth not he that pondereth the heart consider it? and he that keepeth thy soul, doth not he know it? and shall not he render to every man according to his works?

Introduction to Appendices
And A Short Bibliography

When I was in Ghana holding a Bible translation conference with Steve Zeinner, one gentleman asked me a question about the legitimacy of the ending of Mark 16. I learned then that the issues of the Bible text are a problem all over the world. This book was written to present the theology of Bible translating. When I started, I did not intend to get into questions of the Biblical text. However, it is absolutely imperative that a translator know precisely which line of historical "bibles" is the right one, and the translator needs to know which Greek and Hebrew texts are the right ones. To do this, it would help to know the answers to some of the most pressing issues. Furthermore, he needs to know how to find the answers to other issues that arise. Every Christian, not just translators, needs to know these things.

All of this will lead him to the best translation source texts and the best English translation to help him. It is our conviction that the right Hebrew text is the Ginsberg edition of the Ben Chayim Masoretic Text, the right Greek text is the Scrivener edition of the Received Text, and the right English translation is the King James Bible. To help translators and all other Christians to make these decisions, it is necessary to look into these issues. So, I wish to cover the following subjects.

1. We will look at some passages in the Received text that are not based on the majority of manuscripts or are otherwise disputed by scholars.
2. We will look at some passages in the King James that have been disputed. These will only be a few passages, since over the years nearly every verse in the KJB has been criticized.
3. Finally, we will look at several passages that present important translation challenges.
4. We summarize the history of theological liberalism

Introduction to Appendices and Bibliography

      and the connected work of textual criticism.
5.   Finally, we will examine several translation problems so that translators will know how to analyze issues and find answers.

There are many more passages that could be included, than those I have selected. I hope the reader will learn some principles that will help him to face any further challenges that come up.

Below is a list of sources that will give the reader much more information about textual and historical issues about the TR and the KJB.

C. H. Pappas. *In Defense of the Authenticity of 1 John 5:7*. Second Edition. (WestBow Press: Blumington. 2016) also in Kindle
David Brown, *Providential Preservation,* https://kjbrc.org/
David Brown, *What Inspiration is Not.* https://kjbrc.org/
David Brown, *The History of Our English Bible.* https://kjbrc.org/
David Brown, *Why You should Use the King James Bible.* https://kjbrc.org/
David W. Cloud, *The End Times Database*, www.wayoflife.org Bible Believers, www.biblebelievers.com B Web articles, books, links.
David Otis Fuller, ed., *Which Bible*, Grand Rapids: Grand Rapids International Publications, 1970.
David Otis Fuller, ed., *True or False*, Grand Rapids: Grand Rapids International Publications, 1973.
Douglas D. Stauffer, *One Book Stands Alone*, Millbrook, AL: McCowen Mills Publishers, 2001.
Edward F. Hills, *The King James Version Defended*, Des Moines: The Christian Research Press, 1956
Everette Fowler, *Evaluating Versions of the New Testament*, Watertown, WI: Maranatha Baptist Press, 1981.
H.D. Williams, *Word-for Word Translating of the Received Texts*, the old paths publications.com

H.D. Williams, *The Septuagint.* www.theoldpathspublications.com

H.D. Williams, *Producing an Accurate and Faithful Translation of the Word of God.* Theoldpathspublications.com

H.D. Williams. *The Lie that Changed the Modern World.* theoldpathspublications.com

H.D. Williams, *The Miracle of Biblical Inspiration.* The Old Paths Publications.com

H.D. Williams, *The Origin of the Critical Text.* The Old Paths Publications.com Jack Moorman, *Was Sinaiticus Codex Sinaiticus Written in 1840?* The Old Paths Publications.com

Jim Taylor, *In Defense of the Textus Receptus.* Atlanta, GA: Old Paths Publications. 2016.

John W. Burgon, *The Traditional Text of the Holy Scriptures*, Public Domain, Amazon.com.

John W. Burgon, *The Causes of Corruption of the Traditional Text of the New Testament.* Lafayette: Sovereign Grace Publishers. 1998.

John W. Burgon, *The Last Twelve Verses of Mark.* 1871. Public Domain. Google Books.

Kent Bradenburg, Ed. *Thou Shalt Keep Them, A Biblical Theology of the Perfect Preservation of Scripture.* El Sobrante: Pillar and Ground Publishing, 2006.

William P. Grady, *Final Authority*, Schererville, IN: Grady Publications, 1993.

Trinitarian Bible Society, www.trinitarianbiblesociety.org. The Greek and Hebrew Text underlying the KJV, Trinitarian Bible Society.

List of Resources for the Translators

E-Sword (www.e-sword.net) with the following modules (free-there is a similar smart phone app called my-sword):
KJB
KJB with Strong's numbers
Ostervald French Bible
Greek TR with Strong's Numbers
Hebrew Text with Strong's Numbers
King James concordance

Introduction to Appendices and Bibliography

Albert Barnes Notes
Jamieson, Faussett and Brown Commentary
John Gill's Synopsis
John Wesley's Notes on the Bible
Matthew Henry's Commentary
Brown-Driver-Briggs Hebrew Definitions
Scofield Reference Notes
Easton's Bible Dictionary
Fausset's Bible Dictionary
International Bible Encyclopedia
Robinson's Morphological Analysis Codes
Webster's Dictionary of the English Language 1828
Vine's Expository Dictionary of New Testament Words (Not free, but important)
Vine's Expository Dictionary of Old Testament Words (Not free, but important)

Books
Greek and Hebrew Bible (Basis of the KJB) (Trinitarian Bible Society www.tbs-sales.org)
Analytical Greek Lexicon Revised (www.amazon.com)
Vine's Expository Dictionary of Old and New Testament Words (www.amazon.com)
Biblical Bible Translating, Charles Turner (www.amazon.com)
Brown, Driver and Briggs Hebrew Lexicon (www.amazon.com)
Strong's Exhaustive Concordance (www.amazon.com)
Wilson's Old Testament Word Studies (http://www.christianbook.com)
Ancient Hebrew Lexicon of the Bible by Jeff Brenner (www.amazon.com

Appendix 1:

A Bible Believer Asks, Why Use Greek and Hebrew?

Not so long ago, I talked to two Pastors about the source texts for Bible translating. The first asked me, "Why don't you just use the King James Bible to translate?" The second told me not to say much in his church about the Greek New Testament, because his people did not like it. I understand where these questions come from. For many years, I have run in circles that included quite a number of Pastors who saw things this way. The viewpoint is that the King James Bible is the word of God in English. It has no errors. So, it should be sufficient for translation work. Also, for decades, scholars have used "the Greek" to attempt to discredit the KJB. Therefore, Greek is looked at as an enemy. Some of these Pastors believe the KJB is inspired and some believe it has superseded the Greek and Hebrew Bible. My view is a little different and I ask Pastors and Christians of that mind set to read with patience.

If you have read the previous chapters and appendices of this book, you already know that I see value in Greek and Hebrew. I use Greek and I do Hebrew word studies. The reason I do this is that *I can*. I enjoy working with Greek. Also, I personally learn a lot from the exercise. However, there are some things you should know about my use of Greek and Hebrew from the start of this article. First, I do not use Greek and Hebrew to criticize or try to discredit the KJB. I use them to explain and defend the KJB. Second, I do not believe that unless a Christian knows Greek and Hebrew he can't understand the Bible or know the will of God. This is absolutely not true. The English Bible is completely sufficient to perfect the Christian. This whole book is based on the idea that every Christian needs the Word of God in his own language. Third, I believe that the Greek New Testament Received Text and the Ben Chayim Hebrew Masoretic Old Testament is especially valuable for Bible translation work.

There are a number of reasons why I believe a translator must either 1) translate direct from the Greek and Hebrew received

Appendix 1: Why Use Greek and Hebrew?

texts, or 2) make strong reference to them in the process of translating using Greek and Hebrew tools that are available. Please, allow me to explain below.

It is the method used by the King James translators. On the title page of any King James Bible it says. "Newly translated out of the original tongues and with the former translations diligently compared and revised …" Notice that the first thing mentioned is that the King James is a translation from the original languages ("tongues"), that is, from Hebrew, Aramaic, and Greek. The translators based their work on the original inspired Words of God. God promised to preserve them and the KJB translators professed to have them. There had been several previous English translations. They used them as additional sources, but changed them based on their own translation of the original languages ("diligently compared and revised"). They could have based their translation on Tyndale, but they did not. Tyndale's translation had a great influence on the KJB translators, but they translated direct from Hebrew, Aramaic, and Greek. This was their method.

The Hebrew, Aramaic, and Greek words are the original inspired words of God. As we have often repeated, God inspired His Word in Hebrew, Aramaic, and Greek. These inspired texts were, therefore, the Word of God. Every word was from God. They were His words. The Greek and Hebrew Bible is the Word of God as much as is the King James Bible. *So, the words of the Greek New Testament and the Hebrew/Aramaic Old Testament were given by God, they are inspired words, and, therefore, they are perfect words. They ARE the Word of God.*

God is perfect. There is no fault or blemish in Him. As such, all He does is perfect and without error. "*As for God, his **way** is perfect; the word of the LORD is tried: he is a buckler to all them that trust in him*" (2 Sam. 22:31). So, God's way, all He does, is perfect. Part of what God has done is to give us His words. It follows, then, that when He gave His words, those words in Greek, Hebrew, and Aramaic were perfect, without error, and infallible.

God has preserved the Hebrew, Aramaic, and Greek words He inspired. The King James translators apparently believed they had those words and so they did. The inspired words were not lost at anytime in the past. The King James translators had these Hebrew,

Aramaic, and Greek words and the words haven't gotten lost in the last 408 years since. Today, I can pick up the New Testament in Greek and read the inspired Greek words of God. I have them on my book shelf, in my phone, on my computer, and on my Android pad. I also have the Hebrew and Aramaic. God has kept His promise to preserve His words. We still have the original inspired words. We ought to feel perfectly free to use them if we wish.

There is great value in a multitude of counselors. "Where no counsel is, the people fall: but in the multitude of counsellors there is safety (Prov. 11:14). "Without counsel purposes are disappointed: but in the multitude of counsellors they are established" (Prov. 15:22). The King James translators knew the value of many councilors in their translation work. They had all the former English translations available. From those, they saw all the word choices of those translators. They also had foreign translations: the Martin Luther German, the Reina-Valera Spanish, the French, the Latin Vulgate, the Erasmus Latin translation, and the Beza Latin translation. They also had the Complutensian Polyglot. A translator needs all the help he can get. The Greek New Testament and the Hebrew Old Testament are key councilors for the translation of the Bible into any language.

The Greek and Hebrew texts are perfect and pure. "The words of the LORD are pure words (Ps. 12:6). "The law of the LORD is perfect" (Ps. 19:7). The words He was talking about were Hebrew words at the time He said it. His statements clearly apply to the Greek words of the New Testament, as well. We apply the same truths to His English words. My father was a master carpenter. He taught me a few tricks of the trade. If I wanted to cut several lengths of board the same length, I would measure the first one exactly and cut it. Then, I would use the first board, measured exactly, to mark the following boards, so that I can cut them to the exact same length as the original. The Greek and Hebrew texts are the original inspired Words of God for the New and Old Testaments. They are the standard by which all translations are measured. If a translation does not meet that standard, it should be rejected or revised. This was a generally accepted principle when the KJB was translated. There is no basis on which to believe that has changed. Men like William Carey and Adoniram Judson and their associates knew that. Even the King James translators knew it and acted accordingly by translating that standard accurately. In these last days, we have lost sight of it.

Appendix 1: Why Use Greek and Hebrew?

A Word About Lexicons

A Greek or Hebrew dictionary is called a lexicon. These days, there are some who feel that a lexicon is dangerous thing to use. For example, the Greek dictionary by Henry Thayer is considered biased, because Thayer was a Unitarian. He denied the deity of the Lord Jesus Christ. It is possible that Thayer was biased in a few of his entries. If you have been following the notes in this book, you already know that I sometimes use lexicons from the early nineteenth century. I do this in the hope that early lexicons will be less affected by liberal textual criticism and bad doctrine. However, this is also why you should use more than one lexicon. In the multitude of counselors, there is safety. You will find that most lexicons, even the early ones are in agreement on most words.

If you download the "e-sword" program (which I highly recommend) or "the word" program, you will find that they have a module called "King James Concordance' (KJC). The KJC is linked to the numbering system in Strong's Concordance. The KJC lists all the Greek words used in the King James Bible and the various ways the KJB translated those words. The King James translators did not tie themselves to uniformly translate each Greek word by the same English word every time. They made extensive use of synonyms. However, at the same time, they translated consistently with the definitions of the Greek words. The result of this is the KJB is a very good Greek lexicon all by itself. I have found, in the many times I have looked up words, that the various ways a Greek or Hebrew word is translated gives me a very helpful understanding of that word. I find that the KJC gives me information I can trust. However, I still use lexicons, because they can provide additional information. For example, there are some Greek words used only one time in the NT. A lexicon can help in those and other cases.

Appendix 2:

Problems of the Greek Text

There are several major passages of Scripture we will look at in this appendix, 1 John 5:7 is not found in the majority of the Traditional Text copies, and others are disputed by commentators, scholars, or critics. Some of the passages involved are of huge doctrinal importance. One of the great lies of modern scholarship is that none of the textual issues in modern English versions of the Bible involve major doctrine. That is a falsehood. These passages are true textual issues that require a decision to be made. I have chosen a few of them. They are as follows.

1) 1 John 5:7, 8
2) John 1:18
3) John 3:16
4) Mark 16:9-20
5) Romans 8:1
6) 1 Timothy 3:16
7) John 7:53-8:11

1. The Heavenly Witnesses 1 John 5:7-8

For there are three that bear record **in heaven, the Father, the Word, and the Holy Ghost: and these three are one. And there are three that bear witness in earth,** *the Spirit, and the water, and the blood: and these three agree in one.*

The highlighted words are missing in most Traditional Text and Alexandrian Text manuscripts. For many, that is enough reason to reject them. The manuscripts Erasmus had before his first edition did not contain the "Johannine Comma." So, his first two editions did not contain it.
Erasmus inserted the Johannine Comma in the third edition of his Greek text. When Erasmus issued his first and second editions

in 1519, there was a great outcry to include the Comma. His response was that he couldn't find it in any Greek manuscript. If someone would produce a Greek manuscript with the Comma, he declared, he would insert it in his third edition. One such manuscript was soon produced and Erasmus included the Comma in his 1522 edition. It has been there since. That particular manuscript seems to be 61, a copy made in the 15th or 16th century. Erasmus suggested it was made for the purpose of refuting him. Even Scofield in his famous study Bible casts doubt on the passage.

> It is generally agreed that 1Jn 5:7 has no real authority, and has been inserted.

Few of those who reject this passage would be convinced when presented with evidence that it is a genuine Bible reading. Nevertheless, such evidence does indeed exist. Let's approach the question in the manor prescribed by Dean Burgon.

Number, Antiquity, and Variety of 1 John 5:7

Since 1 John 5:7 was dropped (for some reason) from most Greek Manuscripts, we will consider these three things together. There is evidence of the Comma's antiquity and it does exist in a variety of types of evidence. There are a variety of witnesses to the genuineness of the passage: Greek manuscripts, Church fathers, and in the early translations.

We will start with the Greek witnesses. C. H. Pappas tells us:

> The first witnesses that must not be ignored are the Greek manuscripts themselves. This may sound strange, as the Greek manuscripts are often cited as a witness against the Comma. However, at the same time, the Greek manuscripts indisputably bear witness to the Comma. We are told that there are only nine Greek manuscripts that bear witness to the Trinitarian passage. However George Travis in rebuking Gibbon's pointed out that Stephen catalogued 31 Greek manuscripts that bore witness to the disputed passage, (Letters to Edward George

Gibbon, Esq. Forgotten Books p. 285) Hence there are far more Greek Manuscripts that bear witness to 1 John 5:7 than what we are told. [175]

There are only about 500 manuscripts that contain the Book of 1 John. Some of these are in Fragments and many do not contain 1 John 5. Of those that contain 1 john 5, only 11 are dated before the tenth century. Following are eleven of those 31 manuscripts. Notice that some of them include the reading in the margin and included below is a statement by John Gill (1697-1771).

- 629 (14th century)
- 61 (16th century)
- 918 (16th century)
- 2473 (17th century)
- 2318 (18th century)
- 221 margin (10th century)
- 635 margin (11th century)
- 88 margin (12th century)
- 429 margin (14th century)
- 636 margin (15th century)
- 177 margin (11th century) [176]

The evidence of the Greek manuscripts is weak, but it is there, nevertheless. These manuscripts are dated late in history (14th to 17th centuries). However, that does not mean the readings were late. All of these manuscripts were copied from other manuscripts and *no one* knows how far back that goes. The Greek evidence is of late dates, but old dates are not a guarantee of genuineness. A manuscript of any date is genuine if it is an accurate copy of the originals. As we have seen, the oldest manuscript is not necessarily the best.

The passage can also be found in the Old Latin manuscripts. The Old Latin version was translated about 137-150 AD, depending on the scholar you ask. All agree it was an early translation. There are many Old Latin manuscripts, but we only have six that contain 1 John 5. All of them have the Johannine Comma. Latin was the most commonly known language among the Roman Empire countries of

Appendix 2: Problems of the Greek Text

Europe and North Africa. It continued to be a common language for a long time after the Empire collapsed.

> The writer of The *Archon Volume* wrote, "While in Constantinople I found one of these Volumes nicely cased, marked by the Emperor's name (Constantine the Great) and date upon it. To me it was a great curiosity. I got permission with a little bachsach, as they called money, to look through it. It was written on hieotike, which is the finest parchment, in large, bold, Latin characters, quite easy to read…..If the Revision Committee had examined it and published this work, they might have said they were giving the world something new; but so far as we examined it we saw nothing essentially different from our present Bible." What is interesting of this finding, is these two men, Drs. McIntosh and Twyman, in 1887, just six years after the Revised Version was published they had discovered this ancient Old Latin manuscript, dating it back to the time of Constantine the Great. This is the only complete Old Latin manuscript of which the writer is aware. The dating of this manuscript would have to be around AD 325–330. What is of further interest is that men on the Revision Committee had not explored the library in Constantinople while revising the Scripture. Instead they explored the library in Rome! This is indeed interesting. This Old Latin manuscript is said to be essentially the same as our Authorized Version. This is the witness of two separate witnesses. We have the testimony of Drs. McIntosh and Twyman, as well as that of Dr. Frederick Nolan, who was earlier mentioned. They both testified that there is no essential difference in the Old Latin Scriptures and our Authorized Version of the Bible. The Johanneum Comma was in the Latin Scriptures in the Greek Church that predates the oldest manuscript we have in our possession. This Old Latin Manuscript was of Greek origin and thus the same as the Byzantine Text.

And as earlier observed, all of the Old Latin that we have in our possession has the disputed passage of 1 John 5:7. So much for the oldest manuscripts and the verdict of contemporary scholars passed on the Trinitarian passage! [177]

The Latin Vulgate is a witness to the Comma. When Jerome translated the Bible into Latin, starting about 382 AD, the common people rejected it. There was a great outcry over the fact that Jerome had omitted the Comma. Many criticized the Vulgate for numerous errors. It took about 900 years and several persecutions from Rome before the people accepted the Vulgate. They only did that after 1 John 5:7 was added and several other revisions made. Now the vast majority of all the copies of the Latin Vulgate have the Comma. [178] This testifies that the Comma was ingrained in the minds of the Latin speaking churches for many years before Jerome. It would not be in the Latin Versions if it was not translated from Greek.

Other old versions also witness for the Comma. Some say that manuscripts of the Peshitta translation (150 AD) have at least a trace of the Comma. The Old Slavonic of the ninth century has it. And the Waldensian Bible (150-1400 AD) has it.

> Comma. Then there are the Slavic Bibles. These too have the Comma in their translations of the Scriptures. This is not to mention the Russian Bible, which also has the Comma. How did the Comma enter into these translations if it were not in the Greek Bible? After all, these translations were translated from the Greek manuscripts. [179]

Many of the "church fathers" quoted the Comma. Among these are the Latin "Fathers" Tertullian (c. 155-220), Cyprian (c. 200-258), Phoebadius (c. 359), Priscillian (c. 380), Augustine (c. 354-430), Vigilius Tapsensis (c. 450 and 480), Victor Vitensis (c. 485), Fulgentius Ruspensis (died 527), The Greek "Fathers" also made allusions to the Comma including Athenagorus of Athens (c. 177 AD), Origen (C. 184-253), Gregory Nazianzus (c. 329-390), John Chrysostom (c. 349-407), Zacharias Rhetor (born c. 465), Andrew of Crete (born c. 635), John of

Appendix 2: Problems of the Greek Text

Damascus (c. 675-749), Ignatius of Antioch (longer version of writings-4th Century). [180]

1 John 5:7 and Continuity

With this information we can construct a timeline of the evidence to show that the Johannine Comma was known throughout history.

Date	Event or Church Leader
2nd Century	Old Latin translation-Northern Italy
2nd Century	Peshitta Syriac translation
2nd Century	Athenagorus of Athens
3rd Century	Tertullian
3rd Century	Cyprian
3rd Century	Origen
4th Century	Ignatius of Antioch
4th Century	Phoebadius
4th Century	Priscillian
4th Century	Gregory Nazianzus
5th Century	John Chrysostom
5th Century	Augustine
5th Century	Vigilius Tapsensis
5th Century	Victor Vitensis
5th Century	Zacharias Rhetor
5th Century	Council of Carthage referred to it
6th Century	Fulgentius Ruspensis
7th Century	Andrew of Crete
7th-8th Century	John of Damascus
8th Century	Wianburgensis referred to it
9th Century	Latin Vulgate
10th Century	Manuscript 221
11th Century	Manuscript 635
12th Century	Manuscript 88
14th Century	Manuscript 429
15th Century	Manuscript 636
16th Century	Manuscript 61
17th Century	Manuscript 2473

Fig. 27

This historical information proves four things:

1) The Johannine Comma *existed* from the early second century at a minimum,
2) The Comma *was known* throughout history from the second century, less than 50 years after John, the Apostle. It could easily have existed during the life of John, and, of course, it did, because he wrote it.
3) Since most of the evidence consists of quotes and allusions by church ministers and writers, the Comma was not only known, it was *read and used*.
4) The writers used it as the *Word of God*. Therefore, it was considered and accepted to be *Scripture*.

1 John 5:7 and the Church

The Old Testament had its priesthood of Levites descended from Aaron, Moses' brother. There is no such thing in the Church. Rather the entire church is *"a spiritual house, an holy priesthood, a chosen generation, a royal priesthood, an holy nation, a peculiar people"* (1 Peter 2:5, 9). Therefore, it was the body of believers that preserved the New Testament.

> Thus the Holy Spirit guided the early Christians to gather the individual New Testament books into one New Testament canon and to reject all non-canonical books. In the same manner also the Holy Spirit guided the early Christians to preserve the New Testament text by receiving the true readings and rejecting the false. Certainly it would be strange if it were otherwise. [181]

Likewise, the voice of the church was loudly heard in regard to 1 John 5:7.

> The saints in every century, regardless if they were African, Asian, or even European, embraced the

Trinitarian passage without reservation. It was part of their creeds and confessions. It was quoted by the Ante–Nicene Fathers as well as the Post–Nicene Fathers. It was found in their various translations of the Scriptures. All of this indicates, from the earliest dating until 1881, that the Trinitarian passage was never brought into question … [182]

When Jerome left the Comma out, there was an outraged cry to include it. The Vulgate was never accepted by the people for hundreds of years until the Comma was added into it. There was an outcry of the church when Erasmus failed to include the Comma. The voice of the church was ignored by the Revision Committee of the Revised Version, 1881. The voice of the church was ignored by Westcott and Hort. Nestle ignored the church when he followed Westcott and Hort and made his own Greek Text. The UBS ignores the voice of the church today. The voice of the church has been ignored for 138 years since the Revised Version until many Christians are no longer even aware of the issue. Nevertheless, the fight is still raging.

1 John 5:7 and Internal Evidence

When the Comma is left out of the Greek of 1 John 5, there is a serious grammatical problem created. This is a problem strong enough to be a deciding factor. For a discussion of this issue, go back and read the explanation of it in Chapter Eleven.

Why was 1 John 5:7 Removed from the Greek NT?

The Comma is not the majority reading in the Greek manuscripts. However, this does not mean it is a false reading. As we have seen it is strongly attested in the Latin manuscripts and in the Ancient church writings. Nevertheless, we would expect to find it in the Greek manuscripts as well, but we do not, except for a few. Since the Latin Itala version was translated from the Greek New Testament and it has the Comma, how did it disappear from the majority of Greek manuscripts? This is a question we must ask and the answer is in history. There are several historical events that contributed to this situation and the present controversy.

The first event was the imperial Roman persecution that began in 303 AD under Diocletian. I gave a description of this in chapter eleven. Suffice it to say that by the end of the persecution in 312 AD there were few copies of the NT in **Greek** that were not destroyed. What I did not mention is that the Christians of Northern Italy fled into the mountains of north Italy, and they took their Latin copies with them. There they could hide and preserve their Scriptures. Most of the copies of the Old Latin we have were found in northern Italy.

The second event was the ascent of Constantine to the position of Emperor. He issued the Edict of toleration in 313 AD. He went on to become recognized as the head of the church. When he called the bishops of the Empire to Nicea to deal with the Arian controversy in 325 AD, he presided over the bishops as head of the council. This was the time when the churches married the world. It was the real beginning of the Roman Catholic Church. One of Constantine's titles was *Pontifex Maximus*, just as the Pope is called today.

The third event was the Arian controversy and the Council of Nicaea. Arians are said to have believed that Jesus was a begotten God of different substance than the Father. Therefore, He was lesser than the Father. The champion of this doctrine was named Arius (c. 256-336). He seems to have been most popular in Syria, Palestine, and Egypt. Others, including Alexander and Athanasius of Alexandria, disagreed with him and believed that Jesus was equal with God, the Father. It became such a problem that the Council of Nicaea was called by Constantine to deal with it. The Anti-Arian faction prevailed at the council, but Arianism did not go away.

The fourth event was the commission Constantine gave Eusebius, Bishop of Caesarea, in 331 AD to supply fifty Bibles. These Bibles had to be hand copied and were, no doubt, written on parchment. Eusebius turned to the library at Caesarea for the materials to produce the Bibles. Remember, at this time there were few Bibles left because of the Imperial persecution from 303-312. So, Eusebius was called on to provide these Bibles. Eusebius was a disciple of Origen, who had started the library in Caesarea. Origin taught that God had begotten Jesus in eternity past and Eusebius agreed. It is possible that Vaticanus is connected to the fifty Bibles. Some believe it to be one of them or it may be a copy of one of them. If so, then the fifty Bibles left out 1 John 5:7, because Vaticanus does. The fault for this can be traced directly to Adamantius Origen of Alexandria and Caesarea. Both Origen and Eusebius were Arians or semi-Arians.

The fifth historical matter is the growth of Arianism. At the Council of Nicaea, Eusebius of Nicomedia (a different Eusebius) defended Arius, since he was an Arian himself. However, he signed the confession at the council in hand, but not in heart. Constantine was angry with him for his defense of Arius, so he was banished along with Arius. Eusebius was a kinsman with the Emperor and this may have helped him win recall and a renewal of Imperial favor from Constantine. Arius was also recalled. Eusebius became Patriarch of Constantinople. He used the power and tools of government to impose his Arian views on the churches. With the promotion of Eusebius, many other Arian Bishops were promoted and the influence of Arianism spread. This proceeded to the point that Athanasius was falsely accused and exiled. Arius was appointed to take Athanasius' place in Alexandria, but the people rejected him. C. H. Pappas explains further.

> The war over the deity of our Lord was quite apparent, as there were strong debates between the Arians and Gregory of Nazianzus, who in AD 379 was appointed bishop in Constantinople. Up to this time, the Arians held the upper hand in supplying copies of the New Testament to the churches. They were the ones who were supported out of the emperor's coffers. The true church was in desperate need of the Scriptures. They also lacked the financial support the Arians had to produce copies of the Word of God. Furthermore, the copies they produced were upon inferior materials, such as papyrus which had a very short shelf life, especially with use. Not only were the Orthodox bishops without support, but they were also persecuted by these Arian emperors. Therefore, it should not be surprising that the Comma is not as

pronounced as we would like it in the early Greek manuscripts. [183]

Constantine died in 337. Just prior to his death, Eusebius of Nicomedia baptized him. Constantine's son, Constantius II, was convinced by Eusebius to attempt to convert all of Christianity to Arian views. [184] "It was because of Eusebius that 'On the whole, Constantine and his successors made life pretty miserable for Church leaders committed to the Nicene decision and its Trinitarian formula.'" [185]

In 378 AD Orthodoxy began to take the upper hand. An orthodox Emperor, Gratian, came to the throne and appointed an orthodox emperor in the Eastern provinces, Theodosius. Gregory Nazianzus was appointed Patriarch of Constantinople in 379 and the tide began to turn. There were still a lot of hard battles, though. By this time, most of the Bishops of the Greek Church were Arians and Gregory's church was small. Gregory did a great work in Constantinople and the Comma was restored to some of the Greek copies, but it took another two centuries to thoroughly defeat Arianism. Up to this point most Greek manuscripts omitted the Comma. Why 1 John 5:7? The Comma was not the only verse that was attacked, but the Comma is the premier statement of the Trinity in the New Testament. Other verses also affected by this history were John 1:18 and 1 Timothy 3:16.

2. The "Only Begotten God" – John 1:18

The next two issues involve the use of the term "only begotten" and two verses where it is used. In the first one, the argument is not the phrase "only begotten," but it is about *what* is begotten. The King James says it is the "son" that is begotten. The UBS text, Vaticanus, and Sinaiticus say "only begotten god."

Arianism teaches that the Lord Jesus is a god that was created by God the Father as the first act of creation. Yes, He is God, but He is of different substance than the Father and is less than and subordinate to God the Father. It is a form of denial of Jesus' divinity. I restate this, because John 1:18 is another passage affected by this belief.

Appendix 2: Problems of the Greek Text

In 381, the creed of the Council of Constantinople was formulated. It was based on the Nicene Creed, but it added a phrase in regard to the Lord Jesus. It stated that Jesus was "begotten of the Father *before all worlds."* This statement was doubtless an attempt to completely destroy Arianism and to clarify the doctrine of the trinity. However, it introduced an additional heresy that was not even recognized by the Reformers. The 1646 Westminster confession of faith says that Jesus, the Son, was "eternally begotten of the Father." To be "eternally begotten" means begotten in eternity past. The heresy in this is that "begotten" means that the Son had a beginning and, if so, He is not eternal. Therefore, He is not equal to God, the Father. John 1:18 was likely changed in the background of the Arian controversy and the change in the Nicene Creed. The phrase "only begotten god" implies God had a beginning and can only refer to the Lord Jesus.

The phrase "only begotten God" has little manuscript evidence behind it. According to the critical apparatus in the UBS Greek text, it is seen in P66, P75, Vaticanus, Sinaiticus, three other manuscripts (C and L), one Syriac manuscript and the margin of another, a Coptic manuscript, a Georgian manuscript, Origen (in two places out of four), Cyril, and seven other church "fathers."

Next to that, the evidence in favor of "only begotten Son" is overwhelming. The entire Byzantine or Traditional Text includes it. Everything in Chapter eleven that was said about the Traditional text is true for "only begotten Son."

Whether you accept "God" or "son" in John 1:18, depends on whether you believe in the Trinity or not.

When was Jesus Begotten?

Begetting implies a beginning. Those who teach the "eternal begetting of Christ" may say it does not mean a beginning, but that He always existed as the Son. Really? The Bible teaches otherwise. See Psalms 2:7.

> *I will declare the decree: the LORD hath said unto me,*
> *Thou art my Son; this day have I begotten thee.*

The phrase "eternally begotten" is never used in Scripture. That phrase is not simple to understand, but when one takes the Scriptures simply for what they say, *they* are easy to understand. The phrase, "eternally begotten," is NOT a Bible phrase. It is man-made. Psalm 2:7 helps make the truth clear. The begetting is not an eternal *condition*, it is an *action* of God at a *single point*. That point is described as a *day*. As a day, the action of God in begetting the Son could not have taken place in eternity. *There are no days in eternity* (Gen. 1:3-5).

So, when *did* God beget the Son?

Then said Mary unto the angel, How shall this be, seeing I know not a man? And the angel answered and said unto her, The Holy Ghost shall come upon thee, and the power of the Highest shall overshadow thee: **therefore also that holy thing which shall be born of thee shall be called the Son of God.**
(Luke 1:34-35)

The begetting took place in connection with the virgin birth of Christ. The begetting is why a virgin could bare a son. The begetting has to do with how "the Word was made flesh, and dwelt among us" (Jn. 1:14). It has to do with how "God was manifest in the flesh" (1 Tim. 3:16). It is *because* of this begetting that Jesus "shall be called the Son of God." In eternity past, it seems He was not called the Son, but He was the Word (John 1:1; 1 John 5:7). He is the only person in all of history who experienced this kind of begetting, and therefore, He is the *only begotten* Son of God.

Does this mean that Jesus is not God and that the trinity is not true? Of course, it doesn't. It means that the Word existed in eternity as one with the Father and the Spirit; co-eternal, and equal. Then, in time, on a day, the Word was begotten of the virgin as the man, Jesus. So, Jesus is fully man and fully God at the same time. He is the Son of God.

In the context of John 1:18 and the rest of Scripture, "only begotten Son" is the only phrase that makes sense. The virgin birth is the only time God had a son come into the world through a physical birth that was the result of a miracle. The Word "begotten" is the only accurate way to describe Jesus' birth.

Appendix 2: Problems of the Greek Text

3. **Only begotten, Only, or Unique? John 3:16**

The Greek word translated "only begotten" is *monogenes*. The big question is: *what does monogenes really mean*? The NIV translates it "one and only." The New American Standard translates it "only begotten," but has a footnote that tells us it could mean unique, only one of His kind. The ESV simply says "only." The Christian Standard Bible agrees with the NIV as does the Holman Christian Standard Bible. The CEV says "only." The Message tells us it is "one and only." Something called The Passion Translation doubles down with "one and only, unique." They all seem to be arrayed in battle formation against the King James; *anything,* except "only begotten."

Add to this, the fact that the KJB translates the word differently in different contexts. When Jesus came to the city of Nain, he saw a dead man being carried to his burial. He raised the man, who, the KJB tells us, was the "only" son of his mother. The word "only" is *monogenes* (Lk. 7:11-13). Another time, a man had a son who was possessed by a devil. He came to Jesus to get his son delivered and he called his son his "only child" (Lk. 9:38). Again, the Greek word is *monogenes*. So, are the modern versions right, that it should be only, one and only, or unique in John 3:16?

Before we look at Greek definitions, it is imperative to point out a serious doctrinal problem. Any translation that calls the Lord Jesus the "only" or the "one and only" son of God has created a heretical contradiction in Scripture. Jesus is NOT the ONLY son of God. He definitely is NOT the ONE AND ONLY son of God. If we are saved, we are *born again* by the Spirit of God (Jn. 3:1-5) and the result is described below.

> *14 For as many as are led by the Spirit of God,* **they are the sons of God.**
> *15 For ye have not received the spirit of bondage again to fear; but ye have received the Spirit of adoption, whereby we cry,* **Abba, Father.**
> *16 The Spirit itself beareth witness with our spirit, that we are the* **children of God** (Romans 8:14-16).

> *1 Behold, what manner of love the Father hath bestowed upon us, **that we should be called the sons of God:** therefore the world knoweth us not, because it knew him not.*
> *2 Beloved, **now are we the sons of God**, and it doth not yet appear what we shall be: but we know that, when he shall appear, we shall be like him; for we shall see him as he is.*

The other translations listed above either say "children" or "sons" in these verses. According to them, there is only one son of God (John 3:16). Yet, at the same time, Christians are all sons of God by faith. Now hold on a minute! Which is it? Is there one and only one son of God, or are there many? The new versions are trying to have it both ways. This is a *real* contradiction and a serious one.

Now let's look at definitions. The Greek word *monogenes* is a combination of two words *mono* and *genos*. Mono means "only." Genos means:

> **Genos:** "γένος, eos, ovs, ré (γίνουαι), genus, race, i.e. a) offspring, posterity, Acts 17.28. b) family, lineage, stock, Acts 7. 13; so 4.6 ... c) nation, people, Mark 7, 26. d) kind, sort, species, Matt. 13.47." [186]

> **Monogenes:** "μονογενης ... (μονος, γενος), only-born, only-begotten, i.e. only child, Luke 7. 12 ... 8.42, 9, 38, Heb. 11. 17: in John's writings spoken only of ο λογος, the only-begotten Son of God in the highest sense, as alone knowing and revealing the essence of the Father, John 1: 14, 18, 3. 16, 18, 1 John 4.9,-where others, by impl., most dear, only-beloved." [187]

So, based on these definitions, one can say "only son" or "only child," just as the King James did in Luke 7 and 9 and other places. When referring to a human parent child relationship, translating the word that way is sufficient, but it still means that the parent has no other sons or daughters, whichever is the subject. If a man or woman had an only son as in Luke 7 and 9, he or she had *no*

Appendix 2: Problems of the Greek Text

other sons. If a man had only one daughter as in Luke 8:42, then he had *no other daughters*. This is not the case with the Lord Jesus. There are other sons of God. So, His birth needs to be characterized in a way that makes it stand out from all other births.

When it comes to the Lord Jesus, He was the Son of God in a way that no one else could have been. He was truly unique, but to translate *monogenes* as simply "unique" is not enough to express how different His birth truly was. Besides, *monogenes* does not mean *unique* according to the lexicon. To merely say He is *unique* is a massive understatement. The Old Testament says, "Thou art my Son, this day have I **begotten** thee." The Hebrew word for begotten is *yâlad.*

> A verb meaning to give birth, to beget, to deliver. It is commonly used of women bearing children (Gen 3:16) as well as animals who brought forth young (Gen 30:39). In the case of birds, it may refer to the laying or production of eggs (Jer 17:11). In a more general sense, it is used of men becoming the father of children (Gen 4:18). [188]

> **BEGOT', BEGOT'TEN**, pp. of get. Procreated; generated. [189]

The Hebrew word in Psalms 2:7 has to do with *physical* child birth. It matches the definition of *begotten* in English. Therefore, it is the proper word to use in Psalm 2. That verse in the Old Testament is a prophecy of the virgin birth, which was a birth unlike any other that ever happened in the history of the world. "Begotten" is a worthy word to use to describe it. Since it was the word used in the Old Testament for the prophecy, the word used in the New Testament should be the same word, so that there is a connection. It points to the miracle of the virgin birth and it matches the OT prophecy. When we see the word "begotten" in the New Testament, we should be reminded of the prophecy of Psalm 2. If we are spiritually discerning, we will connect that with Luke 1:35, where the miracle of the virgin birth is described and is said to be the **reason** Jesus is called the Son of God. Jesus Christ is the only son God ever physically begat. *The*

Lord Jesus Christ is the only begotten Son of God, and God manifest in the flesh.

4. Mark 16:9-20

Modern scholars have decided that the traditional ending of Mark in verses 19-20 is not a genuine part of the Scriptures. Many of the modern English versions leave these verses in the translation, but add a note casting doubt on the legitimacy of the passage. Even the New King James has a note that says, "Vv. 9–20 are bracketed in NU as not in the original text. They are lacking in Codex Sinaiticus and Codex Vaticanus, although nearly all other mss. of Mark contain them." The initials NU refer to the Nestle-Aland Greek Text (N) and the United Bible Societies Greek Text (U). The two have an identical text and they both reject Mark 16:19-20.

> Mark 16:9-20 has been called a *later addition* to the Gospel of Mark by most New Testament scholars in the past century. The main reason for doubting the authenticity of the ending is that it does not appear in some of the oldest existing witnesses, and it is reported to be absent from many others in ancient times by early writers of the Church. Moreover, the ending has some stylistic features which also suggest that it came from another hand. The Gospel is obviously incomplete without these verses, and so most scholars believe that the final leaf of the original manuscript was lost, and that the ending which appears in English versions today (verses 9-20) was supplied during the second century. [190]

The accusation of inconsistent internal evidence is mainly a matter of opinion. It is said, Mark treats Mary Magdalene as if she had not been mentioned before in verse 9 and the writer used non-Markon vocabulary and grammar. No, siree! That ain't the case. That don't make no never mind. In verse 9, Mark was talkin' 'bout the incident described in John 20:1-2, when Mary came to the tomb before the other women while it was still dark. However, if I were to cogitate reasonably on that intense state of affairs with a cognitive, rational, theoretical, or logical technique, I would have to reject that theory.

Appendix 2: Problems of the Greek Text

Oh! Excuse me! *I just used some words and grammar in this paragraph that I have not used in the entire book.* I used very non-Combsian words and grammar. **I must not have written the previous paragraph** (if I am to believe the twisted imaginations of the scholars). This so called internal evidence is nothing more than *opinion*.

In general there was no problem with Mark 16:9-20 from the publication of the Received Text (1516) until the scholars of the 1800's began to question it. They questioned it primarily because it is missing in Vaticanus and Sinaiticus. After all, they reasoned, these are the oldest manuscripts we have. I find it extremely interesting that both Vaticanus and Sinaiticus leave a large blank space following Mark 16:8. Clearly something had been in that space and was erased in Vaticanus and Sinaiticus. A column and one half was left blank in Vaticanus. Some space after the end of a book was normal. However, this is the only time the writer of Vaticanus left a whole column blank. The space left blank was the exact size needed to include verses 9-20.

External Evidence Against Mark 16:9-20

External evidence has to do with the number, age, and variety of the manuscript evidence. The major evidence is the Vaticanus and Sinaiticus manuscripts, which the scholars date at 325-350 AD. In chapter ten, I gave evidence that they cannot be any older than about 450 AD. Besides these two there is one other ninth century manuscript, designated 130, that omits the ending. There are also four versions that have at least one manuscript omitting the ending and dating back to the third century. Four of the early church fathers questioned its genuineness. One of these was Eusebius of Caesarea and the others merely repeated what he said. This is all the evidence listed in the critical apparatus of the United Bible Societies Greek Text.

There is a short ending in one Latin manuscript. That ending says, "And all that had been commanded them they told briefly to those around Peter. And afterward Jesus himself sent out through them, from east to west, the sacred and imperishable proclamation of eternal salvation. Amen" [191] Only one Latin manuscript has this ending alone. In addition, six Greek manuscripts and at least one manuscript in each of three versions have both endings. The UBS text has both endings also and casts doubt on both of them in the notes.

External Evidence in Favor of Mark 16:9-20

Once again, the manuscript evidence in favor of Mark 16:9-20 is over whelming in comparison to the evidence for omitting it. The ending is found in 99% if all Greek manuscripts and translations. It is found in the majority of manuscripts in each of the major text types: Western, Alexandrian, and Traditional. It is found in the church writers from all over the Mediterranean world: Irenaeus, Asterius, Didymus, Epiphanius, Marcus–Eremita, Severian, Nestorius, Ambrose, and Augustine. It is found in the Apostolic Constitutions. This evidence dates back to the second century, it has the overwhelming number of manuscripts, and it has a variety of kinds of evidence (Greek manuscripts, ancient translations, and "fathers"), and it is found in diverse geographic locations.

The comments of Eusebius of Caesarea do not necessarily mean that most copies of Mark do not include 16:9-20. These are the comments of Eusebius in his Epistle to Marinus.

> He who is for getting rid of the entire passage will say that it is not met with in all the copies of Mark's Gospel: the accurate copies at all events *circumscribe the end* of Mark's narrative at the words of the young man who appeared to the women and said, 'Fear not ye! Ye seek Jesus of Nazareth,' etc.: to which the Evangelist adds, 'And when they heard it, they fled, and said nothing to any man, for they were afraid.' For at these words, in almost all copies of the Gospel according to Mark, *the end has been circumscribed.* What follows, (which is met with seldom, and only in some copies, certainly not in all,) might be dispensed with.
>
> But another, on no account daring to reject anything whatever which is, under whatever circumstance, met with in the text of the Gospels, will say that here are two readings (as is so often the case elsewhere;) and that *both* are to be received,

inasmuch as by the faithful and pious, *this* reading is not held to be genuine rather than *that* nor *that* than *this*. [192]

This sounds, at first look, that Eusebius was saying that the accurate copies ended Mark at verse 16:8, but his second paragraph says that this is not necessarily so. Dr. Edward Hills explains.

> Critics also have interpreted Eusebius as stating that "the accurate copies" and "almost all copies" end Mark's Gospel at 16:8. But Burgon pointed out that Eusebius doesn't say this. Eusebius says that the accurate copies *circumscribe the end* at 16:8 and that in almost all copies *the end has been circumscribed* at this point. What did Eusebius mean by this unusual expression? Burgan's explanation seems to be the only possible one.
>
> Burgon reminded his readers that it was customary, at least in the later manuscript period, to indicate in the New Testament manuscripts the beginning and the end of the Scripture lesson appointed to be read in the worship services of the Church. The beginning of the Scripture lesson was marked by the word beginning (Greek *arche)*, written in the margin of the manuscript, and the end of the reading by the word *end* (Greek *telos)*, written in the text. Burgon argued that this practice began very early and that it was this to which Eusebius was referring when he said that the most accurate copies and almost all copies *circumscribe the end* at Mark 16:8. Eusebius was not talking about the end of the Gospel of Mark but about the liturgical sign indicating the end of a Scripture lesson. He is simply saying that this liturgical sign *end (telos)* was present after Mark 16:8 in many of the manuscripts known to him. [193]

Internal Evidence

There are several considerations regarding the wording of the last twelve verses of Mark. As I previously mentioned, some have said that the style and words of this passage are different than the rest of the book. Metzger said that seventeen non-Markon words were used or used in a non-Markon way. [194] I hope my illustration before in that regard was sufficient to make the point that any writer may and is certainly allowed to vary his style in different parts of his writing. In that illustration, I used some very non-Combsian words. Yet, I wrote it. The well-known nineteenth century scholar, Tregelles, said "that arguments on *style* are often very fallacious, and that by themselves they prove very little." [195] The subject matter of Mark 16:9-20 is different than at any other place in the book, so it is natural that you may find unique words. There is nothing strange in that and it certainly does not automatically mean it is not genuine.

There several other notable things about the passage in favor of its genuineness.

Mark would never have ended his gospel on a note of fear. All the other gospels end with triumph and power, not fear. "All power is given unto me ..." (Mt. 28:19), "And were continually in the temple, praising and blessing God. Amen" (Lk. 24:53), and " there are also many other things which Jesus did, the which, if they should be written every one, I suppose that even the world itself could not contain the books that should be written. Amen" (Jn. 21:25). Compare that with "neither said they any thing to any man; for they were afraid" (Mk. 16:8). God inspired all Scripture. There isn't any possibility that God would have left Mark to end at verse 16:8).

Without verses 9-20, there are no descriptions of the Lord's appearances after the resurrection. All three other gospels, under the inspiration of the Holy Spirit, included a triumphal depiction of the resurrection and the appearances afterward (Mt. 28; Lk. 24; Jn. 20-21). The resurrection of the Lord Jesus is an absolutely necessary part of the gospel and the witnesses were necessary to confirm it (1 Cor. 15:1-5; Rom. 10:9-11).

Mark 16:9-20 describes several appearances of the Lord after His resurrection, consistent with the other Gospels. These include the appearance to Mary Magdalene (Mk. 16:9; Jn. 20:1-2, 11-14), two on the road to Emmaus (Mk. 16:12; Lk. 24:13-16), an appearance to the eleven (Mk. 16:14; Lk. 24:33-49). These are consistent with Mark's quick way of going from one story to the next. His gospel has the shortest number of chapters of them all.

Appendix 2: Problems of the Greek Text

Every other gospel is ended with a command to teach and preach. "Go ye therefore, and teach all nations" (Mt, 28:19), "thus it behoved Christ to suffer, and to rise from the dead the third day: And that repentance and remission of sins should be preached in his name among all nations, beginning at Jerusalem" (Lk. 24:46-47), and "Peace be unto you: as my Father hath sent me, even so send I you" (Jn. 20:21). However, if Mark ends with verse 16:8, we have no command to preach the gospel, but, rather, we have the witnesses of the resurrection cowering in fear.

The list of the signs that will follow believers is consistent with events in the book of acts. The signs include casting out devils (v. 17; Acts 16), speaking with tongues (v. 7; Acts 2, 10, 19), handling poisonous serpents (v. 18; Acts 28:3-7), heal the sick (v. 18; Acts 3, 14). Only drinking deadly things (v. 18) does not have an example in the book of Acts. However, it is clear that the Apostles in particular were given signs they could perform. "Truly the signs of an apostle were wrought among you in all patience, in signs, and wonders, and mighty deeds" (2 Cor. 12:12). Mark 16 does not say these signs would follow believers throughout the Church-Age. It says that the signs were for the purpose of confirming the preached word (v. 20). After the New Testament was complete, they were no longer needed. Mark 16 also does not say that we need to risk our lives by deliberately handling deadly snakes, putting on some vain show. Doing that is not spiritual or obedient. It is a carnal performance and outside the truth revealed in Mark 16.

God LOST It?

The final conclusion some scholars have come to is 1) Mark 16:9-20 is not genuine and 2) that the true ending of Mark has been lost. I can come to only one conclusion about those who say this. *They do not believe in the preservation of Scripture*. They couldn't. What they are saying is that God lost the ending of Mark and He did not preserve it, contrary to His promise of preservation. Anything, but believe what God has said. To me this makes them liberal in their thinking, no matter how conservative they profess to be.

There is no commanding reason to believe that Mark 16:9-20 is not a genuine part of Scripture. There is so little evidence for omitting the passage as to make it insignificant in the extreme. The vastly overwhelming evidence is on the side of including Mark 16:9-20 and accepting it as genuine. The internal evidence is consistent with the other gospels. The short ending was embraced by only one manuscripts and a very few other manuscripts to include it along with the long ending. This only emphasizes the truth that the long ending existed for a long time in the manuscript tradition. The manuscript tradition includes the Alexandrian Text, the Traditional Text (Byzantine), and the Western Text. The scholars have created another text family called Caesarean and that also is overwhelmingly in favor of Mark 16:9-20. The contents of the passage are consistent with the rest of the New Testament.

The conclusion of the matter is that Mark 16:9-20 is genuine Scripture.

5. Romans 8:1 No Condemnation

There is therefore now no condemnation to them which are in Christ Jesus, who walk not after the flesh, but after the Spirit. (Rom. 8:1)

Modern scholarship has rejected the second half of this verse. The phrase "who walk not after the flesh, but after the Spirit" is considered not to be a genuine part of Scripture. After all, it is not true that we have to walk after the Spirit to avoid condemnation. We are free from condemnation simply because we have believed. Right? Therefore, this half of the verse was added by some errant scribe.

> **There is therefore now no condemnation to them which are in Christ Jesus.** (The additional words of this verse in the Textus Receptus have but slight support, having probably been supplied from Rom 8:4. They are out of place here.) [196]
>
> **Who do not walk according to the flesh, but according to the Spirit**: These words are not found in the earliest ancient manuscripts of the Book of Romans and they do not agree with the flow of Paul's context here. There were probably added by a copyist who either made a mistake or thought he

could "help" Paul by bringing in these words from Rom 8:4. [197]

External Evidence for Omission

As it most of the criticisms of the Received Text, this omission is mostly because Sinaiticus and Vaticanus omit it. Nothing else is needed, it seems. These two manuscripts are held up as the supreme authority. Yet, when God began his great work of reformation in 1516-17, he completely ignored both of them. God wasn't interested in them. They were no authority to Him. He gave us what He wanted us to have and it included these disputed words.

The manuscript evidence for omission includes the following, according the compilation of the United Bible Societies.

1. **Six** Uncial Greek Manuscripts including Vaticanus and Sinaiticus.
2. **Five** minuscule Greek manuscripts.
3. **Four** Old Latin manuscripts dating back to the fifth century.
4. It is out in two Coptic (Egyptian) translations (out of eight), the Bohairic and Sahidic, both from the third century.
5. The fifth century Armenian version.
6. The Georgian version of the sixth century.
7. The Ethiopic Version, but apparently the difference is negligible.
8. The following teachers: Marcion (the heretic), Origen, Athanasius, Diodore, Didymus, Cyril, Ambrosiaster, and Augustine. Apparently, these men did not quote the entire verse.

External Evidence for Inclusion

As in our last example, the vast majority of evidence favors inclusion of the last half of the verse.

1. The second corrector of Sinaiticus and the first and second corrector of D plus two other uncials (A and Ψ) support the TR reading.

2. The entire Traditional, Byzantine Text of all three families support the TR reading. That includes an overwhelming number of manuscripts. The UBS apparatus also lists nineteen specific minuscules.
3. The majority of lectionaries.
4. Several Old Latin manuscripts are listed, two of them as correctors to the text. In the UBS eighteen Old Latin manuscripts which have the Pauline Epistles are listed in the introductory material. Only seven are given as evidence for or against Romans 8:1. The other eleven are ignored.
5. Other ancient versions in support of the TR reading are the Vulgate, the Syriac Peshitta, the Harclean Syriac, the Gothic Version, and part of the Armenian version, part of the Georgian, and the Slavic.
5. The following church "fathers:" Victorinus-Rome, Jerome, Pelagius, Speculum, and Chrysostom.

About seventeen manuscripts in the above lists of evidence for inclusion omit the last four words of the text. However, they still constitute evidence that there is more to the verse than modern scholars will permit.

A word about the ancient church writers should be made here. If a writer is included among those who did not quote any of the last half of the verse or the last four words, it means something very important. *It means they did not quote it. It does not necessarily mean they rejected it.* In the course of this work, I have quoted a great many verses of Scripture. I have NOT always quoted the entire verse. Sometimes, I have quoted only the portion of the verse which most helps me make the point. You will see that also in some of what I have written about context below. When I do that, it certainly does NOT mean I reject the rest of the verse. It simply means I had a reason for not quoting it.

The evidence for omitting the disputed words may seem impressive. However, the primary reason for rejecting half the verse is that it is not included in the original text of Vaticanus and Sinaiticus. Those two manuscripts, out of over 5,700 manuscripts, are the authority for modern textual scholars. Once again, the evidence for inclusion is overwhelming in number. That evidence dates back to

150 AD and it come from a large variety of manuscripts from a widespread geographical area. There was no serious question about the verse until Westcott and Hort and several other nineteenth century scholars began to promote liberal theology and thinking in England.

The Internal Context

Sadly, those who reject the last half of the verse (Rom. 8:1) do not understand the context or do not consider it to be important. In reality, one can fight my manuscript against yours, but in this case, the context is the key.

Romans 8 starts out with no condemnation to those in Christ, who walk not after the flesh, but after the Spirit. Is there condemnation then for a Christian, who walks according to the flesh? Paul had already said. "I know that in me (that is, in my flesh,) dwelleth no good thing" (Rom. 7:18) and he called it "the body of this death" (Rom. 7:24). Romans 8:2 says, "For the law of the Spirit of life in Christ Jesus hath made me free from the law of sin and death." The Spirit brings life, but sin brings death as Romans 6:23 says. What is the law of sin and death? Romans 8:13 gives us the answer: "For if ye live after the flesh, ye shall die."

The matter of eternal salvation is a settled issue for a believer. There is no eternal condemnation. However, there is the possibility of *temporal condemnation* to a Christian who fails to walk in obedience to God. Paul cites an example of this when some of the Corinthian believers were abusing the Lord's Supper: "For he that eateth and drinketh unworthily, eateth and drinketh **damnation to himself**, not discerning the Lord's body. *For this cause many are weak and sickly among you, and many **sleep***" (1 Cor. 11:29-30). "Sleep" refers to death. Being weak, sickly, and sleep are part of the Lord's chastening (Heb. 12:5-13).

What is the law of the Spirit of life (v. 2)? Once again this is defined in Roman 8:13: "if ye through the Spirit do mortify the deeds of the body, ye shall live." To "live after the flesh" (v. 13) equals "walk after the flesh" (v. 1). To "mortify the deeds of the body" (v. 13) equals walk "after the Spirit" (v. 1).

This brings us to our major concern. Given the conflict described in Romans seven, how do we "mortify the deeds of the body?" Galatians 5:16 says, "Walk in the Spirit, and ye shall not fulfill the lust of the flesh." The word "mortify" (Rom. 8:13) means "to subdue or bring into subjection." [198] Romans chapter eight has some principles that help us do that.

The first principle is that Christ fulfills the law in us (v. 3-4). Righteousness cannot be fulfilled through the Law. The Law demands righteousness, but it offers no power with which to fulfill its requirements. The Law is weak because the flesh is weak and cannot perfectly obey it. In fact, as we saw in Romans seven, the flesh is opposed to the Law in favor of fulfilling its own lusts. There is only one way the righteousness of the Law can be fulfilled by us. That is because Christ dwells in us. One of the great mysteries of the faith is how that Christ lives in us. The Lord Jesus Christ comes with all his wisdom and strength. "But of him are ye in Christ Jesus, who of God is made unto us wisdom, and righteousness, and sanctification, and redemption: That, according as it is written, He that glorieth, let him glory in the Lord" (1 Cor. 1:30-31). "I can do all things through Christ which strengtheneth me" (Phil. 4:13).

The second principal is the importance of the mind. Romans 8:5 says, "For they that are after the flesh do mind the things of the flesh; but they that are after the Spirit the things of the Spirit. For to be carnally minded is death; but to be spiritually minded is life and peace." We will be either carnally minded or spiritually minded. Those who are seeking to walk in the Spirit are also seeking to be spiritually minded. What a person is depends largely on what his heart's attitudes are centered on and how he thinks. "For as he thinketh in his heart, so is he" (Prov. 23:7). Jesus said that the greatest commandment was to "love the Lord thy God with all thy heart, and with all thy soul, and with all thy *mind*, and with all thy strength" (Mark 12:30). It is certainly a good idea to pray that you will love God like this.

The third principle is that we have the assurance of our special identity in Christ and of a certain and bright hope for the future. There are three distinct promises and several important truths in Romans 8:10-16. One of these promises is unconditional, but you can only have one of the other two. They are dependent on certain conditions. Verse 13 let's you choose either life or death. Verse 11 is the promise of the resurrection.

Fourth, to mortify the deeds of the flesh is a command and a responsibility. It cannot be done without the Spirit's help, but it is our responsibility to do it. Some say, "Let go and let God." However, in this regard, we depend fully on God, but we must face the conflict and fight it. Others say, "Stop trying and start trusting." We must trust, but keep on trying. It is not one or the other.

The fifth principle is to have conviction. We must be convinced that holiness and obedience is necessary and important. We must be convicted that it is God's will for us.

The sixth principle to mortify the deeds of the flesh is to have Commitment. "So likewise, whosoever he be of you that forsaketh not all that he hath, he cannot be my disciple" (Luke 14:33).

The seventh principle is to exercise personal discipline. Discipline or self-control (called "temperance") is a fruit of the Holy Spirit (Gal. 5:22-23).

All of this and more grows out of the context of Romans 7 and 8. The context, in a nut-shell, is that the Christian engages in a great battle within himself daily. He still has an old nature in his flesh that moves him to sin, yet the Spirit of God within moves him to righteousness. Without some help he will lose the battle with the law of sin and death. The answer is to learn to walk after the Spirit, not after the flesh. Romans 8 was written to give him the principles to do that.

Romans 8:1 makes NO SENSE IN THE CONTEXT without the last half of the verse.

6. 1 Timothy 3:16 God Manifest in the Flesh

And without controversy great is the mystery of godliness: God was manifest in the flesh, justified in the Spirit, seen of angels, preached unto the Gentiles, believed on in the world, received up into glory.

The dispute in this verse is about one single word: "God." The TR Greek word is the normal Greek word for God, *theos*. The UBS Greek Text substitutes the word *Os*. A few manuscripts have simply "o." Two manuscripts have *os theos*. The majority, of course, have *theos*. The word *os* is a pronoun and makes the verse read "he was manifest in the flesh." This strips the teaching of Christ's divinity out of the verse.

A Summary of the External Evidence

The evidence in favor of Os: There are five uncials (including Vaticanus, Sinaiticus, and Alexandrinus), four minuscules, the Ethiopic version, and six writers including Origen in the Latin copies.

The evidence in favor of theos: This includes the second corrector of three uncials including Sinaiticus, the corrector of Alexandrinus, plus one more uncial. There are eighteen specific minuscules and the entire Traditional/ Byzantine tradition in support of *theos*. Also included are the majority of the lectionaries, at least one Vulgate manuscript, the second corrector of the Georgian version, the Slavic, and seven writers. Once again, the vast majority of all manuscripts support the word *theos*.

There are even more reasons to believe that 1 Timothy 3:16 reads "God" rather than "who."

A Possible Cause for the Change from Theos to Os

The earliest semi-complete manuscripts were written in capital letters and are called uncial manuscripts. In those manuscripts the name of God, *theos*, was usually abbreviated. The abbreviation for *theos* and the word *Os* are very similar in Greek. The Greek abbreviation for God's name ΘΕΟΣ equals ΘΣ. Observe the difference in Greek between the abbreviation for *theos* and the word *os*:

$$\overline{\text{ΘΣ}} - \text{ΟΣ}$$

The only difference between the two is the line inside the first letter and the line above ΘΣ. These lines could have easily been dropped accidentally. They may have faded with time in some cases. They could have worn off with use. They could even have been deliberately dropped or erased. The same historical conditions that caused 1 John 5:7 to be removed from manuscripts could have affected 1Timothy 3:16. If any of these conditions existed, the scribe who copied the manuscript could have mistaken the ΘΣ to be ΟΣ.

This appears to be what happened to the Alexandrinus manuscript, which the UBS apparatus puts into the "who" column.

Appendix 2: Problems of the Greek Text

There is considerable testimony that the original reading in Alexandrinus was "God."

> The passage has been examined so many times that the parchment is worn away, rendering its present evidence doubtful, but we may refer to the weighty opinions of those who had the copy in their hands long ago. They agreed that it supports the Received Text, "God was manifest in the flesh".
> Patrick Young had custody of this copy from A.D. 1628-1652 and he assured Archbishop Ussher that the original reading was "God". In 1657 Huish collated the manuscript for Walton, who printed "God" in his massive Polyglot. Bishop Pearson wrote in 1659 "we find not 'who' in any copy". Mill worked on his edition of the Greek from 1677 to 1707 and clearly states that he found "God" in the Codex Alexandrinus at this place. In 1718 Wotton wrote, "There can be no doubt that this manuscript always read 'God' in this place". 1n 1716 Wetstein wrote, "Though the middle stroke has been retouched, the fine stroke originally, in the letter is discernible at each end of the fuller stroke of the corrector".
> In his "Lectures on the true reading of 1 Timothy 3:16" (1737-1738) Berriman declared, "If at any time the old line should become all together indiscernible there will never be just cause to doubt but that the genuine and original reading of this manuscript was 'God' ". Woide who edited this Codex in 1785 remarked that he had seen traces of the original stroke in 1765 which had ceased to be clearly visible twenty years later. One of the 1885 Revisers, Prebendary Scrivener, who examined the manuscript at least twenty times, asserted that in 1861 he could still discern the all important stroke which Berriman had seen more clearly in 1741. [199]

Either the editors of the UBS Greek Text did not know this information or they chose to disregard it. This indicates two things.

First, it is certain that the apparatus in UBS does not tell the whole story. Numerous facts are left out and others are slanted. This will become very apparent when we look at the John 7:53-8:11 passage, the woman taken in adultery. Second, there may even be some dishonesty and bias involved.

7. John 7:53-8:11 The Woman Caught in Adultery

> *John 7:53 And every man went unto his own house.*
> *John 8:1 Jesus went unto the mount of Olives.*
> *2 And early in the morning he came again into the temple, and all the people came unto him; and he sat down, and taught them.*
> *3 And the scribes and Pharisees brought unto him a woman taken in adultery; and when they had set her in the midst,*
> *4 They say unto him, Master, this woman was taken in adultery, in the very act.*
> *5 Now Moses in the law commanded us, that such should be stoned: but what sayest thou?*
> *6 This they said, tempting him, that they might have to accuse him. But Jesus stooped down, and with his finger wrote on the ground, as though he heard them not.*
> *7 So when they continued asking him, he lifted up himself, and said unto them, He that is without sin among you, let him first cast a stone at her.*
> *8 And again he stooped down, and wrote on the ground.*
> *9 And they which heard it, being convicted by their own conscience, went out one by one, beginning at the eldest, even unto the last: and Jesus was left alone, and the woman standing in the midst.*
> *10 When Jesus had lifted up himself, and saw none but the woman, he said unto her, Woman, where are those thine accusers? hath no man condemned thee?*
> *11 She said, No man, Lord. And Jesus said unto her, Neither do I condemn thee: go, and sin no more.*

Appendix 2: Problems of the Greek Text

12 ¶Then spake Jesus again unto them, saying, I am the light of the world: he that followeth me shall not walk in darkness, but shall have the light of life.

This passage is often called the *Pericope de Adultera,* because scholars love to give fancy unbiblical names to simple things. I suppose it makes them *feel* scholarly and intelligent. Personally I believe in *"the simplicity that is in Christ"* (2 Cor. 11:3). I also fear for us Christians that our *"minds should be corrupted from the simplicity that is in Christ."* I believe we ought to *"hold fast the form of sound words, which thou hast heard of me, in faith and love which is in Christ Jesus"* (1 Tim. 1:13). Sound words are Biblical words.

This is one of the most disputed passages in the entire New Testament. However, it has not always been so. Until the nineteenth century there were few who argued against it. It is also a passage which shows the bias of the scholars.

External Evidence Relating to John 7:53-8:11

In this section we will compare the external evidence for and against the passage. I will do this because there is a lot of information left out of the UBS apparatus. I am not claiming that the UBS editors were ignorant. It is just that the information they present is incomplete.

First, let's look at the uncial evidence. The UBS apparatus presents the following manuscripts in favor of omitting the passage: Aleph (Sinaiticus-declared to be 4th century), B (Vaticanus-also declared to be 4th century), A (Alexandrinus-5th century), C (5th century), L (8th Century), N (6th Century), T (5th Century), W (5th Century), Delta (9th Century), Theta (9th Century), Psi (9th-10th Centuries), 0141 (10th Century). Let's add to this impressive display of evidence Papyrus 66 (200 AD) and Papyrus 75 (175-220 AD).

This is a very impressive list of evidence that shows us the passage in question was omitted by Alexandrian manuscripts in the early years of church history. That is, on the surface it does. However, there is more to this than meets the eye. Let me list some additional and very pertinent information.

A Practical Theology of Bible Translating

1.   **Codex A, Alexandrinus:** Perhaps thirty-one leaves of the codex are missing. Two of these missing leaves cover the text from John 6:50 to John 8:50, including the passage in question. Therefore no one knows whether Codex A supported the passage or not. Yet the UBS puts it in the evidence against the passage. Codex A can be excused as a witness.

2.   **L and Delta:** Each of these contain a vacant space after John 7:52. This indicates that the scribe was aware that something was missing. This places enough doubt on L and Delta that they are not witnesses of the absence of the passage. We can dismiss them.

3.   **Codex C (Ephraemi Rescriptus):** According to Wikipedia, this manuscript contains the section where the disputed passage would be. However, in examining it (which I attempted to do, I found that it seems to have originally been a uncial manuscript, but is now overwritten by a combination of uncial and minuscule letters, making it extremely hard to read. Two photos are below.

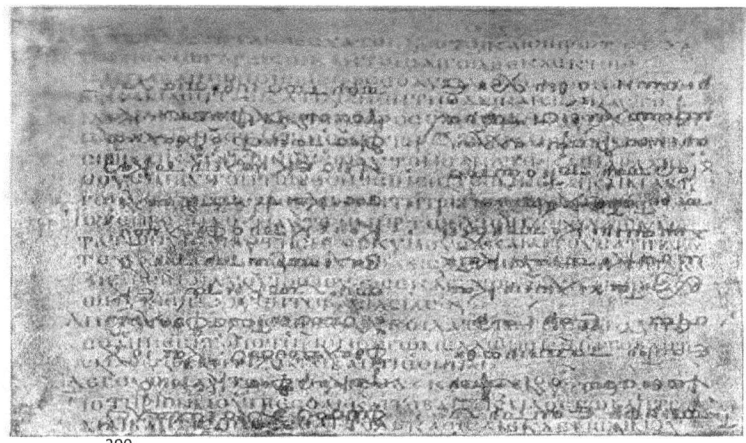
Fig. 28 [200]

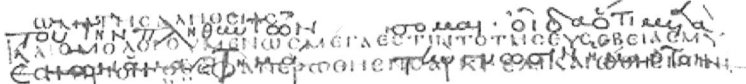
Fig. 29 [201]

Appendix 2: Problems of the Greek Text

Codex C also has *many* blank spaces where text is missing. There is a space where the text we are discussing belongs. There are multiple passages missing from more than 25 NT books. The entire section from John 7:3 – 8:34 is missing, not just the passage about the woman taken in adultery. These missing passages are evidenced by blank spaces and are called Lacunas or Lacunae. This is hardly strong evidence for leaving out John 7:53-8:11.

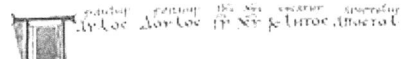

Example of a Lacuna. [202]
Fig. 30

4.   **Codex L, Regius:** John 7 ends with verse 52. However, following this is a small empty space on the same page. On the next page is an entire column and a half empty. The next line starts with John 8:12. The empty space was once filled, but has been erased. It is large enough to contain John 7:53-8:11. Obviously, the Scribe left the space empty with the former words faintly there for a reason. This makes L a weak witness to the omission of the text. Something was there and the faint letters remaining are only partially discernable. This manuscript also has five Lacunae (Matt 4:22-5:14, 28:17-20, Mark 10:16-30, 150:2-20,John 21:15-25).

5.   **Codex N, Petropolitanus Purpureus:** In addition to leaving out John 7:53-8:11, Codex N left out a large number

of other passages and left Lacunae in their place. Twelve of these are in the Book of John alone. So, this manuscript omits a great many legitimate passages. It is not proof that omitting John 7:53-8:1 is justified.

6. **Codex W, Washingtonianus:** Codex W also has numerous missing texts and blank spaces.

7. **Codex Delta, Sangallensis:** Codex Delta is in the same condition as Codex L. The codex is written in one column. The scribe started to write John 8:12 following John 7:52 and stopped. This was followed a large blank space on the rest of the page. The next page starts with a small blank space and the scribe started John 8:12 again. In the blank space, previous writing can be faintly seen. It has been erased. Once again, Codex Delta is a witness that even when scribes leave out or erase John 7:53-8:1, they know something should be in that space. It also has a blank space where John 19:17-35 is omitted.

8. **Codex Theta, Koredethi:** Much of this manuscript is in bad shape. It does seem to omit the passage in dispute, but it also omits other passages. There are blank spaces where Matthew 1:19 and Matthew 1:21-4:4 are also omitted.

So, in looking deeper, we can reduce the twelve uncials UBS claims as evidence for omitting the passage down to four that are certain, Aleph, B, T, and 0141. The rest are doubtful. We can add to that six minuscule manuscripts and two of those are questionable.

The Greek evidence in favor of the passage is heavy. On the other hand, the entire passage is included in D (5th Century), G (9th Century), H (9th Century), M (9th Century), Lambda (9th Century-has 8:3-11 only), and E (8th Century-has 8:2-11). There are also fourteen minuscules listed by UBS and one more that has it in the margin. Then, they admit that it is in the entire Traditional/ Byzantine Text. All of this dates the passage back to some time from 400 AD to 499 AD. This is not the end of the evidence, but this alone proves that the story of the woman caught in adultery was considered a part of Scripture early on.

There are quite a few early church writers marshaled to bear witness to the absence of John 7:53-8:11. The UBS gives Origen, Chrysostom, Cyril, Tertullian, and Cyprian as giving evidence that the

Appendix 2: Problems of the Greek Text

passage should be omitted. Burgon says that the scholars also mention others: Nonnus, Cosmas, and Theophylact. However, claiming these men for evidence is disingenuous. What kind of evidence did they give? They did not mention the passage. Origen, for example, wrote of adultery from the *Song of Suzanna*, but he did not mention this passage. Does the fact that he didn't mention it mean that it did not exist? There were many passages of Scripture that these men did not mention. I have been a teacher, preacher, and writer for fifty years, yet there are many passages I have not used or mentioned. That certainly does not mean that those passages are not Scripture! The Bible is a big book. The silence of these men is no evidence of any kind that the disputed passage did not exist or should not have been part of the Gospel of John.

On the other hand there are many writers who did quote the text. The fact that someone quoted it as Scripture is total proof that it existed as Scripture at that time. The UBS Text lists the following ancient church writers as having quoted part or all of the passage: Ambrosiaster (384), Ambrose (374), Pacian (370), Rufinus (400), Jerome (385), Faustus-Milevis (400), and Augustine (396). Burgon added Chrysologus at Ravenna (433) and Sedulius, a Scot (434). Jerome tells us this passage "is found in many copies both Greek and Latin. [203] This pushes the date much earlier than Jerome. Also, Burgon tells us:

> The unknown authors of two famous treatises written at the same period largely quote this portion of the narrative. It is referred to by Victorius of Victorinus (457), by Vigilius of Tapsus (484) in North Africa, by Gelasius, Bishop of Rome (492), by Cassiodorus in Southern Italy, by Gregory the Great, and by other Fathers of the Western Church. [204]

This proves the existence of John 7:53-8:11 as Scripture as far back as the fourth century. It makes the passage as old as anything claimed for Vaticanus and Sinaiticus. The earliest date listed here is 370 AD. That's 20 to 45 years after the declared date for Vaticanus. This passage did not suddenly pop into existence when it was quoted. It had to be around many years before it was quoted by such a widespread list of people.

The ancient lectionaries are an issue. The majority of lectionaries are listed as support for omitting the passage. Only part of the lectionaries supported the passage. The reason the majority are said to support omitting the passage is that they *do not quote the passage.* The same truth applies here that applied with the church writers who did not mention it. The fact that it is not quoted says nothing about whether it is genuine Scripture or not. The lectionaries only quoted passages planned to be read in church services. Have you never seen responsive readings in the back of some hymn books? The passages printed there certainly do not include the whole Bible. Yet, we don't look at that and say that the passages not included are not Scripture. The principle is the same.

Then, we need to look at the ancient versions (translations). There are versions on both sides. Some Latin manuscripts leave the passage out. However, there are at least seven Old Latin copies that contain the passage.

> But in fact we are not left to Latin authorities. (Out of thirty-eight copies of the Bohairic version the *Pericope de Adultera* is read in fifteen ... In the remaining twenty-three, it is left out.) How is it intelligible that this passage is thus found in nearly half the copies, except on the hypothesis that they formed an integral part of the Memphitic version? ... Once more. The Ethiopic version (fifth century), The Palestinian Syriac (which is referred to the fifth century), the Georgian version (probably fifth or sixth century), to say nothing of the Slavonic, Arabic, and Persian versions, which are of later date, all contain the portion of narrative in dispute. The Armenian version (fourth or fifth century) also originally contained it, though it survives at present in only a few copies. Add that it is found in Codex D, and it will be seen that in all parts of ancient Christendom this portion of Scripture was familiarly known. [205]

Taitian's Diatessaron (160-175) is cited as support for omitting the passage. The Diatessaron does not contain John 7:53-8:11. On the other hand, it omits several passages that are acknowledged as genuine Scripture.

> The ***Diatessaron*** ... (c. 160–175) is the most prominent early gospel harmony, and was created by Tatian, an Assyrian early Christian apologist and ascetic. Tatian sought to combine all the textual material he found in the four gospels—Matthew, Mark, Luke, and John—into a single coherent narrative of Jesus' life and death ... Tatian's harmony follows the gospels closely in terms of text but, in order to fit all the canonical material in, **he created his own narrative sequence**, which is different from both the synoptic sequence and John's sequence; and **occasionally creates intervening time periods** that are found in none of the source accounts ... Where the gospels differ from one another in respect of the details of an event or teaching, the Diatessaron **resolves such apparent contradictions by selecting one or another alternative wording and adding consistent details from the other gospels; while omitting apparent duplicate matter**, especially across the synoptics. Hence, in respect of **the healing of the blind at Jericho the Diatessaron reports only one blind man, Bartimeaus** ... Otherwise, Tatian **originally omitted altogether both of the different genealogies** in Matthew and Luke, as well as Luke's introduction (Luke 1: 1-4); and also **did not originally include Jesus' encounter with the adulteress** (John 7:53–8:11) ... The Diatessaron is notable evidence for the authority already enjoyed by the gospels by the mid- to late-2nd century. Within twenty years after Tatian's harmony was written, Irenaeus was expressly arguing for the authoritative character of the Four Gospels. It is unclear whether Tatian intended the Diatessaron to supplement or replace the four separate gospels; but both outcomes came to pass in different churches. (Emphasis-Author) [206]

No one can get into the mind of someone who lived centuries before his own birth. We do not know what Tatian's thinking was. What we do know is that his harmony of the gospels did not include all the passages from all the gospels and the sequence of events was different from the individual gospels. He left out more than John 7:53-8:11. Therefore, it cannot be honestly used as evidence against that passage. One further thing we learn, is that a number of churches adopted the Diatessaron as their version of the gospels, a version without John 7:53-8:11. Doubtless, this resulted in manuscript copies of John that did not include the disputed passage.

Internal Evidence

The context clearly shows that there is something of significance missing, if the passage, John7:53-8:11, is left out. In the narrative, Jesus went to Jerusalem for the feast of Tabernacles and began to teach in the temple (7:14). A question and answer session ensued (7:15-36). In John 7:37-44, Jesus declared Himself to be the living water and a dispute about Him arose among the people. In verse 7:45, the scene changes to a private location where the officers of the temple came to the Chief Priests and Pharisees. John 7:44-52 is a private discussion. *Jesus was not there*.   Yet, in the absence of John 7:53-8:11, there is a sudden unannounced change to a new location with Jesus in the middle of a declaration. It is so abrupt as to be startling.

> *John 7:52 They answered and said unto him, Art thou also of Galilee? Search, and look: for out of Galilee ariseth no prophet.* (Private conversation-Jesus is not there.)
> *John 8:12 Then spake Jesus again unto **them**, saying, I am the light of the world: he that followeth me shall not walk in darkness, but shall have the light of life.* (This is a public statement at a different public location. Who is "*them*?")

Something is clearly missing between John 7:52 and 8:12. God certainly did not lose a portion of His Word contrary to His promise of preservation. The only available complete passage to include is John 7:53-8:11. Including this passage makes perfect sense of the context. Verse 53 says the Chief Priests and Pharisees went their way to their own homes. In 8:1-11, the scenes changes to a street where the Pharisees bring a woman to Jesus. It all makes perfect contextual sense. Without it, the passage is confusing.

Lessons You Should Remember

There are a number of lessons we can learn from the foregoing discussion. I would like to very briefly list eight of them.

1. ***Don't focus on manuscript evidence, primarily. Focus on Inspiration and Preservation.*** Look for the text God has preserved and made available to us throughout church history. This or that manuscript showing up somewhere in history and briefly used does not indicate God's Providence. But the text (in whatever language) that God has made available to Christians all through church history is the right one. The only thing that qualifies is the Traditional Text and its printed representative, the Received Text. The UBS text is one of the few books we can go to get manuscript evidence. I rarely look at it anymore, because I have settled the issue as to which text is the right one. It is a Greek text that represents the few manuscripts that God allowed to lay unused for centuries. To this lack of use they owe their continued existence.
2. ***The context and internal considerations are often stronger evidence than manuscripts.*** We have seen that in the examples in this appendix.
3. ***Modern scholars are biased toward two manuscripts and one family of manuscripts.*** Those two are Vaticanus and Sinaiticus and the family is the Alexandrian Text. They are often of dubious worth, differing from one another over 3,000 times in the gospels alone.
4. ***Manuscripts are often damaged and uncertain, even though the UBS uses them as evidence.*** Even if a manuscript is damaged beyond knowing what the original reading was, the UBS apparatus often lists it in favor of the Alexandrian reading.
5. ***Modern Scholarship is not entirely honest***. They say the textual issues between the TR and the UBS do not involve major doctrine. This is manifestly false. The examples in this appendix

involve some very major doctrine. They are only a few of many examples.

6. ***Some manuscript evidence listed in UBS has a lot more to it than shows on the surface***. Evidence is judged to simply be on one side or another and placed there, even though the situation is more complicated. For example, see the discussion about the Diatessaron and the early church writers in relation to John 7:53-8:11.

7. ***None of these issues were a serious problem for the churches in general until the nineteenth century.*** The questions and disputes have all been raised by modern textual critics and religious liberals. All of these people doubt a substantial portion of the Bible available today. To them, no Bible, nor manuscript nor text is 100% accurate. They do not encourage people to believe. They encourage them to question the authenticity of the Bible. This does not represent faith. It represents doubt and unbelief.

8. ***The Received text represents the New Testament that was given to the church for nearly 2000 years before modern scholarship began to place doubts on the text.***

I might also point out that most modern evangelical and conservative scholars side with the liberal theologians on these matters. They may hold to certain Biblical truths, but they present many doubts about the accuracy and authenticity of the Bible. We will look at this further in Appendix 2.

Appendix 3:
A Historical Summary of Unbelief

All through the Middle Ages, the Roman Catholic Church was in control of Europe. The Catholic Church is a heretical church. It teaches many things that are contrary to the doctrines of the Bible. It teaches a curious blend of salvation by both works and faith. Paul called this another gospel and said, "If any man preach any other gospel unto you than that ye have received, let him be accursed" (Gal. 1:9). The gospel God gave Paul declares, "For by grace are ye saved through faith; and that not of yourselves: it is the gift of God: Not of works, lest any man should boast" (Eph. 2:8-9). Nevertheless, the Catholic Church held firm in its beliefs and considered anyone who disagreed with it to be a heretic. Several times they conducted crusades against "heretics" in Europe. Tens of thousands of believing Christians were slaughtered.

Throughout that time, the Biblical text the "heretics" held to was the Traditional type text. When God saw fit to free His churches from the clutches of the Catholic Church during the Reformation, he embraced the Received Text to do it. The true churches recognized the Received Text to be the same type of text they had followed for over a thousand years. This same Received Text prevailed until after the middle of the twentieth century. It was the Text God preserved, chose, and used.

The issues we will look at in this chapter are actually recent issues. For hundreds of years they were settled matters for ordinary Christians until the nineteenth century. From then until now the theological landscape has been increasingly filled with theories that lead to doubt about the Word of God. Now, we have arrived at the place where scholars and probably over half the churches do not believe any manuscript, Greek or Hebrew text, or translation is completely accurate or inerrant. They all have errors. Some will allow that God has preserved His message, but not His words. Others will not accept even that. How did this come to pass? It is my purpose in this appendix to summarize the history of theological liberalism and its battle with Bible-believing Christianity.

While you read this appendix, keep in mind the truth from the following Scripture, truth we have looked at before.

> *13 For such are false apostles, deceitful workers, transforming themselves into the apostles of Christ.*
> *14 And no marvel; for Satan himself is transformed into an angel of light.*
> *15 Therefore it is no great thing if **his ministers** also be transformed as the ministers of righteousness; whose end shall be according to their works.*
> (2 Cor. 11:13-15)

What follows is seen by historians as several movements, but is in reality a satanic plan put in place to derail the Protestant Reformation and stop evangelism. Satan initiated an attack from three directions: 1) the Roman Catholic Church, 2) secular philosophers, and 3) biblical scholarship.

First, a word about the Catholic Church's reaction to the Reformation: the Reformation began in 1517, one year after the publication of the Received Greek Text. The Reformation disrupted Catholic control all over Europe. The Catholic Church quickly launched an effort to counter it. First, the order of the Jesuits was organized in 1534 by Ignatius Loyala. Their goals included retaining countries that were still Catholic and to bring back countries that had gone to Protestantism. They had a three-fold strategy: 1) Education through excellent institutions, 2) Indoctrination in Catholic thinking and doctrine, and 3) Infiltration into government, commerce, and military.[207]

Then, the Council of Trent (1545-1563) took place. Basically the Catholic Church entrenched itself in its doctrines and efforts to counter the Protestant Reformation. Its goals were to "preserve the power, influence and material wealth enjoyed by the Catholic Church and to present a theological and material challenge to Reformation."[208] Their reforms included founding seminaries and reforming religious life of the monastic orders. Educational institutions were particularly important as they realized how important it was to control the minds of the youth. It also included the Catholic

Inquisition. Hundreds of thousands of Protestants were expelled and killed as heretics. The Catholic Church also made a greater effort toward foreign missions, but their purpose was to convert the heathen to Catholicism (not Christ).

For centuries, there have been philosophers that oppose the Reformation in particular and Christianity in general. These included Rene Descarte (1596-1650), Baruch Spinoza (1632-1677), G.W. Leibnitz (1646-1716), George Berkeley ((1685-1753), David Hume (1711-1776), Immanuel Kant (1724-1804), and George Hegel (1770-1831). These philosophers conceived of life in purely human and naturalistic terms. They left God out of consideration. They promoted a philosophy of questions, doubt, and agnosticism. This led to carnal materialism and away from spirituality. They were also quite with the theory of evolution. Darwin published *On the Origin of the Species* in 1859. Clearly these philosophers and scientists were the beginning and laid the foundation of Satan's counter-reformation.

Liberalism and what we now call "textual criticism" began in the seventeenth century. The various philosophies led direct to them and strengthened them. Textual criticism is the attempt to restore the Bible to its original condition. It is predicated on the assumption that God did not verbally preserve all his Words. Having come to that conclusion the critics embraced a system of unbelief: rejection of miracles and doubt about nearly everything God has said. Certain men led the way in this process.

The Age of Rationalism

The Age of Rationalism was a period when many educated theologians and scholars and philosophers began to look at the Bible from a purely naturalistic standpoint, as if the Bible was the same as any other human book. Rationalism means "reliance on reason as the basis for establishment of religious truth." They laid aside the supernatural origin of the Bible and sought to analyze it as if it were a completely human book.

Hugo Grotius (1583-1645), a well-known Dutch Theologian, who made a number of guess-work changes in the New Testament.

Stephen Courcelles (1586-1659) became a professor of the Arminian College in Amsterdam in 1658. He published an edition of the New Testament using Grotius' guesses and some of his own mixed with other variant readings from Greek manuscripts.

Thomas Hobbes (1588-1679), an English Philosopher, was among those who first began to level serious doubtful questions toward the Bible. For example, he questioned the Mosaic authorship of the first five books of the Bible, even though Jesus Christ said Moses was the author. So, these attempts to undermine the trust people had in the Bible began during the period when the English Bible was developing.

Richard Simon (1638-1712) was a French *Catholic priest* and an influential Bible critic. He and Baruch Spinoza questioned the Mosaic authorship of the Jewish law. He has been called the founder of Old Testament Criticism. The presence of this man in the ranks of Bible critics indicates the interest of the Catholic Church. From Richard Simon to Cardinal Carlo Martini (1927-2012), editor of the UBS Greek text, the Roman Catholic Church has been involved.

John Fell (1625-1686), Dean of Christ Church, in 1675, taught textual scholars to focus on the activities of the scribes in examining the New Testament to determine what is Scripture and what is not.

Jean Mabillion (1632-1707) was a *Catholic Benedictine monk*. He is considered the founder of Paleography (the study of ancient writing and inscriptions), which every textual critic follows.

Richard Bentley (1662-1742), Cambridge Scholar, proposed in 1720 methods of textual criticism that would abandon the majority of manuscripts in favor of only the oldest.

J. A. Bengel (1687-1752), a German Lutheran, proposed rules to judge the readings of the Bible, such as the hard reading is to be preferred to the easy reading. He thought that Christians themselves had corrupted the New Testament. This amounted to a denial of providential preservation.

Jean Astruc (1684-1766), a *Catholic* physician, disagreed with those who denied Mosaic authorship of the Pentateuch. However, he said Moses borrowed from multiple sources. He embraced methods of textual criticism used by those who examined Greek and Roman secular books. He applied these methods to the Biblical text. They were methods designed for purely secular non-Christian books. Institutions of higher learning all over Germany (and eventually beyond) picked up these methods from Astruc. Christian doctrine began to be expressed in terms of the "scientific method."

Appendix 3: A Historical Summary of Unbelief

Jean Alphonse Turretin (1671–1737), a theologian from Geneva, argued for a critical study of the Bible based solely on reason. He believed that the Bible can be considered authoritative, even if it was not considered to be without error. This is the prevalent view among evangelicals today.

All of these were influenced by many of the unbelieving philosophers listed above. The methods and thinking proposed were designed to depend on the reasoning of the (sinful) human mind rather than God. It all resulted in ever more doubt about the Received Text and the Bible translations that came from it, especially, the KJB. The entire basis for this rationalistic philosophical development was *the presumption that God did not perfectly preserve His words and that it is up to man, using his powers of reason, to find the hidden original wording of the New Testament.* Wasn't it Satan who said, *"Yea, hath God said …?"* (Gen. 3:1).

The Age of Enlightenment-Skepticism

The Age of Enlightenment was an intellectual and philosophical movement that took place in the seventeenth century. One of the movements that developed during the Enlightenment was Biblical Criticism.

> **Biblical criticism** is an umbrella term for those methods of studying the Bible that embrace two distinctive perspectives: the concern to avoid dogma and bias by applying a non-sectarian, reason-based judgment, and the reconstruction of history according to contemporary understanding. Biblical criticism uses the grammar, structure, development, and relationship of language to identify such characteristics as the Bible's literary structure, its genre, its context, meaning, authorship, and origins.[209]

Biblical Criticism was accomplished in four forms: [210]

Textual Criticism: The process of determining the original reading of the Scriptures. (This assumes we do not current know the original readings-Author.)

Source Criticism: This is the process of determining the source of documents or specific portions of the Bible. It is why they kept discussing the authorship of the Pentateuch.

Form Criticism: This "method of biblical criticism classifies units of scripture by literary pattern and then attempts to trace each type to its period of oral transmission." [211]

Literary Criticism: This refers to analyzing the Bible based on its literary value and quality. It is not the same as teaching the Bible as literature. It is judging the Bible based on its style, its importance, and its meaning.

All of these forms of Biblical Criticism developed together. Together they resulted in theological liberalism, the movement that has so devastated the churches in Europe and America. All four forms of Biblical Criticism stem from the same corrupt foundations. The first foundation is a denial and refusal to believe that the Bible has a supernatural origin, inspiration. The second foundation is a denial that the Bible is under supernatural protection, the doctrine of preservation. Without these two foundations, anything can be taught about the Bible. There is, at the core, no certainty about anything philosophical or theological.

Biblical Criticism grew out of the German enlightenment. It was based on Rationalism, which was encouraged by Frederick II, the "Philosopher King" over Prussia from 1740-1786. This was the period that brought all the previous preparations to fruition. In this time, skepticism about the Biblical text was openly expressed and espoused. In Biblical terms and in regard to Biblical truth, it was not an age of *enlightenment*. It was an age of *deception*. Again, wasn't it Satan, who told Eve, *"ye shall be as gods, **knowing** ..."* (Gen. 3:5). Yet, it was Satan, of whom Jesus said, *"When he speaketh a lie, he speaketh of his own: for he is a liar, and the father of it"* (John 8:44).

Johann Semler (1725-1791) was professor at Halle. He "argued for an end to all doctrinal assumptions, giving historical criticism its non-sectarian nature. As a result, Semler is often called the father of historical-critical research." [212] He believed that the New Testament was not merely copied by scribes, but that they edited it. He was very bold in his critical theories. For example, he thought 2 Corinthians 9 was inserted by scribes and Romans 16 was originally part of Corinthians. He questioned the validity of applying certain parts of the gospels to modern life. His theories amounted to one thing: unbelief in the Word of God.

J. J. Griesbach (1745-1812) was a pupil of Semler and a professor in Germany. "In 1771 he wrote, 'The New Testament abounds in more glosses, additions, and interpolations purposely introduced than any other book.' And during his long career there is no indication that he ever changed this view." [213] He produced a critical edition of the Greek New Testament that was different from the Received Text. God never used it, but it did become the basis for the New World Translation. "According to Griesbach, whenever the New Testament manuscripts varied from each other, the orthodox readings were to be ruled out at once as spurious. 'The most suspicious reading of all,' Griesbach wrote, 'is the one that yields a sense favorable to the nourishment of piety (especially monastic piety).' And to this he added another directive: 'When there are many variant readings in one place, that reading which more than the others manifestly favors the dogmas of the orthodox is deservedly regarded as suspicious.'" [214] "Yea, hath God said?"

Johann Leonhard Hug (1765-1846) shared Griesbach's skepticism. In 1787, he became the superintendent of studies in the seminary at the University of Freiberg. In 1808, he taught that by the second century the New Testament had become degenerate and corrupt and that all copies came from this corrupt text. He taught the New Testament was revised by Lucian of Antioch in the fourth century, a theory Westcott and Hort were to pick up later. "Yea, hath God said?"

Carl Lachman (1793-1851) continued the discussion from a similar viewpoint. Lachman did not believe that the New Testament could be known any further back than the fourth century. In order to go any further back one had to guess. These guesses are called "conjectural emendations." In 1831, he published a Greek New Testament based on his ideas. He was the first to completely break from the Received Text. "Yea, hath God said?"

All these men taught and influenced many others.

The Development of Theological Liberalism

None of these movements (the Catholic Counter-Reformation, Rationalism, Enlightenment, Textual Criticism, and

Liberalism or Modernism), developed in isolation and independence from one another. They were interconnected and influenced one another. Often the same men were both textual critics and theological liberals.

Hermann Samuel Reimarus (1694–1768) was one of the first scholars who separated the "historical" Jesus from the theological Jesus. "According to Reimarus, Jesus was a political **Messiah** who failed at creating political change and was executed. His disciples then stole the body and invented the story of the resurrection for personal gain." [215]

Immanuel Kant (1724-1804), following a long line of skeptical unbelieving philosophers, was one of the greatest influences on the theological liberalism that developed in the nineteenth century. He wrote several books trying to destroy the traditional arguments for God's existence. He was an empiricist. That is, he would not accept any evidence that could not be learned from our five senses. He believed there was no empirical evidence that could prove God's existence. No one could know God through the senses.

Frederick Schleiermacher (1768-1834), a German theologian, philosopher, and Bible Scholar, has been called "the founder of theological liberalism." [216] Dr. Jim Eckman says he ...

> maintained that Christianity was not knowledge or propositional truth, nor a system of ethics; it was a "feeling of absolute dependence" on God. This was the essence of Christianity. Gone was any affirmation of Christ's deity, His substitutionary atonement or propositional revelation from God. If Christianity is reduced to feeling and Jesus was merely a suffering man, then the question became, can we trust the New Testament accounts of Jesus? [217]

Schleiermacher taught at the University of Halle and the University of Berlin. Have you noticed how many of these individuals were teachers in institutions of higher learning? It is the place where the most people can be influenced. That's why there are so many socialists in the USA. They learned it in college.

Schleiermacher had a profound effect on "Christian" thought. While many were working on what they called "Lower Criticism," that is, textual criticism, he was influencing "Higher Criticism." Higher criticism is also called the "historical-critical method." This is basically an effort to discover the meaning of the Bible as it was penned in its culture and in its historical time. That's what they say. However, it approached the Bible from the viewpoint that it is an ordinary secular book. No supernatural is allowed and the idea of inspiration is completely ignored and rejected.

> An example of higher criticism is the Documentary Hypothesis which is an attempt to explain the origin of the first five books of Moses: Genesis, Exodus, Leviticus, Numbers, and Deuteronomy. The documentary hypothesis proposes four main authors to the Pentateuch: J (Yahwist), E (Elohist), P (Priestly), and D (Deuteronomic). This is also known as the Graf-Wellhausen hypothesis. This theory proposed that there are sections within the first five books that demonstrate a variety of styles and word concentrations. As an example, it asserts that there are places in the Pentateuch where the word Yahweh occurs more than Elohim. This is because one author tended to use one word or phrase more than another author and these linguistic differences demonstrate multiple authors. [218]

In other words, Jesus Christ, Paul, and the Jews were liars, because they said Moses wrote the Pentateuch (John 5:46; 8:5; 1 Cor. 9:9; 2 Cor. 3:15; Heb. 7:14). "Yea, hath God said?"

David Strauss (1808-1874), a German liberal theologian and writer. He is called a pioneer in the investigation of the "historical" Jesus. [219] He was influenced by Hegel and Schleiermacher. He added the word "myth" to the higher critical discussions of the Pentateuch. He taught at the school in Tübingen. In 1835, he published a book titled *The Life of Jesus,* in which he stripped Jesus of His divinity. The book was strongly influential in Europe. Christianity was becoming nothing more than ethical behavior guided by love. [220] "Yea, hath God said?"

Albrecht Ritschl (1822-1889) was a lecturer of systematic theology at Bonn and Göttingen. He also was influenced by Kant, Hegel, and Schleiermacher. He taught that the core of Jesus' theology was the Kingdom of God and ethics. He argued that faith did not come from facts (such as the Word of God), but from value judgments. [221] "Yea, hath God said?"

Heinrich Julius Holtzmann (1832-1910), was a German Protestant Theologian, who was considered moderately liberal. He taught at the university of Strasbourg and became known as a New Testament critic and exegete. "Yea, hath God said?"

Adolf von Harnack (1851-1930) was a German Lutheran Theologian. By this time, higher and lower criticism was widespread and popular in Germany. Harnack taught in the Tübingen school. He called on Christians to question the truth of doctrines that were taught in the early Christian Church. He rejected the Gospel of John as real history. He "asserted that the essence of the Christian faith was 'the fatherhood of God and the brotherhood of man.'" [222] Christianity was taught as merely a human religion like all others. "Yea, hath God said?" Apparently by this time, it was accepted as fact by some that God never said anything.

Julius Wellhausen (1844-1918) was a German theologian. He developed the Documentary Hypothesis, which questioned the origin of the Pentateuch in a very elaborate way.

Rudolf Bultmann (1884-1976) was a German Lutheran theologian and teacher at the University of Marburg. He taught *nothing is certain* except the simple fact that Jesus existed. The Anti-supernatural teaching of these men reached its greatest with Bultman. "Yea, HATH God said?"

There were many others than these. Notice that these growing theological ideas grew out of a beginning that included questioning the authorship of the Pentateuch. This may seem unimportant, but remember the words of Jesus, *"For had ye believed Moses, ye would have believed me: for he wrote of me. But if ye believe not his writings, how shall ye believe my words?"* (John 5:46-47) The theologians, textual critics, philosophers, and psychologists of this time were growing in agreement with the idea that supernaturalism must be rejected and solutions to the needs of man could be met with human reason alone.

Liberalism and Biblical Criticism in England

We have already seen that liberal ideas regarding textual criticism and theology were gaining strength in Germany and England

Appendix 3: A Historical Summary of Unbelief

as early as the first half of the seventeenth century with Hume, Fell, Bentley, and Bengel. The textual critics rejected the supernatural origin of the Bible. They treated the Bible the same as they would any other ancient book. It was the textual critics who cast doubt on the Bible and paved the way for the theological liberals, as they became liberal themselves. Liberalism and its connection with textual criticism became full-blown in the nineteenth century. By the end of that century it had become well-known and main stream, although rejected by the conservatives of England and the fundamentalists of America.

The textual and Biblical criticism of Germany has continued on to the present day. There were many other things taught that are not described here. The theme that pervades them all is that the Bible is not an inspired book. It is not a supernatural book. It is not inerrant. The reason of man, free from being subservient to the Bible, is totally capable of discovering and understanding truth. To do this, we must question anything and everything.

The attitudes developed in Germany were not confined to Germany and did not remain in Germany. They spread to other countries. Most notably, they spread to England and then America.

Constantin von Tischendorf (1815-1874), the German liberal scholar, was perhaps one of the greatest figures to bridge the gap between German theological endeavors and English theologians. He was a scholar of world renown, because he is credited with the discovery of Codex Sinaiticus at the Monastery of St. Catherine in 1859. He was given honorary doctorates by Oxford and Cambridge. Sinaiticus and Vaticanus are considered the best of all manuscripts by many modern scholars. For many, textual variances are resolved when the two manuscripts agree. Tischendorf hated the Received Text and believed it should be rejected.

Brooke Foss Westcott (1825-1901) was a British Bishop, theologian, textual critic, and scholar. He was Bishop of Durham from 1890 to his death. He and Fenton John Anthony Hort produced a New Testament in Greek that was different from the Received Text and was used as the basis for the Revised Version (1881).

Fenton John Anthony Hort (1828-1898) was an Irish born theologian, textual critic, and scholar. He was a teacher at Emmanuel College, Oxford.

A Practical Theology of Bible Translating

The anti-reformation movement from the Catholic Church, the textual critics, and the liberal theology of two centuries came to rest in Westcott and Hort. Dr. Douglas Stauffer wrote *One Book Stands Alone.* In chapter 14 of that book, he listed the beliefs of these two Anglicans. His source for this information was the personal correspondence of each of them. [223] Their beliefs are listed below.

1. Westcott overwhelmingly rejected the infallibility of Scripture.
2. Westcott did not believe in biblical miracles.
3. Hort rejected the infallibility of the Bible.
4. Hort did not believe in a supernatural creation and Westcott apparently agreed.
5. Hort felt Darwin's evolution was irrefutable.
6. Hort did not believe in the efficacy of the atonement.
7. Hort was a pro-Catholic sympathizer.
8. Hort believed in Purgatory.
9. Westcott was an inner communist.
10. Hort hated democracy and sympathized with communism.
11. Westcott believed in prayers for the dead.
12. Hort believed in the worship of Mary. Westcott apparently agreed. He had his wife, Sarah, add Mary to her name.
13. Hort believed in the sacraments.
14. Westcott and Hort believed in baptismal regeneration.
15. Did not believe in a literal heaven.
16. Did not believe in a literal second coming of the Lord Jesus Christ.
17. Did not believe in the millennial reign of Christ.
18. Did not believe in the literal existence of angels.
19. Denied the Trinity's oneness.
20. Doubted the soul's existence outside the body.
21. Did not believe in a literal devil.

Hort's own mother, Anne Hort, disagreed with his theological positions. This was described in *The Life and Letters of Fenton John Anthony Hort* by his son Arthur.

Appendix 3: A Historical Summary of Unbelief

> Her religious feelings were deep and strong. Circumstances had made her an adherent of the Evangelical school … the Oxford Movement filled her with anxiety and dread as to its possible effect on her son. She was unable to enter into his theological views, which to her school and generation seemed a desertion of the ancient ways; thus, pathetically enough, there came to be a barrier between mother and son. The close intercourse on subjects which lay nearest to the hearts of each was broken, to the loss and sorrow of both … She studied and knew her Bible well, and her own religious life was most carefully regulated. [224]

As if all this was not enough, Westcott and Hort were part of a society called "The Ghostly Guild," which dabbled in the occult, spiritualism, and the supernatural. Hort founded the society and Westcott was a member. Westcott wrote about it in his *Ghostly Circular.*

> The interest and importance of a serious and earnest inquiry into the nature of the phenomena which are vaguely called "supernatural" will scarcely be questioned. Many persons believe that all such apparently mysterious occurrences are due either to purely natural causes, or to delusions of the mind or senses, or to willful deception. But there are many others who believe it possible that the beings of the unseen world may manifest themselves to us in extraordinary ways … If the belief of the latter class should be ultimately confirmed, the limits which human knowledge respecting the spirit-world has hitherto reached might be ascertained with some degree of accuracy. But in any case, even if it should appear that morbid or irregular workings of the mind or senses will satisfactorily account for every such marvel, still some progress will be made towards ascertaining the laws which regulate our being … [225]

Westcott and Hort had numerous scholarly friends who were of a similar theological mindset. All that I have shown heretofore back to the seventeenth century and especially including Westcott and Hort is the fountain from which sprang the UBS Greek Text, the Nestle-Aland Greek text, all the popular modern English translations, and all the foreign translations based on the Westcott and Hort Greek text. This is the Satanic foundation. Would you consider these two men to be full of spiritual discernment or were they blind spiritually? Then, why do you follow them? "If the blind follow the blind ..."

The Westcott and Hort Greek New Testament

These are the men chiefly responsible for every new popular English version of the New Testament. Together they produced **The New Testament in the Original Greek** and published it in 1881. It took them twenty-eight years to publish this New Testament. The chief sources for the text were the manuscripts, Vaticanus and Sinaiticus, although they used a few others. They decided on a joint revision of the Greek text in 1853 and did the work in secret.

Hort had taken his college degree in 1850 and Westcott won his B. A. degree in 1848. Even as young men they had already developed a deep hatred for the Received text. Hort said:

> I had no idea till the last few weeks of the importance of texts having read so little Greek Testament, and dragged on with the villainous *Textus Receptus* ... Think of that vile *Textus Receptus* leaning entirely on late MSS.; it is a blessing there are such early ones ... [226]

In 1870, the convocation of Canterbury decided on a new translation into English, a revision of the King James Version. Over fifty scholars were chosen to participate, but the final number was 99. Westcott and Hort were two of them. The translation committee also included Dr. Vance Smith, a Unitarian pastor; a man who openly denied the deity of Christ! Several thousand Anglican ministers protested this. [227] Westcott and Hort defended him and finally it was decided that he remain on the committee. This man was

Appendix 3: A Historical Summary of Unbelief

responsible for the substitution of "who" in place of "God" in 1 Timothy 3:16. [228]

The beginning of the translation effort coincided with the completion of the Westcott and Hort text (which was not yet published). A question arose about the Greek text and when the Received Text was abandoned, many of the original 99 translators resigned.

> The New Testament revision company was commissioned in 1870 by the convocation of Canterbury.[2] Their stated aim was "to adapt King James' version to the present state of the English language without changing the idiom and vocabulary," and "to adapt it to the present standard of Biblical scholarship." To those ends, the Greek text that was used to translate the New Testament was believed by most to be of higher reliability than the *Textus Receptus*. The readings used were compiled from a different text of the Greek Testament by Edwin Palmer. [229]

This is somewhat misleading. Edwin Palmer was an Archdeacon of Oxford and worked with the committee "producing a Greek New Testament text representing the basis of the *Revised Version*." [230] However, this does not mean he created a Greek text before the translation started. No, he wrote down the readings, which were different from the Received Text, as they were chosen by the translators during the translation work. After the translation was finished, he assembled the chosen readings into one text. The translators made about 30,000 changes in the New Testament alone. Where did they get their alternative readings? They got them from the Westcott and Hort text.

The Revised Version New Testament was published in 1881. The Old Testament was published in 1885. *The New Testament in the original Greek* by Westcott and Hort was published in 1881. In effect, this dethroned the Received Text for the liberal scholars of England.

In 1871, Philip Schaff (1819-1893) chose 30 Americans to work on the Revised Version project. Schaff himself was a Swiss born, German educated Protestant theologian. He lived and taught in the

United States for most of his life. He was also a Unitarian. The Americans worked on the American Standard Version while a part of the RV project. They had to wait fifteen years before publishing it by agreement with the British committee. In 1901, the American Standard Version was published. It was based on the same text as the Revised Version.

As a result the Westcott and Hort Greek text became the standard text for liberal scholars. However, it was NOT accepted by American or British *conservative* scholars. They continued with the Received Text and the KJB. Nevertheless, the Westcott and Hort text was of immense influence on future generations.

The Novum Testamentum Graece or the Nestle-Aland Critical Text: The first edition of the Nestle Aland text was published in 1898 by Eberhard Nestle (1851-1913). He combined the readings of Tischendorf's text, Westcott and Hort's text, and *The Resultant Greek Testament* by Richard F. Weymouth (1822-1902). Erwin Nestle took over his father's work with the 13th edition in 1927. Kurt Aland became associate editor in 1952 with the 21st edition.

The United Bible Societies Greek New Testament: The United Bible Societies was created in 1946 by delegates from 13 countries. The Greek New Testament assembled by the UBS was specifically made for use in Bible translation, so they did not feel they were in competition with the Nestle-Aland text (NA). The first edition was published in 1965, the second in 1968, the third in 1975, the fourth in 1993, and the fifth in 2014. Since the third edition, the Greek text itself has been identical with the NA text. Both of them have come from their great Grandfathers, Westcott and Hort. In chapter thirteen, I provided considerable information about the liberal theology of the members of the UBS.

Liberalism Vs. Fundamentalism in America

Liberalism was firmly established in America by about 1880 and was strongly moved along with the American Standard Version of the Bible of 1871-1901. In those days it was called Modernism. Liberalism or Modernism was embedded deeply in members of both the Revised Version translators and in the ASV translators. That's not to say they were all liberal, but a significant number were. Philip Schaff, the head of the ASV translation committee, denied the deity

Appendix 3: A Historical Summary of Unbelief

of Christ. When English and German theological liberalism invaded the United States, they were met with a solid wall of theological fundamentalists.

Starting from a foundation of skepticism regarding the Bible (led by the textual critics), liberals/ Modernists denied most major doctrinal tenets of the Bible. They denied the inspiration and accuracy of the Bible through their teaching on textual criticism and they denied the truth of the Bible in their teachings of Higher Criticism.

> Modernists taught that the Bible did not come to us by direct revelation from God through the Holy Spirit's ministry to holy men of old, but came, rather, as a purely human evolutionary process. Supposedly, as men's ideas about God became more sophisticated, the writers of the Bible drew an increasingly more sophisticated picture of God, until we come to the allegedly higher theological ideas of the New Testament. Modernists do not believe the Bible's historical accounts are accurate and do not believe the miracles actually happened. They do not believe there actually was an Adam and an Eve, a Garden of Eden, or a worldwide flood. They do not believe the miracles recorded in Exodus and other parts of the O.T. happened as recorded, considering them mere religious myths much like the Hindu fables. Many Modernists do not believe in that Christ was virgin-born, nor that He is truly God, nor that He actually rose from the dead, etc. They do not believe that the Gospel accounts of His life are factual, and they assume that we do not have in the Bible an accurate idea of what Jesus Christ was truly like. [231]

I imagine the readers of this book will not need a definition of fundamentalism, but here it is anyway. A Fundamentalist in any religion or persuasion is basically someone who believes in the "fundamentals." A fundamentalist Christian is someone who believes in the basic Christian truths from the Bible. Since the 1880's, Presbyterians had been fighting battles against the Modernists. The general trend was downhill. In 1910, the general assembly of the Presbyterian Church of the USA passed the "Doctrinal Deliverance of 1910." This declared that there were five doctrines a Christian must hold: 1) the inspiration and inerrancy of the Bible, 2) the virgin birth of Christ, 3) Christ's death was an atonement for sin, 4) the bodily resurrection of Christ, and 5) the historical reality of Christ's miracles. In 1910, Lyman Stewart sponsored a series of booklets called *The Fundamentals: A Testimony to the Truth.* This coined the term "fundamentalist." Anyone rallying around the five "fundamentals" became known as a "fundamentalist."

The battle raged through the first half of the twentieth century. Modernism infiltrated churches, denominational headquarters, and schools of all major denominations. Ultimately little was left of the old mainline denominations of the Lutherans, the Presbyterians, and others that had not fallen into the Modernist camp. Conservative Christians generally separated and created their own organizations and schools. By 1950, liberals and fundamentalists were in separate camps and separate organizations, existing side by side. But great damage had been done. The entire Northern Baptist Convention, for example, became liberal and many left it forming their own organizations, such as the General Association of Regular Baptist Churches (1932).

However, God doesn't need the conventions or the denominations. He wants believers and churches who love Him and believe His Book. Many conservative believers were left and carried on the work of world evangelism.

Unfortunately, the American culture was also affected. The people had a hard time letting go of their hold on the Bible, but it was much weaker than before. The modernists had taught America (and England and Germany, for that matter) that the Bible was not the authoritative book Christians claimed. They taught that the Bible is a fallible human book.

How did all this come about? The liberals slowly infiltrated Christian institutions and churches. One of their most important targets was colleges. Dr. David Brown summarized how one such institution, Princeton Theological Seminary fell into theological liberalism in his booklet, *The Preservation of the Scriptures.*

Appendix 3: A Historical Summary of Unbelief

1. ***1851-78*** - Charles Hodge, 2nd President of Princeton Theological Seminary (a stronghold of Protestant orthodoxy) enters the slippery slope which began the fatal slide to rejection of Providential Preservation by moving toward an Enlightenment and "scientific" apologetic where human mind and human reason are a reliable and authoritative guide to truth, including the truths of the Bible.

2. ***1859*** - Charles Darwin publishes *On The Origin of Species.* Atheist and unbelievers jumped on Darwin's THEORY! ... Hence, the educated "Bible" Scholars looked for a way to syncretize this new theory with the Bible so they did not look anti-scientific and uneducated ...

3. ***1881*** - The stage was set ... Brook Foss Westcott and Fenton John Anthony Hort changed the Greek text of the New Testament to one of their own *'private interpretation.'* ... they forsook the Biblical and historical doctrine of Divine Preservation as held by the early saints, Reformers and our Baptist ancestry as clearly revealed in the Word of God ...

4. ***1878-1886*** - Archibald Alexander Hodge, son of Charles, was the 3rd President of Princeton Theological Seminary who favored higher textual criticism, arguing that Providential Preservation's statement that the text has been kept "pure in all ages" meant "a state of essential purity" where "the essential integrity of our text is ESTABLISHED." And how was ***integrity*** established? It was *"by means of a careful collation and comparison of ...the Ancient manuscripts."* (A. A. Hodge, *A commentary on the Confession of Faith,* 1874). Further, A. A. Hodge shamelessly said the original autographs were not inerrant. *"It is even possible that some of the autographs, if we had them, might not be altogether free from errors as arise from the slip of a pen, as the apostles and ["had"] amanuensis who were not inspired."*(Lefferts Loethscher, *Facing the Enlightenment and Pietism).*

5.   **1887-1921-** Benjamin Breckenridge Warfield was the 4th President of Princeton. He wholly embraced Higher Criticism and the critical text of Westcott & Hort. Dr. Warfield ignored the Providential Preservation of the Scriptures and treated the text of the New Testament as he would the text of any book or writing. *(for* a full treatment of this see - www.febc.edu.sg/VPP12.htm). Warfield adopted the techniques of textual criticism employed by Westcott-Hort. *"Warfield embraced the ability of the apostate editors of the New Testament text to restore the words of God."* (DBS eNews; Vol 1 Issue 94; April 2010).

6.   **Today -** Most of the leading Fundamentalist Leaders, Colleges and Seminaries deny the historic and Biblical view of Providential Preservation of the Scriptures. [232]

Sadly, it was the second half of the twentieth century that did the most damage to faith in the Word of God. At first, most of the Fundamentalists, especially in the Baptist camps, stood for the King James Bible and the Received Text during the great battles. But even they were affected by the doctrines of Modernism. The constant refrain from liberals that the Bible had errors affected them without most of them realizing it.

In the first half of the twentieth century, "fundamentalist" and "evangelical" were basically synonymous terms. However, in 1948, that all began to change. The National Association of Evangelicals was formed in 1942 by a group of fundamentalists that included Bob Jones, Sr., John R. Rice, Charles Woodbridge, Harry Ironside, Harold Okenga, and David Otis Fuller. Later, Harold Okenga said that it was he who preached the sermon that started the "new-evangelical: movement. The sermon was preached at the Civic Auditorium in Pasadena in 1948. He said:

> Neo-evangelicalism was born in 1948 in connection with a convocation address which I gave in the Civic Auditorium in Pasadena. While reaffirming the theological view of fundamentalism, this address

repudiated its ecclesiology and its social theory. The ringing call for a **repudiation of separatism** and the summons to social involvement received a hearty response from many evangelicals. The name caught on and spokesmen such as Drs. Harold Lindsell, Carl F.H. Henry, Edward Carnell, and Gleason Archer supported this viewpoint. We had no intention of launching a movement, but found that the emphasis attracted widespread support and exercised great influence. **Neo-evangelicalism... different from fundamentalism** in its repudiation of separatism and its **determination to engage itself in the theological dialogue of the day**. (Emphasis-Author) [233]

The "repudiation of separatism" and the "determination to engage in the dialogue of the day" came down to two things. First, as schools and denominations and churches went apostate into liberalism, they determined Christians should stay in those institutions and try to change things from within. Unfortunately, fundamentalists had tried to fight modernism from within in many denominations and failed, before they finally decided to separate. Remaining with these apostate institutions was a violation of God's command when He said, *"Be ye not unequally yoked together with unbelievers: for what fellowship hath righteousness with unrighteousness? and what communion hath light with darkness? And what concord hath Christ with Belial? or what part hath he that believeth with an infidel?"* (2 Cor. 6:14-15)

Second, they determined to dialogue with unbelieving liberals and textual critics. Instead of taking a stand against them they decided to discuss theology with them. There is nothing wrong with witnessing and teaching someone who is theologically wrong (2 Tim. 2:24). However, the New-evangelicals met with them on the intellectual and rationalistic playing field of the liberals.

The result of all this was disaster. The evangelicals failed to convince the liberals, but the liberals greatly influenced the evangelicals. In general, evangelicals did not abandon most of their basic Biblical beliefs. However, their own faith in the Bible itself was undermined to the point that they completely accepted lower criticism (textual criticism.) They came to the point that they rejected the providential preservation of Scripture and accepted the idea that all Bibles existing now have errors. The only way they could reconcile their faith to this anomaly (how does a Bible with errors give perfect salvation and doctrine), was to change the definition of "inerrant." To them, the term no longer means that all God's words have been preserved and translated correctly. Its means the "message" *only* of the Bible is true.

America began to hear preachers in evangelical and fundamental pulpits preach the KJB along with statements like, "It is unfortunate it is translated this way..." and "a better rendering would be ..." and "a better translation is ..." and "the older manuscripts say..." These things were heard more and more in the pulpits of men who had a reputation for being orthodox in their beliefs.

All the while, English Bible translation work continued. Every new English translation that came out stated that, while the KJB is the standard, we need a new translation that will speak to America like the old KJB did when it was translated. The comparison was always with the KJB, because every new translation lived a short life. The KJB had that much hold on Christians, because the Spirit of God promoted it. Even the New American Standard Bible lost most of its popularity after a few years. The NIV has now held the field for longer than any other, and the New King James finally broke the hold of the KJB with many believers. However, the KJB continues to be a best seller every year.

There was more going on than the average Christian knows. Modernists have never given up the fight to destroy the KJB and the Textus Receptus. They are continuing their fight right now with very little opposition from fundamentalists or evangelicals. The evangelical leaders and scholars have laid down their arms and surrendered. In fact, they have joined the liberals. I am not saying that evangelicals no longer believe in the atonement, the deity of Christ, the virgin birth, the resurrection, etc. No I am not saying that. Denying those things is what grew out of Rationalism and Higher Criticism. I am sure that most evangelicals would hold to those things. Evangelical leaders and evangelical "scholars" may have rejected Higher Criticism *so far*, but they have *swallowed Lower Criticism hook, line, and sinker*. They don't even seem to think about the fact that Higher and Lower Criticism were interlinked and came from the same rotten source ... unbelief in the Word of God.

Appendix 3: A Historical Summary of Unbelief

To review, what is Lower Criticism? It is defined by The *Merriam-Webster Dictionary* as, "criticism concerned with the recovery of original texts especially of Scripture through collation of extant manuscripts." [234] It is also called textual criticism. Evangelicals in general have accepted this as a legitimate endeavor. Therefore, they have also accepted the need for continual new translations.

Look at the definition again. The very idea that we have to "recover" the Scriptures implies that at least part of the scriptures somehow got lost. How could that be, unless God is a liar? God said He will preserve all His Words for us and for our children (Is. 59:22). The entire discipline of both Higher and Lower (Textual) Criticism is predicated on the belief that God did not keep all His Words. *Today's Evangelicalism agrees.*

In regard to the text of the Bible, Evangelical leaders and many fundamental leaders are on the same road the liberals were on in the days of Hugo Grotius (1583-1645) and Schleiermacher (1768-1834). They are going the same direction. They had the same viewpoint on the Bible: 1) God did not preserve His Words and some say He didn't inspire them, 2) the Bible must be restored to its original condition, because it is corrupted and some words are lost, 3) the Bible is not without error, and 4) human reason is all that's necessary to understand and restore the Bible. All liberal theology begins at these points with a denial of the Bible. Evangelical leaders in the twenty-first century agree with these four points and, so, do not believe we now have an inerrant Bible. To them, *all Bibles* whether English, Greek, Hebrew, or any other language contain errors in the words. They are headed the exact same direction the "Christian" scholars were headed in the enlightenment. History is repeating itself.

In regard to the Bible, there is only one difference between liberals and evangelicals. Evangelicals accept inerrant inspiration, but reject inerrant preservation. Liberals reject both. However, the different doesn't really amount to anything. Both liberals and evangelicals have both ended up with a Bible that has errors and none of them even know where all the errors are. None of them have a Bible they can fully trust. Realizing this, the evangelicals have reduced preservation to the message only, not the words of

Scripture. To them, the Bible has errors, but its message is true. They have no basis whatsoever for this "faith."

Let's take a few moments to see what some prominent evangelicals believe about the Bible.

> In answer to a question about the inerrancy of the Bible, as we have many translations: "However, consider the following point from our statement of faith … Its **assertions** are factually true in all the original autographs … Notice that inerrancy applies **only** to the original autographs (manuscripts). It does not necessarily extend to every single copy." (Answers in Genesis-Emphasis-Author) [235]

Inerrancy is limited to "assertions" rather than "words." Also, inerrancy is limited to *only the original writings (autographs).*

An article by the International Mission Board, after it commented that "a loss of inerrancy cuts at the root of the Great Commission," admitted "***inerrancy belongs, strictly speaking, to the original autographs of Scripture, not the copies*** … Nevertheless, tell national pastors, 'Take this book, my brother. Read it, study it, and teach it to your people, knowing that every word is God's Word: true, trustworthy, and without error.'" (Emphasis-Author) In other words, **lie to them.** [236] Tell them something you don't believe.

These days, you will often see doctrinal statements that say the Bible is inerrant in the original autographs. This means two things: 1) only the first written documents (autographs) of the Bible are inerrant, but we no longer have them, and 2) none of the original language copies we have now, none of the original language texts we have now, and none of the translations are inerrant. In other words, we have NO inerrant Bible today.

> We believe that the sixty-six books of the Old and New Testaments are verbally inspired of God and inerrant in the original writing … (Baptist Mid-Mission) [237]
>
> it is therefore inerrant in the originals and authoritative in all matters. (Liberty University) [238]

Appendix 3: A Historical Summary of Unbelief

There is no perfect English translation (Bob Jones University) [239]

We believe that the Bible is the Word of God; without error as originally written. [240]

No, I don't think we have an infallible, inerrant translation anywhere. (Marquette University) [241]

To say that the Scriptures were inerrant only in the original manuscripts is to admit they are NOT inerrant NOW. There is only one difference between a Modernist Liberal and an Evangelical in regard to his doctrine of the Bible. The evangelical says he believes in the inspiration and inerrancy of the original manuscripts, but the Liberal rejects that. *They both agree* that what we have now is definitely *NOT* inerrant. This includes every translation, printed text, and manuscript in existence.

A growing vanguard of young graduates of evangelical colleges who hold doctorates from non-evangelical divinity centers now question or disown inerrancy and the doctrine is held less consistently by evangelical faculties. ... Some retain the term and reassure supportive constituencies but nonetheless stretch the term's meaning. (Emphasis-Author) [242]

More and more organizations and individuals historically committed to an infallible Scripture **have been embracing and propagating the view that the Bible has errors in it.** This movement away from the historic standpoint has been most noticeable among those often labeled neo-evangelicals. This change of position with respect to the infallibility of the Bible is widespread and has occurred in evangelical denominations, Christian colleges, theological seminaries, publishing houses, and learned societies. (emphasis-author) [243]

Most people outside the evangelical community itself are totally unaware of the profound changes that have occurred within evangelicalism during the last several years--in the movement's understanding of the inspiration and authority of Scripture, in its social concerns, cultural attitudes and ecumenical posture, and in the nature of its emerging leadership. ... **evangelical theologians have begun looking at the Bible with a scrutiny reflecting their widespread acceptance of the principles of Historical and Literary Criticism** ... The position--affirming that Scripture is inerrant or infallible in its teaching on matters of faith and conduct but not necessarily in all its assertions concerning history and the cosmos--is gradually becoming ascendant among the most highly respected Evangelical theologians. ... these new trends ... indicate that evangelical theology is becoming more centrist, more open to biblical criticism and more accepting of science and broad cultural analysis. (Emphasis-Author)[244]

Within Evangelicalism there are a growing number who are modifying their views on the inerrancy of the bible so that the full authority of Scripture is completely undercut. But is happening in very subtle ways. Like the snow lying side-by-side on the ridge, the new views on biblical authority often seem at first glance not to be very far from what evangelicals, until just recently, have always believed. But also, like the snow lying side-by-side on the ridge, the new views when followed consistently end up a thousand miles apart. What may seem like a minor difference at first, in the end makes all the difference in the world ... compromising the full authority of Scripture eventually affects what it means to be a Christian theologically and how we live in the full spectrum of human life. (Emphasis-Author) [245]

Where are we now? More importantly, where does that leave our culture and our youth? Perhaps these questions can be answered in the experience of A. J. Zimmerman, a young man who was led to Christ when he attended youth meetings with a friend. The author of the article, *Evangelicals are Losing the Battle for the*

Appendix 3: A Historical Summary of Unbelief

Bible, And They're Just Fine with That, written in 2016, had this to say after interviewing Zimmerman.

> Since graduating from high school, Zimmermann has undergone a revolution in his thinking about evangelicals' foundational text, the Bible, to the extent that he no longer regards the Bible as inerrant, dictated by God, historically accurate in all of its claims or even internally consistent with itself … I was introduced to Zimmermann by one of his seminary teachers, an Azusa Pacific biblical studies professor named Karen Strand Winslow, who put me in touch with several of her students after I asked her what young evangelicals think about the Bible these days. In addition to his dismissal of biblical inerrancy, Zimmermann told me he no longer believes the biblical book of Genesis is "concerned […] with young-versus-old-earth, literal days of creation stuff." He said biblical passages appearing to condemn homosexuality are products of their time and do not necessarily apply to present-day same-sex couples "committed in a consensual relationship." The same goes for New Testament prohibitions against women in church leadership. "We often forget that Jesus's ministry was founded by women and that the first evangelists were women," he added. Overall, Zimmermann said, the days when evangelicals defined themselves by their uncompromising style of biblical interpretation are over. "Before my generation […] it was like, if you don't believe this doctrine, you're undermining the work of Christ on the cross. [My generation is] not as okay with the simplified answers." [246]

Conclusion? The doubts about the Bible fostered by liberals and embraced within the evangelical community has undermined the world's confidence in Scripture and nearly destroyed the foundations of morality.

I haven't included these quotes to criticize or judge anyone, but rather to show where we are as evangelicals and fundamentalists. All liberalism begins with doubting the Bible and **we are there**. In fact, liberal institutions such as the United Bible Societies, are accepted as legitimate, evangelical institutions. Very few question the beliefs of the leaders and editors or the history of these institutions anymore. Evangelicals embrace the translations they promote and evangelical translators use the UBS Greek text for foreign translations. They are promoting liberalism without realizing it.

The entire movement I have outlined in this appendix is one movement. However, it was not led and planned by one man or one group of men. It was not run by any one organization or one membership. It has the characteristics of a diverse movement, but it has all moved toward one goal: the destruction of the Bible and Biblical Christianity. It had one overall theme: Yea, hath God said? It has all the earmarks of a movement planned, led, and energized by "the god of this world" who has "blinded the minds of them which believe not, lest the light of the glorious gospel of Christ, who is the image of God, should shine unto them" (2 Cor. 4:4).

Appendix 4:

A Few Passages in the KJB Disputed from Greek

Are there places in the King James Bible where questions can legitimately arise? My answer is yes. Questions may be asked, but questions or accusations are *not evidence of error.* Many are eager, even happy, to find errors or difficulties in the KJB text. The difference between me and some others is that I always assume "innocent until proven guilty." That is, I assume the King James Bible is translated correctly until proof is offered that it is not (so far, no one has offered any proof). So, when I look into questions about the text of the KJB, I am looking for reasons why it is right, not why it is wrong.

So, why is this important? The reason is that the KJB stands alone among English Bible translations. The King James is the only true English translation from the TR.

I can hear it now. What about the New King James Version. The NKJV is only partially a translation of the TR. The Old Testament was translated from the Hebraica Stuttgartensia, which is different from the Ben Chayyim Masoretic Text. It is true that the TR was the *basic* source for the New Testament, but many of the passages were translated like the other modern versions.

> We have corresponded with the executive editor of the Old Testament portion of the NKJV, Dr. James Price. In April of 1996 he admitted to me that he is not committed to the Received Text and that he supports the modern critical text in general ... It is obvious that Dr. Price holds the standard eclectic text position that was popularized by Westcott and Hort in the late 1800s and that he is committed to modern textual criticism. By his own testimony, he has no love for or commitment to the Received Text ... With men like this involved; yea in charge; it is not possible

that the New King James Bible could be merely a simple revision of the KJV. I do not know of one man involved with the translation of the NKJV who has a conviction about the absolute authority of the Old and New Testament texts underlying the KJV ... Dr. Price told me that the NKJV translators did not solely follow the Masoretic Hebrew text in the Old Testament of the NKJV but that they introduced textual changes. This is born out in the Preface to the NKJV, which says the New King James Bible modifies the Masoretic Hebrew with the Septuagint, the Latin Vulgate, "a variety of ancient versions," and the Dead Sea Scrolls ... In 1982, Thomas Nelson published "The Greek New Testament According to the Majority Text." The editors, Zane Hodges and Arthur Farstad, were also key players in the New King James Version project. There are almost 1900 differences between the Received Text and the Hodges-Farstad Majority Text ... There are an estimated 100,000 changes, averaging 80 per page. This was probably done for copyright purposes. [247]

Matt 1:1 and Matt 1:17

The book of the generation of Jesus Christ, the son of David, the son of Abraham.

So all the generations from Abraham to David are fourteen generations; and from David until the carrying away into Babylon are fourteen generations; and from the carrying away into Babylon unto Christ are fourteen generations.

Objection: The English word "generation (s)" is used several times in these two verses. However, two different Greek words are used. In Matthew 1:1, the word is *genesis* which means the beginning or production of something. In Matthew 1:17, the word is *genea* and has the idea of a natural descent of procreation.

Appendix 4: A Few Passages in the KJB Disputed from Greek

Answer: First, we want to settle all the definitions involved.
1) **Γένεσις (genesis) – Mt. 1:1**
procreation; in N. T. birth, nativity ... in the sense of descent, lineage ... genealogy, genealogical table,
2) **Γενεά (genea) - Mt. 1:17**
a) offspring, progeny ... b) a descent, degree, i.e. in a genealogical line of ancestors or descendants ... c) spoken of the period of time from one descent to another, i. e. the average duration of human life ... [248]

Since the word "generation" was used for both of these Greek words, we should look at the English definitions of "generation."

GENERATION, n. The act of begetting; procreation, as of animals.
1. Production; formation; as the generation of sounds or of curves or equations.
2. A single succession in natural descent, as the children of the same parents; hence, an age. Thus we say, the third, the fourth, or the tenth generation. Gen 15:16.
3. The people of the same period, or living at the same time.
O faithless and perverse generation. Luke 9.
4. Genealogy; a series of children or descendants from the same stock.
This is the book of the generations of Adam. Gen 5.
5. A family; a race.
6. Progeny; offspring.

The key to understanding the KJB translation is in the English definition of the word "generation" and in the context where the two Greek words are used. The English word has 6 definitions, so it can be used in six different ways in six different contexts. The context determines which definition applies.

Point 1: Meaning of **Γένεσις Mt. 1:1** - In the context, the word points to the **origin and lineage** of Jesus Christ as a man.

Point 2: Meaning of **Γενεά - Mt. 1:17.** In the context, the word points to "an age (i.e. the time ordinarily occupied by each successive generation)."

Point 3: Matt. 1:1 matches the English definition of generation #4 and fits the lexicon definition of Γένεσις. The chapter is about the genealogy of Jesus Christ. **_Therefore, the English word "generation" is accurate in this context._**

Point 4: Matt. 1:17 matches the English definition of generation #2 and the definition of Γενεά. **_Therefore, the English word "generation" is also accurate in this context._**

These are exact definitions of the word generation that exactly fit the usage of the Greek words in these two verses. Therefore, if a translator uses the KJV, he would see "generation" in both places. He would still have the right source word as long as he understood the different usages of the word which can be found in a dictionary. No rule requires a different word for each different Greek word. The example does not illustrate rigidity, but, rather, understanding of words.

The translators of the Chinese Authorized Version have had the same problem in reverse. 2 Timothy 1:5 says, "Now the end of the commandment is charity ..." The problem was with the word "end." The English word has 20 meanings depending on the context. The Greek word, *telos*, has similar meanings. However, Chinese does not have a word that carries all the meanings of "end" in English or Greek. Therefore, a different Chinese word has to be used each time "end" has a different contextual meaning.

Matthew 21:13

> *And said unto them, It is written, My house shall be called the house of prayer; but ye have made it a den of thieves.*

Objection: λεγει is translated in past tense when it is actually in present tense.

Reply: This is not a major concern. I include it because it is another example of the differences between languages. It illustrates the principle that when translating, a different grammar in the target language, may express the meaning of the source language better. So, in Greek it reads, "And says to them." This does not read correctly for English, does it? It reads better in English as, "And said to them."

Appendix 4: A Few Passages in the KJB Disputed from Greek

However, a translator should be aware of the difference. It is possible that a translator who is using the KJB as his primary source text will be working in a language in which the past tense does not work well. He may be tempted to put it in past tense anyway, because that is how it is in the KJB. If he knew that in Greek it is present tense, he might feel better to translate it in present tense.

Matt 27:35 (Mark 15:24; John 19:24)

And they crucified him, and parted his garments, casting lots

Objection: "Casting lots" in the KJB is plural, but in the TR it is singular, "lot."

Answer: "Casting lots" is the English *name* to this activity. The "lot" in Greek is singular, so, apparently the Greek *name* to the activity is "casting a lot." In reality, there were several lots used. Each person involved had a single lot (hence the singular in Greek) and they all cast their lot into someone's lap, so several lots were cast. Each person cast a lot, but all together, they cast lots. Hence, the name given to the activity is "casting lots" in English. I acknowledge that another language may refer to the activity in a different way.

Acts 1:26 uses the same word and it's plural. I checked the NIV, CSV, RSV, NASB, and the NKJV on Mt. 27:35. They all have "casting lots" plural. "Casting a lot" is the Greek idiom for the game and "casting lots" is the English idiom. Trained translators should be able to discern how this is best expressed in the target language.

Acts 19:37

*For ye have brought hither these men, which are neither robbers of **churches**, nor yet blasphemers of your goddess.*

Objection: The Greek word is *hierosulos* which comes from *hieron* which is always *temple* and never *church*. Even the context shows this because they were being accused of crimes against Diana, "temples" would have been a better choice.

Reply: This one calls for some research *beyond the lexicon*. The Greek word *hieron* is used of *pagan* temples only two times in the NT. Those times are Acts 19:27, 37. Every other time it is used of the Jewish temple, the Christian's body, or the church, the body of Christ, and is translated "temple." So, since the KJB translators knew full well the meaning of the word, it is obvious they had some reason to use a different word here.

Here it is. In Elizabethan days, the English word "church" was used freely of both Christian buildings of worship and pagan buildings of worship. It meant both. It was a correct and accurate word at that time.

> These men, which are neither robbers of churches.— Better, robbers of temples. It was not unusual for the writers of the Elizabethan age to apply the term, which we confine to Christian buildings, to heathen temples. They would speak, e.g., of the "church" of Diana, or the "chapel" of Apollo. [249]

> Acts 19:37. γὰρ: "for," *i.e.*, they had done something rash.—τοὺς ἄνδρ. τούτους: Gaius and Aristarchus, ἱεροσύλους, "robbers of temples," R.V., in A.V. "of churches," the word "church" being applied as often in the Elizabethan age to pagan temples. [250]

> The English word "church" refers to congregations or places of worship, Pagan or Christian. For example, the Church of Scientology is not a Christian Church. Furthermore, "church," being derived from the Old English "cirice," which is in turn derived from the Greek "kyrie" (lord), denotes a place dedicated for a lord (*Oxford English Dictionary*). This "church" in Acts 19:37 is a church of Diana, the lady lord of the Pagan Ephesians. [251]

If any translator is using the KJB as his source text, then he should be careful not make a translation error in Acts. 19:37. "Church" is a word that has changed its meaning and is not understood the same way now.

Appendix 4: A Few Passages in the KJB Disputed from Greek

Hebrews 10:23

Let us hold fast the profession of our faith without wavering; (for he is faithful that promised;)

Objection: The Greek word translated faith in Hebrews 10:23 is *elpis*. It does not mean faith. It means hope. The word is translated "hope" over fifty times; every time it's used, but once, Heb. 10:23.

Answer: If the translators did this in a single spot out of over 50 times, then they knew full well the meaning of ***elpis*** and they must have had good reason to translate it different in this verse. Here is my perspective on this.

Many Greek words are flexible in their usage, as you know. The principle of *polysemy* teaches that words have multiple meanings. The verb form of the noun, ***elpis***, is ***elpizo***. It was translated "trust" or "trusteth" 16 times out of 32. Thayer defines *elpizo* as 1) hope and 2) to hopefully trust in. [252] *Trust is faith.* In its definition, the *Word Study Dictionary* uses these words to define ***elpizo***: to hope, expect with desire, to trust in, and confide in. [253]

Elpis is actually defined as 1) Hope, desire of some good with expectation of obtaining it; 2) trust and confidence; [254] 3) expectation and hope; [255] 4) anticipation with pleasure, expectation or confidence. [256] According to Webster, the English word, hope, is desire coupled with expectation and confidence. [257] *All of this includes a strong element of faith*, because faith is also trust, expectation, and confidence. [258]

In addition, Romans 8:24 is a cross reference to Ephesians 2:8. Rom. 8:24 says, "For we are saved by hope" and Eph. 2:8 says, "For we are saved through faith." Hope and faith are synonymous, depending on the context. Rom. 8:24 further states, "but hope that is seen is not hope: for what a man seeth, why doth he yet hope for?" That is the definition of faith. *"Now **faith** is the substance of things **hoped for**, the evidence of things not seen"* (Heb. 11:1). There is an unbreakable connection between the nature of faith and the nature of hope. Faith is hope and hope is part of faith; faith is the *assurance* of the hope.

Then there is the context of Heb. 10:23. Verse 22 says, "Let us draw near with a true heart in full assurance of faith." The word faith is *pistis* in verse 22 and is connected with the *elpis* of verse 23, which is followed up later in verse 23 with, "for he is faithful (pistos) that promised." The subject under discussion is faith, not merely hope. "Let us draw near with a true heart of faith … Let us hold fast the profession of our faith …; (for he is faithful that promised)."

Jude 8

Likewise also these filthy dreamers defile the flesh, despise dominion, and speak evil of dignities.

Objection: The KJV translates 'ενυπνιαζομενοι - *enupniazomoi* as "filthy dreamers." The Greek word literally means "dreamer," not "filthy" dreamer, whereas the Greek word literally does not mean "filthy" dreamers – merely 'dreamer'. (see Acts 2:17) It literally means "in their dreamings". Therefore, the word "filthy" is not necessary.

Reply: This is one of those instances when one should look closer before leaping. I do not mean to be uncharitable, but I want to warn translators and others who judge the texts to be careful. Be "slow to speak." The basic Greek word, *enupniazo*, does mean "dream," but it also means more than that.

> to dream, intrans., spoken of visions in dreams, Acts 2.17; fig… dreamers, i.e. holding vain and empty opinions, deceivers, Jude 8. [259]

> something seen in the sleep, a dream. Used intrans. and spoken of visions in dreams (Act 2:17 [cf. Sept.: Gen 28:12; Joe 2:28]). Pres. mid. part. nom. enupniazómenoi, dreamers, meaning ones holding vain and empty opinions, deceivers (Jud 1:8). [260]

There is also a figurative or idiomatic meaning to the word that includes "empty opinions, deceivers" and as Thayer puts it "metaphorically, to be beguiled with sensual images and carried away to an impious course of conduct." [261] Therefore, the KJB is completely justified to include "filthy" in the translation, considering

Appendix 4: A Few Passages in the KJB Disputed from Greek

the context of Jude, and any translator should consider doing likewise.

The word "filthy" in the KJB is in Italics. So, any translator using the KJB should know it is not a specifically separate word in the Greek text.

The KJB translators did not learn Greek at the same schools we did. Their knowledge of Greek came from the "experts." These were teachers from the Eastern Greek churches and Greeks themselves who fled into Western Europe from the onslaught of the Muslim armies just prior to the Reformation. The KJB translators had a much better understanding of Greek than many of us will ever have.

Revelation 21:9

And there came unto me one of the seven angels which had the seven vials full of the seven last plagues, and talked with me, saying, Come hither, I will shew thee **the bride, the Lamb's wife.**

Objection: In this case, the idea is that the King James Bible agrees with the UBS text over the TR. The UBS says, "the bride the lamb's wife." The Received Text says, "the bride of the lamb the wife." This is a small thing, but it is a difference between the KJB and the TR.

Answer: On the surface, it appears the objection is correct. However, the UBS Text did not exist in 1611, and the KJB did not use the Alexandrian Text or Vaticanus. This is what the UBS Text is based on. They did have several Latin texts available for consulting purposes.

The problem in Rev. 21:9 is with the comma and there are no commas in the original Greek text or in any of the Alexandrian manuscripts. Words in Greek sentences are not required to be in subject-verb-object order. They can be rearranged depending on what the author wishes to emphasize. We can look at this from several angles.

1. The literal translation from the TR is: *the bride of the lamb the wife.*

2.	If we insert the comma after *lamb*, we have "the bride of the lamb, the wife," which is very awkward English. That would be a very bad translation. It does NOT fit English syntax or usage.

3.	If we insert the comma after bride, we literally have: *the bride, of the lamb the wife.* This is literal TR Greek and must be put into proper English. The phrase "of the lamb" put into the usual usage in English becomes "the lamb's." So, in proper English "the bride, of the lamb the wife" becomes:

the bride, the lamb's wife.

… exactly as the KJB has it.

The KJB absolutely matches the TR. The KJB is a correct and accurate translation of the TR. This was translated and matches the KJB, without changing the word order of the TR.

Appendix 5:

Translation Challenge – Acts 19:20 God or Lord?

Acts 19:20 is a verse that contains a controversial translation in the KJV. It is a difficult problem. It's surprising that there has not been more said about it. At the mildest, it has been characterized as a difference between the King James Version and the Greek Received Text. It could be far worse, a translation error. The verse reads:

So mightily grew the word of God and prevailed.

The problem with this verse is the word "God" and the fact that the Greek text does not use the normal word that is translated "God." The normal Greek word for "God" is θεος or *theos.* The word used in Acts 19:20 is κυριος (kurios), which is normally translated "Lord." So, according to the Greek text the translation *should be* "word of the Lord," *rather than* "word of God." On the surface, the only logical conclusion seems to be that the KJV is in error here. The KJV is not an accurate translation, at least not in this verse. There are others who do not agree and defend the translation choice in the KJV.

It is clear and unmistakable that the KJV has "God" and the Greek Received Text has Kurios (Lord). That is indisputable. On the surface, it also seems certain that this verse is proof that the King James Version is not inerrant. Some, who say Acts 19:20 is an incorrect translation, will also say that the KJV is an accurate translation. However, the word "accurate" means "inerrant." Therefore, if Acts 19:20 is not correct, the KJV is neither inerrant nor accurate. There have been some who find certain ancient manuscripts and translations which read theos or a translation of theos, in this verse. However, we accept the Received Text as the preserved word of God in the Greek language. The Received Text has gone through many editions, but no editor was ever led to change Kurios to theos. Scrivener edited the Received Text to match the KJV (1881). Not even he would change it. So, we accept the Greek text as being correct.

However, this does not end the argument. There is another side of the coin to examine. The real question is whether the word Kurios *always and only* is to be translated "Lord" when applied to God or the Lord Jesus Christ. Put another way, *can Kurios ever correctly be translated "God?"* I would say that most people who read Greek would say no. All of us who have attended Greek elementary school have been taught that THE one and only way to translate Kurios, when it applies to God the Father or the Lord Jesus Christ, is "Lord." Therefore, the *only right way* to translate Acts 19:20 is "the word of the Lord." If Kurios *can be translated* "God," then the KJV *is accurate* and the translation of Acts 19:20 is not different from the Received Text.

Many of us have done some study in Greek beyond Greek elementary school and we have discovered that Greek words are often far more flexible than we initially learned. Some words carry general meanings that can be translated many ways in different contexts. These words do not have a single certain meaning and translation in all contexts. So, these words have to be translated according to the context. Doing so is not always easy. One such word is *ekenosen*. The word means "to *make empty*, that is, (figuratively) to *abase, neutralize, falsify.*" The word has a base definition, but it can be translated differently according to the context. Modern versions translate this literally (according to them, but sometimes literal means elementary) in Philippians 2:7 as, "emptied himself." The KJV translates it "made himself of no reputation." The KJV also variously translates the word "made void" and "made of none effect." These various translations of the same word all carry an element of "to neutralize," but the translation must be refined according to the context.

Another example is the Greek word *yinomai*. This word is one of the most flexible words in the New Testament. The basic meaning of the word is "cause to be" and "to become" (Strong's). Once again this word *must* be translated according to its meaning *in the context.* In the KJV, it is variously translated: it came to pass, made, done, become, forbid, been, arose, being, be fulfilled, be married (Rom. 7:3-4), brought, cometh, doing, grow, had, have, past, preferred, seemed, showed, trembled, waxed, wrought, assembled, divided, finished, and others. Once again, there is an element of "becoming" in each of these (in the context), but the word cannot be translated that way in the contexts. Take, for instance, Romans 7:3-4 where the word is translated "be married." Using "becomes" the verse reads, "So then if, while her husband lives, she *becomes* to another man, she shall be called an adulteress." The phrase "she becomes to another man" makes no sense in English nor would it be proper to translate it that way. What does she become to the other man? The context is marriage, so the KJV translators correctly chose to translate it "be married."

How flexible is Kurios? Can it be properly translated "God?" That is the question we will seek to examine in this article. Kurios also has basic meanings which widen its translation possibilities.

Basic Definitions

First, let's take a look at the basic definitions of Kurios given in lexicons, such as Strong's, Abbott-Smith, and Robson. Strong defines it this way: "From κῦρος kuros (*supremacy*); *supreme* in authority, that is, (as noun) *controller*; by implication *Mr.* (as a respectful title)." The *Abbott-Smith* Lexicon says, "having power, authority...lord, master." The flowing is an outlined list from Charles Robson's lexicon.

1.   lord, master, owner. 1. GENERALLY.
   - a)   as possessor, owner, master; of property .
   - b)   of a supreme lord, sovereign; the Roman emperor.
   - c)   as an honorary title of address, especially to superiors, as in Engl. master, sir.
2.   spoken of God and Christ.
   - a)   of God as the supreme Lord and Sovereign of the universe with the art.,
   - b)   of the Lord Jesus Christ.
     - (a) in reference to his abode on earth as a master and teacher.

A Practical Theology of Bible Translating

> (b) as the supreme Lord of the gospel - dispensation, Head over all things to the church, Lord of all. [262]

The word kurios is at base a word that speaks of authority; sometimes supreme authority. It can be applied to both men and God. The KJV translates it with words like sir, master, owner, lord (applied to men), and Lord (applied to God). Since it is translated in various ways and applies to an individual with great, even supreme, power and authority, perhaps it could be translated "God" in the right context. The vast majority of times this word is used in the New Testament, it is translated "Lord" or a variation of it. Once, in Acts 19:20, it is translated "God." The word implies someone who is supreme in authority and of great power and the Lord of the universe. That is its *meaning*, not necessarily the *limit of its translation possibilities.* I believe that it is valid to translate the Greek word Kurios as "God" for the following reasons.

#1 The KJV Translators Were in Good Company

The reading "word of God" in Acts 19:20 is not unique to the King James Version. It has been pointed out that this same translation was typical of the previous English translations. The first English translation from Hebrew and Greek was done by William Tyndale. From 1524 to 1536 (his death) he translated the New Testament and a large part of the Old Testament. After his death up until the King James translators began to translate in 1604, there were several English translations. Producing these versions took a period of about one hundred years. Tyndale's translation of Acts 19:20 was "word of God." The same translation was in Matthew's Bible (1537), The Great Bible (1540), The Bishops Bible (1568), and the Geneva Bible (1587).

Not only do these translations handle Acts 19:20 the same way the KJV does, but the translators of these versions agreed with the forty-seven King James translators. All these translators had lives that covered a period of more than one hundred years. Couple that with the carefulness and knowledge of the KJV translators. In all their scholarship, they believed it proper to translate *kurios* this way. They translated the word *kurios* as "lord" hundreds of times and they translated it as "God" only one time. The decision to translate *kurios* as *God* here had to pass the test with all forty-seven translators. They did not choose the word "God" carelessly. They did not make a mistake. *They did it deliberately, on purpose.* We don't know why they made that choice, but we can reasonably assume they had good reasons. These things don't prove that their choice was correct, but it gives a reasonable assurance that it *could* be. All the other translators of the other versions made the same translation choice. No doubt it was consistent with the understanding of Greek in that day. There was present among all these men a level of learning in Greek and Hebrew that today's scholars should envy.

#2 The Testimony of Others

Those who say that there is a translation error in the KJV in Acts 19:20 or who just say there is "difference" are merely voicing their opinions about the matter. There are other learned individuals who have studied this and other issues regarding the Greek word kurios. They, too, have opinions. One of those is Dr. Jeffrey Khoo, Academic Dean of Far East Bible College in Singapore. Regarding Acts 19:20, he said:

> The KJV is not a mistranslation, and does not differ from the TR. The Greek word kurios can be translated in a number of ways depending on the context. It can be rendered "Lord", "master", "Sir", "God", or "owner". (see The Complete Word Study Dictionary: New Testament, 900-1). Acts 19:20 certainly allows for "God" instead of "Lord" since the context is speaking of the Word of God as a whole. If it is rendered as "the word of the Lord" it might be construed as some specific word from Jesus instead of God's Word or the Holy Scriptures in general. In any case, whether it is "the word of God", or "the word of the Lord", both are perfectly acceptable translations of the original. [263]

Another writer states that the term *kurios*, when applied to Jesus is meant in the highest possible sense, which is God. In his book, *Christian Theology, 2nd Edition,* Millard J. Erickson, Seminary Professor, states:

> There is a more general argument for the deity of Christ. The New Testament writers ascribe the term κυριος (*kurios*-"Lord") to Jesus, particularly in his risen and ascended state. While the term can most certainly be used without any high Christological connotations, there are several considerations that argue that the term signifies divinity when it is applied to Jesus. First, in the Septuagint κυριος is the usual translation of the name יהוה (Jehovah) and of the reverential ארני (Adonai) which was ordinarily substituted for it. Further, several New Testament references to Jesus as "Lord" are quotations of Old Testament texts employing one of the Hebrew names for God (e.g., Acts 2:20-21 and Rom. 10:13 [cf. Joel 2:31-32]; 1 Peter 3:15 [cf. Is. 8:13]). These references make it clear that the apostles meant to give Jesus the title *Lord* in the highest sense. Finally, κυριος is used in the New Testament to designate both God the Father, the sovereign God (e.g., Matt. 1:20; 9:38; 11:25; Acts 17:24; Rev. 4:11), and Jesus (e.g., Luke 2:11; John 20:28; Acts 10:36; 1 Cor. 2:8; Phil. 2:11; James 2:1; Rev. 19:16). William Childs Robinson comments that when Jesus "is addressed as the exalted Lord, he is so identified with God that there is ambiguity in some passages as to whether the Father or the Son is meant (e.g., Acts 1:24; 2:47; 8:39; 9:31; 11:21; 13:10-12; 16:14; 20:19; 21:14; cf. 18:26; Rom. 14:11)." For Jews particularly, the term κυριος suggests that Christ was equal with the Father. [264]

It is clear that one meaning of kurios, when it is applied to Jesus Christ, is "God." 1 Corinthians 12:3 tells us: *"Wherefore I give you to understand, that no man speaking by the Spirit of God calleth Jesus accursed: and that no man can say that Jesus is the Lord, but by the Holy Ghost. "* No one can call Jesus "the Lord" unless it is by the Spirit of God. To call Jesus "the Lord" is to call Jesus "God." The term

Appendix 5: Translation Challenge Acts 19:20-God or Lord?

"the Lord" obviously means "God." Therefore, one definition of the Greek term kurios is "God" when it is applied to Jesus or God the Father.

#3 Kurios is Equivalent to Jehovah

Several writers have equated the term *kurios* with *Jehovah* of Old Testament Hebrew. Dr. Erickson made that statement in the quote above. Another such source is *The Complete Word Study Dictionary,* by Dr. Spiros Zodhiates in the New Testament, which says, "*kúrios*; gen. *kuríou*, masc. noun from *kúros* (n.f.), might, power. Lord, master, owner. Also the NT Gr. equivalent for the OT Hebr. Jehovah." (Emphasis is mine.) [265] Vine's Expository Dictionary of New Testament Words puts it this way: "kurios is the Sept. and NT representative of Heb. Jehovah ('LORD' in Eng. versions), see Mat 4:7; Jam 5:11, e.g., of adon, Lord, Mat 22:44, and of Adonay, Lord, Mat 1:22; it also occurs for Elohim, God, 1Pe 1:25." [266]

This is more significant than it may seem on the surface. The great objection to the idea that *kurios* equals *Jehovah* is that the Old Testament translates *Jehovah* as "LORD" not "God." This would be devastating to any argument that *kurios* can be translated "God," if *Jehovah* can only be translated "Lord." That is, it would be devastating, if it was true. It is not true.

Yes, *Jehovah* is translated in the Old Testament as "LORD;" but, not always. It is translated that way in hundreds of Old Testament passages. However, it is also translated "God" in several places (e.g., Gen.6:5; Ex. 23:17; Ex. 34:23; 2Sam.12:22). In the formula, "Lord God" the Hebrew is usually "*Adon Jehovah*" or a variation. *Adon* is translated "Lord" and *Jehovah* is translated "God" in Exodus 23:17 and Exodus 34:23. However, in Genesis 6:5 and 2 Samuel 12:22, *Jehovah* stands alone and is translated "God" in the KJV. "*And GOD (Jehovah) saw that the wickedness of man was great in the earth, and that every imagination of the thoughts of his heart was only evil continually*" (Gen. 6:5).

Regarding the name Jehovah, the *Complete Word Study Dictionary* says this:

> $y^e h\bar{o}w\bar{a}h$: A noun meaning God. The word refers to the proper name of the God of Israel, particularly the

name by which He revealed Himself to Moses (Exo 6:2-3). The divine name has traditionally not been pronounced, primarily out of respect for its sacredness (cf. Exo 20:7; Deu 28:58). Until the Renaissance, it was written without vowels in the Hebrew text of the Old Testament, being rendered as YHWH. However, since that time, the vowels of another word, *ᵃdōnāy* (H136), have been supplied in hopes of reconstructing the pronunciation. Although the exact derivation of the name is uncertain, most scholars agree that its primary meaning should be understood in the context of God's existence, namely, that He is the "I AM THAT I AM" (Exo 3:14), the One who was, who is, and who always will be (cf. Rev 11:17). Older translations of the Bible and many newer ones employ the practice of rendering the divine name in capital letters, so as to distinguish it from other Hebrew words. It is most often rendered as LORD (Gen 4:1; Deu 6:18; Psa 18:31 [32]; Jer 33:2; Jon 1:9) but also as GOD (Gen 6:5; 2Sa 12:22) or JEHOVAH (Psa 83:18 [19]; Isa 26:4). The frequent appearance of this name in relation to God's redemptive work underscores its tremendous importance (Lev 26:45; Psa 19:14 [15]). Also, it is sometimes compounded with another word to describe the character of the Lord in greater detail (see Gen 22:14; Exo 17:15; Jdg 6:24). [267]

Now we are finally venturing beyond Greek elementary school and boldly stepping into advanced learning. If *kurios* is the New Testament equivalent to *Jehovah* (and it absolutely is) and *Jehovah* in Hebrew is "a noun meaning God" and *Jehovah* is properly translated "God" in the Old Testament (and it is, although in a minority of places), then the Greek word *kurios* most certainly can be rendered "God" in English.

There is further evidence of this. The quotes we have been reading above, have also informed us that *Kurios* is used in the Old Testament Greek version to translate the Hebrew word *Jehovah* (LORD, God). The Greek OT in Vaticanus was reputed to have been written in 350 A.D. and the actual date of translation was probably some years after that. If this is so, the writing of the manuscript took place at a time when New Testament Greek was still in use in everyday life. The Vaticanus Old Testament came from Origin in the third century. Greek was a universal trade language of the Roman Empire. The translator of Vaticanus was no stranger to Greek and he certainly knew how the Greeks used their words and he knew how the church used Greek words.

The Greek Old Testament of Vaticanus freely uses the word *kurios*. *Jehovah* in the Hebrew Old Testament is regularly translated as *kurios* in the Greek Old Testament. However, remember in one of our examples above, Exodus 23:17, *"adon Jehovah"* is used and translated "Lord God" in the KJV. In the Greek Old Testament, the words *kurios theos* are used; *kurios for Lord and theos for Jehovah*. *Theos* is the Greek word for God. In other words, the Greek Old Testament sometimes translates Jehovah as *theos* or God.

Since Jehovah is translated God and Lord and it is the equivalent of kurios, then kurios also means both God and Lord.

#4 Old Testament Quotes in the New Testament

The New Testament quotes or refers to hundreds of verses from the Old Testament. Hidden within those quotes is the final answer to our question. Unfortunately, there is a lot of confusion and ignorance among Christians as to the nature of these quotes. They are generally dismissed by simply saying that they were quotes from the Septuagint, the Old Testament Greek version, not from the Hebrew Old Testament. If they are viewed this way, Christians may miss a great deal of the power and significance of these quotes. I have extensively dealt with the Septuagint in chapter ten. I also gave much information in that chapter about quotes of the OT, but I will repeat some of it here.

The quotes of the Old Testament in the New Testament come in various types. There are many direct and indirect quotes. By indirect quote, I mean a quote that is merely a paraphrase of the teaching of one or more Old Testament verses or a teaching which appeals to one or more Old Testament passages for confirmation or proof. There are allusions and possible allusions. An allusion is "a passing or casual reference; an incidental mention of something, either directly or by implication." [268] There are many allusions in the New Testament.

Another type of quote is similar to an allusion. It is a teaching which appeals to Old Testament Scripture for support. Of course, we do this all the time in teaching and preaching. We make a statement and then refer to what is written for proof. Many times, we don't quote the actual Scripture, but, rather, we paraphrase it. The Scripture says…then we put it in our own words. The New Testament does something similar. This is one of the New Testament equivalents of proof-text teaching.

On the other hand, there are also direct and true quotes from the Hebrew Old Testament. To illustrate, one such quote is in Matthew 1:23, *"Behold, a virgin shall be with child, and shall bring forth a son, and they shall call his name Emmanuel, which being interpreted is, God with us."* This verse is quoted from Isaiah 7:14, *"Therefore the Lord himself shall give you a sign; Behold, a virgin shall conceive, and bear a son, and shall call his name Immanuel. "*

One can readily notice that Matthew 1:23 is not an *exact* quote in every detail. There are differences. See the comments on that in chapter ten.

Now, let's take these principles and apply them to our question about whether kurios can be translated "God." The key quote related to this question is found in 1 Peter 1:25, *"But the word of the Lord endureth for ever. And this is the word which by the gospel is preached unto you."* The quote comes from Isaiah 40:8, *"The grass withereth, the flower fadeth: but the word of our God shall stand for ever."* The verse in the New Testament says "the word of the Lord" (Kurios). The verse in the Old Testament is "the word of our God" (elohim). If one compares all of 1 Peter 1:24-25 with Isaiah 40:6-8, he will find that it falls into the category of exact quote with minor differences. Further, it reveals new understanding of the meaning of words.

The Hebrew word for God in Isaiah 40:8 is *Elohim*. This is THE *primary* Hebrew word for God. When it is applied to God, it is always translated "God." It is never translated "Lord." Yet, when God translates this word in 1 Peter 1:25, He inspired the word "kurios." Make no mistake. This was a deliberate act on the part of God. If we believe in verbal plenary inspiration, we must come to this conclusion. *God deliberately, on purpose, with benevolence aforethought, chose by an act of His sovereign will to translate Elohim into Kurios.* **This clearly means that *kurios* is not just an equivalent for *Jehovah*, but *it is also the equivalent of Elohim, God*.** If Elohim can be translated into *kurios*, then *kurios* can absolutely be translated into *Elohim*. So, "*Kurios*" can be translated into "God."

Conclusion

A deeper understanding of the meaning of "kurios" and its connection with Old Testament Hebrew should settle the question. "Kurios" means *Jehovah* and it means *elohim*. It means "Lord" and it means "God." When Jesus is addressed as the" Lord Jesus Christ," the name includes the truth of His person and nature. It is equal to saying, the "God-Man Anointed One" or "the Anointed God-man." Remember, "no man can say that Jesus is **the Lord**, but by the Holy Ghost" (1 Cor. 12:3). To call Jesus "the Lord" does not mean that He is our Master only. The many uses of the phrase "the Lord" in both Testaments clearly reveals its meaning as "God." To call Jesus "the Lord" is to call Him "God."

The word "*kurios*" not only means God, it can be translated God. *Kurios* is the equivalent of the Old Testament *Jehovah*. *Jehovah* is translated both "LORD" and "God" in the Old Testament. Since *Kurios* is the equivalent of *Jehovah*, then it too can be translated both Lord and God. That *Kurios* is equal to Jehovah is seen in Luke 20:42, "And David himself saith in the book of Psalms, The LORD said unto my Lord, Sit thou on my right hand." In Hebrew (Ps. 110:1) this is "*Jehovah* said to my *Adon*." In the Greek New Testament, it is "*Kurios* said to my *kurios*." *Kurios* is used for both *Jehovah* and *Adon*. This verse clearly shows that *Kurios* is the equivalent of *Jehovah*, as well as *Adon*. 1 Peter 1:25 is the same type of example as Luke 20:42. It reveals that *kurios* is also the equivalent of *Elohim* (God). The Old Testament (Is. 40:8) says, "The word of *Elohim*." 1 Peter 1 says, "The word of *kurios*." The connection here is the same as Luke 20:42. It creates an equivalency. *Kurios* equals *Jehovah*. *Kurios* equals *Elohim*. *Kurios* equals "Lord" and "God."

Appendix 6:

Translation Challenge – John 5:24 Judgment, Condemnation, and Polysemy

The job of a Bible translator or interpreter has many dangers. Suppose that in a certain verse the KJV uses a word and other English versions use a different word in the same place. Many of us would simply choose the KJV word. But, how do we answer a critic when both translated words, though different, came from the same Greek word and *both* translations are *equally valid*? Many Greek words, like words in any language, have more than one meaning. This is called *Polysemy,* the principle that words have multiple meanings. But, how are you to choose between the meanings?

This problem is found many times in the New Testament. One very prominent example is in John 5:24.

> *Verily, verily, I say unto you, He that heareth my word, and believeth on him that sent me, hath everlasting life, and shall not come into* **condemnation***; but is passed from death unto life.* (John 5:24)

This seems to be a straight forward and clear verse. It is in perfect accord with the teachings about salvation in the entire Bible. However, there is an issue with the word "condemnation." The New King James and other modern versions translate the Greek word, *krisis* as "judgment." It would not be so bad if it stopped there. But, early Received Text Bibles also translate it that way. The Tyndale, Coverdale, Bishops, and Geneva translations all use the words condemnation or damnation. One the other hand, the 1744 French Ostervald Bible says "judgment" (that is, the text as available on e-

Appendix 6: Translation Challenge John 5:24

sword.net; the 2018 Revision of the Ostervald by Pastor Mario Monette says "condemnation"). The 1545 Martin Luther German translation uses the word Gericht, which means "court or judgment." J. P. Green's so-called "literal" translation says "judgment." Even the King James has a difference in how it translates *krisis*. In John 5:29, the KJV translates *krisis* as "judgment." Then, again the word is used in verse 30 and translated "damnation."

How are you to know which is correct? Once again, some of you would point to the way the KJV does it and say the KJV is right. I also agree the KJV translated this correctly. But, how are you to *explain* it? How would you explain the difference in how the KJV translated this word to a young or ignorant Christian? How do you *know* which is right?

It's easier than you think. But, many miss it.

First, the Greek word, *krisis*, is an example of *polysemy*. It has multiple meanings which depend on the context. According to the *Complete Word Study Dictionary,* the word means both "the act of judging" and "sentence pronounced." *Vine's Complete Expository Dictionary of New Testament Words* says it "primarily denotes 'a separating,' then, 'a decision.' "*Thayer's Greek Definitions* tells us the word means a "trial or contest" and an "opinion or decision." So, it has more than one meaning. It means the process of examining someone in court (judgment) and the sentence or decision made after the examination (either condemnation or acquittal). Therefore, on the bare surface, both translations of "judgment" and "condemnation" are *technically* correct.

So, how are we to choose between the definitions? Many words have multiple meanings. Which definition applies in a given place in a document depends entirely on *context.* In the Bible, that contextual information may come from the verse in which we find the word or it may come from the nearby verses or even other chapters in the same book. It may even be found in other Bible books.

The context of John 5:24 and the word *krisis* is an example of the last one and it depends on a correct understanding of the verse itself.

The subject of John 5:24 is *eternal life* and *how one obtains it*. Salvation depends on 1) hearing the word and 2) believing it. By doing this you ensure your eternal safety. The viewpoint in this verse is eternity. So, the result of believing is 1) you have eternal life right now and 2) you will never be condemned. That is the teaching of the verse as it stands in the KJV. However, the translations that use "judgment" do not guarantee a freedom from condemnation, but they guarantee freedom from judgment.

You may say, isn't freedom from judgment the same as freedom from condemnation? That is not the problem. Using "judgment" in John 5:24 is saying that believers will never go through the process of being judged. The *real difficulty* is that the statement, "you shall never come into judgment," **is not true**. *In fact, it is a flat out lie.* Moreover, it sets up a *contradiction* in Scripture. The greater Scriptural context contradicts the idea that you, as a believer, will *never* come into judgment. The proof of this is found in 2 Corinthians 5:10, *"For* **we must all appear before the judgment seat of Christ;** *that every one may receive the things done in his body, according to that he hath done, whether it be good or bad."* We will be judged at the Judgment Seat of Christ to determine our rewards, but we will never be condemned. Therefore, all of us who have believed are going to a future judgment to determine what rewards we will get. *Judgment cannot be avoided.*

So, the decision of which definition of *Krisis* to use is settled by cross references. To translate *krisis* as "judgment" in John 5:24 is to create a lie and a contradiction in Scripture. This is a danger that all translators must carefully avoid and of which all Christians should be aware.

Appendix 7:

Translation Challenge: 2 Timothy 2:15 Diligent Study

Study to shew thyself approved unto God,
a workman that needeth not to be ashamed,
rightly dividing the word of truth.

This verse has been discussed for many years. The point of intense controversy is focused on the very first word, "study." Many have criticized the King James' choice of translation here. Of course, the King James is always immediately considered to be wrong in any question, without spending the necessary *study* to find out the real truth. However, the issue of the correctness or wrongness of the KJB is not the only issue. The question extends to all languages, because translators must also decide how to translate the Greek word *spoudazo*. The difference is seen below in several other English translations.

NIV: *Do your best* to present yourself to God as one approved, a worker who does not need to be ashamed and who correctly handles the word of truth.

CSB: *Be diligent* to present yourself to God as one approved, a worker who doesn't need to be ashamed, correctly teaching the word of truth.

CEV: *Do your best* to win God's approval as a worker who doesn't need to be ashamed and who teaches only the true message.

ESV: *Do your best* to present yourself to God as one approved, a worker who has no need to be ashamed, rightly handling the word of truth.

NKJV: *Be diligent* to present yourself approved to God, a worker who does not need to be ashamed, rightly dividing the word of truth.

These are only five modern translations. They all agree that the word should be translated "be diligent" or "do your best." So which should it be? First, let's look at how the King James translated this Greek word in the other places it is used.

"diligence" – 2 Timothy 4:9, 21
"diligent" – Titus 3:12; 2 Peter 3:14
"endeavour" – 2 Peter 1:15
"endeavouring" – Ephesians 4:3
"was forward" – Galatians 2:10
"Let us labour" – Hebrews 4:10-11
"Study" – 2 Timothy 2:15

Several things should be clear from these examples. First, one meaning of the Greek word is to be diligent. Second, the KJB translators knew this. They translated the same word as "diligence" and "diligent" in the same epistle, 2 Timothy. Third, that should tell you they had a reason to translate it differently in 2 Timothy 2:15. In other words, they chose a different word **on purpose and with full knowledge**. It was not a mistake. What could their reason be?

At this point, it would be good to look at some definitions of the Greek word, *spoudazo*.

> to hasten, accelerate, expedite; to use one's endeavours; to be anxious. [269]

> to be in earnest; to endeavor, to strive, to hasten. [270]

> To be diligent, earnest, or eager ... To make every effort to do one's best, to be eager. [271]

Appendix 7: Translation Challenge -Diligent Study 2 Tim. 2:15

it signifies "to hasten to do a thing, to exert oneself, endeavor, give diligence" [272]

Here are two older lexicons (1828 and 1832) along with *Vine's* and the *Word Study*. They all say the same thing. All four seem to be in agreement with how the King James translated the Greek word in all, but one place, 2 Timothy 2:15. It seems to mean diligence and earnest endeavor or effort. How do we account for the one difference?

Remember, a lexicon does not give us a list of words we are to use in our translations. It gives us the *meaning* of the word. The *meaning* is to be used to *find* the correct target language word that fits the context. It is the same as a definition of a modern word in a dictionary. It is a definition. It is not the word.

A translator and anyone who wishes to learn God's word should always consider **the context** of a word when trying to determine its meaning, and what is the best word to use for the target translation.

For example, the context of 2 Timothy 4:9, 21 is different than the context of 2 Timothy 2:15. In chapter four, Paul is expressing his desire that Timothy come to him before winter and come soon. His advice for Timothy is that he *is diligent* to do this. The same is true of the advice he gave Titus in Titus 3:12; "be diligent to come unto me." However, the emphasis is a little different in 2 Peter 1:15, 1 Thessalonians 2:17, and Ephesians 4:3. In these passages something was to be attempted, but the ability to accomplish it depended too much on others or other circumstances. So, the word is translated "endeavor," which means "To attempt to gain; to try to effect." [273] The word endeavor fits nicely within the definition of the Greek word. In Galatians 2:10, the KJB uses the word *forward*, which means "Ardent; eager; earnest; violent." [274] The word *forward* also agrees well with the definition of the Greek word and fits the context of Galatians 2:10 nicely. Finally, Hebrews 4:10-11 seems to be talking about qualifying to enter rest. In this regard, the KJB translates the Greek word as "labor." This word labor means *exertion* mentally, physically, or any other way to do work. Again, this agrees well with the definition of the Greek word.

The particular choice of English term used to translate spoudazo depends on its use in the context.

The contexts of all other uses of *spoudazo* are different from that in 2 Timothy 2:15. None of the others speak about learning to *"rightly divide the word of truth."* Remember, God inspired the New Testament in Greek. Therefore, *spoudazo* is the word God chose. It is the word that God inspired. Therefore, it is a perfect word of God. The question is whether the word "study" fits within the definitions of this Greek word. If it does, then it is a true and correct translation of the God inspired Greek word.

What is the definition of the English word, *study*?

> To fix the mind closely upon a subject ... To apply the mind ... To endeavor diligently. [275]
> Devote time and attention to gaining knowledge ... Investigate and analyse (a subject or situation) in detail ... Apply oneself to study ... Learn intensively about something. [276]

So, the word *study* meant "to endeavor diligently" at the time the KJB was translated. *That alone would make it an accurate term to use in 2 Timothy 2:15.*

However, the truth goes much deeper. The term *study* means to *use the mind* and the verbs attached to this use are *fix, apply, endeavor diligently, devote (time), give attention, investigate, analyze, and learn intensively*. All of that fits well into the definition of the Greek word. Furthermore, the context teaches that to be approved of God one must "rightly divide the word of truth." He must learn the Bible. Tell me, if you are diligently endeavoring to apply your mind with intense effort to gain knowledge of the Bible, WHAT ARE YOU DOING? *YOU ARE STUDYING*!

In summary, The English word, *study*, means "an application of mind" and *application* is "intenseness of thought" and "the employment of means."[277] I repeat. If one is to make every effort and does his best to diligently rightly divide the word of truth so that he is approved of God, there is only one way to do it. He must intensely apply his mind and employ methods to learning the truth. *In other words, he must **study**!* Therefore, in the context, to "study" to show yourself approved by rightly dividing the word is defined as a diligent effort to learn the word.

"Study" is a correct and accurate translation of the Greek word *spoudazo* in the context of 2 Timothy 2:15.

Appendix 8:

Translation Challenge: Romans 3:3 Faith or Faithful?

For what if some did not believe? shall their unbelief make the <u>faith</u> of God without effect? (Rom. 3:3)

There is a disagreement among translators and commentators about whether the word "faith" should actually be "faithfulness," making the translation read "shall their unbelief make the faithfulness of God without affect?" It sounds good that someone's unbelief cannot interfere with God's faithfulness. After all we don't want anything to interfere with His faithfulness toward us, do we?

But is it the right way to translate the Greek word?

Regarding this question, it is my opinion that the best translation is "faith." The Greek word "pistin" (accusative form of pistis) is used in both the Received Text and the UBS Critical text. The translation "faithfulness" is typical in the critical text English translations. *This is not a translation problem. It is an interpretation problem.* Below are some reasons why I have concluded that the correct translation is "faith."

The Meaning of "pistis"

The definition of *pistis* is:

Faith. Subjectively meaning firm persuasion, conviction, belief in the truth, veracity, reality or faithfulness (**though rare**). Objectively meaning that which is believed, doctrine, the received articles of faith. [278]

Notice that *pistis* can be translated "faithfulness," but that is rare. In other words, the word hardly ever means faithfulness.

> '*pistis* ... , primarily, 'firm persuasion,' a conviction based upon hearing (akin to peitho, "to persuade"), is used in the NT always of 'faith in God or Christ, or things spiritual.' [279]

The Greater Context

The word *pistis* is used in the New Testament 244 times. In all but two places the King James version translates the word "faith," "belief," "believes," or "believe." In Acts 17:31, it is translated "assurance" in a context where God is encouraging or persuading people to believe. In Titus 2:10, it is translated "fidelity" (which means faithfulness). The context in Titus is about a servant who doesn't steal but shows good fidelity. The word *pistis* is used, because it means this person is one who can be believed in, he can be trusted.

Therefore, the greater use of the word *pistis* is faith and that is weighty evidence that Romans 3:3 most likely also means faith.

There is a different word that means "faithful" - pistos (See Ephesians 1:1 for example). This word, *pistos,* is defined in the Word Study dictionary as, "True, sure, trustworthy, believable, worthy of credit ... Faithful in duty to oneself and to others, of true fidelity." [280] The word is used 66 times and is translated *faithful* or *faithfully* almost every time. In a few places, it is translated believe or believer.

The NT Use of the Phrase "the faith"

This phrase is always used in the NT to mean one of two things:
1) A belief that someone holds in their heart, or
2) Something someone believes in; the object of faith, usually the Gospel.

Appendix 8: Translation Challenge Faith or Faithful Romans 3:3

When the phrase is pointing to *something believed in*, it always points to God, Christ, or the Word of God, particularly the Gospel. Examples of this are: Acts 6:7; 13:8; 16:5 and many others. "The faith" also refers to *the faith in a person's heart*. "The faith of Abraham" means faith Abraham had in his heart in what God promised him (Rom. 4:16). In Acts 24:24.

There is a use of this phrase that is almost exactly like Romans 3:3 in Galatians 2:16; "that we might be justified by the faith of Christ." The "faith of Christ" is not *faith that Christ has*. Nor is it the *faithfulness of Christ.* Rather, it involves the *faith we have in Christ.* We know this because it has to do with how we are justified. "Being justified freely by his grace through the redemption that is in Christ Jesus … Therefore we conclude that a man is **justified by faith** without the deeds of the law" (Romans 3:24, 28). Therefore, justification requires that a sinner have faith in the Gospel of Christ. So, the "faith of Christ" involves two things: the gospel and our belief in it. Therefore, the phrase "the faith of Christ" means having faith in the gospel of Christ. We are not justified by the works of the law, but by faith in the gospel of Christ.

Romans 3:3 in Its Immediate Context

Romans 2:28-3:4, is one connected train of thought.
Romans 2:28-29 – The point of these verses is that a true Jew is not one who is only a Jew physically. He must be a Jew inwardly by faith in Jesus Christ.
Romans 3:1 – So, the logical question is asked. What is the advantage of being a physical Jew?
Romans 3:2 –Paul points out only one advantage. The oracles of God, the Scriptures, were given to and through them.
Romans 3:3 – Back to the key issue of chapter two, Paul points them to the issue of belief or unbelief. That is the difference between a merely physical Jew and a true physical and spiritual Jew.

"For what if some did not believe?" Believe what? The oracles of God (v.2). Some of the Jews did not believe the Word of God, especially those parts about salvation in Christ.

"Shall it make the faith of God of no effect?" Here (just as in other places "the faith" refers to the oracles of God) "the faith," which belongs to God, refers to the "Oracles of God." God has given the Jews the *Oracles of God* and *that* is "the faith" to them and to God. Yet, some of the Jews do not believe those Oracles. Does their unbelief make the Oracles of no effect? Of course not. Does their unbelief make the Oracles ineffective in the lives of those who do believe? Of course not.

Romans 3:4 - God forbid: yea, let God be true, but every man a liar. Whether you believe or not, God's Oracles are true. Those who speak against His Word are liars.

"The faith" is the truth of God's Word, which we believe. You see, Paul was not concerned about God's faithfulness in these verses. He was concerned about God's truth and whether we believe it or not. He was concerned about faith.

About the Author

Dr. Steve Combs is an ordained minister. He spent his early years in Kentucky, Virginia, and finally Ohio. He was not raised in a Christian home. He had some Christian influence from his grandmother, but that had little effect on him. Due to discussions with a Baptist preacher and a Sunday School teacher, who visited his home, he began to read the Bible. The Word of God had its effect. He came under strong conviction of his sins. A friend invited him to a nearby church during revival meetings, where he heard the gospel preached.

God showed him that Jesus Christ, the Son of God, paid for his sins when he died on the cross and, afterward, rose physically from the dead. He believed it with all his heart and, as a result, he was born spiritually into the family of God and saved from condemnation for his sins.

Since then there have been major transformations to his life. God called him to preach and enabled a backward shy individual suffering from an inferiority complex to stand before crowds and confidently proclaim the Word of God. God gave him a business background as a CPA and God put him in several ministry positions. He has served as a Bible Institute teacher and Dean, a youth pastor, assistant pastor, and a senior pastor. He holds a Doctor of Theology from Covington Theological Seminary.

Currently Steve Combs is Assistant Director and a Global Translation Advisor for Bearing Precious Seed Global/ Global Bible Translators, www.bpsglobal.com. BPS Global starts and assists Bible translation projects around the world.

He is married and has four married children.

Index of Key Words

1689 Baptist Confession of Faith, 33, 206
Aland, 201, 214, 215, 216, 217
Alexandria, 7, 9, 136, 137, 138, 139, 140, 141, 142, 143, 144, 149, 151, 152, 173, 186, 187, 188, 189, 193, 195, 272, 273
Alexandrian Text, 7, 168, 187, 188, 195, 198, 264, 286, 303, 341
Alexandrinus, 7, 11, 140, 149, 158, 159, 168, 171, 181, 182, 198, 292, 293, 295, 296
Allegorical Interpretation Allegory, 7
Amoraim, 164
Apparatus, 7
Aramaic, 35, 36, 39, 42, 50, 53, 63, 78, 79, 80, 82, 89, 90, 133, 163, 202
Arianism, 272, 273, 274
Aristeas, 136, 138, 139, 140, 142, 143, 144, 153, 154, 155
Aristobulus, 138, 141, 142, 143, 144, 150
authority, 33, 39, 44, 45, 46, 47, 50, 53, 93, 207, 210, 221, 235. 258
Babel, 5, 19, 21, 22, 24, 31, 52, 62
Babylon, 21, 22, 243, 244
Baptist Bible Translators Institute, 230, 233, 236
Bearing Precious Seed Global, 236
Bearing Precious Seed ministries, 235
Ben Chayim, 102, 162, 164, 165, 210, 256, 260
Bengel, 214
Beza, 204, 205, 206, 207, 208
Bible League International, 229, 230
Bible study, 114, 119, 120, 121, 123
Bibles International, 229, 231, 235, 251
Biblical Criticism, 309, 310, 314
Biblical nation, 20, 24, 25
Blind leaders, 210, 217
BPS Global, 236
Byzantine Text, 167, 193, 267, 298
Cardinal Francisco Jiménez de Cisneros, 202
church planting, 28, 29, 30, 64, 230, 235, 236, 252
Clement, 138, 142, 151, 185, 186
Codex, 7, 9, 11, 141, 148, 152, 153, 158, 168, 170, 171, 179, 182, 190, 198, 204, 205, 258, 280, 293, 296, 297, 298, 300, 315
Colinaeus, 204
Complutensian Polyglot, 202, 203, 204, 206, 208, 209
confusion of languages, 20
Constantine, 149, 152, 153, 193, 267, 272, 273, 274
Copies, 35
Corrupt text, 92
Cursive, 8, 176, 179
Dating methods, 147

Index

David Christian Ginsberg, 165
Dead Sea Scrolls, 165
Dynamic equivalence, 7, 8, 76, 77, 85, 86, 87, 88, 92, 94, 97, 99, 108, 113, 136, 161
Dynamic Equivalent, 11, 87
Egypt, 19, 22, 51, 52
Elzevir, 206, 209
English, 20, 34, 42, 45, 56, 59, 60, 61, 62, 77, 79, 80, 85, 86, 88, 92, 102, 103, 106, 107, 108, 109, 110, 113, 118, 133, 206, 209, 211, 215, 223, 225, 230, 360, 375
Enlightenment, 309, 311, 323
Erasmus, 201, 202, 203, 204, 205, 206, 208
Essentially literal, 7, 11, 86, 87, 113, 236
Ethnic, 19, 20, 24, 27, 28
Ethnolinguistic, 28, 29
Ethnos360, 230
Evangel Bible Translators, 229, 230
Exemplar, 7
False views of modern readers, 99
Families, 20, 24, 25, 26, 27, 28, 30, 31
Family, 7, 19, 26, 27, 127, 132, 179, 206, 375
First Translator, 5, 51, 52
FirstBible International, 235
Five Judgments, 126
Formal Equivalence, 7, 8, 10, 76, 85, 88
Formal equivalent, 82, 89, 90, 91, 92, 108, 113

Four and twenty elders, 239, 240
Functional equivalence, 87
Functional Equivalent, 8
God is the God of history, 203
God's Plan, 67
Graceway Bible Society, 234
Grammar, 79, 83, 84, 85, 88, 102, 105, 106, 108, 113, 115, 215
Great Commission, 5, 25, 56, 63, 64, 65, 66, 130, 219, 235
Greece, 22, 23, 24
Greek, 22, 32, 34, 35, 39, 42, 43, 50, 53, 54, 55, 58, 63, 77, 78, 79, 80, 82, 85, 93, 102, 103, 105, 106, 107, 109, 110, 111, 112, 117, 118, 133, 135, 163, 167, 200, 201, 202, 203, 205, 206, 207, 208, 209, 210, 211, 212, 214, 215, 217, 218, 220, 229, 231, 234, 236, 246, 248, 252, 253, 258
Griesbach, 214
Heart language, 20, 226
Hebrew, 19, 20, 22, 24, 25, 34, 35, 36, 39, 42, 50, 52, 53, 54, 55, 58, 63, 78, 79, 80, 82, 89, 90, 102, 133, 135, 162, 163, 164, 202, 206, 209, 210, 211, 218, 231, 236, 252, 253, 258
Hermeneutics, 114, 115
Historical-grammatical method, 115
History, 5, 24, 52, 219, 251
Holy men, 33, 36, 39, 130, 131

Hort, 11, 150, 168, 170, 174, 178, 198, 214, 215, 271, 289, 311, 315, 316, 317, 318, 319, 320, 323, 324, 333
Idiom(s), 7, 8, 83, 89, 102, 107, 108, 109, 110, 111, 113
Idiomatic, 84, 86
Idiomatic translation, 8
Inerrant, 8, 35, 59, 60, 61, 66, 217, 305, 315, 323, 326, 327, 328, 329, 330, 331, 343
Inspiration, 33, 34, 35, 38, 39, 42, 48, 50, 54, 62, 90, 97, 101, 116, 131, 132, 167, 210, 214, 216, 217, 234, 236
International Mission Board, 29, 229, 231, 375
interpretation, 21, 36, 77, 79, 80, 81, 82, 89, 100, 108, 113, 115, 130, 133
Jew, Gentile, and Church, 123
Jews, 20, 51, 53, 54, 58, 68, 123, 164, 211, 232, 240, 249, 375
King James Concordance', 263
Knowledge, 120, 122
Language, 19, 20, 21, 22, 23, 24, 25, 26, 27, 28, 31, 32, 34, 43, 44, 51, 52, 53, 54, 55, 56, 57, 58, 59, 60, 61, 62, 63, 65, 66, 68, 70, 71, 72, 74, 76, 77, 78, 81, 82, 83, 84, 85, 86, 87, 88, 91, 94, 100, 101, 102, 103, 105, 107, 108, 111, 113, 114, 128, 133, 167, 206, 213, 219, 220, 222, 223, 224, 225, 227, 228, 229, 230, 233, 234, 235, 236, 237, 241, 245, 246, 247, 248
Latin, 22, 53, 94, 168, 202, 203, 205, 206, 209, 220, 223, 224
Liberalism
 liberals, 307, 311, 312, 314, 315, 320
Literal, 84, 86, 103, 106, 109, 110, 111
Literal Translation, 8
Lutheran Bible Translators, 229
Majority Text, 18, 167, 169, 183, 198, 231, 334
Manuscript evidence, 204, 207, 209
Manuscript(s), 8, 10, 11, 43, 164, 167, 188, 201, 202, 209, 210, 212, 215, 267, 269
Martin Luther, 203, 210, 220, 223
Martini, Cardinal, 216, 217
Masoretes, 164
Masoretic, 102, 162, 164, 165, 209, 210, 218, 231, 236
Meaning, 76, 88, 100, 101
Message, 45, 46, 88, 92, 93, 94
Method, 7, 8, 18, 37, 84, 85, 86, 87, 88, 89, 90, 91, 102, 113, 115, 120, 134, 143, 148, 222, 308, 310, 313
Method of Translating, 8, 84
Metzger, 137, 216, 284
Middle Ages, 94, 95, 164, 220
Minuscule, 8, 180, 182, 287, 296, 298
Modified literal, 84, 85

Mother tongue, 8, 15, 20, 53, 61, 62, 226, 237
Nation(s), 8, 17, 19, 20, 21, 23, 24, 25, 26, 27, 28, 29, 30, 31, 34, 36, 44, 51, 52, 54, 56, 57, 58, 59, 60, 62, 63, 64, 72, 74, 125, 206, 207, 238, 240, 241, 243, 244, 245, 246, 253, 285, 375
Naturalistic, 215
Nestle-Aland, 196, 198, 216, 280, 318, 320
New Tribes, 229, 230
Origen, 115, 139, 151, 152, 153, 154, 186, 187, 193, 268, 269, 272, 275, 287, 292, 298
Palimpsest, 8, 190
Peoples, 7, 26, 27, 28, 29, 30, 226, 228, 241, 244, 251
Perfect, 33, 34, 39, 44, 48, 50, 55, 58, 59, 60, 61, 62, 63, 65, 66, 70, 72, 73, 74, 75, 77, 90, 96, 97, 98, 106, 107, 113, 116, 126, 131, 163, 171, 179, 201, 303, 329, 354, 360
Peshitta, 168, 220
Philo, 138, 139, 142, 143, 144, 150, 151, 153
Philosophers, 307, 309, 312, 314
Post Apostolic Age, 220
Practical, 17, 97
Preservation, 5, 33, 39, 40
Preserved, 34, 39, 42, 43, 44, 50, 97, 116, 133, 162, 163, 164, 208, 236

Providential preservation, 41, 132, 214
Providentially guided translation, 35
Rapture, 127, 238, 240, 242, 245
Rationalism, 307, 310, 311, 326
Received Text, 9, 11, 14, 18, 35, 102, 133, 135, 140, 150, 167, 171, 172, 174, 195, 198, 199, 200, 201, 202, 203, 204, 205, 206, 207, 209, 210, 212, 213, 214, 217, 218, 220, 229, 230, 231, 232, 233, 235, 236, 256, 281, 287, 293, 303, 305, 309, 311, 315, 319, 324, 333, 341, 343, 344, 354, 361
  Textus Receptus, 9, 11, 133, 150, 171, 175, 189, 198, 206, 214, 258, 286, 318, 319, 326
Reformation, 203, 209, 210, 220, 223, 224
Satanic plan, 306
Scrivener, 205, 206, 207, 208, 209, 211
Seed Company, 229, 231
Septuagint, 5, 9, 11, 14, 39, 135, 136, 138, 139, 140, 141, 142, 143, 144, 145, 146, 151, 152, 153, 154, 155, 156, 157, 158, 159, 161, 162, 163, 258, 334, 348, 351
Seven Covenants, 123
Seven Dispensations, 124

A Practical Theology of Bible Translating

SIL, 229, 231, 248
Sinaiticus, 7, 9, 140, 141, 148, 149, 150, 158, 159, 168, 170, 172, 178, 180, 196, 210, 212, 258, 274, 275, 280, 281, 287, 288, 292, 295, 299, 303, 315, 318
Source Language, 9
Source Text, 9
Stephanus, 204, 208
Sufficiency., 71
Syriac, 168, 205, 209, 220
Tannaim, 164
Target Language, 9
Target Text, 9
Textual Criticism, 9, 183, 217, 309, 311, 327
Tischendorf, 9, 141, 148, 149, 176, 179, 315, 320
Tongue(s), 9, 20, 25, 26, 51, 57, 238, 240, 243
Traditional Text, 5, 11, 43, 150, 167, 168, 169, 170, 171, 172, 174, 176, 177, 179, 180, 181, 182, 183, 184, 185, 186, 187, 188, 190, 191, 193, 194, 195, 197, 198, 199, 200, 209, 210, 258, 264, 275, 286, 303
Translate, 7, 8, 13, 14, 17, 18, 44, 46, 55, 65, 75, 76, 84, 85, 88, 89, 96, 97, 99, 101, 102, 104, 106, 107, 108, 109, 111, 113, 114, 129, 131, 132, 133, 143, 159, 161, 214, 232, 237, 245, 246, 247, 252, 255, 279, 319, 337, 339, 344, 345, 346, 350, 353, 354, 356, 357, 358, 359, 361
Translating, 1, 3, 5, 8,9, 10, 14, 24, 31, 38, 54, 58, 63, 64, 65, 66, 74, 76, 77, 79, 82, 83, 84, 85, 88, 89, 90, 91, 95, 96, 101, 102, 103, 105, 109, 113, 114, 130, 132, 133, 134, 162, 213, 219, 222, 223, 230, 231, 232, 233, 235, 236, 238, 246, 251, 257, 375
Tribulation, 208, 240, 242, 243, 244, 245
Trinitarian Bible Society, 165, 211, 214, 234, 235, 258
Two Advents of Christ, 127
UBS, 5, 216, 341
    United Bible Societies, 5, 7, 9, 175, 194, 195, 196, 198, 200, 210, 212, 214, 215, 216, 217, 218, 228, 229, 230, 231, 232, 246, 248, 264, 271, 274, 275, 282, 288, 291, 292, 293, 294, 295, 296, 298, 299, 303, 304, 308, 318, 320, 332, 341, 361
Uncial, 10, 182, 287
Understanding, 38, 88, 100, 101, 108, 111, 114, 115, 116, 117, 118, 119, 121, 122, 128, 233, 252
United Bible Societies, 72, 133, 211, 212, 213, 214, 217, 218, 229, 232, 234
United Bible Societies Greek Text, 18, 133, 135, 194, 212, 214, 280, 281

Index

Unreached, 28, 29, 30, 57, 232, 235, 236, 251, 252, 253
Vaticanus, 7, 9, 10, 11, 140, 146, 147, 149, 150, 152, 153, 158, 159, 168, 178, 180, 188, 194, 195, 196, 202, 203, 210, 212, 273, 274, 275, 280, 281, 287, 288, 292, 295, 299, 303, 315, 318, 341, 350, 351
Verbal Plenary Inspiration, 10
Verbal plenary preservation, 10, 42, 116, 217
Westcott, 11, 150, 168, 170, 174, 178, 198, 214, 215, 271, 289, 311, 315, 316, 317, 318, 319, 320, 323, 324, 333
What Can Individual Christians Do, 253
What Can Mission Agencies Do, 251
What Can the Bible Schools Do, 252
What Can the Churches Do, 249
William Carey, 27, 56, 57, 210
Wisdom, 33, 49, 71, 72, 84, 96, 98, 100, 101, 114, 117, 118, 119, 122, 127, 128, 242
Word, 4, 10, 35, 40, 41, 44, 45, 46, 47, 48, 49, 50, 51, 59, 62, 65, 66, 71, 72, 73, 74, 79, 84, 88, 91, 93, 94, 96, 97, 98, 100, 102, 103, 116, 117, 118, 119, 122, 123, 128, 131, 132, 133, 134, 135, 162, 164, 207, 209, 210, 232, 234, 235, 236, 245, 251
Word of God, 10, 18, 25, 28, 34, 35, 40, 41, 42, 46, 48, 49, 57, 63, 65, 66, 67, 70, 71, 74, 93, 94, 98, 110, 111, 112, 116, 119, 122, 132, 133, 142, 161, 186, 188, 209, 211, 218, 224, 225, 234, 236, 246, 247, 248, 250, 251, 258, 260, 261, 270, 273, 305, 311, 314, 323, 324, 326, 329, 347, 363, 365
Words of God, 10, 13, 39, 42, 46, 50, 66, 74, 75, 90, 92, 95, 96, 99, 132, 134, 261, 262
Worldview ministries, 235
Wycliffe, 31, 32, 57, 72, 229, 230, 231, 232, 248, 375
Ximenes, 202, 203
Yea, hath God said, 309, 311, 313, 314, 332

371

Notes

_____

[1] See https://www.bible-history.com/maps/2-table-of-nations.html. Jan. 17, 2018

[2] Larry Pierceon. *In the Days of Peleg.* Answers in Genesis. Dec. 1, 1999. Web. Jan. 16, 2019.

[3] Pierceon

[4] Flavius Josephus. The Antiquities of the Jews, Book I, Chapter 6. 93-94 AD. E-Sword. Rick Meyers. Version 10.2.1. Franklin, Tn.: 2013. Downloaded computer software. Jan. 2019.

[5] Wikipedia. Sargon of Akkad. https://en.wikipedia.org/wiki/Sargon_of_Akkad. 2019. Web. Jan. 26, 2019.

[6] Charles V. Turner, Biblical Bible Translating (Lafayette, Indiana: Sovereign Grace Publishers, 2001). Print. 11-12.

[7] Turner. 12

[8] "Nation." New World Dictionary of American English, 1988 ed. Webster, Noah. "Webster's Dictionary of American English." 1828 edition. E-Sword. Rick Meyers. Version 10.2.1. Franklin, Tn.: 2013. Downloaded computer software.

[9] Winter, Ralph D. and Koch, Bruce. *Finishing the Task: the Unreached People Challenge.* Mission Frontiers. June 2000. Web. 14 June 2000.

[10] Winter and Koch

[11] Global Research. International Mission Board. (www.peoplegroups.org). 2019. Web. January 2019.

[12] JP Deutillo. The Toulambi. http://jpdutilleux.com/ the work/toulambi/index.html. Web. 2004, 2005

[13] Global Research. International Mission Board. (www.peoplegroups.org). Web. Web. January 2019.

[14] Global Research. International Mission Board. (www.peoplegroups.org). 2019. Web. January 2019.

[15] Ethnologue. https://www.ethnologue.com/statistics/ family. Jan. 17, 2019.

[16] Wycliffe Global Alliance. 2018 Bible Translation Statistics FAQ, http://resources.wycliffe.net/statistics/2018_Statistics_FAQs_EN.pdf. Jan. 17, 2019.

Notes

[17] Wycliffe. Scripture and Language Statistics 2018. http://www.wycliffe.net/statistics Web. July 2017

[18] The 1689 Baptist Confession of Faith. https://www.the1689confession.com/1689/chapter-1. Jan. 19, 2019.

[19] H.D. Williams. The Miracle of Biblical Inspiration. (The Old Paths Publications: Cleveland, GA) 2009. PDF download. Jan. 2019.

[20] Merriam-Webster Dictionary online. Merriam-webster.com. Web. 5-2019

[21] Gary La More. *Thou Shalt Keep Them: A Biblical Theology of the Perfect Preserrvation of Scripture.* Cited. David Brown. *Providential Preservation: the Doctrine that Virtually Disappeared.* Print. Jan. 23, 2019.

[22] Andy Stanley. At Exponential a conference. 2014. Cited. *God's Word: The Authority over Us.* Answers in Genesis. 2017. Web. Jan. 24, 2019.

[23] Christianity Today. *Should Pastors Stop Saying 'God says?'* 2014. Cited. *God's Word: The Authority Over Us.* Answers in Genesis. 2014. Web. Jan. 24, 2019.

[24] Ruth A. Tucker, From Jerusalem to Iryan Jaya, (Grand Rapids: Zondervan 1983) 115

[25] Vedder, 251.

[26] Ruth A. Tucker, From Jerusalem to Iryan Jaya, (Grand Rapids:Zondervan1983)115

[27] King James Version translators. *The Translators to the Reader.* 1611. Bible-Reseacher.com. Web. 2017.

[28] Wycliffe. *Scripture and Language Statistics 2018.* Wycliffe.net/statistics. 2018. Web. Jan. 2019.

[29] *Global Status and Trends of Evangelical Christianity.* 2018.http://www.peoplegroups.org/258.aspx. Web. Jan. 2019

[30] Sam Gipp. *The Answer Book.* Chick Publications. Web. 2002.

[31] Merriam Webster. https://www.merriam-webster.com/dictionary/perfect. Web. Mar. 2019.

[32] Merriam Webster

[33] Merriam Webster

[34] Dennis List, A Writing Global English, 2004. (http://www.audiencedialogue.org/english.html). Web. 23 June 2004.

[35] English Language All About the English Language. *English Language Statistics.* Englishlanguageguide. Com. Web. 5-2019.

[36] Wikipedia. *English Language.* Wikipedia.com. Web. 5-2019.
[37] Editors of Encyclopedia Britannica. *Biblical Translation.* 2019. Web. Jan. 26, 2019.
[38] Kevin Gary Smith. *Bible Translation and Relevance Theory A Translation of Titus.* A Dissertation submitted to the University of Stellenbach (South Africa). Dec. 2000. Web. https://www.sats.edu.za/userfiles/BibleTranslationandRelevance Theory.pdf.Jan. 2019
[39] Joseph Henry Thayer. Thayer's Greek Definitions. *E-Sword.* Rick Meyers. Version 10.2.1. Franklin, Tn.: 2013. Downloaded computer software.
[40] Strong's Exhaustive Concordance. *E-Sword.* Rick Meyers. Version 10.2.1. Franklin, Tn.: 2013. Downloaded computer software.
[41] Strong's
[42] Thayer
[43] John Beekman and John Callow. *Translating the Word of God.* (Zondervan Publishing House: Grand Rapids. 1974) Print. p21. Jan. 28, 2019.
[44] Eugene Nida and Charles Taylor. *The Theory and Practice of Translation, With Special Reference to Bible Translating*, 1969. Cited. Wikipedia. *Dynamic and Formal Equivalence.* 2018. Web. Jan. 28, 2019.
[45] Leland Ryken. The Word of God in English: Criteria for Excellence in Bible Translation (Kindle Locations 99-101). Kindle Edition.
[46] Leland Ryken. The Word of God in English: Criteria for Excellence in Bible Translation (Kindle Locations 161-166). Kindle Edition.
[47] Leland Ryken. The Word of God in English: Criteria for Excellence in Bible Translation (Kindle Locations 253-257). Kindle Edition.
[48] One Word. https://www.oneword.de/en/sae-j2450-quality-metric. Web. Jan. 2019.
[49] Oxford Dictionaries. *Paraphrase.* https://en.oxforddictionaries.com/ definition/paraphrase. 2019. Web. Jan. 2019.
[50] Leland Ryken. The Word of God in English: Criteria for Excellence in Bible Translation (Kindle Locations 258-263). Kindle Edition.
[51] Ryken, chapter 6.
[52] Merriam-Webster. *Idiom.* merriam-webster.com/dictionary/idiom. Web. 6-2019.

Notes

[53] The Complete Word Study Dictionary. E-Sword. Rick Meyers. Version 10.2.1. Franklin, Tn.: 2013. Downloaded computer software.

[54] Walter Bauer, *A Greek-English Lexicon Of The New Testament And Other Early Christian Literature*, 403. Cited. AV1611.com. 2 Corinthians 2:17 - "which corrupt the Word of God." Web. Feb. 2019.

[55] Joseph Thayer, *A Greek-English Lexicon Of The New Testament* (Grand Rapids: Baker Book, 1977 edition), 324-325. Cited. AV1611.com. 2 Corinthians 2:17 - "which corrupt the Word of God." Web. Feb. 2019.

[56] Gerhard Kittle. *Theologisches Wörterbuch zum Neuen Testament*. Vol. III. P 605. Cited. AV1611.com. 2 Corinthians 2:17 - "which corrupt the Word of God." Web. Feb. 2019.

[57] Athanasius, *Apologia Contra Arianos (Defence Against The Arians)*, III:49. Cited. AV1611.com. 2 Corinthians 2:17 - "which corrupt the Word of God." Web. Feb. 2019.

[58] Gregory Nazianzus, *Oratition 2* ("In Defence Of His Flight To Pontus"), 46. Cited. AV1611.com. 2 Corinthians 2:17 - "which corrupt the Word of God." Web. Feb. 2019.

[59] What is wrong with the allegorical interpretation method? Gotquestions.org. 2002-2019. Web. Feb. 2019.

[60] The Complete Word Study Dictionary, spoudázō. *E-Sword*. Rick Meyers. Version 10.2.1. Franklin, Tn.: 2013. Downloaded computer software.

[61] Webster 1828. Study.

[62] Harry Ironsides. Ironside's notes on Selected Books, Proverbs 2. StudyLight.org. Web. Feb. 2019.

[63] Webster 1828. Knowledge.

[64] Mel Lawrenz. *How to Study the Bible: Observation*. Bible Gateway Blog. https://www.biblegateway.com/blog/ 2015/11/ how-to-study-the-bible-observation. Nov. 2015. Web. Feb. 2019.

[65] Wikipedia. *Letter of Aristeas*. https://en.wikipedia.org/ wiki/Letter_of_Aristeas. 2018. Web. Jan. 28, 2019.

[66] Metzger, B., *The Bible in Translation* (Baker Academic, 2001), p. 15. Cited. Wikipedia. *Letter of Aristeas.* 4-9-2019.

[67] Kaufmann Kohler, Paul Wendland. *Aristeas, Letter of.* Jewishencyclopedia.com. 2002-2011. Web. 4-2019.

[68] HOIM Staff. *The Septuagint-Is It a Fraud or Forgery?* http://hope-of-israel.org/lxx.htm. 2018. Web. Jan. 28, 2019.

[69] Wikipedia. *Septuagint.* Web. 3-2019.
[70] IBID
[71] IBID
[72] IBID
[73] Daniels, David W.. Is The "World's Oldest Bible" A Fake? . Chick Publications. Kindle Edition/ James Snapp, Jr. *Erasmian Myths: Codex Vaticanus.* Confessionalbibliology.com. June 2016. Web. 3-2019.
[74] Daniels, David W.
[75] Early Jewish Writings. *Information on Aristobulus.* early jewishwritings.com. 2001-2013. Web. 4-2019.
[76] Editors, Jewish Virtual Library. *Gnosticism.* Jewish virtual library.org. 1998-2019. Web. 4-2019.
[77] Wikipedia. *Philo of Alexandria.* Web. 4-2019.
[78] Wikipedia. *Septuagint Manuscripts.* Wikipedia.com. Last edited April 2019. Web. 4-2019.
[79] *Dead Sea Scrolls.* Brittanica.com. Web. 4-2019
[80] Source= https://commons.wikimedia.org/wiki/File:Pap_266. Jpg. Public domain in the United States. Copyright term life of author plus 70 years. Web. 4-2019.
[81] Source=https://commons.wikimedia.org/wiki/File: Codex_ vaticanus. Jpg. Public Domain in the United States. Copyright term life of author plus 70 years. Web. 4-2019.
[82] Norman L. Geisler and William E. Nix. *A General Introduction.* (Chicago: Moody Press, 1978) p. 259. Print. 4-2019.
[83] J. C. Trevor. "The Discovery of the Scrolls." *Biblical Archaeologist, Vol. XI.* (Sept. 1948). Cited. Geisler and Nix. p. 260. Print. 4-2019.
[84] Daniels, David W. *Is The "World's Oldest Bible" A Fake?* . Chick Publications. Kindle Edition. 4-2019.
[85] Edward F. Hills. *The King James Version Defended.* (Des Moines: Christian Research Press. 1979) Print. p. 119. 4-2019.
[86] Geisler and Nix. p. 260. 4-2019.
[87] "Hexapla." Wikipedia. Web. 3-2019.
[88] Jerome. *De Viris Illustribus* (*On Illustrious Men*), Chap. 54. Posted by Thomas Yonan. August 9, 2013. ecclesiaepatres. blogspot.com/2013/08/jerome-on-origen.html. Web. 4-2019.
[89] Wikipedia, "Eusebius." Web. 3-2019.

Notes

[90] Dr. Phil Stringer. *Was the Septuagint the Bible of Christ and the Apostles?* http://www.scionofzion.com/septuagint2.htm. Web. 4-2019.

[91] Wikipedia. "Hexapla." Web. 3-2019.

[92] *Codex Vaticanus.* 1611 King James Bibl.com. Web. 3-2019.

[93] *Codex Vaticanus.* Textus Receptus. http://textus-receptus.com/wiki/Codex_Vaticanus. Web. 3-2019.

[94] Dr. Phil Stringer

[95] IBID

[96] Donald Waite, *Defending the King James Bible.* Cited. Dr. H. D. Williams. *The Character of God's Words are Not Found in the Septuagint.* Theoldpathspublications.com. Web. 4-2019.

[97] Dr. Craig A. Evans, *From Prophecy to Testament:the Foundation of the Old Testament in the New.* Cited. *Does the New Testament quote from the Greek Septuagint?* KJV Today. Web. Jan. 28, 2019.

[98] "Allusion. dictionary.reference.com. Web.

[99] David W. Daniels. *Was There a BC Septuagint? Part 1 of 5.* Chick Publications. Youtube.com. 2017. Web. 4-2019.

[100] Jim Taylor. Unpublished study notes. 3-2019.

[101] Burgon, John William. The Traditional Text of the Holy Gospels (p. 29). Kindle Edition.

[102] Edward F. Hills

[103] Ibid

[104] Dr. Jim Taylor, *In Defense of the Textus Receptus.* theoldpathspublications.com. 2016. Nook Edition. P. 260. 4-2019.

[105] Biblical Archaeology. www. la-via.es/english/archivo/ MagdalenEN.htm. Web. 2014.

[106] Dr. Edward Hills.

[107] Dr. Jim Taylor, p. 180.

[108] Burgon, John William. *The Traditional Text of the Holy Gospels* (p. 18). Kindle Edition.

[109] Burgon, John William. The Traditional Text of the Holy Gospels (pp. 21-22). Kindle Edition.

[110] Burgon, John William. The Traditional Text of the Holy Gospels (p. 41). Kindle Edition.

[111] Burgon, John William. The Traditional Text of the Holy Gospels (p. 44). Kindle Edition.

[112] Burgon, John William. The Traditional Text of the Holy Gospels (p. 43). Kindle Edition.
[113] Burgon, John William. The Traditional Text of the Holy Gospels (p. 45). Kindle Edition.
[114] Dr. D. A. Waite. *Summary of the Traditional Text.* Deanburgonsociety.org. 1997. Web. 4-2019.
[115] Burgon, John William. The Traditional Text of the Holy Gospels (pp. 45-46). Kindle Edition.
[116] Dr. Wilbur Pickering. *In Defense of the Objective Authority of the Sacred Text.* Walkinhiscommandments.com. 2009. Web. 4-2019.
[117] Wikipedia. *Byzantine text-type.* Web. 4-2019.
[118] Dr. David L. Brown. *Early Witnesses to the Received Text.* Logosresourcepages.org. Web. 4-2019.
[119] Burgon, John William. The Traditional Text of the Holy Gospels (p. 91). Kindle Edition.
[120] IBID
[121] IBID
[122] Frederick H. A. Scrivener. *A Plain Introduction to the Criticism of the New Testament.* Ed. iv (1894), Vol. II. pp. 264-265. Cited. Burgon, John William. The Traditional Text of the Holy Gospels (p. 37). Kindle Edition. 4-2019.
[123] John Foxe. Fox's Book of Martyrs Or A History of the Lives, Sufferings, and Triumphant Deaths of the Primitive Protestant Martyrs: The Original Classics - Illustrated (pp. 43-44). Unknown. Kindle Edition
[124] James Snapp, Jr. *Byzantine Manuscripts: Where Were They Before the 300's?* thetextofthegospels.com. 2017. Web. 4-2019.
[125] Burgon, John William. The Traditional Text of the Holy Gospels (pp. 49-50). Kindle Edition.
[126] Edward F. Hills
[127] Maurice Robinson and William Pierpont. "Introduction." *The New Testament in the Original Greek According to the Byzantine / Majority Textform.* Skypoint.com. (Published in print by: The Original Word Publishers: Atlanta. 1991). Web. 4-2019.
[128] IBID
[129] Edward F. Hills, The King James Version Defended. (Des Moines, Iowa: Christian research Press. 1973). Print. p. 197.

Notes

[130] Frederick H. A. Scrivener, *Scrivener's Annotated Greek New Testament*. 1881. (Dean Burgon Society Press: Collingswood, New Jersey. 1999). Print. pp. vii-viii.

[131] (1689 Baptist Confession of Faith, Chapter 1, section 8. http://www.arbca.com/1689-chapter1. 8-23-18.

[132] Jonathan Petersen. Billy Graham: 1918-2018. Bible Gateway. 2018. https://www.biblegateway.com/ blog/ 2018/ 02/ billy-graham-1918-20. Web. Feb. 2019.

[133] The Bible Societies. Trinitarian Bible Society Quarterly Record. Jan-Mar 1979. Pgs. 13-14. Cited: The UBS Greek New Testament. Prophets-See-All. http://prophets-see all.tripod.com/46645.htm. Web. 17 August 2017.

[134] Brown, Andrew, The Word of God Among All Nations: a Brief History of the Trinitarian Bible Society, 1831-1981. P.122. 1981. Trinitarian Bible Society. Cited: The UBS Greek New Testament. Prophets-See-All. http://prophets-see-all.tripod.com/46645.htm. Web. 17 August 2017.

[135] Brown, Andrew, The Word of God Among All Nations: a Brief History of the Trinitarian Bible Society, 1831-1981. P 12. 1981. Trinitarian Bible Society. Cited: The UBS Greek New Testament. Prophets-See-All. http://prophets-see-all.tripod.com/46645.htm. Web. 17 August 2017.

[136] Metger, Bruce. Cited: Brooks, James. Bible Interpreters of the Twentieth Century. p. 64. Cited: "Aren't Newer Translations Based on a Better Greek Text." KJV Today. 2017. Web. 17 August 2017

[137] "Aren't Newer Translations Based on a Better Greek Text." KJV Today. 2017. Web. 17 August 2017.

[138] Westcott and Hort. The New Testament in the Original Greek, the Text Revised by B.F. Westcott and F.J.A. Hort. (Cambridge: MacMillan & Co., 1882), p. 20. Cited: "Aren't newer translations based on a better Greek text?" KJV Today. 2017. Web. 17 August 2017.

[139] La More, Gary E, Ph. D. (in Greek Philosophy and M. Div. in Greek and Hebrew). Bruce Metzger: a Princeton Apostate. Pastor's Helps. Grace Missionary Baptist Church. Web. 22 July 2017.

[140] La Moore

[141] La Moore

[142] La Moore

[143] Introduction, Nestle-Aland: Novum Testamentum Graece , 27th revised edition. 2006. Cited. Aren't Newer Translations Based on a Better Text? The King's Bible. www.kingsbible.org.Web. 14 July 2017

[144] Fowler, Everette W. Evaluating Versions of the New Testament. (Watertown, WI: Maranatha Baptist Press, 1981) p. 28-66. Print. 19 August 2014.

[145] Geisler and Nix 316-328

[146] Foxe, Foxe's Book of Martyrs, 27 June 2004 (http://biblebelievers. com /foxes/fox104.htm).

[147] Richard Bennett, The Pattern of Papal Persecutions, Then and Now. 27 June 2004. (http://biblebelievers.com/bennett/

[148] Tucker. 38,39.

[149] Tucker. 40

[150] Geisler and Nix. 326.

[151] Robert L. Webb, "Waldenses and the Bible", The Primitive Baptists Library. (http://www.giveshare.org/ library/ bible/waldensesandbible.html). 13 July 2017.

[152] Bunn, Danny D. "The Bible the Waldenses Used,: Ekklesia Communicator. (http://www.ekkcom.com/gail17.htm). 27 June 2004.

[153] Author Unknown, Martin Luther the Reformer, (Chicago: Moody Press). Print. 53.

[154] Webb, "Waldenses and the Bible."

[155] Don Richardson, Eternity in their hearts, (Ventura, CA: Regal Books, 1981) 73-92.

[156] About, Lutheran Bible Translators. (www.us.lbt.org). 13 July 2017

[157] About, Pioneer Bible Translators. www.pioneerbible.org. 13 July 2017.

[158] Ethnos360 web site. www.ethnos360.org. 13 July 2017.

[159] Charles Turner, "Wycliffe Bible Translators," Way of Life. 1994, www.wayoflife.org/fbns/wycliffe.htm.13 Jul 2017.

[160] About, Evangel Bible Translators. (http://evangelbible.org/). 13 July 2017.

[161] About. www.bibleleague.org. 13 July 2017

[162] About, The Seed Company, theseedcompany.org.   13 July 2017.

[163] About. www.IMB.org. 13 July 2017.

[164] About. Baptist Mid-Missions. www.bmm.org. 13 July 2017

Notes

http://biblesint.org/biNew/be-informed-toptabs-138/bi-beliefs/translation-philosophy. 13 July 2017

[165] Zane C. Hodges, The Greek Text of the King James Version, Which Bible, ed. David Otis Fuller, (Grand Rapids: Grand Rapids Intl Publications,1975)25,26

[166] Charles Turner, "Wycliffe Bible Translators," Way of Life, 1994, 27 June 2004, (www.wayoflife.org/fbns/wycliffe.htm)

[167] David W. Cloud, *Wycliffe-Whither Bound?* 1991 (www.wayoflife.org/fbns/wycliffebible.htm). 27 June 2004.

[168] Baptist Bible Translators Institute. History. Bowie, Texas:2017. https://baptisttranslators.com/history. Web. Jan. 13, 2019.

[169] Trinitarian Bible Society. https://www.tbsbibles.org/default.aspx. Web. Jan. 13, 2019.

[170] Graceway Bible Society. Mississauga, Ontario. http://www.graceway.com. Web. Jan. 13, 2019.

[171] FirstBible. Milford, Ohio. https://www.firstbible.net/about. Web. Jan. 13, 2019.

[172] Worldview Ministries. http://worldviewonline.net. 20 August 2017.

[173] Bearing Precious Seed Global. www.bpsglobal.org. Jan. 13 2019.

[174] C. I. Scofield, ed., The Scofield Reference Bible, (New York: Oxford University Press, 1996), 1343.

[175] Pappas ThM, C. H.. In Defense of the Authenticity of 1 John 5:7 (pp. 1-2). WestBow Press. Kindle Edition. 5-2019.

[176] KJV Today. *Johannine Comma (1 John 5:7).* Kjvtoday.com. Web. 5-2019.

[177] Drs. McIntosh and Twyman, The Archko Volume (New Canaan, CT: Keats Publishing Inc., 1998), 34. Cited. Pappas ThM, C. H.. In Defense of the Authenticity of 1 John 5:7 (pp. 124-126). WestBow Press. Kindle Edition. 5-2019.

[178] Pappas ThM, C. H.. In Defense of the Authenticity of 1 John 5:7 (p. 6-8). WestBow Press. Kindle Edition. 5-2019.

[179] G. H. Orchard, Essay by J. R. Graves, History of Baptist (Texarkana, TX, Bogard Press, 1987), xxi. Cited. Pappas ThM, C. H.. In Defense of the Authenticity of 1 John 5:7 (pp. 16-17). WestBow Press. Kindle Edition.

[180] Pappas

[181] Dr. Edward F. Hills

[182] Pappas ThM, C. H.. In Defense of the Authenticity of 1 John 5:7 (p. 20). WestBow Press. Kindle Edition.
[183] Pappas ThM, C. H.. In Defense of the Authenticity of 1 John 5:7 (pp. 36-37). WestBow Press. Kindle Edition.
[184] Wikipedia. *Eusebius of Nicomedia.* Wikipedia.com. Web. 5-2019.
[185] IBID
[186] Charles Robson. *A Greek Lexicon to the New Testament.* (Whitaker and Co: London. 1839). Google facsimile version. Web. 5-2019.
[187] IBID
[188] Word Study
[189] Webster
[190] Bible-Researcher. *Mark 16:9-20.* Bible-researcher.com. Web. 5-2019.
[191] *The Shorter Ending of Mark.* Ex-christian.net. Web. 5-2019.
[192] Dr. Edward Hills, *Defended.* Chapter 7.
[193] IBID
[194] IBID
[195] IBID
[196] The Pulpit Commentary. 1880-1897. Public Domain. E-Sword. Rick Meyers. Version 10.2.1. Franklin, Tn.: 2013. Downloaded computer software. 5-2019.
[197] David Guzik. David Guzik's Enduring Word Commentary. 2014. E-Sword. Rick Meyers. Version 10.2.1. Franklin, Tn.: 2013. Downloaded computer software. 5-2019.
[198] Webster
[199] Terrance H. Brown. *God was Manifest in the Flesh (1 Timothy 3:16).* True or False? David Otis Fuller. Ed. (Grand Rapids, Michigan: Grand Rapids International Publications, 1973). Print. Pg. 32-33. 5-2019.
[200] Wikipedia. *Codex Ephraemi Rescriptus*, at the Bibliothèque Nationale, Paris, Département des manuscrits, Grec 9, fol. 60r (rotated) Public Domain in the USA. 5-2019
[201] **Wikipedia.** Scrivener's facsimile with text of 1 Tim 3:15–16. Codex Ephraemi Rescriptus. Public Domain in the USA. 5-19.
[202] **Wikipedia.** First page of the **Codex** with lacuna in **Romans** 1:1-4. Public Domain in the USA. 5-2019.

Notes

[203] John W. Burgon. *Pericope De Adultera. Counterfeit or Genuine Mark 16? John 8?* David Otis Fuller, Ed. (Grand Rapids International Publishers: Grand Rapids. 1975) Print. Pgs. 131-158. 5-2019.
[204] IBID
[205] IBID
[206] Wikipedia. *Diatessaron.* Wikipedia.com. Web. 5-2019.
[207] William P. Grady. *Final Authority a Christian's Guide to the King James Version.* (Grady Publications: Schererville, Indiana. 1993). Print. Pg. 197. 5-2019.
[208] Wikipedia. *Counter Reformation.* Wikipedia.com. Web. 5-2019.
[209] Wikipedia. *Biblical Criticism.* Wikipedia.com. Web. 5-2019.
[210] IBID
[211] IBID
[212] Wikipedia. Biblical Criticism. Wikipedia.com. Web. 5-2019.
[213] Hills. *Defended.* Chapter three. 5-2019.
[214] IBID
[215] Wikipedia. *Biblical Criticism.* Wikipedia.com. Web. 5-2019
[216] Dr. Jim Eckman. *Nineteenth Century Theological Liberalism and Modern Evangelicalism.* Issues in Perspective with Dr. Jim Eckman. April 23, 2011. Graceuniversity.edu. Web. 5-2019.
[217] IBID
[218] Matt Slick. *What is higher criticism and the historical critical method of examining the Bible?* Christian Apologetics and Research Ministry (CARM). May 22, 2016. Web. 5-2019.
[219] Wikipedia. *David Strauss.* Wikipedia.com. Web. 5-20019.
[220] Eckman
[221] Wikipedia. *Albrecht Ritschl.* Wikipedia.com. Web. 5-2019.
[222] Eckman
[223] Dr. Douglas Stauffer. *One Book Stands Alone The Key to Believing the Bible.* (McCowen Mills Publishers: Millbrook, Alabama. 2001) Print. Pgs. 231-233. 5-2019.
[224] Arthur Fenton Hort. *Life and Letters of Fenton John Anthony Hort.* (London: Macmillan & Co. 1896) Pg. 7-8. Cited. William P. Grady. *Final Authority a Christian's Guide to the King James Version.* (Grady Publications: Schererville, Indiana. 1993). Print. Pg. 214-215. 5-2019.
[225] Arthur Westcott. *Life and Letters of Brooke Foss Westcott.* (London: Macmillan and Co. 1901) Pg. 56-57, Cited. William P. Grady.

Final Authority a Christian's Guide to the King James Version. (Grady Publications: Schererville, Indiana. 1993). Print. Pg. 218. 5-2019.

[226] Fenton John Anthony Hort. Cited. William P. Grady. Pg, 245.

[227] William Grady. Pg. 250.

[228] IBID. Pg. 251.

[229] Wikipedia. *Revised Version.* Wikipedia.com. Web. 5-2019.

[230] Wikipedia. *Edwin Palmer.* Wikipedia.com. Web. 5-2019.

[231] David Cloud. Fundamentalism, Modernism, and New-Evangelicalism. Way of Life Literature. 2001. Web. 1-14-2005.

[232] David L. Brown. *Providential Preservation: The Doctrine that Virtually Disappeared.* www.kjbrc.org.

[233] Cited by Harold LIndsell. Introduction, *Battle for the Bible.* Also cited by David Cloud. *Neo-Evangelicalism-Its History.* Way fo Life Literature. 2001. Web. 1-14-2005.

[234] Merriam-Webster Dictionary. *Lower Criticism.* Merriam-Webster.com. Web. 5-2019.

[235] Tim Chaffey, *Is the Bible Authoritative and Inerrant.* answersingenesis.org. 2010, Web. 6-2019.

[236] Derick Brown. *Why Inerrancy Matters for Mission.* imb.org/2018/08/02/why-inerrancy-matters-missions. 2018. Web. 6-2019.

[237] Baptist Mid-Mission. *Our Beliefs.* Web. 6-2019.

[238] Liberty University. *Doctrinal statement.* Web. 6-2019.

[239] A letter to Ronnie Powell from Stewart Custer, Chairman, Division of Bible, Bob Jones University, May 1978. Facsimile. Peter Ruckman. *Problem Texts. Appendix Ten.* (Pensacola: Pensacola Bible Institute Press. 1980) Print. Pg. 475. 6-2019.

[240] Evangelical Beliefs. *What Evangelical Christians Believe.* evangelicalbeliefs.com. 2011. Web. 6-2019.

[241] IBID, Pg. 477

[242] Carl F.H. Henry, first editor of *Christianity Today*, chairman for the 1966 World Congress on Evangelism, "Conflict Over Biblical Inerrancy," *Christianity Today*, May 7, 1976) cited. David Cloud. *Evangelicalism's Apostasy.* Way of Life Literature. 2001. Web. 2005.

[243] Harold Lindsell, former vice-president and professor Fuller Theological Seminary and Editor Emeritus of *Christianity Today, The Battle for the Bible*, 1976, p. 20. cited. David Cloud. *Evangelicalism's Apostasy.* Way of Life Literature. 2001. Web. 2005.

Notes

[244] Richard Quebedeaux, author of *The Young Evangelicals* and *The Worldly Evangelicals*, "The Evangelicals: New Trends and Tensions," *Christianity and Crisis*, Sept. 20, 1976, pp. 197-202. cited. David Cloud. *Evangelicalism's Apostasy*. Way of Life Literature. 2001. Web. 2005.

[245] Francis Schaeffer, *The Great Evangelical Disaster*, 1983, p. 44. . cited. David Cloud. *Evangelicalism's Apostasy*. Way of Life Literature. 2001. Web. 2005.

[246] Jim Hinch. *Evangelicals Are Losing the Battle for the Bible. And They're Just Fine with That.* Los Angeles Review of Books. (Author wrote for Guideposts Magazine). lareviewofbooks.org/article. 2006. Web. 6-2019.

[247] David Cloud. *What About the New King James Version? (*Way of Life Literature: Port Huron. 2003). Web. 5-2019.

[248] Charles Robson. *A Greek Lexicon to the New Testament.* (Whitaker and Co: London. 1839). Google facsimile version. Web. 5-2019.

[249] Charles John Ellicott. *Ellicott's Commentary For English Readers.* Studylight.org. Web 2-2019.

[250] Expositor's Greek Testament. E-Sword. Rick Meyers. Version 10.2.1. Franklin, Tn.: 2013. Downloaded computer software. 2019.

[251] Churches" or "Temples" in Acts 19:37? KJV Today,com. Web 2019.

[252] Thayer

[253] Word Study

[254] Word Study

[255] Thayer

[256] Strong's

[257] Webster

[258] Webster

[259] Charles Robson.

[260] The Complete Word Study dictionary. E-Sword. Rick Meyers. Version 10.2.1. Franklin, Tn.: 2013. Downloaded computer software. 5-2019.

[261] Thayer. Greek Dictionary.

[262] Charles Robson

[263] Dr. Jeffrey Khoo, Academic Dean of Far East Bible College in Singapore.

[264] *Christian Theology, 2nd Edition,* Millard J. Erickson

[265] Word Study

[266] Vine's

[267] Word Study
[268] dictionary.reference.com
[269] John Pickering. A Greek English Lexicon. (Hilliard, Gray, Little, and Wilkins: Boston. 1832). Google Edition. 5-2019.
[270] Samuel C. Loveland. *A Greek Lexicon Adapted to the New Testament with English Definitions.* (Printed by David Watson: Woodstock, Vt. 1828). Google Edition. 5-2019.
[271] Word Study
[272] Vine's
[273] Webster
[274] Webster
[275] Webster
[276] Oxford Dictionary
[277] Webster 1828. Study.
[278] Word Study
[279] Vine's
[280] Word Study

www.ingramcontent.com/pod-product-compliance
Lightning Source LLC
Chambersburg PA
CBHW071949220426
43662CB00009B/1066